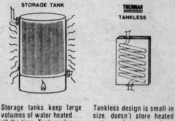

FEATURES

INDEX OF CHARTS, TABLES, FORECASTS, AND DEPARTMENTS

1 **Basket King Hybrid.** Early variety. For containers. A Burpee exclusive.

2 **Big Girl Hybrid VF.** Sweet. Many over 1 lb. Burpee exclusive. Great main-crop tomato.

3 **Supersteak Hybrid VFN.** Extra-meaty. Most weigh 1-2 lbs. Tolerant to disease.

4 **Sweet 100 Hybrid.** Amazingly sweet. Bears early. Long season.

5 **Early Girl Hybrid.** Sweet yet tart. Heavy crop sooner. Longer season.

6 **Delicious.** Its seed grew the world's largest tomato. Excellent flavor.

7 **Long Keeper.** Best-storing tomatoes we've seen. A Burpee exclusive.

8 **Roma VF.** Superior pasta-type. Big crops. Few seeds. Plum-shaped.

9 **Gardener's Delight.** Rich and abundant. Our favorite cherry-sized tomato.

10 **Tiny Tim.** Grows only 15 inches tall. Many ¾-inch fruits. Fine for garden or pots.

11 **Yellow Pear.** Mild and pleasing for salads, preserving or pickling.

12 **Floramerica Hybrid VF 1 & 2.** All-America Winner. Tolerant to 15 diseases.

12 juicy reasons to send for Burpee's free 1985 Garden Catalog!

Tomatoes! Burpee's 1985 Garden Catalog offers you seeds for these 12 different varieties—and 23 more! Early starters. Late stoppers. New and exclusive varieties. Salad and pasta types. Big beauties and bite-sized gems. Long keeper. Easy slicers. Yellows. Pinks. Oranges. And all guaranteed to satisfy. **Send for your free catalog now.**

They're all described in detail and guaranteed to satisfy. This is gardening's most-wanted catalog! It gives you 184 color pages! 400 varieties of vegetables! 650 varieties of flowers! Plus fruit trees…bulbs…shrubs…supplies! All backed by Burpee's famous guarantee of money back or full replacement any time within a year.

If you ordered from our 1984 catalog, you needn't request the 1985 catalog—you will receive it automatically. Burpee's 1985 Garden Catalog will be mailed in January.

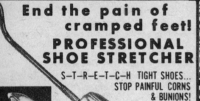

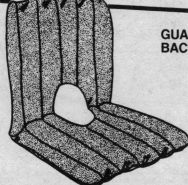

REWARD $3,000.00
FOR THIS PENNY!

OUR COIN
CATALOGUE TELLS
YOU HOW TO
SHIP COINS
TO US AND
QUICKLY
GET THE MOST
MONEY WE PAY
FOR COINS! SEND
FOR IT TODAY!

**We'll Pay You $3,000.00
For A 1943 Copper Penny
Like this One;**

FOR CERTAIN COINS WE PAY UP TO: CERTAIN	
Gold Coins Before 1939	$89,000.00
Nickels Before 1969	$96,000.00
Silver Dollars Before 1964	$76,000.00
Half Dollars Before 1967	$ 5,000.00
Pennies Before 1970	$ 4,800.00
Dimes Before 1966	$20,900.00
Quarters Before 1967	$ 5,000.00
Half Cents Before 1910	$ 3,700.00
Lincoln Pennies Before 1973	$ 250.00

Stop spending valuable coins worth hundreds of dollars. New 1985 catalogue with NEW HIGHER PRICES, lists hundreds of coins we want to buy and gives the price range we will pay for these United States Coins. Certain half cent coins are worth up to $3,500.00 for Canadian Coins. Our valuable Coin Book may reward you many thousands of dollars. Coins do not have to be old to be valuable. Thousands of dollars have been paid for coins dated as recently as 1940 to 1956. Now you too can learn the rare dates and how to identify rare coins in your possession with our new 1985 catalogue. A fortune may be waiting for you. Millions of Dollars have been paid for rare coins. Send your order for this valuable coin catalogue now. Hold on to your coins until you obtain our catalogue. Send $4.50 plus 50¢ postage and handling for 1985 Coin Catalogue to:

Best Values Co., Dept. D-806
P.O. Box 802, E. Orange, N.J. 07019

$500,000 SEARCH
FOR RARE COINS!
OLD and NEW!
MAIL MONEY-SAVING NO-RISK
FREE TRIAL COUPON NOW!

Best Values Co., Dept D-806
P.O. Box 802, E. Orange, N.J. 07019
Rush your latest 1985 catalogue listing the actual price range you will pay for United States Coins listed in the catalogue. I enclose $4.50 plus 50¢ postage and handling.

NAME _____

ADDRESS _____

CITY _____ STATE _____

*Your Money Will Be Refunded in Full
If You Are Not Satisfied With This Catalogue*

"Have never seen anything anywhere quite like it!"

MARGUERITE CARTER

"Going Bald?"
Try This At No Risk

HOUSTON, Texas — If you have symptoms of "Sebum" hair loss; oily or greasy forehead; dandruff, dry or oily; itchy scalp; and if your hair pulls out easily on top of your head, chances are excellent that you can now stop your hair loss ... and grow more hair in the privacy of your own home.

A firm of laboratory consultants has developed a treatment for "Sebum" hair loss that has been so successful, they don't even ask you to take their word for it. They invite you to try the treatment for 32 days, at their risk, and see for yourself!

Naturally, they would not offer this opportunity unless the treatment worked. However, it is impossible to help everyone.

The great majority of cases of excessive hair fall and baldness are the beginning and more fully developed stages of male pattern baldness and cannot be helped.

But, how can you be sure what is actually causing your hair loss? Even if baldness may seem to "run in the family," it is certainly not proof of the cause of YOUR hair loss. Many conditions can cause hair loss.

Everyone starts out with a full head of hair and usually has no problem retaining it until sometime after puberty. In the case of hair loss caused by "sebum", the problem starts when the male hormone production reaches its peak. This causes an excessive discharge of toxic sebum, which if not properly controlled, will gradually destroy the hair roots.

Hair loss caused by sebum can also run in your family by simply inheriting an over-abundance of male hormone. In any case, if you wait until you are slick bald and your hair roots are dead, you are beyond help.

So, if you still have any hair on top of your head, and would like to stop your hair loss and grow more hair ... now is the time to do something about it before it's too late.

Loesch Laboratory Consultants, Inc., will supply you with treatment for 32 days ... at their risk ... if you have the sebum symptoms and are not already bald. Just send them the information listed below. All inquiries are answered confidentially by mail.   ADV.

NO OBLIGATION COUPON

To: Loesch Laboratory Consultants, Inc.
    Dept. F40, 3311 West Main Street
    P.O. Box 66001   Houston, Texas 77266

I am submitting the following information with the understanding that it will be kept strictly confidential and that I am under no obligation whatsoever.

Does your forehead become oily or greasy? _____

How soon after washing? _____

Do you have dandruff? _____ Dry or oily? _____

Does hair pull out easily on top of head? _____

Any thin areas? _____ Where? _____

Any slick bald areas? _____ Where? _____

NAME _____ Sex _____ Age _____

ADDRESS _____

CITY _____ STATE _____ ZIP _____

Discover All The Pure Fresh Water You Will Ever Need. . . In Your BACKYARD!

FREE BOOK

How to drill your own water well

USED WORLD-WIDE TO DRILL 100,000 WATER WELLS SINCE 1962

© 1984 DeepRock Mfg. Co.

SIMPLE
The *Hydra-Drill* is as easy operate as a power lawn mow Tested and proven by thousan of homeowners from coast coast and around the wor

ECONOMICAL
You can SAVE money even if y drill only one water well for y home. You can MAKE money you drill wells for othe

GOES EVERYWHERE
No backyard is too small for *Hydra-Drill* well. The *Hydra-D* can be transported easily locations where commercial w drilling equipment can't

ABSOLUTELY FREE
You can get a big informati package about the *Hydra-D* absolutely free. Write today! just call the toll-free number.

DeepRock Mfg. Co.
Opelika, Alabama 36802

CALL TOLL-FREE
1-800-821-770
(Ask for Extension 5643)

Call anytime including Sundays
OR CLIP COUPON AND MAIL TODAY!

DeepRock
Since 1962

5643 Anderson Road
Opelika, Alabama 36802

PRINT NAME

ADDRESS

CITY   STATE   ZIP

PHONE

CONVERT YOUR HOUSE WIRING INTO A
Giant TV Antenna
JUST PLUG INTO ANY OUTLET....

* **USES NO ELECTRICITY**
* **NO TOOLS REQUIRED**
* **COMPLETLY SAFE TO USE**
* **SHARP, CLEAR CHANNELS**

Only
4⁷⁵

An electronic invention that will let you tune every black & white TV channel in your area sharp & clear without an expensive roof antenna or unsightly rabbit ears! Attaches to your black & white TV set in seconds — plugs into an electric outlet. Uses no current—100% safe to use! Use with FM radios, too. Complete instructions included.

No. 4250—Giant TV Antenna $4.75 **2 for only** $7.49

Professional Extra Leverage
TOENAIL CLIPPER

Only... **$2⁹⁸**

Spring Action Clipper

Extra Leverage For Tough, Thickened Nail

Special Contour Head Gets Under Ingrown Nails

Problem Nails? Use these specially designed Clippers to cut through thickened nails safely and easily! Here's the answer to ingrown nails. Contoured Clipper Blades cut nails at the right angle — reduces the chance of ingrown nails. Fine quality Surgical Steel.

No. 3167—Toenail Clipper $2.98

ELECTRIC CARD SHUFFLER
Shuffles Deck in 3 Seconds

PRICE SLASH

Only
9⁹⁵

BE FIRST WITH THE LATEST! This new electrical marvel shuffles a deck in mere seconds. Does it far more thoroughly than by hand! Also **shuffles 2 decks**, merging them to perfection. Lay cards in 2 holders, push the button and the **lightning action begins.** A quality item made of metals and high impact plastic housing. Equipped with a **powerful** rotary motor for years of top performances. Uses 2 D cell batteries (not included). Adds new enjoyment to Canasta, Poker, Bridge, Gin, etc. Gift Boxed. Compare our price!

No. 2002A—Electric Card Shuffler $9.95

Foster-Trent INC.
2345 Post Road, Dept. 304PG Larchmont, N.Y. 10538

RUSH the items ordered below on **30 DAY TRIAL** — complete satisfaction **GUARANTEED** or my money back promply (except postage & handling). My payment is enclosed including 1.40 for postage & handling. (Sorry! No C.O.D.)

QUAN.	SIZE	ITEM NO.	DESCRIPTION	PRICE	
			SHIPPING & HANDLING	1	40
		N.Y.S. Customers MUST add Sales Tax			
			Total Enclosed		

Please use Street Address and Apt. No. for **FASTER** U.P.S. Delivery!

Name _____
Address _____ Apt. # ____
City _____
State _____ Zip Code ____

DO YOU HAVE A SORE KNEE?
Free Yourself From Crippling Pai

If you suffer from knee pain, we don't have to tell you how distressing it can be, how disabling it is, and how it can curtail even such simple, basic activities as walking or gettin out of a chair.

And you have learned, by now, that such pain is not limited to athletes. The office worke who does nothing more strenuous than sit at his desk all day is just as likely to suffer fror what he calls "my bum knee acting up" as the tennis player or the housewife. Merely per forming ordinary, every-day movements such as walking or climbing stairs or even just sittin in one position can bring on that familiar, painful sensation.

Familiar and frequent and agonizing — but now needless.

Because now you can wear a revolutionary new knee strap and free yourself of this pair

Designed by orthopedic surgeon Dr. Jack Levine, Director of the Department of Orthc pedic Surgery, Brookdale Hospital, Brooklyn, N.Y., the strap has been described in paper published in the American Journal of Sports Medicine and in Clinical Orthopaedics.

The principle of the Levine Knee Strap is that by wearing it you reduce the pressure between the knee cap and the thigh bone, and in that way you relieve the pain and get com fort and — most important — mobility of action. You can walk, you can sit, you can stand, yo can run, you can even play ball or dance.

Who needs the Levine Knee Strap?

If your knee hurts when you climb stairs . . .

If you have pain in your knee when sitting in one position for any length of time — an even worse pain when you get up . . .

If you have pain when playing tennis, when jogging, when engaging in any form o physical exercise — and even more pain after the exercise . . .

If you occasionally feel your knee buckling when you're walking or running or dancing..

And if you have found the ordinary elastic supports and traditional treatments of littl or no help . . .

You need the Levine Knee Strap.

You no longer have to resign yourself to pain, you don't have to learn to live with i Thousands of people who have used the Levine Knee Strap have found blessed relief fror this needless suffering —and the chances are you will, too.

Wear the Levine Knee Strap and you'll be able to move about freely once again. Wea it when you're walking, when you're sitting. Wear it when playing tennis, baseball, even foot ball. It is worn just below the knee cap, it is thin and light-weight — only one ounce — an will not be visible under your clothing.

We are so sure that the Levine Knee Strap will help you that we make this no-risk offe Wear the Levine Knee Strap for ten days, following our simple instructions, and if you are no satisfied, if you feel that it has not helped you, send it back to us and we will refund your fu purchase price — no questions asked.

You now have the opportunity to free yourself from that crippling pain—at no risk. Th Levine Knee Strap can be purchased only by ordering it directly from us. Simply send you name, address and $15.00 (cash, check or money order) to:

PATELL-EASE CORP., DEPT. 1810C, P.O. BOX 315, JENKINTOWN, PA. 1904

PARK SEED
High Performers™
CATALOG

Get beautiful, carefree blooms and better tasting, high-yield vegetables with Park's Flower and Vegetable **High Performers™** Catalog. Over 3000 to choose on 124 PAGES . . . exciting NEW introductions and your proven all-time favorites. Send for your FULL COLOR CATALOG TODAY.

It's Yours FREE!

PARK SEED
Flower & Vegetable
High Performers
1984

© 1984 Park Seed Co., Inc.

985   OLD FARMER'S ALMANAC   21

CUCUMBER & BEAUTY

BY ANA MAHER

Every woman, at some time in her life, faces the spectre of an aging skin. Most women never solve the problem, and finally become resigned. A fortunate few find the answer and are rewarded with a complexion that remains fresh and youthful all their lives.

I had this skin problem 23 years ago. Nothing very serious, but when I took my mirror over to a bright light, I could detect evidence of dryness and tell-tale signs of advancing years. And I didn't like it. I knew that these were danger signals that warned of an aging skin.

I was also very bewildered. I had always taken the best care of my skin. And no matter what I did, my complexion showed no improvement. Finally I became resigned. After all, everybody gets older and most of us show our age.

A VITAL BEAUTY DISCOVERY FOR ME

Then one day I had a visit from an elderly widowed neighbor. This charming lady was about seventy, but she had the most beautiful, moist, youthful skin. I remarked about it and mentioned my own skin problem.

She told me she used a marvelous cream which had been formulated by her late husband, a physician, and that she made it herself. "Try it," she said, and then she left and returned with a jar of this cream.

So I tried using my neighbor's cream.

In only three weeks, I began to see a marked improvement. My skin was fresher, clearer, smoother. After two months, my former dry, dull skin was revitalized. My skin now had a youthful, almost translucent quality. I was thrilled with my neighbor's formula.

For six years, this kind lady kept me supplied with this cream. And I want to tell you that my skin was more vital and younger looking than it had been when I first started to use it, six years before.

Then my neighbor died suddenly —and with her went that wonderful cream and its secret ingredients. I was saddened by the loss of a good friend— and dejected by the loss of a miracle cream. Her family told me that her personal papers revealed no formulas of any kind. I was desperate. But I did have three jars left from the last batch she had made.

So I took the cream to one of the best known analytical cosmetic chemists. The cost of the analysis was enormous, but I got what I wanted. I had the wonder cream formula

PURE, SAFE INGREDIENTS FOUND ONLY IN NATURE

It had a base of cucumber juice, two super-moisturizers, three natural lubricants, and a special component to keep the cucumber juice fresh. My chemist told me that the formula consisted of only safe, pure ingredients— no hormones, estrogens or steroids.

I made a batch of cream for myself, following the chemist's instructions. Then my friends and relatives began using it. And in every case, the results were absolutely astounding.

Soon friends began insisting that the cream should be made known and available to all women, since the problem of aging skin is universal.

So my cream was put on the market 17 years ago, with the financial help of an uncle. It is called Cucumbre Frost.

The same wonderful results experienced by me, my friends and relatives were repeated time and time again by women all over the country. I have in my file hundreds of letters from grateful women telling of the remarkable results obtained with Cucumbre Frost.

NO SPECIAL TIME CONSUMING TREATMENT

Treatment is not a complicated ritual. I don't have time for that and the chances are you don't, either. You apply Cucumbre Frost at bedtime. Leave it on all night. It feeds, protects and nourishes your skin while you sleep.

AND IT'S ABSOLUTELY GUARANTEED

I know what Cucumbre Frost can do for you. Therefore, I offer you this UNCONDITIONAL GUARANTEE. Try it. See for yourself in your own mirror how, after a few treatments, Cucumbre Frost helps revitalize dull, dry, aging skin. How, when used regularly, Cucumbre Frost helps facial skin to regain lost smoothness, moistness and freshness. Many women wrote me of astonishing results after only two weeks. Some take longer. But I say this to you: if, for any reason you are not delighted with Cucumbre Frost—return the unused portion to me for a complete refund. No questions asked.

You now have the opportunity to have a vital, youthful, lovely skin—at no risk. Cucumbre Frost can be purchased only by ordering it directly from me. Just fill out the coupon below. Be sure to indicate which size Cucumbre Frost you want.

THE

OLD FARMER'S ALMANAC

CALCULATED ON A NEW AND IMPROVED PLAN
FOR THE YEAR OF OUR LORD

1985

Being 1st after BISSEXTILE or LEAP YEAR, and (until July 4)
209th year of American Independence

FITTED FOR BOSTON, AND THE NEW ENGLAND STATES, WITH SPECIAL COR-
RECTIONS AND CALCULATIONS TO ANSWER FOR ALL THE UNITED STATES.

Containing, besides the large number of Astronomical Calculations
and the Farmer's Calendar for every month
in the year, a variety of

NEW, USEFUL, AND ENTERTAINING MATTER.
ESTABLISHED IN 1792

BY ROBERT B. THOMAS

I love a life whose plot is simple,
And does not thicken with every pimple,
A soul so sound no sickly conscience binds it,
That makes the universe no worse than't finds it.
— *Henry David Thoreau*

COPYRIGHT 1984 by YANKEE PUBLISHING INCORPORATED

COVER T.M. REGISTERED
IN U.S. PATENT OFFICE   ISSN 0078-4516

LIBRARY OF CONGRESS
CARD NO. 56-29681

Address All Correspondence to
Publisher   THE OLD FARMER'S ALMANAC   *Editor*
Rob Trowbridge   DUBLIN, NH 03444, U.S.A.   Jud Hale

To Patrons

The first advertisements in *The Old Farmer's Almanac* featured Dutch quills, penknives, ink powder, writing paper, and various books, including a "cheap edition of *Watt's Psalms and Hymns* and "a novel by an American Lady." The year was 1794. Other than in our annual Special Edition (sold in bulk and without advertising to companies who give it to their customers), advertisements have been an integral part of every regular newsstand edition of this publication since that year. (Arm & Hammer Baking Soda has been with us for more than a hundred of those years!)

Some people, cynical by nature, may tend to disbelieve those almanac advertisements that, for instance, promise to "drive fish crazy," restore vim and vigor, provide 60 percent more juice from apples, aid your hearing, remove your corns, stretch your shoes, or provide a peek into the "afterlife." Those same people, however, may accept the notion that romance, social status, and financial success will automatically be theirs if, like the beautiful folks in the slick four-color magazine ads, they drink a certain brand of whiskey.

The advertisements in this publication *deliver*. Those chickens really *do* lay colored eggs. Last year someone wrote to complain about that particular advertisement, saying, "You can't call the color" before the hen lays her eggs. Evidently he had experimented by loudly shouting "red!", "blue!" or whatever directly at the hen as she was commencing to lay her egg. To no avail. The hen would lay an egg in whatever color she felt appropriate to the moment. We patiently pointed out to the complainer that the advertisement for these chickens has never *claimed* you can "call the color."

We won't say that Jimmy Carter's ads for fishing worms and "raising instructions" in this almanac during the early 1970s enabled him to ascend to the presidency. That would be silly. But we do know people from all over the country were well satisfied with those worms from Plains, Georgia.

There are lots of advertisements we will not accept. They include those for mind altering drugs (like liquor), cigarettes, sexual items, or "sex literature," and advertising that, in our opinion, is otherwise in bad taste, dangerous, or deceptive. The latter category occasionally creates argument. However, in our view a metal "golden hand" that promises "good luck" is not deceptive. A pill that promises to turn body fat into plain water *is* deceptive. Potentially dangerous, too. This year we refused to print little more than 14 pages of such advertising.

Not long ago, Charles Kuralt of CBS News devoted a portion of his national television program to our advertisements. After describing a number of them, he concluded by saying, "There's not a brittle, sophisticated ad in this whole edition. *The Old Farmer's Almanac* is willing to leave that market to *Playboy* and *The New Yorker*. These ads speak to the real America, the one that is worried about its false teeth falling out or its pants falling down . . . Publications come and go with their ads for designer gowns. *The Old Farmer's Almanac* offers remedies for aching feet. That's why it's lasted for over 190 years."

One hundred and ninety-three, to be exact, and still counting! With the help of a few "rooster pills" from time to time, we hope to go on forever . . .   J.D.H.

* * *

We're indebted to: Dr. Richard Head for all the weather data; Susan Mahnke, assisted by Mary Sheldon, Dougald MacDonald, Anna Larson, Mary Lewis, and Jody Saville for the editorial work; John Pierce as managing editor; Jill Shaffer as designer; Steve Klett and staff for graphic services; Marilyn White, ad production; George Greenstein, astronomical calculations; Fred Schaaf, astronomical consultant; and Castle Freeman, Jr., Farmer's Calendar essays.

However, it is by our works and not our words that we would be judged. These, we hope, will sustain us in the humble though proud station we have so long held in the name of   Your ob'd. servant,

June 1984

INTRODUCTION
Including How to Use This Almanac Anywhere in the U.S.A.
THE LEFT-HAND CALENDAR PAGES
(Pages 48-74)

These pages will provide you with the phases of the moon; the hour and minute of the sun's rising and setting for each day of the year and month; the length of each day; the times of high tides in Boston in the morning and evening ("11¼" under "Full Sea Boston, A.M.," means that the high tide that morning will be at 11:15 A.M. — with the number of feet of high tide shown for some of the dates on the right calendar pages); the hour and minutes of the moon's rising and setting; the declination of the sun in degrees and minutes (angular distance from the celestial equator); the moon's place in the heavens; and finally, in the far right column, the moon's age. The moon's place and age apply, without correction, throughout the United States.

The moon's place given on the left-hand pages is its *astronomical* place in the heavens. (*All* calculations in this almanac, except for the astrological information on pages 173 and 201-203, are based on astronomy, not astrology.) As well as the 12 constellations of the Zodiac, four other abbreviations appear in this column: Ophiuchus (OPH) is a constellation primarily north of the Zodiac, but with a small corner between Scorpio and Sagittarius. Orion (ORI) is a constellation whose northern limit just reaches the Zodiac between Taurus and Gemini. Sextans (SEX) lies south of the Zodiac except for a corner that just touches it near Leo. Cetus (CET) lies south of the Zodiac, just south of Pisces and Aries.

Eastern Standard Time is used throughout this Almanac. (Be sure to add one hour for Daylight Saving Time between April 28 and October 27.) **All of the times on the left-hand calendar pages are calculated for Boston.** Key letters accompany much of the data; they are provided so that the Boston times can easily be corrected for anywhere in the United States — including Alaska and Hawaii — and selected cities in Canada. Here's how . . .

Sunrise, Sunset

Note the Key letter to the right of each time for sunrise and sunset in the column entitled "Key." To find the time of sunrise or sunset for your area, consult the Time Correction Tables (pages 86-90). Find your city or the city nearest you and locate the figure, expressed in minutes, in the appropriate Key letter column. Add, or subtract, that figure to the time given for Boston. The result will be accurate to within 5 minutes for latitudes north of 35°, 10 minutes for latitudes 30-35°, and 15 minutes for latitudes 25-30°.

Example: April 7 (Easter) sunrise in Boston is 5:17 A.M., EST, with Key letter B (p. 58). To find the time of sunrise in Denver, Colorado, look on page 87. Key letter B for Denver is +21 min., so sunrise in Denver is 5:38 A.M., MST. Use the same process for sunset. (Add one hour for Daylight Saving Time April 28-October 27.)

Moonrise, Moonset

Moonrise and moonset are figured the same way except that an additional correction factor (see table below) based on longitude should be used. For the longitude of your city, consult pages 86-90.

Longitude of city	58°-76°	77°-89°	90°-102°	103°-115°	116°-127°	128°-141°	142°-155°
Correction minutes	0	+1	+2	+3	+4	+5	+6

Example: To determine moonrise in Little Rock, Arkansas, for September 22, 1985, see page 68. Moonrise in Boston is 2:45 P.M., EST, with Key letter E. For Little Rock, time correction E (page 88) is −3 min., moving back moonrise to 2:42 P.M. The longitude of Little Rock is 92° 17′, so the additional correction is +2 minutes. Moonrise in Little Rock is therefore 2:44 P.M., CST. (Add one hour for Daylight Saving Time.) Follow the same procedure for moonset.

Sundials

Also in the left-hand calendar pages is a column headed "Sun Fast." This is for changing sundial time into local clock time. A sundial reads natural, or sun, time which is neither Standard nor Daylight time except by coincidence. Simply *subtract* Sun Fast time to get local clock time and use Key letter C (pages 86-90) to correct the time for your city. (Add one hour for Daylight Saving Time April 28-October 27.)

Example:	Boston	Los Angeles
Sundial reading, Mar. 1	12:00	12:00
Subtract Sun Fast	−3	−3
Add Key C (for Los Angeles)		+10
Clock Time	11:57 EST	12:07 PST

Rising and Setting of the Planets

The times of rising and setting of naked-eye planets, with the exception of Mercury, are given for Boston on pages 36-37. To convert these times to those of other localities (pages 86-90), follow the same procedure as that given for finding the times of sunrise and sunset.

Length of Day

The "Length of Day" column for Boston (pages 48-74) tells how long the sun will be above the horizon. Use the Time Correction Tables (pages 86-90) to determine sunrise and sunset times for your city. Add 12 hours to the time of sunset, subtract the time of sunrise, and you will have the length of day.

Length of Twilight

Subtract from time of sunrise for dawn. Add to time of sunset for dark.

Latitude	25°N to 30°N	31°N to 36°N	37°N to 42°N	43°N to 47°N	48°N to 49°N
	h m	h m	h m	h m	h m
Jan. 1 to Apr. 10	1 20	1 26	1 33	1 42	1 50
Apr. 11 to May 2	1 23	1 28	1 39	1 51	2 04
May 3 to May 14	1 26	1 34	1 47	2 02	2 22
May 15 to May 25	1 29	1 38	1 52	2 13	2 42
May 26 to July 22	1 32	1 43	1 59	2 27	—
July 23 to Aug. 3	1 29	1 38	1 52	2 13	2 42
Aug. 4 to Aug. 14	1 26	1 34	1 47	2 02	2 22
Aug. 15 to Sept. 5	1 23	1 28	1 39	1 51	2 04
Sept. 6 to Dec. 31	1 20	1 26	1 33	1 42	1 50

Dawn and Dark

The approximate times dawn will break and dark descend are found by applying the length of twilight taken from the table above to the times of sunrise and sunset at any specific place. The latitude of the place (see pages 86-90) determines the column from which the length of twilight is to be selected.

Boston (latitude 42° 22′)		Las Vegas (latitude 36° 10′)	
Sunrise Apr. 1	5:27 A.M.	Sunrise Apr. 1	5:36 A.M.
Length of twilight	−1:33	Length of twilight	−1:26
Dawn breaks	3:54 A.M.	Dawn breaks	4:10 A.M.
Sunset Apr. 1	6:10 P.M.	Sunset Apr. 1	6:07 P.M.
Length of twilight	+1:33	Length of twilight	+1:26
Dark descends	7:43 P.M.	Dark descends	7:33 P.M.

THE RIGHT-HAND CALENDAR PAGES
(Pages 49-75)

These pages are a combination of astronomical data: specific dates in mainly the Anglican church calendar, inclusion of which has always been traditional in American and English almanacs (though we also include some other religious dates); tide heights at Boston (the left-hand calendar pages include the daily times of high tides; the corrections for your locality are on pages 78-79); quotations; anniversary dates; appropriate seasonal activities; and a rhyming version of the weather forecasts for the Northeast. (Detailed forecasts for the entire country are presented on pages 114-144.)

The following is a short summary of the highlights from this year's right-hand calendar pages, the signs used, and a sample (the first part of December 1984) of a calendar page explained. . . .

Movable Feasts and Fasts for 1985

Epiphany	Jan. 6	Low Sunday	Apr. 14
Septuagesima Sunday	Feb. 3	Rogation Sunday	May 12
Shrove Tuesday	Feb. 19	Ascension Day	May 16
Ash Wednesday	Feb. 20	Whit Sunday-Pentecost	May 26
Palm Sunday	Mar. 31	Trinity Sunday	June 2
Good Friday	Apr. 5	Corpus Christi	June 6
Easter Day	Apr. 7	1st Sunday in Advent	Dec. 1

The Seasons of 1985

Winter (1984)	Dec. 21	11:23 A.M.	E.S.T.	(Sun enters Capricorn)
Spring	Mar. 20	11:14 A.M.	E.S.T.	(Sun enters Aries)
Summer	June 21	5:44 A.M.	E.S.T.	(Sun enters Cancer)
Fall	Sept. 22	9:07 P.M.	E.S.T.	(Sun enters Libra)
Winter (1985)	Dec. 21	5:08 P.M.	E.S.T.	(Sun enters Capricorn)

Chronological Cycles for 1985

Golden Number (Lunar Cycle) . . 10
Epact 8
Solar Cycle 6
Dominical Letter . . . . F
Roman Indiction 8
Year of Julian Period 6698

ERA	Year	Begins
Byzantine	7494	Sept. 14
Jewish (A.M.)*	5746	Sept. 15

Roman (A.U.C.)	2738	Jan. 14
Nabonassar	2734	Apr. 27
Japanese	2645	Jan. 1
Grecian	2297	Sept. 14
(Seleucidae)		(or Oct. 14)
Indian (Saka)	1907	Mar. 22
Diocletian	1702	Sept. 11
Islamic (Hegira)*	1406	Sept. 15
Chinese (Lunar)	Ox	Feb. 20

*Year begins at sunset.

Determination of Earthquakes

Note, on right-hand pages 49-75, the dates when the moon (☾) "runs high" or "runs low." The date of the high begins the most likely five-day period of earthquakes in the northern hemisphere; the date of the low indicates a similar five-day period in the southern hemisphere. You will also find on these pages a notation for moon on the Equator (☾ on Eq.) twice each month. At this time, in both hemispheres, is a two-day earthquake period.

Names and Characters of the Principal Planets and Aspects

Every now and again on these right-hand calendar pages, you will see symbols conjoined in groups to tell you what is happening in the heavens. For example, ♅♂☌ opposite November 14 on page 73 means that Uranus ♅ and the Moon ☾ are on that date in conjunction ☌ or apparently near each other.

Here are the symbols used . . .

☉ The Sun	♀ Venus	♃ Jupiter	♆ Neptune
○ ● ☾ The Moon	⊕ The Earth	♄ Saturn	♇ Pluto
☿ Mercury	♂ Mars	♅ Uranus	

☌ Conjunction, or in the same degree   ☊ Ascending Node
♂ Opposition, or 180 degrees   ☋ Descending Node

Sample Page
(from December 1984—page 51)

Day of the month.   Day of the week.   For detailed regional forecasts, see pages 114-144.

The moon is at apogee, or its farthest point from the earth.

Conjunction — closest apparent approach — of Uranus and the Sun.

The moon is at the ascending node, crossing from-below to above the ecliptic plane (the plane in which the earth travels in its yearly motion around the sun).

The Dominical Letter for 1984 was A during January and February because the first Sunday of the year fell on the first day of January; after Leap Year Day it became G. The letter for 1985 is F.

2nd Sunday of Advent. Events in the church calendar generally appear in this typeface.

Moon runs high — day of the month in which the moon is highest above the south point of the observer's horizon.

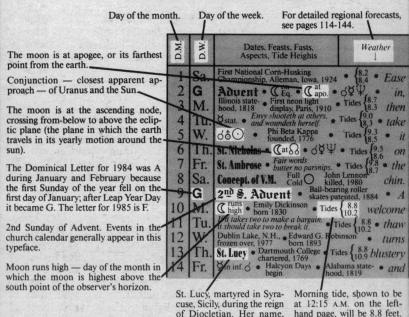

St. Lucy, martyred in Syracuse, Sicily, during the reign of Diocletian. Her name, meaning "light," and her December 13th feastday, gave rise to the folk saying, "Lucy light, shortest day, longest night."

Morning tide, shown to be at 12:15 A.M. on the left-hand page, will be 8.8 feet. Evening tide, at 12:15 P.M., will be 10.2 feet.

NOTE: The values of Key Letters are given in the Time Correction Tables.
     (See pages 86-90.)

Earth at Aphelion and Perihelion 1985

The Earth will be at Perihelion on January 3, 1985, when it will be 91,400,005 miles from the Sun. The Earth will be at Aphelion on July 5, 1985, when it will be 94,512,258 miles from the Sun.

How the Almanac Weather Forecasts Are Made

Our weather forecasts are determined both by the use of a secret weather forecasting formula devised by the founder of this almanac in 1792 and by the most modern scientific calculations based on solar activity. We believe nothing in the universe occurs haphazardly; that there is a cause-and-effect pattern to all phenomena, including weather. It follows, therefore, that we believe weather is predictable. It is obvious, however, that neither we nor anyone else has as yet gained sufficient insight into the mysteries of the universe to predict weather with anything resembling total accuracy.

Holidays, 1985

(*) Are recommended as holidays with pay for all employees. (**) State observances only.

Jan. 1 (*) New Year's Day
Jan. 15 (**) Martin Luther King's Birthday
Jan. 19 (**) Robert E. Lee's Birthday (Ala.,
    Ark., Miss., S.C., Tenn.);
    Lee-Jackson Day (Va.); Confederate
    Heroes Day (Tex.)
Feb. 2 Groundhog Day
Feb. 12 (**) Abraham Lincoln's Birthday
Feb. 14 Valentine's Day
Feb. 18 (*) George Washington's Birthday
    (Presidents' Day)
Feb. 19 (**) Mardi Gras (Ala., La.)
Mar. 2 (**) Texas Independence Day
Mar. 15 (**) Andrew Jackson Day (Tenn.)
Mar. 17 St. Patrick's Day
Mar. 18 (**) Evacuation Day (Boston and
    Suffolk Co., Mass.)
Mar. 25 (**) Seward's Day (Alaska)
Apr. 6 Passover
Apr. 7 Easter
Apr. 13 (**) Thomas Jefferson's Birthday
    (Ala., Okla.)
Apr. 15 (**) Patriots Day (Me., Mass.)
Apr. 21 (**) San Jacinto Day (Tex.)
Apr. 22 (**) Fast Day (N.H.);
    (**) Oklahoma Day;
    (**) Arbor Day (Nebr.)
Apr. 29 (**) Confederate Memorial Day
    (Ala., Ga., Miss.)
May 1 May Day
May 6 (**) Harry S. Truman's Birthday
    (Mo.)
May 12 Mother's Day
May 18 Armed Forces Day
May 20 Victoria Day (Canada)
May 27 (*) Memorial Day
June 1 (**) Statehood Day (Tenn.)
June 3 (**) Jefferson Davis's Birthday
June 11 (**) King Kamehameha I Day
    (Hawaii)

June 14 (**) Robert M. La Follette, Jr., Day
    (Wis.)
June 14 Flag Day
June 16 Father's Day
June 17 (**) Bunker Hill Day (Boston and
    Suffolk Co., Mass.)
June 20 (**) West Virginia Day
July 1 Canada Day
July 4 (*) Independence Day
July 24 (**) Pioneer Day (Utah)
Aug. 4 (**) American Family Day (Ariz.)
Aug. 5 (**) Colorado Day
Aug. 12 (**) Victory Day (R.I.)
Aug. 16 (**) Bennington Battle Day (Vt.)
Aug. 27 (**) Lyndon B. Johnson's Birthday
    (Tex.)
Sept. 2 (*) Labor Day
Sept. 9 (**) Admission Day (Calif.)
Sept. 12 (**) Defenders Day (Md.)
Sept. 16 Rosh Hashanah
Sept. 25 Yom Kippur
Sept. 27 American Indian Day
Sept. 28 (**) Frances Willard Day
    (Minn., Wis.)
Oct. 14 (*) Columbus Day;
    (**) Pioneers Day (S. Dak.)
Oct. 18 (**) Alaska Day
Oct. 24 United Nations Day
Oct. 31 Halloween;
    (**) Nevada Day
Nov. 5 General Election Day
Nov. 11 (*) Veterans Day (Armistice Day)
Nov. 16 Sadie Hawkins Day
Nov. 28 (*) Thanksgiving Day
Dec. 8 Chanukah
Dec. 10 (**) Wyoming Day
Dec. 15 Bill of Rights Day
Dec. 17 Wright Brothers Day
Dec. 21 (**) Forefathers Day (New England)
Dec. 25 (*) Christmas Day

Aph. — Aphelion: Planet reaches point in its orbit farthest away from the sun.

Apo. — Apogee: Moon reaches point in its orbit farthest from the earth.

Conj. — Conjunction: Time of apparent closest approach to each other of any two heavenly bodies.

Declination: Measure of angular distance any celestial object lies perpendicularly north or south of celestial equator; analogous to terrestrial latitude. The Almanac gives the sun's declination at noon E.S.T.

Dominical Letter: Used for the ecclesiastical calendar and determined by the date on which the first Sunday of the year falls. If Jan. 1 is a Sunday, the Letter is A; if Jan. 2 is a Sunday, the Letter is B; and so to G when the first Sunday is Jan. 7. In leap years the Letter applies through February and then takes the Letter before.

Eclipse, Annular: An eclipse in which sunlight shows around the moon.

Eclipse, Lunar: Opposition of sun and moon with the moon at or near node.

Eclipse, Solar: Conjunction of sun and moon with the moon at or near node.

El. — Elongation: Apparent angular distance of a member of the solar system from the sun as seen from the earth.

Epact: A number from 1 to 30 to harmonize the lunar year with the solar year, used for the ecclesiastical calendar. Indicates the moon's age on Jan. 1.

Eq. — Equator: A great circle of the earth equidistant from the two poles.

Equinox, Fall: Sun passes from northern to southern hemisphere.

Equinox, Spring: Sun passes from southern to northern hemisphere.

Evening Star: A planet that is above the horizon at sunset and less than 180° east of the sun.

Golden Number: Denoting the year in the 19-year cycle of the moon. The moon phases occur on the same dates every nineteen years.

Gr. El.: Greatest Elongation.

Inf. — Inferior: Conjunction in which the planet is between the sun and the earth.

Julian Period: A period of 7,980 Julian years, being a period of agreement of solar and lunar cycles. Add 4,713 to year to find Julian year.

Moon's Age: The number of days since the previous new moon. First Quarter: Right half of moon illuminated. Full Moon: Moon reaches opposition. Last Quarter: Left half of moon illuminated. New Moon: Sun and Moon in conjunction.

Moon Runs High or Low: Day of month moon is highest or lowest exactly above the South point of observer's horizon.

Morning Star: A planet that is above the horizon at sunrise and less than 180° west of the sun in right ascension.

Node: Either of the two points where the moon's orbit intersects the ecliptic.

Occultations: Eclipses of stars by the moon.

Opposition: Time when the sun and moon or planet appear on opposite sides of the sky (El. 180 degrees).

Perig. — Perigee: Moon reaches point in its orbit closest to the earth.

Perih. — Perihelion: Planet reaches point in its orbit closest to the sun.

R.A. — Right Ascension: The coordinate on the celestial sphere analogous to longitude on the earth.

Roman Indiction: A cycle of 15 years established Jan. 1, A.D. 313 as a fiscal term. Add 3 to the number of years in the Christian era and divide by 15. The remainder is the year of Roman Indiction — no remainder is 15.

Solar Cycle: A period of 28 years, at the end of which the days of the month return to the same days of the week.

Solstice, Summer: Point at which the sun is farthest north of the celestial equator: Sun enters Cancer. **Winter:** Point at which the sun is farthest south of the celestial equator: Sun enters Capricorn.

Stat. — Stationary: Halt in the apparent movement of a planet against the background of the stars just before the planet comes to opposition.

Sun Fast: Subtract times given in this column from your sundial to arrive at the correct Standard Time.

Sunrise & Sunset: Visible rising and setting of the sun's upper limb across the unobstructed horizon of an observer whose eyes are 15' above ground level.

Sup. — Superior: Superior Conjunction; indicates that the sun is between the planet and the earth.

Twilight: Begins or ends when stars of the sixth magnitude disappear or appear at the zenith; or when the sun is about 18 degrees below the horizon.

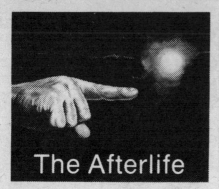

The Afterlife

Is there too much emphasis on the afterlife? Are the heaven and hell men anticipate figments of their own minds—and conditions which they create *here*? Are men forfeiting the divine opportunities this life affords by merely making it a preparation for a future existence? Is it not possible that here—on Earth—men can become the real images of their god by understanding and expressing the infinite element within them? If deity is universal in its essence, not isolated in remote space, then all the elements of spiritual ecstasy and beatitude are possible in this life.

FREE BOOK

Too long have men placed their god beyond the galaxies and closed their consciousness to the divinity residing within themselves. Not beyond the threshold of death, but in *this world* does it lie within the province and power of man to experience that supreme state of Peace Profound. For those who think tradition should be reexamined in the light of our times, we offer the fascinating free book, *The Mastery of Life.* Address: Scribe ASL

The ROSICRUCIANS
(AMORC)
San Jose, California
95191, U.S.A.
(Not A Religion)

For 50 years, people have chosen Thompson vitamins for the same reasons you grow your own crops – to get absolute freshness and the best that nature has to offer.

The Thompson Company is celebrating 50 years of providing the purest, most natural vitamins available. Thompson offers a complete line of vitamin and mineral supplements in a variety of dosages, bottle sizes and forms, including tablets, capsules and easy-to-swallow soft capsules. They are all double-sealed to provide guaranteed freshness and full labeled potency through the freshness date clearly marked on each bottle.

As part of our 50 year celebration, we are offering readers of "The Farmer's Almanac" free coupons worth $5.00 on Thompson products. Simply send a self-addressed stamped envelope to: The Thompson Company, Box 1, 475 Alaska Ave., Torrance, CA 90503. Please allow 4 to 6 weeks for mailing and handling.

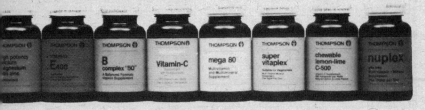

THOMPSON
The vitamin company.

THE PLANETS, 1985

The times of rising or setting of the planets Venus, Mars, Jupiter, and Saturn on the 1st, 11th, and 21st of each month are given below. The approximate time of rising or setting of these planets on other days may be found with sufficient accuracy by interpolation. For an explanation of Key Letters (used in adjusting the times given here for Boston to the time in your town), see page 27 and pages 86-90. Key Letters appear as capital letters beside the time of rising or setting. (For definitions of morning and evening stars, see page 32.)

VENUS is brilliant in the evening sky from the beginning of the year until the end of March, when it becomes too close to the sun for observation. It reappears as a morning star just before mid April and can thereafter be seen in the morning sky until just before mid December, when it again becomes too close to the sun. Venus is in conjunction with Mars on February 8, February 15, and October 4, and with Mercury on March 23 and December 4.

Boldface — P.M.   Lightface — A.M.

Jan. 1	set	**8:10**	B	May 1	rise	3:09	B	Sept. 1	rise	2:15	A
Jan. 11	"	**8:29**	B	May 11	"	2:47	B	Sept. 11	"	2:36	B
Jan. 21	"	**8:45**	B	May 21	"	2:29	B	Sept. 21	"	2:59	B
Feb. 1	set	**8:59**	C	June 1	rise	2:11	B	Oct. 1	rise	3:22	B
Feb. 11	"	**9:07**	D	June 11	"	1:56	B	Oct. 11	"	3:46	B
Feb. 21	"	**9:07**	D	June 21	"	1:44	B	Oct. 21	"	4:10	C
Mar. 1	set	**9:00**	D	July 1	rise	1:34	A	Nov. 1	rise	4:36	D
Mar. 11	"	**8:37**	D	July 11	"	1:28	A	Nov. 11	"	5:01	D
Mar. 21	"	**7:53**	D	July 21	"	1:27	A	Nov. 21	"	5:27	D
Apr. 1	rise	4:57	B	Aug. 1	rise	1:31	A	Dec. 1	rise	5:53	D
Apr. 11	"	4:12	B	Aug 11	"	1:40	A	Dec. 11	"	6:18	E
Apr. 21	"	3:36	B	Aug. 21	"	1:55	A	Dec. 21	"	6:40	E
								Dec. 31	rise	6:58	E

MARS can be seen only in the evening sky for the first five months of the year, passing 6° N. of Aldebaran on May 11. At the end of May it becomes too close to the sun for observation. Mars reappears in the morning sky in early September, passing 0.8° N. of Regulus on September 9, then moving through Virgo, passing 3° N. of Spica on December 2. Mars is in conjunction with Venus on February 8, February 15, and October 4, and with Mercury on September 4. Mars is distinguished by its reddish tint.

MARS

Jan. 1	set	**8:55**	B	May 1	set	**8:39**	E	Sept. 1	rise	3:53	B
Jan. 11	"	**8:55**	B	May 11	"	**8:35**	E	Sept. 11	"	3:47	B
Jan. 21	"	**8:55**	C	May 21	"	**8:29**	E	Sept. 21	"	3:40	B
Feb. 1	set	**8:55**	C	June 1	set	**8:21**	E	Oct. 1	rise	3:34	B
Feb. 11	"	**8:54**	C	June 11	"	**8:11**	E	Oct. 11	"	3:27	B
Feb. 21	"	**8:53**	C	June 21	"	**8:09**	E	Oct. 21	"	3:20	C
Mar. 1	set	**8:52**	C	July 1	set	**7:47**	E	Nov. 1	rise	3:12	C
Mar. 11	"	**8:51**	D	July 11	"	**7:31**	E	Nov. 11	"	3:04	C
Mar. 21	"	**8:50**	D	July 21	" rise	4:18	A	Nov. 21	"	2:57	C
Apr. 1	set	**8:48**	D	Aug. 1	rise	4:12	A	Dec. 1	rise	2:49	D
Apr. 11	"	**8:46**	D	Aug. 11	"	4:06	A	Dec. 11	"	2:42	D
Apr. 21	"	**8:43**	E	Aug. 21	"	4:00	A	Dec. 21	"	2:34	D
								Dec. 31	rise	2:26	D

JUPITER is briefly visible as an evening star early in January and then becomes too close to the sun for observation until it reappears in the morning sky at the end of January. It is at opposition on August 4, when it can be seen throughout the night. Thereafter its eastern elongation gradually decreases, and from early November until the end of 1985 it is visible only in the evening sky. Jupiter is in conjunction with Mercury on January 31.

IVPITER

Jan. 1	set	5:09	A	May 1	rise	1:19	D	Sept. 1	set	2:38	A
Jan. 11	"	4:41	A	May 11	"	12:42	D	Sept. 11	"	1:55	A
Jan. 21	rise	6:53	E	May 21	"	12:05	D	Sept. 21	"	1:13	A
Feb. 1	rise	6:19	E	June 1	rise	11:19	D	Oct. 1	set	12:28	A
Feb. 11	"	5:47	E	June 11	"	10:40	D	Oct. 11	"	11:50	A
Feb. 21	"	5:15	E	June 21	"	9:59	D	Oct. 21	"	11:13	A
Mar. 1	rise	4:49	E	July 1	rise	9:18	D	Nov. 1	set	10:34	A
Mar. 11	"	4:16	D	July 11	"	8:37	D	Nov. 11	"	10:00	A
Mar. 21	"	3:42	D	July 21	"	7:54	D	Nov. 21	"	9:28	A
Apr. 1	rise	3:05	D	Aug. 1	rise	7:07	D	Dec. 1	set	8:56	A
Apr. 11	"	2:30	D	Aug. 11	set	4:14	A	Dec. 11	"	8:26	A
Apr. 21	"	1:55	D	Aug. 21	"	3:28	A	Dec. 21	"	7:57	A
								Dec. 31	set	7:28	B

SATV RN9

SATURN rises well before sunrise at the beginning of the year in Libra, and remains in this constellation for most of the year. It is at opposition on May 15, when it is visible all night. From early August until early November it is visible only in the evening sky. Saturn then moves too close to the sun to be seen until just before mid December, when it reappears at morning in Scorpius. Saturn is in conjunction with Mercury on October 30 and December 16.

Jan. 1	rise	3:33	D	May 1	rise	7:42	D	Sept. 1	set	9:23	B
Jan. 11	"	2:58	D	May 11	"	6:59	D	Sept. 11	"	8:45	B
Jan. 21	"	2:23	D	May 21	set	4:19	B	Sept. 21	"	8:08	A
Feb. 1	rise	1:43	D	June 1	set	3:33	B	Oct. 1	set	7:31	A
Feb. 11	"	1:06	D	June 11	"	2:52	B	Oct. 11	"	6:55	A
Feb. 21	"	12:28	D	June 21	"	2:11	B	Oct. 21	"	6:19	A
Mar. 1	rise	11:53	D	July 1	set	1:30	B	Nov. 1	set	5:39	A
Mar. 11	"	11:14	D	July 11	"	12:49	B	Nov. 11	"	5:04	A
Mar. 21	"	10:34	D	July 21	"	12:09	B	Nov. 21	"	4:28	A
Apr. 1	rise	9:49	D	Aug. 1	set	11:22	B	Dec. 1	rise	6:11	D
Apr. 11	"	9:07	D	Aug. 11	"	10:43	B	Dec. 11	"	5:38	D
Apr. 21	"	8:25	D	Aug. 21	"	10:05	B	Dec. 21	"	5:04	D
								Dec. 31	rise	4:30	E

MERCURY can be seen low in the east only before sunrise, or low in the west after sunset. It is visible in the mornings between these approximate dates: January 1-February 6, April 11-May 31, August 19-September 13, and December 4-December 31. The planet is brighter at the end of each period; best viewing conditions in northern latitudes occur around mid December. It is visible in the evenings between these approximate dates: March 2-March 27, June 15-August 4, and October 6-November 23. The planet is brighter at the beginning of each period; best viewing conditions in northern latitudes occur around mid March.

DO NOT CONFUSE 1) Jupiter with Mercury around mid January and with Mars at mid October; on both occasions, Jupiter is the brighter object. 2) Venus with Jupiter in late January and late November, with Mercury in late April and early May, and with Saturn in early October; in each case Venus is the brighter. 3) Mars with Saturn around mid February, when Mars is distinguished by its reddish tint, and again from late May until late June, when Mars is brighter.

LETTERS TO THE ASTRONOMER

Dr. George Greenstein, astronomer
for *The Old Farmer's Almanac,* answers readers' questions

How does the moon cause tides, and why is there also a high tide on the side of the earth opposite the moon?

Tides are caused by the moon's gravity. As it passes overhead it pulls the ocean slightly towards it, and the ocean bulges upwards. At the same time, though, the moon is also pulling the entire earth upwards towards it, although this pull is weaker because the earth as a whole is farther from the moon than the ocean, and gravity is weaker over great distances than over short ones. It is a double motion: the ocean directly underneath the moon lifts upwards and we get a high tide, and the entire earth pulls away from the ocean on the *far* side and we get a high tide there, too. So there are two high tides a day.

The earth is nearest to the sun in January and farthest in July. Does this have any effect on temperatures in either the southern or the northern hemisphere?

Seasons are caused by the tilt of the earth's axis: when the northern hemisphere is tilted away from the sun, it is winter here. So happens that at just this time we are closest to the sun. If we were *much* closer, this would entirely cancel out the winter; similarly, six months later when we are farthest from the sun, summer would be canceled. But because the earth drifts only a relatively slight distance towards and away from the sun, we experience only a slight moderation of the seasons. The situation is reversed in the southern hemisphere though: there the seasons are a little more severe than here.

What are the astronomical events of 1985 to watch for?

On September 4 climb out of bed just before dawn to see one of the closest conjunctions of all time between Mercury and Mars. They will appear to be nearly touching. On October 4, Venus and Mars will be in conjunction just before dawn, both very brilliant.

What would happen if the earth were struck by a comet? Has it ever happened?

It would be a disaster of unparalleled magnitude. The force with which it struck would be incomparably greater than that of any hydrogen bomb. Comets contain great amounts of methane, ammonia, and carbon dioxide, and enough would be released into the atmosphere to render the air poisonous for miles around the point of impact. Since most of the earth is covered by oceans, it would probably land there, and so much water would be vaporized that the worldwide humidity level would be drastically raised.

It may be that such a collision did occur in the far distant past and was responsible for the extinction of the dinosaurs. Luckily, however, these disasters are exceedingly unlikely and there is no appreciable chance of one happening within hundreds of thousands of years. Certainly we are *not* on a collision course with Halley's comet.

Are new stars being formed, or did they all form at the same time?

They are continually being formed. The Pleiades are an example of a group of newly formed stars: when the dinosaurs walked the earth, the Pleiades did not exist.

Do any heavenly bodies ever move in an unpredictable way — i.e., haphazardly?

No. Their motion may be complicated, but it is comprehensible. □□

How Young a Moon Can You See?
by Chet Raymo

☐ THE SPORT OF LOOKING FOR VERY young and very old moons was a popular pastime in Britain at the turn of the century. In 1971 Joseph Ashbrook described some of the British observations in *Sky and Telescope* magazine. His article sparked a revival of interest in the art of spotting thin lunar crescents.

Very old moons can be observed in the east at dawn. It is somewhat more challenging (and convenient) to look for young moons in the west at sunset. The moon is exactly new at the moment it passes between the earth and the sun. You are unlikely to notice the young moon until three or four days after it is new, when the fattening crescent has moved out of twilight into the dark night sky. A two-day-old moon is not difficult to see, if you know where to look. To see a moon one day old requires planning and patience.

The record for the youngest moon seen with the naked eye belongs to Lizzie King and Nellie Collinson, two housemaids of Scarborough, England, who saw a moon 14½ hours old on May 2, 1916. Their claim was checked by the amateur astronomer Charles Whitwell, who had a passionate interest in such matters, and it appears to be genuine. The best observations of recent years are mostly far behind.

To find a young moon, check the last column of the *Almanac*'s monthly left-hand calendar for moons one or two days old. To obtain an approximate age for a moon less than a day old, subtract the time of the new moon from the time of sunset at your locality. For example, the moon will be new on January 20, 1985, at 9:30 P.M. EST. At sunset on January 21 (4:44 P.M.), the moon will be about 19 hours old.

The age of the moon is not the only factor that will determine your chance of seeing it. The altitude of the moon above the horizon is critical. Young moons are best sought in the spring, when the plane of the moon's orbit is steeply inclined to the western horizon. (For the same reason, look for old moons on fall mornings.) An unobstructed horizon, clear skies, and good eyesight are also important.

A one-day-old moon will be closer to the just-set sun than your spread fingers held at arm's length. If you see such a moon, you can rightly take pride in the achievement. (Of course, *never* look directly at the sun.) Any moon younger than 18 or 19 hours is worth reporting. You can write to *Sky and Telescope,* 49 Bay State Rd., Cambridge, MA 02238. To be useful, any report should include precise information on time, place, and atmospheric conditions. Binoculars will help you find the young moon, but to count as a record the crescent must be seen with the naked eye.   ☐ ☐

ECLIPSES FOR 1985

There will be four eclipses in 1985, two of the sun and two of the moon. Lunar eclipses technically are visible from the entire night side of the earth; solar eclipses are visible only in certain local areas. Of the 1985 eclipses, none will be visible from the United States, except for the partial solar eclipse of May 19, which will be visible in Alaska.

1. Total eclipse of the moon, May 4. The eclipse of the full moon will be visible in Australasia, Asia, Europe, and Africa.

2. Partial eclipse of the sun, May 19. The partial solar eclipse will be visible across northeastern Asia, Japan, the extreme northern regions of North America, Greenland, Iceland, northern Scandinavia, and arctic regions. The area of greatest eclipse will be at longitude 80° 53.0′ east and latitude 63° north.

3. Total eclipse of the moon, October 28. This second total lunar eclipse of the year will be visible across Australasia, Asia, Europe, and Africa.

4. Total eclipse of the sun, November 12. This total solar eclipse will be limited to viewers in Antarctica and southern South America. The area of greatest eclipse will be at longitude 165° 7.6′ west and latitude 62° south.

FULL MOON DAYS

	1985	1986	1987	1988	1989		1985	1986	1987	1988	1989
Jan.	6	25	14	3	21	July	2/31	21	10	28	18
Feb.	5	24	13	2	20	Aug.	30	19	9	27	16
Mar.	6	25	15	3	22	Sept.	28	18	7	25	15
Apr.	5	24	13	2	20	Oct.	28	17	6	24	14
May	4	23	13	1/31	20	Nov.	27	16	5	23	13
June	2	21	11	29	19	Dec.	27	16	5	23	12

PRINCIPAL METEOR SHOWERS

Shower	Best Hour (EST)	Radiant Direction*	Date of Maximum**	Approx. Peak Rate (/hr.)	Associated Comet
Quadrantid	5 A.M.	N.	Jan. 4	40-150	—
Lyrid	4 A.M.	S.	Apr. 21	10-15	1861 I
Eta Aquarid	4 A.M.	S.E.	May 4	10-40	Halley
Delta Aquarid	2 A.M.	S.	July 30	10-35	—
Perseid	4 A.M.	N.	Aug. 11-13	50-100	1862 III
Draconid	9 P.M.	N.W.	Oct. 9	10	Giacobini-Zinner
Orionid	4 A.M.	S.	Oct. 20	10-70	Halley
Taurid	midnight	S.	Nov. 9	5-15	Encke
Andromedid	10 P.M.	S.	Nov. 25-27	10	Biela
Leonid	5 A.M.	S.	Nov. 16	5-20	1866 I
Geminid	2 A.M.	S.	Dec. 13	50-80	—
Ursid	5 A.M.	N.	Dec. 22	10-15	—

* Direction from which the meteors appear to come.
** Date of actual maximum occurrence may vary by one or two days in either direction.

BRIGHT STARS, 1985

The upper table shows the Eastern Standard Time when each star transits the meridian of Boston (i.e., lies directly above the horizon's south point there), and its altitude above that point at transit on the dates shown. The time of transit on any other date differs from that on the nearest date listed by approximately four minutes of time for each day. For a place outside Boston the local time of the star's transit is found by correcting the time at Boston by the value of Key Letter "C" for the place. (See footnote.)

Star	Constellation	Magni-tude	Time of Transit (E.S.T.) Boldface—P.M. Lightface—A.M.						Alt.
			Jan. 1	Mar. 1	May 1	July 1	Sept. 1	Nov. 1	
Altair	Aquila	0.8	**12 49**	8 57	4 57	**12 57**	**8 49**	**4 49**	56.3
Deneb	Cygnus	1.3	**1 39**	9 48	5 48	**1 48**	**9 40**	**5 40**	87.5
Fomalhaut	Psc. Austr.	1.2	**3 54**	**12 02**	8 02	4 02	**11 55**	7 55	17.8
Algol	Perseus	2.2	**8 05**	**4 13**	**12 13**	8 13	4 09	12 10	88.5
Aldebaran	Taurus	0.9	**9 32**	**5 40**	**1 40**	9 40	5 37	1 37	64.1
Rigel	Orion	0.1	**10 10**	**6 18**	**2 19**	10 19	6 15	2 15	39.4
Capella	Auriga	0.1	**10 12**	**6 20**	**2 20**	10 21	6 17	2 17	85.4
Bellatrix	Orion	1.6	**10 21**	**6 29**	**2 29**	10 30	6 26	2 26	54.0
Betelgeuse	Orion	0.7	**10 51**	**6 59**	**2 59**	10 59	6 56	2 56	55.0
Sirius	Can. Maj.	-1.4	**11 41**	7 49	3 49	11 49	7 45	3 46	31.0
Procyon	Can. Min.	0.4	12 39	**8 43**	**4 43**	**12 43**	8 39	4 39	52.9
Pollux	Gemini	1.2	12 45	**8 49**	**4 49**	**12 49**	8 45	4 45	75.7
Regulus	Leo	1.4	**3 08**	**11 12**	**7 12**	**3 12**	11 08	7 08	59.7
Spica	Virgo	1.0	6 24	2 39	**10 28**	**6 28**	**2 24**	10 25	36.6
Arcturus	Bootes	-0.1	7 15	3 23	**11 19**	**7 19**	**3 15**	11 16	66.9
Antares	Scorpius	var.09	9 28	5 36	1 36	**9 32**	**5 28**	**1 28**	21.3
Vega	Lyra	0.0	11 35	7 43	3 43	**11 39**	7 36	3 36	86.4

Risings and Settings. The times of the star's rising and setting at Boston on any date are found by applying the interval shown to the time of the star's transit on that date. Subtract the interval for the star's rising; add it for its setting. The times for a place outside Boston are found by correcting the times found for Boston by the values of the Key Letters shown. (See footnote.) The directions in which the star rises and sets shown for Boston are generally useful throughout the United States. Deneb, Algol, Capella, and Vega are circumpolar stars — this means that they do not appear to rise or set but are above the horizon.

Star	Int. hr.m.	Rising Key Dir.		Setting Key Dir.		Star	Int. hr.m.	Rising Key Dir.		Setting Key Dir.	
Altair	6 36	B	EbN	D	WbN	Sirius	5 00	D	ESE	B	WSW
Deneb		A	NNE	E	NNW	Procyon	6 23	B	EbN	D	WbN
Fomalhaut	3 59	E	SE	A	SW	Pollux	8 01	A	NE	E	NW
Algol	9 28	A	NNE	E	NNW	Regulus	6 49	B	EbN	D	WbN
Aldebaran	7 06	B	ENE	D	WNW	Spica	5 23	D	EbS	B	WbS
Rigel	5 33	D	EbS	B	WbS	Arcturus	7 19	A	ENE	E	WNW
Capella		A	NNE	E	NNW	Antares	4 17	E	SEbE	A	SWbW
Bellatrix	6 27	B	EbN	D	WbN	Vega	9 08	A	NNE	E	NNW
Betelgeuse	6 31	B	EbN	D	WbN						

NOTE: The values of Key Letters are given in the Time Correction Tables.
  (See pages 86-90.)

Earth's Most Mysterious Visitor

Halley's comet returns from the depths of the solar system every 76 years or so to remind us how little we know about comets – and how much there is to fear within ourselves.

by Donald Gropman and Kenneth Mirvis
illustrated by Carl Kirkpatrick

□ THE SMALL GROUP OF PEOPLE SI-lently watched their leader as he got ready to perform the ritual. It is impossible to know what was in their minds, but we can imagine they expected immediate relief from the dread of annihilation that had gripped them for weeks. They must also have been awestruck, for they were about to witness one of humankind's most awful deeds — a human sacrifice.

Perhaps the young virgin on the makeshift altar was numb with fear as the leader of the Sacred Followers hovered over her, knife in hand. In every direction beyond the small cluster of people, the flat scrub stretched to the horizon. Overhead the glowing, spectral tail of Halley's comet, the angry god whose wrath they were about to appease with an offering of human blood, cast its eerie, ominous light on the scene.

We tend to associate the practice of human sacrifice with pre-historic people and primitive fears. But the fact is that the Sacred Followers, a Halley's comet cult, were about to perform their bloody ritual in the 20th century, in Oklahoma, U.S.A. Theirs was among the more extreme responses to Halley's 1910 visit, but it did not stand alone. It was a bizarre event on a worldwide continuum of extraordinary behavior of the kind that usually accompanies a visit by Halley's comet.

Halley's comet, the Earth's most famous visitor from the depths of the solar system, will return to our skies toward the end of 1985 and again in the early part of 1986, after it has circled the sun. This will be Halley's first visit since 1910, but it will not arrive as a stranger; almost everyone has heard of it. As Dr. Brian Marsden, Director of the Harvard-Smithsonian Astrophysical Observatory, has remarked, "To the man in the street, the solar system consists of Mars, the rings of Saturn, and Halley's comet."

Like all comets, Halley orbits the sun. After it circled the sun in 1910, it turned and headed out toward the other end of its elliptical orbit, which lies somewhere between Neptune and Pluto, the two farthest known planets in the solar system. In 1948, when it reached that distant point, the sun's gravitational pull turned it around and caused it to head back in toward the center. It has been on its way back to us since then.

Also like all comets, the exact physical nature of Halley is unknown, though many theories have been advanced over the centuries. From ancient times through the Middle Ages, comets were believed to be optical illusions, or exhalations of the Earth which caught fire in the upper atmosphere.

These early fanciful theories were based, in part, on the assumption that comets originated on Earth and were phenomena that occurred within the Earth's atmosphere. It was not until the 16th century that Danish astronomer Tycho Brahe discovered that comets were, in fact, celestial. He demonstrated that they occurred far beyond the moon, somewhere among the planets in solar space. For the next century, the flight path of comets occupied astronomers: did a comet fly in a straight line through space, or did it follow a predetermined orbit?

Enter Edmond Halley, probably the most famous name in astronomy. He was both a Fellow and Secretary of the Royal Society and Astronomer Royal to King George I of England. Among Halley's scientific interests were the

ideas of his friend, Isaac Newton. He not only admired and championed Newton's work, but he also edited Newton's monumental *Philosophiae Naturalis Principia Mathematica* and paid for its publication out of his own pocket. In the *Principia,* Newton propounded the Law of Gravitation and the Laws of Motion. Proceeding from a suggestion offered by Newton about the orbit of comets and employing the concepts presented in the *Principia,* Halley set out to calculate the orbit of a great comet seen in 1682. After years of collecting and analyzing data, he announced in 1705 that the very same comet that had appeared in 1682 would reappear at the end of 1758.

The prediction caused little excitement. When Halley died in 1742, at the age of 86, the obituary notices dwelt on his many accomplishments, but no mention was made of "his" comet or his prediction that it would return.

When it did return on schedule to fulfill his prediction, it was immediately given Halley's name. And now that the orbital nature of comets was proven, astronomers returned to the physical problem. What *was* a comet? The most widely held view today is the "dirty snowball theory" proposed by astronomer-cometologist Dr. Fred Whipple in 1950. As its name implies, this theory holds that a comet is a relatively small, solid object composed mainly of dust and stones, ice, and a small percentage of volatile substances. More recently, scientists at the Jet Propulsion Laboratory of NASA have tentatively described the head of Halley as being five kilometers in diameter and weighing at least 65 billion tons.

This sounds very heavy, but comparatively speaking it is a featherweight. The Earth, for example, weighs 6.6 sextillion tons (6.6 followed by 21 zeros) and is one hundred billion times heavier than the estimated weight of Halley. Its relative lightness makes Halley vulnerable to numerous gravitational pulls, each of which causes a slight alteration in its orbit and speed, thus making precise predictions of its arrival time difficult. And once it arrives, its physical behavior from day to day (the shape, length, and brightness of its tail) will also defy prediction.

As soon as Halley's 1758 return revealed its periodicity (on average, it returns every 76 years), cometologists began to search for indications of its previous visits in historical records, chronicles, and illustrations. The earliest recorded appearance accepted by today's scientific community is 240 B.C., when it was described in the ancient Chinese chronicles, *Outline of the Universal Mirror.* Following the age-old belief that comets presaged momentous events, many writers tried to correlate Halley's visits with great historical incidents. Some of these coincidences are actual and definite. During Halley's A.D. 451 visit, for example, Attila the Hun was defeated at the Battle of Chalons in France, thus changing the course of history.

More famous and better documented was Halley's visit of 1066. Six months after it flashed across the skies, the English were defeated at the Battle of Hastings. Halley's appearance earlier that year was quickly interpreted as a cosmic prediction of that pivotal event.

Other purported coincidences are subject to doubt. For example, some believe Halley was the Star of Bethlehem, as depicted by Giotto in his famous painting, "The Adoration of the Magi." Others claim that the notorious Roman Emperor Nero executed all of his lively successors (which he definitely did) because his astrologers told him Halley signified imminent treachery from within the royal family.

Another theme, this one played by the popular press of 1909-1910, was Halley's potential for causing catastrophe. The fear of an encounter with an object from space, particularly a comet, has long been a destruction fantasy entertained by the human imagination, and the popular press soon created the conditions for the 1910 epidemic of comet fever. The fever rose markedly when a spectrographic analysis of Halley's light revealed the presence of deadly cyanogen gas in its tail. The anxiety caused by this discovery quickly turned to dread and terror when the world's leading astronomers announced that the Earth would actually pass through the tail of Halley's comet on the night of May 18-19, 1910.

Aware of the panic that could result

from the announcement of our coming encounter with Halley's tail and its poisonous gases, many "enlightened" spokesmen, including the editors of *Scientific American,* tried to defuse the situation with calm reassurances. They repeatedly pointed out that Halley's tail, which could exceed 100 million miles in length and 50 trillion cubic miles in volume, weighed only one-half of one ounce. It was so insubstantial that each cubic yard of its volume contained only one molecule of solid matter or gas. "The whole tail could be packed in a suitcase," declared Harvard astronomer Percival Lowell. In Cambridge, England, Professor R. S. Ball scoffed, "A rhinoceros in full charge does not fear collision with a cobweb."

While *Scientific American* and other apparently responsible publications addressed the enlightened, the popular press, particularly publications that specialized in yellow journalism, spoke to the great masses of people given to superstition and most vulnerable to irrational fears. One masterpiece of mixed message, which inflamed as it calmed, was delivered by the Hearst newspapers. A week before the Earth passed through the tail, Hearst's *Boston American* proclaimed, "The Earth will pass through the tail, which is composed of masses of deadly cyanogen gas, without any danger . . . The brilliancy of this ball of cyanide gas is the hope of astronomers and the nemesis of the superstitious."

By this time comet fever was rampant and had been for six months. Superstitious people everywhere watched for signs of Halley's curse. They found one in the death of Mark Twain. On its 1835 visit, Halley had reached perihelion (its closest approach to the sun) on November 14. Two weeks later, on November 30, Samuel Clemens was born

---

He gathered some timbers and erected a crude crucifix. Then he took his hammer, a few long spikes, and methodically nailed himself to the cross.

---

in Hannibal, Missouri. The boy who was to become Mark Twain had a lifelong fascination with Halley, believing it to be his talisman.

By 1909 Twain was an internationally loved humorist and author, but he was a bitter and tired man. Two of his four children were already dead, as was his beloved wife Livy. His finances were shaky and he was ill. At Christmastime his daughter Jean died suddenly. He never recovered from this blow. A short time later he wrote a letter to a friend in which he imagined God to be talking about Mark Twain and Halley's comet: " 'Here are those

unaccountable freaks. They came in together, they must go out together.' Oh! I am looking forward to that." On April 21, 1910, the day after Halley reached perihelion, Mark Twain died at the age of 75.

Another death was more dramatic. On May 6, as Halley began its spectacular outward passage, Edward VII, King of Great Britain and Ireland and Emperor of India, died suddenly at the age of 67. Here at last was a catastrophe that the cometophobes could sink their teeth into. Just as Halley had brought doom to King Harold in 1066, they claimed, so had it done in King Edward in 1910.

King Edward died on the 6th. For the next 12 days, two stories shared world headlines: the preparations for Edward's funeral, for which the crowned heads of Europe would gather, and Earth's approaching encounter with Halley's tail, scheduled for the 18th-19th. Doomsayers warned the human race to prepare for the end.

The Sacred Followers of Oklahoma tried to prevent disaster by offering a human sacrifice. As the story goes, however, they were foiled by the local sheriff and his posse, who galloped onto the macabre scene at the last minute and rescued the fair maiden.

Other worriers, who turned to self-sacrifice, were more successful. As Halley got closer and closer, a rash of suicides attributed to comet phobia broke out in nations everywhere. In California, a brooding prospector named Paul Hammerton took matters into his own hands. He was convinced he knew how to save the world. At the site of his mining claim he gathered some timbers and erected a crude crucifix. Then he took his hammer, a few long spikes, and methodically nailed himself to the cross.

The night of May 18-19, 1910, was unique in human history, witnessing what was perhaps the largest simultaneously shared event in the history of the human race. The world was split between those who partied and those who prepared. In Chicago tens of thousands sealed their windows with tape, rags, and whatever else was available, hoping to avoid the cyanogen. In the Midwest and Southwest, thousands of families took shelter in cyclone cellars. In Wilkes-Barre, Pennsylvania, miners refused to enter the mines and flocked to churches instead. In San Juan, Puerto Rico, tobacco plantations, factories, and loading docks came to a standstill. Parades and torchlight processions

---

In different sections of Talladega, Alabama, a white woman and a black man looked up at Halley and dropped dead.

---

were joined by thousands of people chanting prayers. In Stanford, Kentucky, all-night services were held at every church.

On board the liner *Germania* in mid-Atlantic, the 370 steerage passengers, "greatly disturbed," spent the night on deck wailing, praying, and brandishing crucifixes. In different sections of Talladega, Alabama, a white woman and a black man looked up at Halley and dropped dead. In Bermuda inhabitants fell to their knees in prayer, refusing to work, certain that the end of the world was upon them.

In Brooklyn, New York, a teenage girl, entranced by Halley while standing on a crowded tenement roof, fell through a skylight to her death. In Paris, France, many people bought bottled oxygen as a hedge against cyanogen and retired to the cellars of Paris for safety. In St. Petersburg, Russia, while the pious prayed, epicureans partook of elegant "comet suppers" in the finest restaurants; these were followed by "comet dances."

In Switzerland there was a rush to the highest Alpine resorts, where the view

was best. Most of the leading Swiss hotels arranged for "comet dances," many of them rooftop affairs, which commenced at midnight. The Swiss Aero Club arranged midnight balloon ascents from Lausanne.

In Manhattan, hotel rooftop "comet dinners" featuring "comet menus," "comet favors," "comet cocktails," and "comet dances" were the order of the day.

In London, England, masses of people roamed through the streets waiting for 4:00 A.M. when Halley, with its invisible cyanogen tail, would be most visible. Their vigil changed to celebration at 4:15. The English had more than just Halley on their minds. After one day of recuperation, they would witness the May 20th pageant of King Edward's funeral.

Two weeks earlier, at the time of Edward's death, doomsayers had read Halley's behavior as a definite sign that war would break out during the reign of Edward's successor, King George. And strangely enough, after the funeral the *New York Tribune* had described Archduke Ferdinand of Austria as a man "destined to make history in southeastern Europe." Four years later, in the summer of 1914, these predictions came true.

Halley's 1910 visit was one of the most memorable events of the 20th century to date. There is no telling how much excitement it will cause in 1985-86. This will be its first visit in the electronic age, and media coverage will be profuse. A new generation of telescopes and cameras will watch its every move. Space probes will approach it in attempts to solve its physical mysteries. Wherever it is visible, people will gather to view it. We do not know how deeply Halley will affect our imaginations. Comet fever is a mysterious ailment, and we are vulnerable to it any time a comet is in view. ▫ ▫

© 1984 by Donald Gropman and Kenneth Mirvis. Adapted from *Comet Fever*, to be published by Warner Books in September 1985.

When your knees go bad ...you're in trouble!

Now thanks to Coach "Cotton" Barlow, there's an answer!

Nobody knows more about crippling knee pain, stiffness and strain than "Cotton" Barlow.

The veteran football coach has seen plenty of it in his years on and off the field.

He's also discovered that ordinary knee supports and elastic bandages just can't do the job. So he finally set to work to find a way to add strength and stability directly to the joint where support and protection are needed most.

FOR PEOPLE OF ALL AGES
Today, thanks to his unique invention, thousands of men, women and children of all ages lead active, pain-free lives despite serious knee problems.

Coach Barlow's fantastic invention uses no metal yet it provides maximum lateral and cap support. This incredibly lightweight support absorbs shocks and prevents twisting. And the BARLOW™ knee support provides soothing warmth to injured or arthritic joints.

So comfortable you can wear it for hours and non-allergenic too. Choose from five sizes for your perfect fit.

NO RISK OFFER
We urge you to try Coach Barlow's remarkable knee supports for 30 days. If it doesn't bring you pain-free relief, we'll refund your money without questions.

Don't let the pain and anxiety of "bad" knees get you down. Order today. Specify size in coupon.

© 1984 BARLOW INC.

Custom form fitting pad design prevents slipping and affords maximum mobility and comfort.

Absorbs shock that is continually applied to the front, sides and back of the joint.

Adds strength and stability directly to where support and protection is needed.

Lightweight non-metal construction allows full range of motion and can be comfortably worn for hours.

Significantly reduces impact from a blow to the side of the knee.

Comes in 5 different sizes to ensure proper fit for either knee.

WHAT FOLKS SAY ABOUT MY KNEE SUPPORT:

"I'm 80 years old and certainly not an athlete... but now I can garden again and be active 'cause I wear your brace."
L.W. Oconto Falls, WI

"At first I wasn't sure... now I want a brace for the other knee. I've had knee problems for the last 5 years. I only wish I had known of this brace 5 years ago. I'm so grateful. Thank you."
J.N. Hartwell, GA

"This support is a great help to me. I could hardly get around before I got it. Thank you."
A.J. Springfield, OR

NOVEMBER, THE ELEVENTH MONTH

At around 8:37 P.M. EST on the 18th, Venus will be so close to the bright star Lambda Sagittarii that only a good telescope will show any gap between the two. With the unaided eye watch Venus approach the star the night before, then appear to merge with the star on the 18th. A very bright and spectacular conjunction occurs on the evening of the 24th when Venus is 2° south of Jupiter and a slender moon is in the west with them (watch that moon pass them on following nights). The Great Square of Pegasus is high in the southwest; the misty patch of the Andromeda Galaxy is almost overhead around 9 P.M. South of the Andromeda Galaxy is little Triangulum the Triangle and Aries the Ram. The Milky Way has swung around since summer to run east and west. The brilliant K-shape of Perseus is high in the northeast sky.

ASTRONOMICAL CALCULATIONS

○	Full Moon	8th day	12th hour	43rd min.
☾	Last Quarter	16th day	2nd hour	0 min.
●	New Moon	22nd day	17th hour	58th min.
☽	First Quarter	30th day	3rd hour	1st min.

FOR POINTS OUTSIDE BOSTON SEE KEY LETTER CORRECTIONS—PAGES 86-90

Day of Year	Day of Month	Day of Week	☉ Rises h. m.	Key	☉ Sets h. m.	Key	Length of Days h. m.	Sun Fast m.	Full Sea Boston A.M.	Full Sea Boston P.M.	☽ Rises h.m.	Key	☽ Sets h.m.	Key	Declination of sun ° ′	☽ Place	☽ Age
306	1	Th.	6 17	D	4 38	B	10 21	31	5½	5¾	2 P.M. 02	E	— —	–	14S.38	CAP	8
307	2	Fr.	6 19	D	4 37	B	10 18	31	6½	6¾	2 28	D	12 A.M. 04	B	14 57	AQU	9
308	3	Sa.	6 20	D	4 35	B	10 15	31	7½	7¾	2 50	D	1 06	C	15 16	AQU	10
309	4	G	6 21	D	4 34	B	10 13	31	8¼	8½	3 10	D	2 07	C	15 34	AQU	11
310	5	M.	6 22	D	4 33	B	10 11	31	9	9¼	3 29	C	3 07	D	15 52	PSC	12
311	6	Tu.	6 24	D	4 32	B	10 08	31	9½	10	3 49	B	4 08	D	16 10	PSC	13
312	7	W.	6 25	D	4 31	B	10 06	31	10¼	10½	4 10	B	5 09	E	16 28	PSC	14
313	8	Th.	6 26	D	4 30	B	10 04	31	10¾	11¼	4 34	B	6 12	E	16 46	ARI	15
314	9	Fr.	6 27	D	4 28	B	10 01	31	11¼	11¾	5 03	A	7 17	E	17 03	TAU	16
315	10	Sa.	6 29	D	4 27	A	9 58	31	—	12	5 38	A	8 23	E	17 20	TAU	17
316	11	G	6 30	D	4 26	A	9 56	31	12½	12¾	6 21	A	9 27	E	17 36	TAU	18
317	12	M.	6 31	D	4 25	A	9 54	31	1¼	1¼	7 13	A	10 28	E	17 52	GEM	19
318	13	Tu.	6 32	D	4 24	A	9 52	31	2	2	8 14	A	11 A.M. 22	E	18 08	GEM	20
319	14	W.	6 34	D	4 23	A	9 49	31	2¾	3	9 22	B	12 P.M. 09	E	18 23	CAN	21
320	15	Th.	6 35	D	4 23	A	9 48	30	3¾	4	10 35	B	12 47	E	18 39	CAN	22
321	16	Fr.	6 36	D	4 22	A	9 46	30	4¾	5	11 P.M. 50	C	1 19	E	18 53	LEO	23
322	17	Sa.	6 37	D	4 21	A	9 44	30	5¾	6	— —	–	1 47	D	19 08	LEO	24
323	18	G	6 38	D	4 20	A	9 42	30	6½	7	1 A.M. 05	D	2 13	D	19 22	LEO	25
324	19	M.	6 40	D	4 19	A	9 39	30	7½	8	2 19	D	2 38	C	19 36	VIR	26
325	20	Tu.	6 41	D	4 19	A	9 38	29	8½	9	3 29	E	3 04	B	19 50	VIR	27
326	21	W.	6 42	D	4 18	A	9 36	29	9¼	9¾	4 56	E	3 33	B	20 03	VIR	28
327	22	Th.	6 43	E	4 17	A	9 34	29	10¼	10¾	6 15	E	4 07	B	20 16	LIB	0
328	23	Fr.	6 45	E	4 17	A	9 32	29	11	11½	7 34	E	4 48	A	20 29	SCO	1
329	24	Sa.	6 46	E	4 16	A	9 30	28	11¾	—	8 47	E	5 37	A	20 41	OPH	2
330	25	G	6 47	E	4 15	A	9 28	28	12½	12¾	9 52	E	6 34	A	20 52	SAG	3
331	26	M.	6 48	E	4 15	A	9 27	28	1¼	1½	10 46	E	7 38	A	21 03	SAG	4
332	27	Tu.	6 49	E	4 14	A	9 25	27	2	2¼	11 A.M. 29	E	8 44	B	21 14	CAP	5
333	28	W.	6 50	E	4 14	A	9 24	27	3	3¼	12 P.M. 02	E	9 50	B	21 25	CAP	6
334	29	Th.	6 51	E	4 14	A	9 23	27	4	4	12 30	E	10 54	C	21 35	AQU	7
335	30	Fr.	6 52	E	4 13	A	9 21	26	4¾	5	12 P.M. 54	D	11 P.M. 56	C	21S.45	AQU	8

NOVEMBER hath 30 days. 1984

I saw old Autumn in the misty morn
Stand shadowless like Silence, listening
To silence, for no lonely bird would sing
Into his hollow ear from woods forlorn.
— *Thomas Hood*

D.M.	D.W.	Dates, Feasts, Fasts, Aspects, Tide Heights	Weather ↓
1	Th.	**All Saints** • George Blanda completed 37 passes for Houston, 1964	*Scudding*
2	Fr.	**All Souls** • Luftwaffe bombed London for 57th consecutive night, 1940	*clouds*
3	Sa.	Linus Pauling won Nobel Prize for chemistry, 1954 • Beef 3¢ a pound, Ill., 1837 • {8.4 / 8.7 •	*fly,*
4	G	**21st S. af. P.** • ☾ at apo. • {8.7 / 8.8 •	*throwing*
5	M.	☾ on Eq. • Roy Rogers born 1912 • Guy Fawkes' Plot, 1605 • {9.0 / 8.9 •	*rain*
6	Tu.	**St. Leonard** • General Election Day • Tides {9.3 / 9.0	*in your*
7	W.	*He that hath a good harvest may be content with a few thistles.* • Tides {9.6 / 9.1 •	*eye.*
8	Th.	Full Beaver ○ • Eclipse ○ • Patti Page born 1927	*Brightening*
9	Fr.	☾ at ☊ • Giant panda discovered in China, 1936 • {9.9 / 9.0 •	*sky,*
10	Sa.	*Old friends to meet, old wine to drink, and old wood to burn.* • Stanley found Livingstone, 1871	*then*
11	G	**22nd S. af. P.** • ☌♄☉ • **St. Martin**	*mud*
12	M.	Auguste Rodin born, 1840 • U.S. exported first oil to Europe, 1861 • {8.7 / 9.8 •	*knee-*
13	Tu.	☾ runs high • ☌♀♆ • Paul Simon born 1942 • Tides {8.5 / 9.7	*high.*
14	W.	Lech Walesa freed after 11 months in prison, Poland, 1982 • Tides {8.4 / 9.6 •	*Scurry*
15	Th.	☌☿♅ • Niagara Falls power plant began generating, 1896 • {8.4 / 9.4 •	*through*
16	Fr.	*If a man could have half his wishes, he would double his troubles.* • Tides {8.5 / 9.4 •	*a*
17	Sa.	46,000 meteoroids fell over Ariz. in 20 minutes, 1966 • Tides {8.9 / 9.5 •	*flurry.*
18	G	**23rd S. af. P.** • Imogene Coca born 1908 • {9.4 / 9.7 •	*Give*
19	M.	☾ on Eq. • Pres. Lincoln delivered Gettysburg Address, 1863 • {10.0 / 9.9 •	*thanks*
20	Tu.	☾ at peri. • *Deeds are fruits, words but leaves.* • RFK born 1925 • {10.7 / 10.1	*this*
21	W.	Moses F. Gale patented cigar lighter, 1871 • Goldie Hawn born 1945 •	*verse*
22	Th.	**Thanksgiving Day** • ☾ at ☋ • New ● • Eclipse ☉	
23	Fr.	**St. Clement** • Severe earthquake, Naples, Italy, 1980 • Tides {11.7 / 10.1	*isn't*
24	Sa.	☌♀♃ • ☌♆☾ • ☌☿☾ • Scott Joplin born 1868	*worse!*
25	G	**24th S. af. P.** • ☿ Gr. Elong. 22° East •	☌♃☾
26	M.	*Marrying for love is risky, but God smiles on it.* • Charles Schultz born 1922 •	*Gray*
27	Tu.	☌♅☾ • John Walker invented friction match, England, 1826 • {9.0 / 10.1	*as a*
28	W.	Debut of "Hopalong Cassidy," NBC television, 1948 • {8.7 / 9.5 •	*banker's*
29	Th.	King Tutankhamen's tomb opened, 1922 • Louisa May Alcott born 1832 • {8.4 / 9.0	*suit,*
30	Fr.	**St. Andrew** • Cleopatra committed suicide, 30 B.C. •	*to boot.*

Three things are difficult: to keep a secret, to bear an injury patiently, and to spend leisure well.

Farmer's Calendar

I must tear out the vegetable garden. It is finished now. I'll till it if I have time and can borrow a machine, but first I must clean out all the old vegetation, wire, strings, and stakes. I'll pick a nice afternoon, one when the sun shines; but it's a cold job anyway. My hands get cold.

The pea wire has to come down. I'll strip the dried vines from the chicken wire, then pull the poles that support the wire. The poles are old. Some of them break off at the ground when I try to pull them up. I'll have to cut some new poles for the peas next year. At the bottoms of their wire cylinders the tomato plants lie dead on the ground like exhausted serpents in a run-down menagerie. I'll uproot the old plants and carry off the cages. I'll yank the bean plants, the peppers, the sunflowers. I'll pull the cucumber vines off their fence and pack the fence away. I see I missed a couple of cucumbers. They're enormous now, the size of footballs, and about as good to eat, having gone soft within, and their hides yellow and leathery. I'll give one of them a kick.

The sun is getting down and the cold is in my feet and fingers, but I'm about done. All the leaves are off the trees. From the top of the garden I can see a white house, one I can't see during the summer, on the side of the mountain to the east. In another month the garden will be under snow. I'm up in the squash patch now, among the ruined leaves and the dead vines that run over the ground, everywhere crossing and tangling. I've never been a neat gardener. There are a number of old squashes lying about still. Now I grab a vine and give it a tug. Twenty feet away, across the confusion of mingled vines, an acorn squash gives a bob, and the vine comes taut where I'm connected to the squash as though it were a fish.

1984 DECEMBER, THE TWELFTH MONTH

Venus is now approaching its greatest eastern elongation as the Evening Star, visible high in the west after sunset. High in the south the Pleiades cluster sparkles with the V-shaped Hyades star cluster and orange Aldebaran (the Bull's eye) in Taurus. High in the north is Cassiopeia's bright M, and Perseus is overhead, followed by yellow Capella in Auriga. In the southeast springs mighty Orion with his Belt and his bright stars, blue Rigel and red Betelgeuse. Observation of the Geminid meteors is spoiled by the moon on the 14th. Jupiter disappears into the sun's afterglow, while Mars is dim high in the southwest in the evening. Saturn is now emerging in the pre-dawn sky. Winter solstice occurs at 11:23 A.M. EST on the 21st.

ASTRONOMICAL CALCULATIONS

○ Full Moon	8th day	5th hour	54th min.
☾ Last Quarter	15th day	10th hour	26th min.
● New Moon	22nd day	6th hour	48th min.
☽ First Quarter	30th day	0 hour	28th min.

FOR POINTS OUTSIDE BOSTON SEE KEY LETTER CORRECTIONS—PAGES 86-90

Day of Year	Day of Month	Day of Week	☉ Rises h. m.	Key	☉ Sets h. m.	Key	Length of Days h. m.	Sun Fast m.	Full Sea Boston A.M.	Full Sea Boston P.M.	☽ Rises h.m.	Key	☽ Sets h.m.	Key	Declination of sun ° ′	☽ Place	☽ Age
336	1	Sa.	6 54	E	4 13	A	9 19	26	5¾	6	1 P.M. 15	D	— —	–	21s.54	AQU	9
337	2	**G**	6 55	E	4 13	A	9 18	25	6½	7	1 34	C	12 A.M. 57	D	22 03	PSC	10
338	3	M.	6 56	E	4 12	A	9 16	25	7½	7¾	1 53	C	1 57	D	22 11	CET	11
339	4	Tu.	6 57	E	4 12	A	9 15	25	8¼	8½	2 14	B	2 58	E	22 19	PSC	12
340	5	W.	6 58	E	4 12	A	9 14	24	9	9¼	2 37	B	4 00	E	22 26	ARI	13
341	6	Th.	6 59	E	4 12	A	9 13	24	9½	10	3 04	B	5 04	E	22 33	ARI	14
342	7	Fr.	7 00	E	4 12	A	9 12	23	10¼	10¾	3 37	A	6 11	E	22 40	TAU	15
343	8	Sa.	7 01	E	4 12	A	9 11	23	10¾	11½	4 17	A	7 17	E	22 47	TAU	16
344	9	**G**	7 01	E	4 12	A	9 11	23	11½	—	5 07	A	8 20	E	22 53	TAU	17
345	10	M.	7 02	E	4 12	A	9 10	22	12¼	12¼	6 06	B	9 17	E	22 58	GEM	18
346	11	Tu.	7 03	E	4 12	A	9 09	22	12¾	1	7 14	B	10 07	E	23 03	GEM	19
347	12	W.	7 04	E	4 12	A	9 08	21	1¾	1¾	8 26	B	10 49	E	23 07	CAN	20
348	13	Th.	7 05	E	4 12	A	9 07	21	2½	2¾	9 40	C	11 22	E	23 11	LEO	21
349	14	Fr.	7 06	E	4 12	A	9 06	20	3¼	3½	10 P.M. 54	C	11 A.M. 51	D	23 15	LEO	22
350	15	Sa.	7 06	E	4 12	A	9 06	20	4¼	4½	— —	–	12 P.M. 17	D	23 18	LEO	23
351	16	**G**	7 07	E	4 13	A	9 06	19	5¼	5¾	12 A.M. 08	D	12 41	C	23 20	VIR	24
352	17	M.	7 08	E	4 13	A	9 05	19	6¼	6¾	1 21	D	1 06	B	23 22	VIR	25
353	18	Tu.	7 08	E	4 13	A	9 05	18	7¼	7¾	2 36	E	1 33	B	23 24	VIR	26
354	19	W.	7 09	E	4 14	A	9 05	18	8	8¾	3 52	E	2 03	B	23 25	LIB	27
355	20	Th.	7 10	E	4 14	A	9 04	17	9	9½	5 09	E	2 39	A	23 26	SCO	28
356	21	Fr.	7 10	E	4 14	A	9 04	17	9¾	10½	6 24	E	3 23	A	23 26	OPH	29
357	22	Sa.	7 11	E	4 15	A	9 04	16	10¾	11¼	7 33	E	4 17	A	23 26	SAG	0
358	23	**G**	7 11	E	4 16	A	9 05	16	11½	—	8 32	E	5 19	A	23 25	SAG	1
359	24	M.	7 11	E	4 16	A	9 05	15	12¼	12¼	9 21	E	6 24	B	23 24	SAG	2
360	25	Tu.	7 12	E	4 17	A	9 05	15	1	1	9 59	E	7 32	B	23 22	CAP	3
361	26	W.	7 13	E	4 18	A	9 05	14	1¾	2	10 30	E	8 38	B	23 20	CAP	4
362	27	Th.	7 13	E	4 18	A	9 05	14	2½	2¾	10 56	D	9 42	C	23 17	AQU	5
363	28	Fr.	7 13	E	4 19	A	9 06	13	3¼	3½	11 18	D	10 44	C	23 14	AQU	6
364	29	Sa.	7 13	E	4 20	A	9 07	13	4	4¼	11 37	C	11 P.M. 44	D	23 11	PSC	7
365	30	**G**	7 13	E	4 20	A	9 07	12	5	5¼	11 A.M. 57	C	— —	–	23 07	CET	8
366	31	M.	7 13	E	4 21	A	9 08	12	5¾	6	12 P.M. 17	B	12 A.M. 45	D	23s.03	PSC	9

DECEMBER hath 31 days. 1984

Ring out, wild bells, to the wild sky,
The flying cloud, the frosty light:
The year is dying in the night;
Ring out, wild bells, and let him die.
— *Alfred Tennyson*

D.M.	D.W.	Dates, Feasts, Fasts, Aspects, Tide Heights	Weather ↓
1	Sa.	First National Corn-Husking Championship, Alleman, Iowa, 1924 • {8.2 8.4 •	*Ease*
2	G	**Advent** • ☾ on Eq. • ☾ at apo. • ☌☿♆ •	*in,*
3	M.	Illinois statehood, 1818 • First neon light display, Paris, 1910 • Tides {8.7 8.3	*then*
4	Tu.	☿ stat. • *Envy shooteth at others, and woundeth herself.* • Tides {9.0 8.3 •	*take*
5	W.	☌♅☉ • Phi Beta Kappa founded, 1776 • Tides {9.3 8.5 •	*it*
6	Th.	**St. Nicholas** • ☾ at ☊ • ☌☿♆ • Tides {9.5 8.6	*on*
7	Fr.	**St. Ambrose** • *Fair words butter no parsnips.* • Tides {9.8 8.7 •	*the*
8	Sa.	**Concept. of V.M.** Full Cold ○ John Lennon killed, 1980	*chin.*
9	G	**2nd S. Advent** • Ball-bearing roller skates patented, 1884 •	*A*
10	M.	☾ runs high • Emily Dickinson born 1830 • Tides {8.8 10.2	*welcome*
11	Tu.	*If it takes two to make a bargain, it should take two to break it.* • Tides {8.8 10.2 •	*thaw*
12	W.	Dublin Lake, N.H., frozen over, 1977 • Edward G. Robinson born 1893 •	*turns*
13	Th.	**St. Lucy** • Dartmouth College chartered, 1769 • Tides {8.8 10.9	*blustery*
14	Fr.	☿ in inf. ☌ • Halcyon Days begin • Alabama statehood, 1819 •	*and*
15	Sa.	James Naismith invented basketball, Canada, 1891 • *Argo Merchant* oil spill, 1976 • {9.1 9.5	*raw.*
16	G	**3rd S. Advent** • ☾ on Eq. • {9.4 9.3 •	*A corker*
17	M.	*You can lead a boy to college, but you cannot make him think.* • Tides {9.8 9.3 •	*of a*
18	Tu.	☾ at peri. • Liberty Bell, muffled, tolled for Washington's death, 1799 •	*storm,*
19	W.	☾ at ☋ • ☌♄☾ • **Chanukah** • Ember Day • {10.6 9.4	*as*
20	Th.	Missouri levied tax on bachelors, 1820 • Tides {10.9 9.4 •	*holiday*
21	Fr.	**St. Thomas** • Winter solstice 11:23 A.M. EST • Ember Day •	*plans*
22	Sa.	New ● • ☌♆☉ • Ember Day • Tides {11.2 9.4	*form.*
23	G	**4th S. Advent** • ☾ runs low • ☌♃☾ • ☌☿♅	
24	M.	☿ stat. • *Tolerance should spring from charity, not from indifference.* •	*Crystal*
25	Tu.	**Christmas** • ☌♅☾ • Tides {9.1 10.4 •	*cold,*
26	W.	**St. Stephen** • ☌☿♅ • ☌♅☾ • Tornadoes, Georgia, 1964	*then*
27	Th.	**St. John** • Ether first used as childbirth anaesthetic, 1845 • {8.7 9.5 •	*sleet*
28	Fr.	**Holy Innocents** • Comet Kohoutek at perihelion, 1973 •	*foretold.*
29	Sa.	**St. Thomas à Becket** • Battle of Wounded Knee, S.D., 1890 •	*Hail*
30	G	**1st S. af. Christmas** • ☾ on Eq. • ☾ at apo. •	
31	M.	**St. Sylvester** • *With bounteous cheer conclude the year.*	*and farewell!*

Farmer's Calendar

Somebody said, "You know, the snow really brings out the rabbits." Of course, he's right about what he sees. When the first snow has been down for a night, you can go out around the meadow edges and into the pine woods and find the tracks of rabbits thick on the snow. The tracks are a string of orderly dots, most often arranged two in a line and two side by side, as though the rabbits were trying to leave a message for you in garbled Morse. The tracks wind in and out under the pines in a tangle of loops and doublings and figures in the snow that looks like the diagram of an intricate ballroom dance performed by clumsy madmen. Rabbits are busy animals.

The rabbits I know are the little brown cottontails, not the big hares that turn white in the winter. The cottontails are the ones that eat gardens (though they've never touched mine); the ones that children's literature has depended on from the beginning. Cottontails are the rabbits whose reproductive prowess you can demonstrate by one of those fancy mathematical manipulations. You can prove that if rabbits were not meat for every carnivore that breathes — if they could breed with 100 percent survival — there would in a year be no room on earth for anything but rabbits.

I'm not tracker enough to know how many rabbits are in the population that leaves the tracks I find in the snow. There are enough to make it clear that the rabbit is a common animal in my neighborhood, as common, surely, as the chipmunk, the red squirrel, the deer. But the curious thing is that I've hardly seen a rabbit in the flesh. I'd scarcely know they were around in numbers if I didn't find their tracks in winter. If I were a strict empiricist, then, like the observer above, I might believe that the snow brings the rabbits out. I know better.

1985 JANUARY, THE FIRST MONTH

Orion the Hunter, highest in the south at mid-evening, is conspicuous with his Belt of three stars in a row and his brightest stars, blue Rigel and red Betelgeuse. Blue-white Sirius, to the lower left from Orion, is the most brilliant of all stars. Much brighter is the planet Venus, which reaches a greatest elongation (farthest distance from the sun) of 47° on the 21st. Early risers on the year's first days can see Saturn in the southeast before morning twilight and Mercury rather low at a greatest elongation of 23° on the 3rd. The earth is at perihelion — closest to the sun — at 3 P.M. EST on the 3rd. On the 3rd and 4th of the month a few dozen silver-trailed Quadrantid meteors can be glimpsed in the northeast in the hour before morning twilight begins.

ASTRONOMICAL CALCULATIONS

○	Full Moon	6th day	21st hour	18th min.
☾	Last Quarter	13th day	18th hour	27th min.
●	New Moon	20th day	21st hour	30th min.
☽	First Quarter	28th day	22nd hour	31st min.

FOR POINTS OUTSIDE BOSTON SEE KEY LETTER CORRECTIONS—PAGES 86-90

Day of Year	Day of Month	Day of Week	☉ Rises h. m.	Key	☉ Sets h. m.	Key	Length of Days h. m.	Sun Fast m.	Full Sea Boston A.M.	Full Sea Boston P.M.	☽ Rises h.m.	Key	☽ Sets h.m.	Key	Declination of sun ° '	☽ Place	☽ Age
1	1	Tu.	7 14	E	4 22	A	9 08	11	6½	7	12 P.M. 39	B	1 A.M. 46	E	22s.58	ARI	10
2	2	W.	7 14	E	4 23	A	9 09	11	7¼	8	1 03	B	2 49	E	22 52	ARI	11
3	3	Th.	7 14	E	4 24	A	9 10	10	8¼	8¾	1 33	A	3 54	E	22 46	TAU	12
4	4	Fr.	7 14	E	4 25	A	9 11	10	9	9½	2 11	A	5 01	E	22 40	TAU	13
5	5	Sa.	7 14	E	4 26	A	9 12	10	9¾	10¼	2 57	A	6 05	E	22 34	TAU	14
6	6	**F**	7 14	E	4 27	A	9 13	9	10½	11	3 54	A	7 07	E	22 26	GEM	15
7	7	M.	7 13	E	4 28	A	9 15	9	11¼	11¾	5 00	A	8 00	E	22 19	GEM	16
8	8	Tu.	7 13	E	4 29	A	9 16	8	—	12	6 13	B	8 46	E	22 10	CAN	17
9	9	W.	7 13	E	4 30	A	9 17	8	12½	12¾	7 28	B	9 23	E	22 02	LEO	18
10	10	Th.	7 13	E	4 31	A	9 18	7	1¼	1½	8 44	C	9 55	D	21 53	LEO	19
11	11	Fr.	7 13	E	4 32	A	9 19	7	2	2½	9 59	D	10 22	D	21 43	LEO	20
12	12	Sa.	7 12	E	4 33	A	9 21	7	3	3¼	11 P.M. 12	D	10 46	C	21 33	VIR	21
13	13	**F**	7 12	E	4 34	A	9 22	6	3¾	4¼	— —	–	11 10	C	21 23	VIR	22
14	14	M.	7 12	E	4 36	A	9 24	6	4¾	5¼	12 A.M. 25	E	11 A.M. 35	B	21 13	VIR	23
15	15	Tu.	7 11	E	4 37	A	9 26	6	5¾	6¼	1 40	E	12 P.M. 04	B	21 02	LIB	24
16	16	W.	7 11	E	4 38	A	9 27	5	6¾	7¼	2 55	E	12 37	B	20 51	LIB	25
17	17	Th.	7 10	E	4 39	A	9 29	5	7¾	8½	4 09	E	1 17	A	20 39	OPH	26
18	18	Fr.	7 10	E	4 40	A	9 30	5	8¾	9½	5 18	E	2 06	A	20 27	OPH	27
19	19	Sa.	7 09	E	4 42	A	9 33	4	9½	10¼	6 21	E	3 03	A	20 14	SAG	28
20	20	**F**	7 08	E	4 43	A	9 35	4	10½	11	7 13	E	4 07	B	20 01	SAG	0
21	21	M.	7 08	E	4 44	A	9 36	4	11¼	11¾	7 55	E	5 15	B	19 48	CAP	1
22	22	Tu.	7 07	D	4 45	A	9 38	3	—	12	8 29	E	6 22	B	19 34	CAP	2
23	23	W.	7 06	D	4 47	A	9 41	3	12½	12¾	8 56	E	7 27	C	19 20	AQU	3
24	24	Th.	7 05	D	4 48	A	9 43	3	1¼	1½	9 20	D	8 31	C	19 06	AQU	4
25	25	Fr.	7 05	D	4 49	A	9 44	3	2	2¼	9 41	D	9 32	D	18 51	AQU	5
26	26	Sa.	7 04	D	4 50	A	9 46	2	2¾	3	10 00	C	10 32	D	18 36	PSC	6
27	27	**F**	7 03	D	4 52	A	9 49	2	3¼	3¾	10 19	C	11 P.M. 33	E	18 20	PSC	7
28	28	M.	7 02	D	4 53	A	9 51	2	4	4½	10 40	B	— —	–	18 04	PSC	8
29	29	Tu.	7 01	D	4 54	A	9 53	2	5	5¼	11 03	B	12 A.M. 35	E	17 48	ARI	9
30	30	W.	7 00	D	4 56	A	9 56	2	5¾	6¼	11 A.M. 30	B	1 38	E	17 31	TAU	10
31	31	Th.	6 59	D	4 57	A	9 58	1	6½	7¼	12 P.M. 03	A	2 A.M. 43	E	17s.15	TAU	11

Old Winter sad, in snow yclad,
Is making a doleful din;
But let him howl till he crack his jowl,
We will not let him in.
— *Thomas Noel*

Farmer's Calendar

On the coldest day of winter I'll light a fire in the stove in this room, and presently, when the heat from the stove has had time to soften the cold, there will come a slow, intermittent buzzing from somewhere in the room, as though a patient salesman were ringing the doorbell. Then a fly the size of a Piper Cub will appear at the window inside, buzzing weakly, climbing up the window pane, falling back down onto the sill, buzzing.

All winter long the cracks of the house yield up an endless train of fat, lazy flies that issue forth to gather at the windows whenever the room they're living in gets warm enough. Long after most of the housefly class of 1984 have succumbed to winter outdoors, these individuals survive past their natural date inside the house. In the way they gather at the windows to look out at the inhospitable winter, they remind me of elderly, well-stuffed gentlemen, members of a venerable and aristocratic club, who from the windows of the drawing room look out at the street, and seeing the changed world out there, are grateful to be old. I expect any minute one of these flies will abruptly rustle the pages of his *Times* and ring for a brandy.

It's not all Easy Street for the flies that move indoors for the winter. They are still flies, and I squash them when they bother me. The cats in the house love to chase them, especially the kittens, who are electrified by the noisy, struggling flies and try to climb right up the window after them. By springtime the number of indoor flies has been cut down. But there are always a few left around, and it's one of the year's little ceremonies on a warm early spring day to open the window for the first time in six or seven months and watch those aged flies at last buzz heavily away.

D.M.	D.W.	Dates, Feasts, Fasts, Aspects, Tide Heights	Weather ↓
1	Tu.	𝕮ircumcision • New Year's Day •	*Snow*
2	W.	14°F., Haleakala, Hawaii, 1961 • Tides {8.8 / 7.8	*and ice,*
3	Th.	☾ at ☍ • ☿ Gr. Elong. W. (23°) • ⊕ at perihelion 3:00 P.M. EST	*no*
4	Fr.	*In a calm sea every man is a pilot.* • Tides {9.4 / 8.2	*school —*
5	Sa.	Nellie Ross became first woman governor of a state, Wyoming, 1925 • {9.8 / 8.4	*that's*
6	F	𝕰piphany • Full ☾ Wolf • ☾ runs high	*nice!*
7	M.	Plough Monday • Fanny Farmer published her first cookbook, 1896 • Tides {10.4 / 8.9	*No*
8	Tu.	*To believe a thing impossible is to make it so.* • Tides {— / 10.7	*law*
9	W.	"The Seeing Eye" dog training school incorporated, 1929 • Richard Nixon born, 1913	*against*
10	Th.	-28°F., Sheboygan, Wisconsin, 1982 • First aerial photography, 1911 • {9.4 / 10.7	*a thaw.*
11	Fr.	☾ at peri. • Francium discovered, 1930 • Tides {9.6 / 10.4	*Icy*
12	Sa.	☾ on Eq. • Jack London born, 1876 • Tides {9.8 / 10.0	*chill,*
13	F	1ˢᵗ 𝕊. af. 𝕰piph. • ☌☿Ψ • St. Hilary	*winter's*
14	M.	☌2⟂☉ • "The Today Show" debuted on N.B.C., 1952 • {10.0 / 9.1	*a*
15	Tu.	*Wisdom is knowing what to do next; virtue is doing it.* • {10.0 / 8.8	*bitter*
16	W.	☾ at • ☍♂☾ • A. J. Foyt born, 1935 • Tides {10.1 / 8.6	*pill.*
17	Th.	St. Antony • ☌♂☾ • 135 mph winds, Boulder, Colo., 1982	*Your*
18	Fr.	☌Ψ☾ • Francisco Pizarro founded Lima, Peru, 1535 • {10.3 / 8.7	*bicycle*
19	Sa.	☾ runs low • ☌♂☾ • Dolly Parton born, 1946 • {10.4 / 8.8	*grows*
20	F	2ⁿᵈ 𝕊. af. 𝕰piph. • New ● •	*icicles;*
21	M.	St. Agnes • ♀ Gr. Elong. E. (47°) • Tides {10.4 / 8.9	*seize*
22	Tu.	St. Vincent • Allied troops landed at Anzio, 1944 • {— / 10.3	*your*
23	W.	Tornado killed 28 in Hazelhurst, Miss., 1969 • Humphrey Bogart born, 1899	*skis.*
24	Th.	St. Timothy • ☌♀☾ • ☌♂☾ • {8.9 / 9.7	*Flurry*
25	Fr.	Conv. of Paul • First Winter Olympics, Chamonix, France, 1924 •	*worries.*
26	Sa.	☾ on Eq. • George F. Green patented the electric dental drill, 1875	*Snow's*
27	F	3ʳᵈ 𝕊. af. 𝕰piph. • ☾ at apo. • {8.7 / 8.4	*hush*
28	M.	*Laziness travels so slowly that poverty soon overtakes him.* • {8.6 / 8.0	*turns*
29	Tu.	U.C.L.A. won its 88th consecutive basketball game, 1974	*quickly*
30	W.	☾ at ☍ • First known sighting of Antarctica, 1820 • Tides {8.5 / 7.5	*to*
31	Th.	☌♂2⟂ • "Scotch Tape" went on sale, 1928 • Tides {8.6 / 7.5	*slush.*

1985 FEBRUARY, THE SECOND MONTH

During the first half of February Venus shines at its brightest and highest in the southwest as darkness falls, and does not set for more than three hours after the sun. At this pinnacle of its current apparition as the Evening Star, Venus has conjunctions with Mars on both the 7th and 15th (quite unusual), though in both cases Venus is about 3° north of Mars and the latter is not very bright. Later in the month Venus will begin to set sooner than Mars, but continues to brighten until the 26th, when it is a splendid beacon at its greatest brilliancy. In the south with Orion and Sirius are the bright stars Aldebaran (in Taurus), Capella (in Auriga), Pollux and Castor (in Gemini), and Procyon (in Canis Minor). Now observers will be able to see the planet Jupiter emerge into visibility in the southeast before dawn. A short time after sunset on the 20th an extremely slender crescent moon may be glimpsed low in the west.

ASTRONOMICAL CALCULATIONS

○	Full Moon	5th day	10th hour	19th min.
☾	Last Quarter	12th day	2nd hour	57th min.
●	New Moon	19th day	13th hour	44th min.
☽	First Quarter	27th day	18th hour	42nd min.

FOR POINTS OUTSIDE BOSTON SEE KEY LETTER CORRECTIONS—PAGES 86-90

Day of Year	Day of Month	Day of Week	☉ Rises h. m.	Key	☉ Sets h. m.	Key	Length of Days h. m.	Sun Fast m.	Full Sea Boston A.M.	Full Sea Boston P.M.	☽ Rises h.m.	Key	☽ Sets h.m.	Key	Declination of sun ° ′	☽ Place	☽ Age
32	1	Fr.	6 58	D	4 58	A	10 00	1	7½	8¼	12 P.M. 45	A	3 A.M. 48	E	16s.58	TAU	12
33	2	Sa.	6 57	D	4 59	A	10 02	1	8¼	9	1 37	A	4 51	E	16 40	GEM	13
34	3	F	6 56	D	5 01	B	10 05	1	9¼	9¾	2 39	B	5 48	E	16 23	GEM	14
35	4	M.	6 55	D	5 02	B	10 07	1	10	10½	3 50	B	6 37	E	16 05	CAN	15
36	5	Tu.	6 54	D	5 03	B	10 09	1	10¾	11¼	5 07	B	7 19	E	15 47	CAN	16
37	6	W.	6 53	D	5 05	B	10 12	1	11½	—	6 25	C	7 53	E	15 28	LEO	17
38	7	Th.	6 52	D	5 06	B	10 14	1	12¼	12½	7 43	C	8 22	D	15 10	LEO	18
39	8	Fr.	6 50	D	5 07	B	10 17	1	1	1¼	8 59	D	8 48	D	14 51	VIR	19
40	9	Sa.	6 49	D	5 09	B	10 20	1	1¾	2	10 15	D	9 13	C	14 31	VIR	20
41	10	F	6 48	D	5 10	B	10 22	1	2½	3	11 P.M. 31	E	9 38	B	14 12	VIR	21
42	11	M.	6 47	D	5 11	B	10 24	1	3½	4	— —	-	10 06	B	13 52	VIR	22
43	12	Tu.	6 45	D	5 12	B	10 27	1	4¼	5	12 A.M. 46	E	10 38	B	13 32	LIB	23
44	13	W.	6 44	D	5 14	B	10 30	1	5¼	6	2 00	E	11 A.M. 16	A	13 12	SCO	24
45	14	Th.	6 43	D	5 15	B	10 32	1	6¼	7	3 11	E	12 P.M. 01	A	12 52	OPH	25
46	15	Fr.	6 41	D	5 16	B	10 35	1	7½	8¼	4 14	E	12 55	A	12 31	SAG	26
47	16	Sa.	6 40	D	5 18	B	10 38	1	8½	9¼	5 08	E	1 56	B	12 10	SAG	27
48	17	F	6 38	D	5 19	B	10 41	1	9½	10	5 53	E	3 01	B	11 50	CAP	28
49	18	M.	6 37	D	5 20	B	10 43	1	10¼	10¾	6 29	E	4 08	B	11 28	CAP	29
50	19	Tu.	6 36	D	5 21	B	10 45	1	11	11½	6 58	E	5 14	C	11 07	CAP	0
51	20	W.	6 34	D	5 23	B	10 49	1	11¾	—	7 22	D	6 18	C	10 45	AQU	1
52	21	Th.	6 33	D	5 24	B	10 51	1	12¼	12¼	7 44	D	7 21	C	10 24	AQU	2
53	22	Fr.	6 31	D	5 25	B	10 54	1	12¾	1	8 03	C	8 21	D	10 02	PSC	3
54	23	Sa.	6 30	D	5 26	B	10 56	2	1½	1¾	8 23	C	9 22	D	9 40	CET	4
55	24	F	6 28	D	5 28	B	11 00	2	2	2¼	8 43	B	10 23	E	9 17	PSC	5
56	25	M.	6 26	D	5 29	B	11 03	2	2¾	3	9 04	B	11 P.M. 26	E	8 55	ARI	6
57	26	Tu.	6 25	D	5 30	B	11 05	2	3½	3¾	9 29	B	— —	-	8 33	ARI	7
58	27	W.	6 23	D	5 31	B	11 08	2	4¼	4¾	9 59	A	12 A.M. 29	E	8 10	TAU	8
59	28	Th.	6 22	D	5 33	B	11 11	2	5	5½	10 A.M. 36	A	1 A.M. 33	E	7s.47	TAU	9

Thank God who seasons thus the year,
And sometimes kindly slants his rays;
For in his winter he's most near
And plainest seen upon the shortest days.
— *Henry David Thoreau*

Farmer's Calendar

Thirty or forty yards from my house, at the edge of a meadow, I keep a kitchen garbage dump that I call a compost pile. Four bluejays who live on the property call it a free lunch and avail themselves of its provender liberally in all seasons, but especially so in winter. They rise from the pile with a great flap and squawk as I approach with a new pail of table scraps. When I return to the house, they descend immediately and commence flinging the stuff all over the snow, keeping up a loud palaver the whole time, like a hall full of drunken undergraduates.

Bluejays are the most human of birds. We recognize them easily as creatures that are more like us than most other birds are. What is it we recognize? It's sin. The qualities we think birds have that make them resemble us are never good qualities. The cock is proud, the crow thieving, the goose a bully. Whoever felt kinship with any bird for its charity, devotion, or high-mindedness? The principle extends to animals, but not perfectly. Domestic animals we say may have human traits that are admirable: dogs are loyal and loving, cats dignified, horses stalwart. Wild animals, however, when we find them to have human qualities, have qualities we hesitate to praise: the fox's low cunning, the weasel's blood lust, the bear's clownishness.

Still, we admire them; we admire them all. Bluejays are rapacious, greedy, disorderly, noisy, evidently irresponsible. They are also beautiful; but that bright outfit and that rakish crest could not belong to a good citizen. Birds and animals do for us what certain characters in fiction do. The qualities we admire in creatures, like those we admire in some people in novels, are ones we are not so apt to admire in our friends and neighbors.

D.M.	D.W.	Dates, Feasts, Fasts, Aspects, Tide Heights	Weather ↓
1	Fr.	*Accusing the times is but excusing ourselves.* • Tides {8.9 / 7.7	*Keep*
2	Sa.	**Candlemas** • Cub Scouts founded, 1914 • Tides {9.3 / 8.0	*fingers*
3	F	**Septuagesima** • ℂ runs high	*crossed,*
4	M.	Auspicious day for marriage and repair of ships. • Tides {10.3 / 8.9	*we're*
5	Tu.	**St. Agatha** • Full Snow ○ • Ella Grasso died, 1981	*in*
6	W.	**St. Dorothea** • Society for the Protection of N.H. Forests formed, 1901	*for*
7	Th.	♂♀☌ • ℂ at peri. • Eubie Blake born, 1883 • Tides {9.9 / 11.1	*a*
8	Fr.	ℂ on Eq. • *He that lives on hope alone will die fasting.* • {10.3 / 11.0	*frost.*
9	Sa.	-63°F., Moran, Wyo., 1933 • Dean Rusk born, 1909 • Tides {10.5 / 10.7	*Heavy*
10	F	**Sexagesima** • Civilian auto production halted, 1942 • snow,	*snow,*
11	M.	℗ stat. • Ruth Carol Stewart hired as first black airline stewardess, 1958	*sledders*
12	Tu.	ℂ at ☍ • ♂♃ℂ • Lincoln's Birthday • Tides {10.2 / 8.9	*go!*
13	W.	♂♃ℂ • Ice jammed the Mississippi River in New Orleans, La., 1784	*Warm*
14	Th.	**St. Valentine** • First California oranges arrived on East Coast, 1886	*heart,*
15	Fr.	ℂ runs low • ♂♆ℂ • ♂♀☌ • Tides {9.7 / 8.2	*but*
16	Sa.	Flooded coal mine in Braidwood, Ill., 69 drowned, 1883 • {9.8 / 8.3	*the*
17	F	**Quinquagesima** • ♂♃ℂ • Tides {9.9 / 8.6	*car*
18	M.	Presidents Day holiday • The planet Pluto discovered, 1930 • {10.0 / 8.8	*won't*
19	Tu.	**Shrove Tues.** • ☿ at sup. ☌ • New ●	*start.*
20	W.	**Ash Wed.** • Wind today continues through Lent.	*start.*
21	Th.	First telephone directory (fifty names), New Haven, Conn., 1878 • {9.1 / 9.8	*Rime*
22	Fr.	ℂ on Eq. • *The sting of a reproach is the truth of it.* • Tides {9.2 / 9.6	*time.*
23	Sa.	♂♀ℂ • ♂♃ℂ • ℂ at apo. • Tides {9.2 / 9.3	*Days*
24	F	**1st S. Lent** • **St. Matthias**	*growing*
25	M.	91.6°F. Los Angeles, Calif., 1921 • George Harrison born, 1943	*longer,*
26	Tu.	ℂ at ☌ • ♀ greatest brilliancy • *Avoid popularity.*	*wind*
27	W.	Ember Day • Saccharin discovered, 1879 • {8.7 / 7.7	*blowing*
28	Th.	Bachelors Day • Zero Mostel born, 1915 • {8.6 / 7.5	*stronger!*

History is something that never happened, written by a man who wasn't there. — *Anon.*

1985 MARCH, THE THIRD MONTH

As Venus approaches the earth it presents more of its night side to us and loses some of its brightness but becomes large enough to see as a crescent in steadily held binoculars. Observers will be able to see it get noticeably lower in the west with each successive twilight. Meanwhile, Mercury attains its best altitude of the year in the evening sky, becoming visible early in the month and reaching a greatest elongation (farthest distance from the sun) of 18.5° on the 17th. Venus passes 5° north of Mercury on the evening of the 22nd. Both planets are joined by the moon the next night. The spring equinox is reached at 11:14 A.M. EST on the 20th when the sun rises due east and sets due west, and days and nights are about equally long.

ASTRONOMICAL CALCULATIONS

○	Full Moon	6th day	21st hour	14th min.
☾	Last Quarter	13th day	12th hour	35th min.
●	New Moon	21st day	6th hour	59th min.
☽	First Quarter	29th day	11th hour	12th min.

FOR POINTS OUTSIDE BOSTON SEE KEY LETTER CORRECTIONS—PAGES 86-90

Day of Year	Day of Month	Day of Week	☉ Rises h. m.	Key	☉ Sets h. m.	Key	Length of Days h. m.	Sun Fast m.	Full Sea Boston A.M.	Full Sea Boston P.M.	☽ Rises h.m.	Key	☽ Sets h.m.	Key	Declination of sun ° '	☽ Place	☽ Age
60	1	Fr.	6 20	D	5 34	B	11 14	3	6	6½	11 A.M. 21	A	2 A.M. 36	E	7S. 24	TAU	10
61	2	Sa.	6 19	D	5 35	B	11 16	3	6¾	7½	12 P.M. 18	A	3 35	E	7 01	GEM	11
62	3	F	6 17	D	5 36	B	11 19	3	7¾	8½	1 24	B	4 27	E	6 38	GEM	12
63	4	M.	6 15	D	5 38	B	11 23	3	8¾	9¼	2 38	B	5 11	E	6 15	CAN	13
64	5	Tu.	6 14	D	5 39	B	11 25	3	9½	10¼	3 56	C	5 48	E	5 52	LEO	14
65	6	W.	6 12	D	5 40	B	11 28	4	10½	11	5 16	C	6 20	D	5 29	LEO	15
66	7	Th.	6 10	C	5 41	B	11 31	4	11¼	11¾	6 36	D	6 47	D	5 06	LEO	16
67	8	Fr.	6 09	C	5 42	B	11 33	4	—	12	7 54	D	7 13	C	4 43	VIR	17
68	9	Sa.	6 07	C	5 43	B	11 36	4	12½	1	9 13	E	7 38	C	4 19	VIR	18
69	10	F	6 05	C	5 45	B	11 40	5	1¼	1¾	10 32	E	8 06	B	3 56	VIR	19
70	11	M.	6 04	C	5 46	B	11 42	5	2¼	2¾	11 P.M. 49	E	8 37	B	3 32	LIB	20
71	12	Tu.	6 02	C	5 47	B	11 45	5	3	3½	— —	–	9 13	A	3 09	SCO	21
72	13	W.	6 00	C	5 48	B	11 48	5	4	4¾	1 A.M. 03	E	9 57	A	2 45	OPH	22
73	14	Th.	5 58	C	5 49	B	11 51	6	5	5¾	2 10	E	10 49	A	2 21	SAG	23
74	15	Fr.	5 57	C	5 50	C	11 53	6	6	6¾	3 08	E	11 A.M. 48	A	1 58	SAG	24
75	16	Sa.	5 55	C	5 52	C	11 57	6	7¼	8	3 55	E	12 P.M. 53	B	1 33	SAG	25
76	17	F	5 53	C	5 53	C	12 00	7	8¼	9	4 32	E	1 59	B	1 10	CAP	26
77	18	M.	5 52	C	5 54	C	12 02	7	9¼	9¾	5 02	E	3 05	B	0 47	CAP	27
78	19	Tu.	5 50	C	5 55	C	12 05	7	10	10½	5 27	D	4 09	C	0S. 23	AQU	28
79	20	W.	5 48	C	5 56	C	12 08	7	10¾	11	5 49	D	5 12	C	0N.01	AQU	29
80	21	Th.	5 46	C	5 57	C	12 11	8	11¼	11¾	6 09	D	6 13	D	0 24	PSC	0
81	22	Fr.	5 45	C	5 59	C	12 14	8	—	12	6 28	C	7 14	D	0 48	PSC	1
82	23	Sa.	5 43	B	6 00	C	12 17	8	12¼	12½	6 47	C	8 14	E	1 12	PSC	2
83	24	F	5 41	B	6 01	C	12 20	9	12¾	1¼	7 08	B	9 16	E	1 35	ARI	3
84	25	M.	5 39	B	6 02	C	12 23	9	1½	1¾	7 32	B	10 19	E	1 58	ARI	4
85	26	Tu.	5 38	B	6 03	C	12 25	9	2	2½	7 59	B	11 P.M. 23	E	2 22	TAU	5
86	27	W.	5 36	B	6 04	C	12 28	10	2¾	3¼	8 32	A	— —	–	2 46	TAU	6
87	28	Th.	5 34	B	6 05	C	12 31	10	3½	4¼	9 13	A	12 A.M. 26	E	3 09	TAU	7
88	29	Fr.	5 32	B	6 06	C	12 34	10	4¼	5	10 04	A	1 25	E	3 33	GEM	8
89	30	Sa.	5 31	B	6 08	C	12 37	11	5¼	6	11 A.M. 04	B	2 18	E	3 56	GEM	9
90	31	F	5 29	B	6 09	C	12 40	11	6¼	7	12 P.M. 14	B	3 A.M. 05	E	4N.19	CAN	10

MARCH hath 31 days. 1985

Slayer of winter, art thou here again?
O welcome, thou that brings't the summer nigh!
The bitter wind makes not thy victory vain,
Nor will we mock thee for thy faint blue sky.
— *William Morris*

D.M.	D.W.	Dates, Feasts, Fasts, Aspects, Tide Heights	Weather ↓
1	Fr.	**St. David** • Dinah Shore born, 1918 • Ember Day •	*A*
2	Sa.	☾ runs high • Car crossed frozen Penobscot Bay, Maine, 1918 • Ember Day •	*bit*
3	F	**2nd S. Lent** • National Anthem Day • Tides {9.3 8.2 •	*of*
4	M.	Voyager I spacecraft revealed rings of Jupiter, 1979 • Tides {9.9 8.8 •	*snow*
5	Tu.	*Necessity never made a good bargain.* • Tides {10.4 9.5 •	*ere*
6	W.	Full Worm ○ • Hector S. Cyrano de Bergerac born, 1619 •	*winter*
7	Th.	♄ stat. • Charles Miller patented button-hole sewing machine, 1854 •	*goes.*
8	Fr.	☾ on Eq. • ☾ at peri. • Tides {— 11.3 •	*Sun*
9	Sa.	*False friends and shadows attend only when the sun is shining.* • {11.1 11.1 •	*is*
10	F	**3rd S. Lent** • First U.S. paper money issued, 1862 •	*showing,*
11	M.	☾ at ☋ • ☌♄☾ • 451″ of snow on ground, Tamarack, Calif., 1911 •	*sap*
12	Tu.	**St. Gregory** • ♀ stat. • Jack Kerouac born, 1922 • {10.8 9.4 •	*is*
13	W.	☌♅☾ • "Uncle Sam" first seen in cartoons, 1852 • {10.3 8.7 •	*flowing,*
14	Th.	☌♆☾ • *Brevity is the soul of wit.* • Tides {9.8 8.3 •	*flowers*
15	Fr.	☾ runs low • First indoor flycasting tournament, N.Y.C., 1897 • {9.5 8.1	*growing;*
16	Sa.	☌♃☾ • West Point Military Academy established, 1802 •	*Whoops —*
17	F	**4th S. Lent** • **St. Patrick** • ☿ Gr. Elong. E. (18°)	*it's*
18	M.	Schick, Inc. sells first electric shavers, 1931 • Tides {9.5 8.7 •	*snowing!*
19	Tu.	**St. Joseph** • Wyatt Earp born, 1848 • *The Caine Mutiny* published, 1951 •	*Icy*
20	W.	Spring Equinox 11:14 A.M. EST • U.S. Marines landed in Nicaragua, 1896 • {9.6 9.2 •	*grip*
21	Th.	**St. Benedict** • ☾ on Eq. • New ● •	*begins*
22	Fr.	☌☿☾ • ☌♀☾ • ♅ stat. • ☌☿♀ • {— 9.5 •	*to*
23	Sa.	☾ at apo. • U.S. Army sold its homing pigeons, 1957 • Tides {9.5 9.4 •	*slip.*
24	F	**5th S. Lent** • **Passion** • ☿ stat. • ☌♅☾	
25	M.	**Annunciation** • ☾ at ☊ • Tides {9.4 8.8 •	*Out*
26	Tu.	*As we grow old, beauty steals inward.* • Bangladesh declared independence, 1971 •	*like*
27	W.	Mt. St. Helens erupted, Washington, 1980 • Kerosene patented, 1855 • {9.1 8.1 •	*a*
28	Th.	Edmund Muskie born, 1914 • Tibet's Dalai Lama fled to India, 1959 •	*lamb;*
29	Fr.	☾ runs high • *Little boats should keep near shore.* • Tides {8.8 7.7 •	*thank*
30	Sa.	Vincent van Gogh born, 1853 • Queensboro Bridge opened, 1909 • {8.8 7.8 •	*you,*
31	F	**Palm Sun.** • Civilian Conservation Corps authorized, 1933	*Ma'am.*

Farmer's Calendar

I was out for a walk one day around this time some years ago when I found a place where it looked as if someone had thrown a handful of iron filings or black pepper down on the snow. I took a closer look and found a patch of minute black grains scattered thickly over the snow. I knelt down close to get a good look. There was just time to note that each grain of the black dust was a little smaller than the small letter "o" on this page when something happened. The grain of dust I was looking at vanished. It was there and then it wasn't there. I found another grain. Shortly it too vanished. I stood up and soon saw that the handful of black pepper on the snow was really some enormous number of *things* that were continually hopping or flipping about. This is something, I thought.

It is at this point in experience that you go to books, there to find that the marvel you've happened on is a commonplace. My disappearing pepper is an insect called the snow flea *(Achorutes nivicolus),* a northern member of the big group of insects called springtails. These little guys are shaped like tiny grains of rice, and at their back end they have a stiff tail that bends around underneath them, where it's held in tension by a catch on their belly. Imagine an upside-down mouse trap, set. Released, the tail snaps the snow flea up and back, and they are so small that the sudden movement makes them appear to vanish. They develop from an immature form, a nymph, in the late winter and creep up through the snow to throng on the surface in the earliest spring sun. Like any other bug, snow fleas love what's sweet. You can find them swimming around in the maple sap that gathers in the buckets in March. A widespread, well-understood subject, then, the snow flea. But even so, not an ordinary one.

1985 APRIL, THE FOURTH MONTH

The Milky Way has almost passed from sight, setting early in the evening now. New constellations are beginning to appear in the spring skies: Corona the crown, Hercules, and Libra low in the east in early evening. The Big Dipper, part of the larger constellation Ursa Major (the Great Bear), is now high in the north above Polaris in the evening. Opposite the Big Dipper in the south is Leo the Lion with his sickle-shaped front part and his bright heart-star Regulus. Look for Lyrid meteors from high in the sky after midnight on the 21st and 22nd. Venus is 7.7° north of the sun on the 4th and sets right after it on the first few days of April. Venus then quickly becomes prominent in the east as the Morning Star. The moon has seven conjunctions with planets this month, a number surpassed in 1985 only during October.

ASTRONOMICAL CALCULATIONS

○	Full Moon	5th day	6th hour	33rd min.
☾	Last Quarter	11th day	23rd hour	42nd min.
●	New Moon	20th day	0 hour	22nd min.
☽	First Quarter	27th day	23rd hour	26th min.

ADD 1 hour for Daylight Saving Time at 2 A.M. April 28th.

FOR POINTS OUTSIDE BOSTON SEE KEY LETTER CORRECTIONS—PAGES 86-90

Day of Year	Day of Month	Day of Week	☉ Rises h. m.	Key	☉ Sets h. m.	Key	Length of Days h. m.	Sun Fast m.	Full Sea Boston A.M.	Full Sea Boston P.M.	☽ Rises h.m.	Key	☽ Sets h.m.	Key	Declination of sun ° ′	☽ Place	☽ Age
91	1	M.	5 27	B	6 10	C	12 43	11	7¼	8	1 P.M. 28	B	3 A.M. 43	E	4N.42	CAN	11
92	2	Tu.	5 26	B	6 11	C	12 45	11	8¼	8¾	2 46	C	4 16	E	5 05	LEO	12
93	3	W.	5 24	B	6 12	C	12 48	12	9¼	9¾	4 05	C	4 45	D	5 28	LEO	13
94	4	Th.	5 22	B	6 13	C	12 51	12	10	10½	5 24	D	5 11	D	5 51	VIR	14
95	5	Fr.	5 20	B	6 14	C	12 54	12	11	11¼	6 44	E	5 37	C	6 14	VIR	15
96	6	Sa.	5 19	B	6 15	C	12 56	13	11¾	—	8 05	E	6 04	B	6 37	VIR	16
97	7	**F**	5 17	B	6 17	C	13 00	13	12	12½	9 27	E	6 33	B	6 59	LIB	17
98	8	M.	5 15	B	6 18	D	13 03	13	1	1½	10 46	E	7 08	A	7 21	LIB	18
99	9	Tu.	5 14	B	6 19	D	13 05	13	1¾	2¼	11 P.M. 59	E	7 50	A	7 44	OPH	19
100	10	W.	5 12	B	6 20	D	13 08	14	2¾	3¼	— —	–	8 40	A	8 06	OPH	20
101	11	Th.	5 10	B	6 21	D	13 11	14	3½	4¼	1 A.M. 01	E	9 39	A	8 28	SAG	21
102	12	Fr.	5 09	B	6 22	D	13 13	14	4¾	5½	1 53	E	10 44	A	8 50	SAG	22
103	13	Sa.	5 07	B	6 23	D	13 16	14	5¾	6½	2 34	E	11 A.M. 50	B	9 12	CAP	23
104	14	**F**	5 05	B	6 24	D	13 19	15	6¾	7½	3 07	E	12 P.M. 57	B	9 33	CAP	24
105	15	M.	5 04	B	6 26	D	13 22	15	8	8½	3 33	E	2 02	C	9 55	AQU	25
106	16	Tu.	5 02	B	6 27	D	13 25	15	8¾	9¼	3 56	D	3 04	C	10 16	AQU	26
107	17	W.	5 01	B	6 28	D	13 27	15	9½	10	4 16	D	4 05	D	10 37	AQU	27
108	18	Th.	4 59	B	6 29	D	13 30	16	10¼	10½	4 35	C	5 06	D	10 58	CET	28
109	19	Fr.	4 57	B	6 30	D	13 33	16	11	11	4 54	B	6 07	E	11 19	PSC	29
110	20	Sa.	4 56	B	6 31	D	13 35	16	11½	11¾	5 13	B	7 08	E	11 39	PSC	0
111	21	**F**	4 54	B	6 32	D	13 38	16	—	12	5 36	B	8 11	E	12 00	ARI	1
112	22	M.	4 53	B	6 33	D	13 40	16	12¼	12¾	6 01	B	9 15	E	12 20	TAU	2
113	23	Tu.	4 51	B	6 35	D	13 44	17	1	1½	6 32	A	10 18	E	12 40	TAU	3
114	24	W.	4 50	B	6 36	D	13 46	17	1½	2	7 11	A	11 P.M. 18	E	13 00	TAU	4
115	25	Th.	4 48	B	6 37	D	13 49	17	2¼	2¾	7 58	A	— —	–	13 20	GEM	5
116	26	Fr.	4 47	B	6 38	D	13 51	17	3	3¾	8 54	A	12 A.M. 14	E	13 39	GEM	6
117	27	Sa.	4 45	B	6 39	D	13 54	17	3¾	4½	9 58	A	1 01	E	13 58	CAN	7
118	28	**F**	4 44	B	6 40	D	13 56	18	4¾	5½	11 A.M. 09	B	1 42	E	14 17	CAN	8
119	29	M.	4 43	B	6 41	D	13 58	18	5¾	6½	12 P.M. 22	C	2 15	E	14 35	LEO	9
120	30	Tu.	4 41	B	6 42	D	14 01	18	6¾	7½	1 P.M. 38	C	2 A.M. 44	D	14N.54	LEO	10

With what a still, untroubled air,
The spring comes stealing up the way,
Like some young maiden coyly fair,
Too modest for the light of day.
— *Ellery Channing*

Farmer's Calendar

Every spring there is one last all-out snowstorm, but this time people don't meet the weather with any of the varieties of resignation they have perfected over a long winter of successive snows. This time a big snowfall is, well, funny. Spring blizzards are a lark. Why? Snow is snow: if you're sick of it in February, you ought by rights to be even sicker of it in April. Besides, spring blizzards — at least around here — are often among the biggest storms of the year in terms of inches dumped. Last year we had two feet in one April storm. Oughtn't their volume alone make them particularly oppressive, never mind their timing?

No. The argument above starts from a false premise, that snow is all alike. It isn't. Every snow is different, and the big spring snow is the most different of all. That big accumulation doesn't weigh on your soul; on the contrary, the magnitude of a spring blizzard is one of the aspects of it that make it a joke. These storms are like an outrageous dessert that winds up a seven-course dinner: General Grant life-size in blue ice cream at the G.A.R. banquet.

And anyway, you can enjoy anything if you know it isn't real. Spring blizzards are like painted scenes of storefronts on a stage set. You enter the illusion knowing you could punch your fist right through their brick walls, knowing that very soon someone will come and pack all the sets away. These are white storms. The sky is bright in spite of the snow, and the sun that will be out tomorrow is a spring sun that means business: in a day all this snow will be gone. You needn't take it seriously, then. The birds don't. The summer birds have already arrived, and you can hear the robins singing through the middle of the storm.

D.M.	D.W.	Dates, Feasts, Fasts, Aspects, Tide Heights		Weather ↓
1	M.	All Fools Day • Louis Marx began selling the yo-yo, 1929	{9.4 {8.7	Blue
2	Tu.	*He who stumbles twice over one stone deserves to break his shins.*	{10.0 {9.4	sky,
3	W.	☿ in inf. ♂ • ♀ in inf. ♂ • Marlon Brando born, 1924		no
4	Th.	**St. Ambrose** • ☾ on Eq. • Ψ stat.	{10.9 {10.9	lie!
5	Fr.	**Good Fri.** • Full Pink ○ • ☾ at peri.		Clouds
6	Sa.	**Passover** • U.S. declared war on Germany, 1917	{11.1	are
7	F	**Easter** • ☾ at ☋ • Tides	{11.7 {10.9	scudding,
8	M.	♂☌☾ • 85°F. in New York City, 1929	{11.7 {10.4	springtime
9	Tu.	♂☌☾ • T. S. Hudson caught a 4 lb. 12 oz. bluegill in Alabama, 1950		mudding.
10	W.	♂Ψ☾ • U.S. occupied Greenland, 1941 • Tides	{10.9 {9.2	Steady
11	Th.	☾ runs low • Ethel Kennedy born, 1928 • Barber Shop Quartet Day		rain,
12	Fr.	*You can live well, whether you're rich or poor, but it's cheaper if you're poor.* • Tides	{9.7 {8.3	kids
13	Sa.	♂♃☾ • First J.C. Penney store, Kemmerer, Wyoming, 1902		complain;
14	F	**Low Sun.** • Pete Rose born, 1941	{9.1 {8.3	parents
15	M.	☿ stat. • Income tax returns due • Coca Cola opened plant in Peking, China, 1981		use
16	Tu.	*You get what you pay for.* • Charlie Chaplin born, 1889	{9.1 {8.9	profanity,
17	W.	♂♀☾ • ♂☿☾ • Tides	{9.2 {9.2	teachers
18	Th.	☾ on Eq. • Eddie A. Rommel became first major league umpire to wear glasses, 1956		risk
19	Fr.	☾ at apo. • 3' of snow on the ground in southern N.H., 1785	{9.2 {9.6	insanity!
20	Sa.	New ● • Adolph Hitler born, 1889	{9.2 {9.7	Sunshine —
21	F	**2ⁿᵈ S. af. E.** • ☾ at ☋ • Tides	{9.1	just
22	M.	♀ stat. • ♂☌☾ • R. J. Tylers patented roller skates, 1823	{9.7 {8.9	in
23	Tu.	**St. George** • ♀ at ☍ • Tides	{8.6 {8.7	time!
24	W.	*The worst deluded are the self-deluded.* • Shirley MacLaine born, 1934		Now
25	Th.	**St. Mark** • St. Lawrence Seaway opened, 1959		comes
26	Fr.	☾ runs high • Arbor Day (most states) • Tides	{9.2 {8.0	the
27	Sa.	Apache War ended, 1873 • *Ignorance is the mother of suspicion.*		umpire's
28	F	**3ʳᵈ S. af. E.** • Daylight Saving Time begins, 2 A.M.		call —
29	M.	First performance of Haydn's "The Creation," 1798 • Tides	{9.3 {8.7	Play
30	Tu.	Casey Jones killed, 1900 • South Vietnam surrendered to Vietcong, 1975		ball!

If you would sleep soundly, take a clear conscience to bed. — *B. Franklin*

1985 MAY, THE FIFTH MONTH

Saturn comes to opposition on the 15th, a golden point of light in Libra rising at sunset and visible all night long. Jupiter is brilliant when it rises in the southeast in the middle of the night. Early risers can behold Venus adorning the east, attaining greatest brilliancy on the 9th, but Mercury probably will not be spotted. The Eta Aquarid meteors, derived from Halley's Comet, will be mostly spoiled by the full moon on the 3rd and 4th. A total lunar eclipse on the 4th will not be visible from the contiguous 48 states, but Alaskans can see a partial solar eclipse at its best around 11 A.M. local time on the 19th. The brightest star in the evening sky is orange Arcturus in the southeast far above and slightly brighter than the planet Saturn.

ASTRONOMICAL CALCULATIONS

○	Full Moon	4th day	14th hour	54th min.
☾	Last Quarter	11th day	12th hour	35th min.
●	New Moon	19th day	16th hour	41st min.
☽	First Quarter	27th day	7th hour	56th min.

ADD 1 hour for Daylight Saving Time.

FOR POINTS OUTSIDE BOSTON SEE KEY LETTER CORRECTIONS—PAGES 86-90

Day of Year	Day of Month	Day of Week	☉ Rises h. m.	Key	☉ Sets h. m.	Key	Length of Days h. m.	Sun Fast m.	Full Sea Boston A.M.	Full Sea Boston P.M.	☽ Rises h.m.	Key	☽ Sets h.m.	Key	Declination of sun ° ′	☽ Place	☽ Age
121	1	W.	4 40	B	6 44	D	14 04	18	7¾	8¼	2P.M.55	D	3A.M.11	D	15N.12	LEO	11
122	2	Th.	4 39	A	6 45	D	14 06	18	8¾	9¼	4 13	D	3 35	C	15 30	VIR	12
123	3	Fr.	4 37	A	6 46	D	14 09	18	9¾	10	5 33	E	4 00	C	15 48	VIR	13
124	4	Sa.	4 36	A	6 47	D	14 11	18	10½	10¾	6 56	E	4 28	B	16 05	VIR	14
125	5	F	4 35	A	6 48	D	14 13	18	11½	11¾	8 18	E	5 01	B	16 23	LIB	15
126	6	M.	4 33	A	6 49	D	14 16	18	—	12¼	9 36	E	5 39	A	16 39	SCO	16
127	7	Tu.	4 32	A	6 50	D	14 18	18	12½	1¼	10 47	E	6 27	A	16 56	OPH	17
128	8	W.	4 31	A	6 51	D	14 20	19	1½	2	11P.M.46	E	7 24	A	17 12	SAG	18
129	9	Th.	4 30	A	6 52	D	14 22	19	2¼	3	— —	-	8 29	A	17 28	SAG	19
130	10	Fr.	4 29	A	6 53	E	14 24	19	3¼	4	12A.M.32	E	9 38	B	17 44	CAP	20
131	11	Sa.	4 27	A	6 54	E	14 27	19	4¼	5	1 09	E	10 46	B	17 59	CAP	21
132	12	F	4 26	A	6 55	E	14 29	19	5¼	6	1 37	E	11A.M.52	B	18 14	AQU	22
133	13	M.	4 25	A	6 57	E	14 32	19	6¼	7	2 01	D	12P.M.56	C	18 29	AQU	23
134	14	Tu.	4 24	A	6 58	E	14 34	19	7¼	7¾	2 22	D	1 58	C	18 43	AQU	24
135	15	W.	4 23	A	6 59	E	14 36	19	8¼	8½	2 41	C	2 58	D	18 57	PSC	25
136	16	Th.	4 22	A	7 00	E	14 38	19	9	9¼	3 00	C	3 59	D	19 11	PSC	26
137	17	Fr.	4 21	A	7 01	E	14 40	19	9¾	10	3 19	B	5 00	E	19 25	PSC	27
138	18	Sa.	4 20	A	7 02	E	14 42	19	10¼	10½	3 41	B	6 03	E	19 38	ARI	28
139	19	F	4 19	A	7 03	E	14 44	19	11	11¼	4 05	B	7 07	E	19 51	ARI	0
140	20	M.	4 18	A	7 04	E	14 46	19	11¾	11¾	4 35	A	8 11	E	20 04	TAU	1
141	21	Tu.	4 17	A	7 05	E	14 48	18	—	12¼	5 10	A	9 13	E	20 16	TAU	2
142	22	W.	4 17	A	7 06	E	14 49	18	12½	1	5 55	A	10 10	E	20 28	TAU	3
143	23	Th.	4 16	A	7 07	E	14 51	18	1	1¾	6 48	A	11 00	E	20 39	GEM	4
144	24	Fr.	4 15	A	7 07	E	14 52	18	1¾	2½	7 50	A	11P.M.42	E	20 50	GEM	5
145	25	Sa.	4 14	A	7 08	E	14 54	18	2½	3¼	8 58	B	— —	-	21 01	CAN	6
146	26	F	4 14	A	7 09	E	14 55	18	3½	4¼	10 10	B	12A.M.17	E	21 12	LEO	7
147	27	M.	4 13	A	7 10	E	14 57	18	4½	5	11A.M.22	C	12 47	E	21 22	LEO	8
148	28	Tu.	4 12	A	7 11	E	14 59	18	5½	6	12P.M.36	D	1 13	D	21 32	LEO	9
149	29	W.	4 12	A	7 12	E	15 00	18	6½	7	1 50	D	1 37	D	21 41	VIR	10
150	30	Th.	4 11	A	7 13	E	15 02	18	7½	7¾	3 07	E	2 01	C	21 50	VIR	11
151	31	Fr.	4 11	A	7 13	E	15 02	17	8¼	8¾	4P.M.26	E	2A.M.26	B	21N.58	VIR	12

Hail, bounteous May, that doth inspire
Mirth, and youth, and warm desire;
Woods and groves are of thy dressing,
Hill and dale doth boast thy blessing.
— *John Milton*

D.M.	D.W.	Dates, Feasts, Fasts, Aspects, Tide Heights	Weather ↓
1	W.	**Sts. Philip and James** • ☿ Gr. Elong. W. (27°) • {9.9 10.1 •	*A*
2	Th.	☾ on Eq. • *Little strokes fell great oaks.* • Tides {10.3 10.8 •	*maypole*
3	Fr.	**Invent. of Cross** • Tides {10.6 11.5 •	*celebration —*
4	Sa.	☾ at ☋ • Full Flower ○ • Eclipse ○ • ☾ at peri.	
5	F	**4th S. af. E.** • ☌♄☾ • Tides {10.7 11.9 •	*no*
6	M.	☌♂☾ • Babe Ruth hit his first home run, 1915 •	*precipitation!*
7	Tu.	☌♆☾ • Edwin H. Land born, 1909 • Tides {11.8 10.1 •	*Spoke*
8	W.	☾ runs low • Tornadoes in ten states, 1961 • Storks return to Ribe, Denmark •	*too*
9	Th.	♀ greatest brilliancy • Pancho Gonzales born, 1928 • {10.8 9.1 •	*soon,*
10	Fr.	*Faith is to man what gravity is to planets and suns.* • {10.2 8.7 •	*ring*
11	Sa.	☌♃☾ • ☌♂ Aldebaran • *Three* • Tides {9.6 8.4	
12	F	**Rogation S.** • *Chilly* • {9.1 8.4 •	*around*
13	M.	U.S. declared war on Mexico, 1846 • *Saints* • Tides {8.8 8.5 •	*the*
14	Tu.	*Go where he will, the wise man is always at home.* • Tides {8.7 8.8 •	*moon.*
15	W.	☾ on Eq. • ♄ at ☍ • ☌♀☾ •	*Seasonable*
16	Th.	**Ascension** • ☾ at apo. • Tides {8.7 9.3 •	*seems*
17	Fr.	☌☿☾ • First Kentucky Derby, 1875 •	*reasonable —*
18	Sa.	☾ at ☊ • Bertrand Russell born, 1872 • Tides {8.8 9.7 •	*with*
19	F	**1st S. af. Ascen.** • Partial Eclipse ☉ • New ●	
20	M.	Weights and Measures Day • Victoria Day (Canada) •	*forecasts*
21	Tu.	☌♂☾ • *A sneer is the weapon of the weak.* • {— 8.7 •	*like*
22	W.	Dr. Sheffield invented the toothpaste tube, 1892 • Tides {9.8 8.6 •	*this,*
23	Th.	☾ runs high • Captain Kidd hanged in London, 1701 • {9.8 8.5 •	*we'll*
24	Fr.	Snowstorm in Kentucky, 1894 • Ohio Anti-Saloon League formed, 1893 •	*never*
25	Sa.	U.S. Narcotic Farm dedicated in Lexington, Kentucky, 1935 • Tides {9.6 8.4 •	*miss!*
26	F	**Whit Sun.** • **Pentecost** • **Shebuoth**	
27	M.	**Memorial Day** • Sam Snead born, 1912 •	*Listen*
28	Tu.	*He who knows little, and knows it, knows much.* • Tides {9.5 9.4 •	*for*
29	W.	☾ on Eq. • Severe sandstorm in Yuma, Arizona, 1877 • Ember Day •	*the*
30	Th.	First known automobile crash, New York City, 1896 • {9.7 10.6 •	*dandelion's*
31	Fr.	Adolph Eichmann hanged, 1962 • Walt Whitman born, 1819 • Ember Day	*roar.*

Farmer's Calendar

The year turns to full spring, and some days look exactly like summer, but in protected places the last of the winter's snow can still be found. Under north walls, in cold hemlock thickets, beside fallen trunks in the woods, the old snow lies in scattered atolls that dwindle away like the last remnants of the submerged continent of winter. The old snow is icy, gray, coarse. It is stained and dirty, full of fallen pine needles and bits of bud scales and other trash.

Coming on a patch of old snow in the green woods in May is a surprise, and it's an embarrassment: as though you have met a beggar in the street whom you know to be the last unfortunate representative of a once aristocratic family now fallen into decay. Four months ago snow was everywhere. It ruled and its reign was splendid, the whole world its ermine robe; but now it's overthrown and it has fled into exile in the cool shadows where it wastes away. You can imagine the old snow remembering its lost glory; listen for it mumbling away like a senile Cavalier dreaming of Bonnie Prince Charlie and The Forty-Five.

Old snow hides in the same places every year. Around my house I know there will be a lump of it beside the north wall of our shed when dandelions have begun to grow in the grass a few feet away, and I know a place in the angle of a stone wall in the woods where the snow may remain into June. Some curious place names in this area have come from the old settlers' noticing that the snow and ice endured long past their natural term in dark, deep defiles where the sun never lingered. So we have Greenland Gulf, the Freezing Hole, and Frigid Ridge — although I confess that the old settler who named the last of these was I.

JUNE, THE SIXTH MONTH

Summer begins at 5:44 A.M. EST on the 21st, which is therefore the longest day of the year. Once darkness is fully fallen, look for Leo in the west, the Big Dipper in the northwest, and Arcturus in the south. Summer stars now coming into view include reddish Antares in the southeast (left of Saturn) and brilliant blue Vega in the east. Hercules and Corona Borealis, the Northern Crown, lie between Arcturus and Vega. Corvus the Crow and the bright star Spica are now in the southwest, ahead of the still brilliant Saturn. Distant Uranus and Neptune are at opposition but their observation will generally require the use of charts and binoculars. Jupiter still rises late but not so late as the even brighter Venus, which is striking in the eastern skies when morning twilight starts. Venus is at greatest elongation, 46° from the sun, on the 12th.

ASTRONOMICAL CALCULATIONS

- ○ Full Moon — 2nd day, 22nd hour, 51st min.
- ☾ Last Quarter — 10th day, 3rd hour, 20th min.
- ● New Moon — 18th day, 6th hour, 59th min.
- ☽ First Quarter — 25th day, 13th hour, 54th min.

ADD 1 hour for Daylight Saving Time.

FOR POINTS OUTSIDE BOSTON SEE KEY LETTER CORRECTIONS—PAGES 86-90

Day of Year	Day of Month	Day of Week	☉ Rises h. m.	Key	☉ Sets h. m.	Key	Length of Days h. m.	Sun Fast m.	Full Sea Boston A.M.	Full Sea Boston P.M.	☽ Rises h.m.	Key	☽ Sets h.m.	Key	Declination of sun ° ′	☽ Place	☽ Age
152	1	Sa.	4 10	A	7 14	E	15 04	17	9¼	9½	5 P.M. 48	E	2 A.M. 55	B	22N.06	LIB	13
153	2	**F**	4 10	A	7 15	E	15 05	17	10¼	10½	7 08	E	3 30	A	22 14	SCO	14
154	3	M.	4 09	A	7 16	E	15 07	17	11¼	11¼	8 24	E	4 13	A	22 21	OPH	15
155	4	Tu.	4 09	A	7 16	E	15 07	17	—	12	9 30	E	5 06	A	22 28	SAG	16
156	5	W.	4 08	A	7 17	E	15 09	17	12¼	1	10 24	E	6 09	A	22 35	SAG	17
157	6	Th.	4 08	A	7 18	E	15 10	16	1	1¾	11 05	E	7 18	B	22 42	SAG	18
158	7	Fr.	4 08	A	7 18	E	15 10	16	2	2¾	11 P.M. 38	E	8 29	B	22 47	CAP	19
159	8	Sa.	4 08	A	7 19	E	15 11	16	2¾	3½	— —	–	9 38	B	22 53	CAP	20
160	9	**F**	4 07	A	7 20	E	15 13	16	3¾	4½	12 A.M. 05	D	10 44	C	22 58	AQU	21
161	10	M.	4 07	A	7 20	E	15 13	16	4¾	5¼	12 27	D	11 A.M. 48	C	23 02	AQU	22
162	11	Tu.	4 07	A	7 21	E	15 14	15	5¾	6¼	12 46	D	12 P.M. 49	D	23 06	PSC	23
163	12	W.	4 07	A	7 21	E	15 14	15	6½	7	1 05	C	1 50	D	23 10	CET	24
164	13	Th.	4 07	A	7 22	E	15 15	15	7½	7¾	1 24	C	2 51	E	23 14	PSC	25
165	14	Fr.	4 07	A	7 22	E	15 15	15	8¼	8½	1 45	B	3 53	E	23 17	ARI	26
166	15	Sa.	4 07	A	7 23	E	15 16	15	9	9¼	2 08	B	4 56	E	23 19	ARI	27
167	16	**F**	4 07	A	7 23	E	15 16	14	9¾	10	2 36	A	6 01	E	23 21	TAU	28
168	17	M.	4 07	A	7 23	E	15 16	14	10½	10¾	3 10	A	7 04	E	23 23	TAU	29
169	18	Tu.	4 07	A	7 24	E	15 17	14	11¼	11¼	3 51	A	8 04	E	23 24	TAU	0
170	19	W.	4 07	A	7 24	E	15 17	14	—	12	4 42	A	8 57	E	23 25	GEM	1
171	20	Th.	4 07	A	7 24	E	15 17	14	12	12¾	5 43	A	9 42	E	23 26	GEM	2
172	21	Fr.	4 07	A	7 24	E	15 17	13	12¾	1¼	6 50	B	10 19	E	23 27	CAN	3
173	22	Sa.	4 08	A	7 25	E	15 17	13	1½	2	8 01	B	10 51	E	23 26	CAN	4
174	23	**F**	4 08	A	7 25	E	15 17	13	2¼	3	9 13	C	11 17	D	23 25	LEO	5
175	24	M.	4 08	A	7 25	E	15 17	13	3¼	3¾	10 25	D	11 P.M. 41	D	23 24	LEO	6
176	25	Tu.	4 08	A	7 25	E	15 17	12	4	4¾	11 A.M. 39	D	— —	–	23 22	VIR	7
177	26	W.	4 09	A	7 25	E	15 16	12	5	5½	12 P.M. 52	D	12 A.M. 04	C	23 20	VIR	8
178	27	Th.	4 09	A	7 25	E	15 16	12	6	6½	2 07	E	12 28	B	23 18	VIR	9
179	28	Fr.	4 10	A	7 25	E	15 15	12	7	7½	3 25	E	12 55	B	23 15	LIB	10
180	29	Sa.	4 10	A	7 25	E	15 15	12	8	8½	4 44	E	1 26	B	23 12	LIB	11
181	30	**F**	4 10	A	7 25	E	15 15	11	9	9¼	6 P.M. 01	E	2 A.M. 04	A	23N.08	SCO	12

Our seasons have no fixed returns,
Without our will they come and go;
At noon our sudden summer burns,
Ere sunset all is snow.
—James Russell Lowell

D.M.	D.W.	Dates, Feasts, Fasts, Aspects, Tide Heights	*Weather* ↓
1	Sa.	☾ at ☋ • ☾ at peri. • ☌♄☾ • Ember Day •	*Slip*
2	F	**Trinity** • Full Strawberry ○ • Lou Gehrig died, 1941 •	*on*
3	M.	☌♅☾ • *A little knowledge is a dangerous thing.* • {10.1 / 11.7} •	*galoshes*
4	Tu.	☌♆☾ • Evacuation of Dunkirk completed, 1940 • Tides {— / 9.9}	*for*
5	W.	**St. Boniface** • ☾ runs low • ♃ stat. •	*summer*
6	Th.	**Corpus Christi** • ♅ at ☍ • Tides {11.1 / 9.4} •	*slish-*
7	Fr.	☿ in sup. ☌ • ☌♃☾ • Mt. McKinley climbed, 1913 •	*sloshes.*
8	Sa.	*An ass is but an ass though laden with gold.* • Vacuum cleaner patented, 1869 •	*Cold*
9	F	**2nd S. af. P.** • Cole Porter born, 1893 • Tides {9.5 / 8.7} •	*and*
10	M.	First tornado recorded in New Haven, Conn., 1682 • Tides {9.0 / 8.6} •	*then*
11	Tu.	**St. Barnabas** • ☾ on Eq. • Vince Lombardi born, 1913 •	*a*
12	W.	♀ Gr. Elong. W. (46°) • Gas mask patented, 1849 •	*toaster,*
13	Th.	☾ at apo. • First telecast of a moving object, 1925 • Tides {8.3 / 9.1}	*June's*
14	Fr.	☌♀☾ • Magna Carta adopted in England, 1215 • Tides {8.3 / 9.3} •	*a*
15	Sa.	**St. Bernard** • ☾ at ☊ • Tides {8.3 / 9.5} •	*roller-*
16	F	**3rd S. af. P.** • 1¾ lb. hailstone fell, Dubuque, Iowa, 1882	*coaster!*
17	M.	**St. Alban** • Igor Stravinsky born, 1882 • Tides {8.5 / 9.9} •	*Watch*
18	Tu.	New ● • *One woman's poise is another woman's poison.* • {8.6 / 10.0} •	*out*
19	W.	☾ runs high • Blaise Pascal born, 1623 • Tides {— / 8.6} •	*for*
20	Th.	Stephen Schwenk caught 51 lb. crevalle jack in Florida, 1978 •	*thunderheads,*
21	Fr.	Summer solstice 5:44 A.M. EST • Tides {10.2 / 8.8} •	*dunderhead!*
22	Sa.	118°F., Bullhead City, Arizona, 1981 • Karl Malden born, 1913 • {10.2 / 8.9}	*So*
23	F	**4th S. af P.** • ♆ at ☍ • Tides {10.1 / 9.1} •	*long*
24	M.	**Nativ. of John the Baptist** •	*ambition—*
25	Tu.	☾ on Eq. • Battle of Little Big Horn, 1876 • Tides {9.7 / 9.6} •	*we're*
26	W.	*A fish is not a fish until it's on the bank.* • Tides {9.5 / 10.0} •	*going*
27	Th.	Larry Corcoran pitched third no-hitter, 1884 • Helen Keller born, 1880 •	*fishin'.*
28	Fr.	☾ at ☋ • Charles Dumas was first man to high jump seven feet, 1956 •	*Hot's*
29	Sa.	**St. Peter** • ☌♄☾ • ☾ at peri. • Tides {9.3 / 11.0} •	*our*
30	F	**5th S. af. P.** • **St. Paul** • ☌♅☾ •	*lot.*

Love is like a dizziness; it winna
let a poor body gang about his biziness!

Farmer's Calendar

Time was, I tilled my garden by hand with a stout garden fork, but I am no longer a kid, and last year when I thrust my fork into the earth and bore down upon it, my back said, "No." I borrowed a rototiller for the job. I would till by machine. My garden is on a hill, as are, I suppose, two thirds of the gardens in northern New England, a fact that has formed an obstacle to agriculture in these parts for nearly 300 years. Sidehill farming is an obstacle, furthermore, that mechanization has not entirely removed.

I started the rototiller and set out across the garden at right angles to the incline. The tiller flipped over. Okay, I would till down the hill, I thought, avoiding having the machine turn turtle and also allowing gravity to help. Gravity helped more than I expected. I got the tiller pointed downhill and gave it the gas. Reader, it got away from me. Emitting a whoop, the machine wrenched itself from my grasp and churned off down the garden. It tilled an erratic swath through the unplanted ground. It tilled my new peas, too, very thoroughly, and when it reached the garden fence, it tilled that as well, and it tilled a good bit of the lawn. It would have tilled the house, but it hit a rock and went over. I now think the rototiller as we know it is not a trustworthy implement on a hill.

We need a rototiller that we can use up here, one designed on the principle of the well-known Vermont sheep, which has longer legs on one side so it can stand upright on a hill. This Improved Vermont Tiller would have to have a big rotating set of blades at one end of the axle and a little bitty one at the other. That way, you could go across the hill without flipping, and you wouldn't have to risk making gravity your friend.

The full moons on both the 2nd and 31st are the last time two will occur in one calendar month until May 1988. In the east before dawn, Venus remains spectacular and is amazingly close to the top star in the Hyades star cluster of Taurus on the 13th and 14th. Jupiter rises in the southeast in mid-evening and Scorpius with its red heart-star Antares is in the south. The Summer Triangle of bright stars Vega, Deneb, and Altair is prominent in the east. After midnight and moonset from about the 24th to the 28th, look for Delta Aquarid and Capricornid meteors gliding out of the south. The earth is at aphelion (most distant from the sun) on the 5th at 5 A.M. EST.

ASTRONOMICAL CALCULATIONS

○	Full Moon	2nd day	7th hour	9th min.
☾	Last Quarter	9th day	19th hour	50th min.
●	New Moon	17th day	18th hour	58th min.
☽	First Quarter	24th day	18th hour	40th min.
○	Full Moon	31st day	16th hour	42nd min.

ADD 1 hour for Daylight Saving Time.

FOR POINTS OUTSIDE BOSTON SEE KEY LETTER CORRECTIONS—PAGES 86-90

Day of Year	Day of Month	Day of Week	☉ Rises h. m.	Key	☉ Sets h. m.	Key	Length of Days h. m.	Sun Fast m.	Full Sea Boston A.M.	Full Sea Boston P.M.	☽ Rises h.m.	Key	☽ Sets h.m.	Key	Declination of sun ° ′	☽ Place	☽ Age
182	1	M.	4 11	A	7 25	E	15 14	11	10	10¼	7 P.M. 11	E	2 A.M. 51	A	23N.05	OPH	13
183	2	Tu.	4 11	A	7 25	E	15 14	11	11	11	8 11	E	3 50	A	23 00	SAG	14
184	3	W.	4 12	A	7 24	E	15 12	11	11¾	—	8 58	E	4 57	A	22 55	SAG	15
185	4	Th.	4 13	A	7 24	E	15 11	11	12	12½	9 35	E	6 08	B	22 50	CAP	16
186	5	Fr.	4 13	A	7 24	E	15 11	10	12¾	1½	10 04	E	7 19	B	22 44	CAP	17
187	6	Sa.	4 14	A	7 24	E	15 10	10	1½	2¼	10 28	D	8 29	B	22 38	AQU	18
188	7	F	4 14	A	7 23	E	15 09	10	2½	3	10 50	D	9 34	C	22 32	AQU	19
189	8	M.	4 15	A	7 23	E	15 08	10	3¼	3¾	11 09	C	10 37	D	22 26	PSC	20
190	9	Tu.	4 16	A	7 23	E	15 07	10	4	4¾	11 28	C	11 A.M. 39	D	22 18	PSC	21
191	10	W.	4 16	A	7 22	E	15 06	10	5	5½	11 P.M. 48	B	12 P.M. 40	E	22 11	PSC	22
192	11	Th.	4 17	A	7 22	E	15 05	10	5¾	6¼	— —	–	1 41	E	22 03	ARI	23
193	12	Fr.	4 18	A	7 21	E	15 03	9	6¾	7	12 A.M. 10	B	2 44	E	21 54	ARI	24
194	13	Sa.	4 19	A	7 21	E	15 02	9	7½	8	12 36	A	3 48	E	21 45	TAU	25
195	14	F	4 20	A	7 20	E	15 00	9	8½	8¾	1 07	A	4 52	E	21 36	TAU	26
196	15	M.	4 20	A	7 19	E	14 59	9	9¼	9½	1 46	A	5 53	E	21 27	TAU	27
197	16	Tu.	4 21	A	7 19	E	14 58	9	10	10¼	2 34	A	6 50	E	21 17	GEM	28
198	17	W.	4 22	A	7 18	E	14 56	9	10¾	11	3 32	A	7 38	E	21 07	GEM	0
199	18	Th.	4 23	A	7 17	E	14 54	9	11½	11¾	4 38	B	8 19	E	20 57	CAN	1
200	19	Fr.	4 24	A	7 17	E	14 53	9	—	12¼	5 49	B	8 52	E	20 46	CAN	2
201	20	Sa.	4 25	A	7 16	E	14 51	9	12½	1	7 03	B	9 21	D	20 35	LEO	3
202	21	F	4 26	A	7 15	E	14 49	9	1¼	1¾	8 16	C	9 46	D	20 23	LEO	4
203	22	M.	4 27	A	7 14	E	14 47	9	2	2½	9 30	D	10 09	C	20 11	VIR	5
204	23	Tu.	4 28	A	7 13	E	14 45	9	2¾	3¼	10 43	D	10 32	C	19 59	VIR	6
205	24	W.	4 28	A	7 12	E	14 44	9	3¾	4¼	11 A.M. 57	E	10 57	B	19 46	VIR	7
206	25	Th.	4 29	A	7 11	E	14 42	9	4¾	5¼	1 P.M. 13	E	11 P.M. 26	B	19 33	VIR	8
207	26	Fr.	4 30	A	7 10	E	14 40	9	5¾	6¼	2 30	E	— —	–	19 20	LIB	9
208	27	Sa.	4 31	A	7 09	E	14 38	9	6¾	7	3 45	E	12 A.M. 00	B	19 07	SCO	10
209	28	F	4 32	A	7 08	E	14 36	9	7¾	8¼	4 57	E	12 43	A	18 53	OPH	11
210	29	M.	4 33	A	7 07	E	14 34	9	8¾	9	6 00	E	1 36	A	18 39	SAG	12
211	30	Tu.	4 34	A	7 06	E	14 32	9	9¾	10	6 51	E	2 39	A	18 24	SAG	13
212	31	W.	4 35	A	7 05	E	14 30	9	10¾	10¾	7 P.M. 31	E	3 A.M. 48	B	18N.09	CAP	14

> Through all the long midsummer-day
> The meadow-sides are sweet with hay.
> I seek the coolest sheltered seat,
> Just where the field and forest meet.
> — *John Townsend Trowbridge*

Farmer's Calendar

To this observer, evolution seems to be a process that is far from stern, far from having the solemnity becoming a fundamental principle of life on earth. Rather, the profusion of forms of plants and animals, the variety and cleverness of their behavior, the fullness and complexity with which earth, air, and water are packed with life — all these seem to belong to an evolution that is always experimenting, improvising, being playful. The origin of species is something like a game, and in my neighborhood one of its best sports is the creature called the flying squirrel. This is an otherwise rather dumpy, stubby little quadruped that has, for no good reason, wings. It's as though nature gave the squirrel wings casually, for fun, with the randomness of a bright child drawing horns and mustachios on people in magazines to make a rainy afternoon pass. Let's see what this guy looks like with an elephant nose. Let's make this one fly.

The flying squirrels are abroad on summer nights. They're the size of a big red squirrel; they have fine, fancy gray fur, enormous liquid eyes, and long flaps of loose skin that run between their fore and hind quarters on each side. They extend these flaps like sails to fly. When the squirrel is at rest, the folds of soft, furred skin lie opulently around its shoulders: it's fur that looks as though it belongs inside a long, black car on Park Avenue. All the books agree that the flying squirrel can't really fly. It only glides, falling on its wide sails, the experts insist. Ignore them. The experts are jealous, that's all. If you or I could jump out of a tall tree and float for 100 feet, sometimes carrying the kids with us; if we could in the process turn, stall, even gain a bit of altitude, as the flying squirrel can, would we hesitate to call it flight?

D.M.	D.W.	Dates, Feasts, Fasts, Aspects, Tide Heights	Weather ↓
1	M.	♂♀☾ • **Canada Day** • Tides {9.5 {11.4	Blue
2	Tu.	**Visit. of Mary** • ☾ at peri. • Full Buck ○ {9.5 {11.3	sky
3	W.	*Be careful how you spend and what you lend.* • Tides {9.5	and
4	Th.	**Independence Day** • ♂24☾ • Tides {11.2 {9.4	corn
5	Fr.	⊕ at aphelion 5:00 A.M. EST • First U.S. soldier killed in Korea, 1950 •	knee-
6	Sa.	George Wyman, first transcontinental motorcyclist, arrived in New York, 1903 • {10.4 {9.2	high.
7	F	**6th S. af. P.** • U.S. occupied Iceland, 1941 •	Steady
8	M.	☾ on Eq. • The Liberty Bell cracked, 1835 • Tides {9.4 {8.9	drizzle,
9	Tu.	*Full cups must be held steady.* • Tides {8.9 {8.8	campfires
10	W.	134°F. in Greenland Ranch, Calif., 1913 • Tides {8.4 {8.8	fizzle.
11	Th.	☾ at apo. • Alexander Hamilton killed in a duel by Aaron Burr, 1804 •	A
12	Fr.	☾ at ☊ • Andrew Wyeth born, 1917 {7.9 {8.9	midsummer
13	Sa.	☿ Gr. Elong. E. (27°) • U.S. Patent No. "One" issued, 1836 •	night's
14	F	**7th S. af. P.** • ♂♀☾ • Tides {8.0 {9.3	dream,
15	M.	**St. Swithin** • ♂♀ Aldebaran • Tides {8.1 {9.6	vanilla
16	Tu.	☾ runs high • *To virtues be kind, to faults be blind.* • Tides {8.3 {9.9	ice
17	W.	New ● • ♂♂⊙ • Disneyland opened, 1955 •	cream!
18	Th.	℞ stat. • S.I. Hayakawa born, 1906 • Tides {8.8 {10.5	Sun
19	Fr.	♂♀☾ • *He that is warm thinks all men so.* • Lizzie Borden born, 1860 •	and
20	Sa.	**St. Margaret** • Colombia Independence Day •	showers
21	F	**8th S. af. P.** • Tides {10.6 {9.7	together:
22	M.	**St. Mary Magdalen** • Tides {10.5 {9.9	rainbow
23	Tu.	☾ on eq. • Bunker Hill Monument completed, 1841 •	weather!
24	W.	118°F. in Minden, Neb., 1936 • Amelia Earhart born, 1898 • Tides {9.9 {10.2	A
25	Th.	**St. James • St. Christopher** • ☾ at ☊ • ☾ at peri.	
26	Fr.	**St. Anne** • ♂♄☾ • ♄ stat. • ☿ stat. •	soaking,
27	Sa.	♂♂☾ • Norman Lear born, 1922 • Tides {8.9 {10.5	and
28	F	**9th S. af. P.** • Rudy Vallee born, 1901 •	we're
29	M.	♂♀☾ • ☾ runs low • Tides {8.9 {10.7	not
30	Tu.	Dr. W. J. Cook caught a 14½ lb. brook trout, Ontario, 1916 • Tides {9.1 {10.8	joking.
31	W.	**St. Ignatius of Loyola** • Full Sturgeon ○ • ♂24☾	

Jupiter is superbly bright and visible all night long in Capricornus when it comes to opposition on the 4th. More than 60 Perseid meteors per hour can be observed in the best periods after midnight on the 12th and 13th (though slightly disturbed by a late crescent moon). Mercury has its best morning apparition of the year in the second half of August, featuring its greatest elongation of 18° on the 28th when it is best seen in the east about 45 minutes before sunup. Amateur astronomers with large telescopes should get their first looks at Halley's Comet on these mornings. Vega in little Lyra the Lyre passes near the zenith around mid-evening.The Milky Way reaches its broadest and brightest in the south at Sagittarius the Archer.

ASTRONOMICAL CALCULATIONS

☾	Last Quarter	8th day	13th hour	29th min.
●	New Moon	16th day	5th hour	7th min.
☽	First Quarter	22nd day	23rd hour	38th min.
○	Full Moon	30th day	4th hour	28th min.

ADD 1 hour for Daylight Saving Time.

FOR POINTS OUTSIDE BOSTON SEE KEY LETTER CORRECTIONS—PAGES 86-90

Day of Year	Day of Month	Day of Week	☉ Rises h. m.	Key	☉ Sets h. m.	Key	Length of Days h. m.	Sun Fast m.	Full Sea Boston A.M.	Full Sea Boston P.M.	☽ Rises h.m.	Key	☽ Sets h.m.	Key	Declination of sun ° '	☽ Place	☽ Age
213	1	Th.	4 36	A	7 04	E	14 28	9	11½	11¾	8ᴘ04	E	5ᴀ00	B	17ɴ.54	CAP	15
214	2	Fr.	4 37	A	7 03	D	14 26	9	—	12¼	8 30	D	6 10	B	17 39	AQU	16
215	3	Sa.	4 38	A	7 02	D	14 24	9	12½	1	8 52	D	7 18	C	17 23	AQU	17
216	4	F	4 39	A	7 00	D	14 21	9	1¼	1¾	9 12	D	8 23	D	17 07	AQU	18
217	5	M.	4 40	A	6 59	D	14 19	9	2	2½	9 31	C	9 26	D	16 51	PSC	19
218	6	Tu.	4 42	A	6 58	D	14 16	9	2¾	3	9 51	B	10 28	D	16 34	PSC	20
219	7	W.	4 43	A	6 57	D	14 14	9	3½	3¾	10 12	B	11ᴀ29	E	16 17	PSC	21
220	8	Th.	4 44	A	6 55	D	14 11	9	4¼	4½	10 36	B	12ᴘ32	E	16 00	ARI	22
221	9	Fr.	4 45	A	6 54	D	14 09	10	5	5½	11 05	A	1 35	E	15 43	ARI	23
222	10	Sa.	4 46	A	6 53	D	14 07	10	6	6¼	11ᴘ39	A	2 38	E	15 26	TAU	24
223	11	F	4 47	A	6 51	D	14 04	10	7	7¼	—	—	3 41	E	15 08	TAU	25
224	12	M.	4 48	A	6 50	D	14 02	10	7¾	8	12ᴀ23	A	4 39	E	14 50	GEM	26
225	13	Tu.	4 49	A	6 49	D	14 00	10	8¾	9	1 17	A	5 31	E	14 32	GEM	27
226	14	W.	4 50	A	6 47	D	13 57	10	9½	9¾	2 20	A	6 15	E	14 13	GEM	28
227	15	Th.	4 51	A	6 46	D	13 55	11	10¼	10½	3 31	B	6 52	E	13 55	CAN	29
228	16	Fr.	4 52	A	6 44	D	13 52	11	11	11¼	4 45	B	7 22	E	13 36	LEO	0
229	17	Sa.	4 53	A	6 43	D	13 50	11	11¾	—	6 01	C	7 48	D	13 16	LEO	1
230	18	F	4 54	B	6 41	D	13 47	11	12	12½	7 16	D	8 12	D	12 57	LEO	2
231	19	M.	4 55	B	6 40	D	13 45	11	12¾	1¼	8 31	D	8 36	C	12 37	VIR	3
232	20	Tu.	4 56	B	6 38	D	13 42	12	1¾	2	9 47	E	9 01	B	12 18	VIR	4
233	21	W.	4 57	B	6 37	D	13 40	12	2½	3	11ᴀ03	E	9 29	B	11 58	VIR	5
234	22	Th.	4 58	B	6 35	D	13 37	12	3½	3¾	12ᴘ20	E	10 01	B	11 38	LIB	6
235	23	Fr.	4 59	B	6 33	D	13 34	12	4¼	4¾	1 36	E	10 41	A	11 17	SCO	7
236	24	Sa.	5 01	B	6 32	D	13 31	13	5½	5¾	2 49	E	11ᴘ30	A	10 57	OPH	8
237	25	F	5 02	B	6 30	D	13 28	13	6½	7	3 53	E	—	—	10 36	SAG	9
238	26	M.	5 03	B	6 29	D	13 26	13	7¾	8	4 47	E	12ᴀ28	A	10 16	SAG	10
239	27	Tu.	5 04	B	6 27	D	13 23	14	8¾	9	5 30	E	1 34	A	9 55	SAG	11
240	28	W.	5 05	B	6 25	D	13 20	14	9½	9¾	6 04	E	2 44	B	9 33	CAP	12
241	29	Th.	5 06	B	6 24	D	13 18	14	10½	10¾	6 32	E	3 55	B	9 12	CAP	13
242	30	Fr.	5 07	B	6 22	D	13 15	14	11¼	11¼	6 55	D	5 04	C	8 51	AQU	14
243	31	Sa.	5 08	B	6 20	D	13 12	15	11¾	—	7ᴘ16	D	6ᴀ09	C	8ɴ.29	AQU	15

Fairest of months! ripe Summer's Queen
The hey-day of the year.
With robes that gleam with sunny sheen,
Sweet August doth appear.
— *R. Cambe Miller*

Farmer's Calendar

In August the butternut fall begins where I live, providing food for rodents. For people, the large nuts, which lie in the grass like green golf balls, furnish a kind of welcome wild candy, but they also are hazards to travel and to lawn care. Trod on, a butternut can turn your ankle, and run over with a lawn mower, the nuts can make an alarming racket rather like what would result from dropping a handful of nuts and bolts into a kitchen blender. Of course you can plod about the yard to pick the butternuts up and cart them away, but that is idiot work. You can also ignore them and let the squirrels gather them for you, but that's too easy for most of us; sitting back and letting nature do our work for us is not the way we Americans got where we are today. We constantly seek a better way, even to dispose of butternuts.

Last summer I discovered a heavy fall of fresh butternuts in the yard on a day when a kid happened to have left a plastic whiffle baseball bat lying handy. Immediately I thought of ballplayers nonchalantly hitting fungoes into the outfield before a game. You know: you hold the bat at your shoulder with one hand, then toss the ball up in the air with your other hand, grab the bat, and cream the ball as it falls. I used to think of myself as being pretty good at that. I tried it with my butternuts, and the results were most satisfactory. I clean missed the first nut, but the next one I socked. It took off like a bird and landed in the meadow an impressive distance away. I find I can drive a butternut about 80 feet, which takes it well off my lawn. Now every evening I go out after supper and hit 15 or 20. In a week the lawn is as clear of butternuts as it needs to be, and I have honored what was the major sport of my childhood.

D.M.	D.W.	Dates, Feasts, Fasts, Aspects, Tide Heights	Weather ↓
1	Th.	**Lammas Day** • Shredded wheat biscuits invented, 1893 •	*Open*
2	Fr.	Carl D. Anderson discovered the positron, 1932 •	*an*
3	Sa.	*If you would be loved, love and be lovable.* • {10.5 9.4} •	*umbrella,*
4	F	**10th S. af. P.** • ♃ at ☍ • {10.2 9.3} •	*that's*
5	M.	☾ on Eq. • First transatlantic helicopter flight, 1952 • Tides {9.7 9.2} •	*a*
6	Tu.	**Transfiguration** • Lucille Ball born, 1911 •	*good*
7	W.	**Name of Jesus** • ☾ at apo. • Tides {8.8 8.9} •	*fella!*
8	Th.	☾ at ☍☍ • Theophilus Vankannel patented the revolving door, 1888 •	*Don't*
9	Fr.	Tornado in Wallingford, Conn., 1878 • Tides {8.0 8.7} •	*pout,*
10	Sa.	**St. Laurence of Rome** • ☿ in inf. ♂ •	*the*
11	F	**11th S. af. P.** • Movie star Rin Tin Tin died, 1932 •	*sun*
12	M.	*Fair and softly* • Construction began *go far in a day.* • on Berlin Wall, 1961 • Tides {7.8 9.2} •	*is*
13	Tu.	☾ runs high • ♂☾☾ • Great Minneapolis fire, 1893 •	*out.*
14	W.	Liberty Tree Day (Mass.) • Tides {8.4 10.1} •	*Precipitation*
15	Th.	Panama Canal opened, 1914 • Julia Child born, 1912 •	*anticipation*
16	Fr.	New ● • Octuplets born in Naples, Italy, 1979 • Tides {9.4 10.8} •	*spells*
17	Sa.	*Nature and books belong to the eyes that see them.* • Tides {9.8} •	*vacation*
18	F	**12th S. af. P.** • **St. Helena** • Tides {11.0 10.3}	
19	M.	☾ on Eq. • ☾ at peri. • Tides {11.0 10.6} •	*hesitation.*
20	Tu.	♀ stat. • H.P. Lovecraft born, 1890 • Soviets invaded Czechoslovakia, 1968 •	*Lazy*
21	W.	☾ at ☍☍ • 26-day drought ends, Portland, Maine, 1961 • Tides {10.3 10.7} •	*days.*
22	Th.	♂♄☾ • ☿ stat. • Carl Yastrzemski born, 1939 •	*Hot,*
23	Fr.	♂♀ Pollux • First hotel elevator installed, 1859 • {9.3 10.4} •	*muggy,*
24	Sa.	**St. Bartholomew** • ♂☌☾ • Tides {8.8 10.2} •	*and*
25	F	**13th S. af. P.** • ♂♇☾ • Tides {8.6 10.1} •	*buggy!*
26	M.	☾ runs low • Island of Krakatoa erupted, 1883 • Tides {8.5 10.1} •	*Sunny*
27	Tu.	♂♃☾ • Federal income tax declared unconstitutional, 1894 •	*day,*
28	W.	**St. Augustine of Hippo** • ☿ Gr. Elong. W. (18°) • Tides {8.9 10.4} •	*make*
29	Th.	Billy "Pop" Shriver caught a ball dropped from Washington Monument, 1892 •	*some*
30	Fr.	Full ○ Corn • *Diligence is the mother of good fortune.* • {9.4 10.3} •	*hay.*
31	Sa.	Earthquake in Charleston, S.C. destroyed 95% of city's chimneys, 1886 •	

1985 SEPTEMBER, THE NINTH MONTH

On the morning of the 4th Venus is so near the star Delta Cancri that binoculars on a tripod or a small telescope will be necessary to show the star. That morning and the following five, look low in the east and close to sunrise to see Mercury, the star Regulus, and Mars all passing very close to one another. On the morning of the 21st observers will be able to see quite easily the extremely beautiful meeting of Venus and Regulus. Autumn begins with the equinox at 9:07 P.M. EST on the 22nd, after which nights are longer than days. The full moon on the 28th, which is the full moon closest to the autumnal equinox, is called the Harvest Moon; notice how it comes up at about the same time each night around this date. The Milky Way is shifting from its midsummer north-south position toward its November east-west orientation.

ASTRONOMICAL CALCULATIONS

☾	Last Quarter	7th day	7th hour	17th min.
●	New Moon	14th day	14th hour	21st min.
☽	First Quarter	21st day	6th hour	4th min.
○	Full Moon	28th day	19th hour	9th min.

ADD 1 hour for Daylight Saving Time.

FOR POINTS OUTSIDE BOSTON SEE KEY LETTER CORRECTIONS—PAGES 86-90

Day of Year	Day of Month	Day of Week	☉ Rises h. m.	Key	☉ Sets h. m.	Key	Length of Days h. m.	Sun Fast m.	Full Sea Boston A.M.	Full Sea Boston P.M.	☽ Rises h.m.	Key	☽ Sets h.m.	Key	Declination of sun ° '	☽ Place	☽ Age
244	1	F	5 09	B	6 19	D	13 10	15	12	12½	7 P.M. 35	C	7 A.M. 13	D	8N.07	PSC	16
245	2	M.	5 10	B	6 17	D	13 07	15	12¾	1	7 54	C	8 16	D	7 45	PSC	17
246	3	Tu.	5 11	B	6 15	D	13 04	16	1½	1¾	8 14	B	9 17	E	7 23	PSC	18
247	4	W.	5 12	B	6 14	D	13 02	16	2	2½	8 18	A	10 19	E	7 01	ARI	19
248	5	Th.	5 13	B	6 12	D	12 59	16	2¾	3	8 45	A	11 A.M. 22	E	6 39	ARI	20
249	6	Fr.	5 14	B	6 10	D	12 56	17	3½	4	9 35	A	12 P.M. 26	E	6 16	TAU	21
250	7	Sa.	5 15	B	6 08	C	12 53	17	4½	4¾	10 14	A	1 28	E	5 54	TAU	22
251	8	F	5 16	B	6 07	C	12 51	17	5¼	5¾	11 P.M. 03	A	2 28	E	5 31	TAU	23
252	9	M.	5 17	B	6 05	C	12 48	18	6¼	6½	— —	–	3 22	E	5 09	GEM	24
253	10	Tu.	5 19	B	6 03	C	12 44	18	7¼	7½	12 A.M. 01	A	4 08	E	4 46	GEM	25
254	11	W.	5 20	B	6 01	C	12 41	18	8¼	8½	1 08	B	4 47	E	4 23	CAN	26
255	12	Th.	5 21	B	6 00	C	12 39	19	9	9¼	2 21	B	5 20	E	4 00	CAN	27
256	13	Fr.	5 22	B	5 58	C	12 36	19	9¾	10	3 37	C	5 48	D	3 37	LEO	28
257	14	Sa.	5 23	B	5 56	C	12 33	19	10½	10¾	4 53	C	6 14	D	3 14	LEO	0
258	15	F	5 24	B	5 54	C	12 30	20	11¼	11¾	6 10	D	6 38	C	2 51	VIR	1
259	16	M.	5 25	B	5 53	C	12 28	20	—	12	7 28	D	7 02	B	2 28	VIR	2
260	17	Tu.	5 26	B	5 51	C	12 25	21	12½	12¾	8 47	E	7 30	B	2 05	VIR	3
261	18	W.	5 27	B	5 49	C	12 22	21	1¼	1¾	10 06	E	8 01	B	1 42	LIB	4
262	19	Th.	5 28	B	5 47	C	12 19	21	2¼	2½	11 A.M. 26	E	8 39	A	1 18	LIB	5
263	20	Fr.	5 29	B	5 46	C	12 17	22	3	3½	12 P.M. 41	E	9 25	A	0 55	SCO	6
264	21	Sa.	5 30	B	5 44	C	12 14	22	4	4½	1 49	E	10 21	A	0 32	SAG	7
265	22	F	5 31	B	5 42	C	12 11	22	5¼	5½	2 45	E	11 P.M. 25	A	0N.08	SAG	8
266	23	M.	5 32	C	5 40	C	12 08	23	6¼	6¾	3 31	E	— —	–	0S. 14	SAG	9
267	24	Tu.	5 33	C	5 39	C	12 06	23	7½	7¾	4 08	E	12 A.M. 34	B	0 38	CAP	10
268	25	W.	5 34	C	5 37	C	12 03	23	8½	8¾	4 36	E	1 44	B	1 01	CAP	11
269	26	Th.	5 36	C	5 35	C	11 59	24	9¼	9½	5 00	D	2 53	B	1 24	AQU	12
270	27	Fr.	5 37	C	5 33	C	11 56	24	10	10¼	5 21	D	3 59	C	1 47	AQU	13
271	28	Sa.	5 38	C	5 31	C	11 53	24	10¾	11	5 40	C	5 02	C	2 11	PSC	14
272	29	F	5 39	C	5 30	C	11 51	25	11¼	11¾	5 59	C	6 05	D	2 34	PSC	15
273	30	M.	5 40	C	5 28	C	11 48	25	—	12	6 P.M. 18	B	7 A.M. 07	D	2S. 58	PSC	16

Frost is but slender weeks away,
Tonight the sunset glow will stay,
Swing to the north and burn up higher,
And Northern Lights wall earth with fire.
—*Robert P. Tristram Coffin*

Farmer's Calendar

Every time I took a piece of wood from the pile beside the woodshed, another creature fled deeper into the dwindling heap. Each spring a big pile of short round pieces of firewood gets dumped for me to split and put away over the summer. By September the pile is getting down, and by September, too, it has become the home of a considerable stock of creepers, leapers, and crawlers who like the damp dark spaces between the pieces of wood, as well as the ease of refuge the woodpile offers. As I get down to the end of the pile, I drive these creatures into a smaller and smaller place, and population pressure builds up. I wonder whether on my picking up the last stick half the animal kingdom will burst out and race off in all directions, leaving me flat on my back.

You could outfit a high-school biology course with the life that moves into my woodpile each summer. Working down from stick to stick I have exposed: orange salamanders, green salamanders, snails, slugs, centipedes, brown wood frogs, bullfrogs, toads, garter snakes, little red-bellied snakes, spiders, big black beetles, crickets, ants, and earthworms. You never know what you'll uncover. Given the nature of woodpile life (not always high-class from the evolutionary point of view), and given the modes of locomotion of much of that life (scuttling, crawling, squirming), I know there are those who would find the whole project offensive. I think it's exciting. And the climax, when just one piece of wood remains, is curious as well. For invariably I have moved the last stick to find — nothing. No bug, no worm, no toad. No empty bottles or old newspapers. At the last moment all the animals, after their kind, boarded the ark and sailed away.

D.M.	D.W.	Dates, Feasts, Fasts, Aspects, Tide Heights	Weather ↓
1	F	**14ᵗʰ S. af. P.** • ☾ on Eq. • Tides {10.2 / 9.6}	*Dry*
2	M.	**Labor Day** • *Be not forward in words and slack in deeds.*	*as*
3	Tu.	Pineapple season in Bahamas • Frederick Douglass escaped from slavery, 1838	*a*
4	W.	☾at ☍ ☌ • ♂♀☿ • ☾ at apo. • Tides {9.1 / 9.3}	*bone,*
5	Th.	Hay fever now at its worst • Jesse James born, 1847 • {8.7 / 9.0}	*grass*
6	Fr.	*A wager is a Fool's argument.* • Urban C. "Red" Faber born, 1888 • {8.2 / 8.8}	*stops*
7	Sa.	Margaret Gorman, aged 15, won the first Miss America contest, 1921	*growin'.*
8	F	**15ᵗʰ S. af. P.** • **Nativ. of Mary** • ☌ ☾ Regulus	
9	M.	☾ runs high • William the Conqueror died, age 60, Rouen, France, 1087	*Children*
10	Tu.	The Lincoln Highway, first coast-to-coast paved road in U.S., opened, 1913 • {7.8 / 9.2}	*chime*
11	W.	Allied forces entered Germany, 1944 • Tides {8.2 / 9.7}	*schoolyard*
12	Th.	☌♀☾ • ♅ stat. • Tides {8.8 / 10.2}	*rhymes:*
13	Fr.	☌♂☾ • World record high temperature: 136.4° in shade, Libya, 1922 • {9.4 / 10.7}	*a*
14	Sa.	**Holy Cross** • New ● • Tides {10.1 / 11.0}	*tisket,*
15	F	**16ᵗʰ S. af. P.** • ☾ on Eq. • Agatha Christie born, 1891	*a*
16	M.	**Rosh Hashanah** • ☾ at peri. • Tides {11.1}	*tasket,*
17	Tu.	**St. Lambert** • ☾at ☍ • Warren Burger born, 1907	*fill*
18	W.	☌♄☾ • *To avoid criticism, do nothing, say nothing, be nothing.* • Ember Day	*a*
19	Th.	New York State College of Forestry founded, 1898 • Tides {10.3 / 11.1}	*harvest*
20	Fr.	☌♂☾ • Upton Sinclair born, 1878 • Ember Day	*basket.*
21	Sa.	**St. Matthew** • ☌♅☾ • ☌♀ Regulus	*Apple-*
22	F	**17ᵗʰ S. af. P.** • ☾ runs low • Autumn equinox 9:07 P.M. EST	*dappled*
23	M.	Christ's Hospital opened, London, 1552 • Tides {8.4 / 9.7}	*dappled*
24	Tu.	☌♃☾ • *The cat in gloves catches no mice.* • Salathé Wall climbed, Yosemite Valley, California, 1961	*hills,*
25	W.	**Yom Kippur** • {8.7 / 9.8}	*fields*
26	Th.	**St. Cyprian** • David O. Saylor patented cement, 1871	*awash*
27	Fr.	American Indian Day • Santa Claus School opened, Albion, N.Y., 1937 • {9.4 / 9.9}	*with*
28	Sa.	Full Harvest ○ • ☾ on Eq. • Tides {9.6 / 9.8}	*squash.*
29	F	**18ᵗʰ S. af. P.** • **St. Michael** •	*Shower*
30	M	**St. Jerome** • **Succoth** • Tides { / 9.8}	*power!*

When the press is free, and every man able to read, all is safe. — T. Jefferson

1985 OCTOBER, THE TENTH MONTH

The star Altair, in Aquila the Eagle, is in the southwest, much higher than Saturn, which is lost in evening twilight. Especially conspicuous in early evening is Deneb in Cygnus the Swan, up near the zenith. The Great Square of Pegasus is high in the south, with Andromeda (and the naked-eye galaxy M31) following. Around 3 to 5 A.M. on the 20th and 21st, Orionid meteors are at their best and, it is hoped, more numerous because they are probably fragments from Halley's Comet, now visible in small telescopes here near Orion. A spectacular conjunction of Venus and the much dimmer Mars occurs in the eastern sky before morning twilight on the 4th.

ASTRONOMICAL CALCULATIONS

☾	Last Quarter	7th day	0 hour	5th min.
●	New Moon	13th day	23rd hour	34th min.
☽	First Quarter	20th day	15th hour	13th min.
○	Full Moon	28th day	12th hour	38th min.

ADD 1 hour for Daylight Saving Time until 2 A.M. October 27th.

FOR POINTS OUTSIDE BOSTON SEE KEY LETTER CORRECTIONS—PAGES 86-90

Day of Year	Day of Month	Day of Week	☉ Rises h. m.	Key	☉ Sets h. m.	Key	Length of Days h. m.	Sun Fast m.	Full Sea Boston A.M.	Full Sea Boston P.M.	☽ Rises h.m.	Key	☽ Sets h.m.	Key	Declination of sun ° ′	☽ Place	☽ Age
274	1	Tu.	5 41	C	5 26	B	11 45	25	12¼	12½	6 P.M. 40	B	8 A.M. 09	E	3s.21	ARI	17
275	2	W.	5 42	C	5 25	B	11 43	26	1	1	7 04	B	9 12	E	3 44	ARI	18
276	3	Th.	5 43	C	5 23	B	11 40	26	1½	1¾	7 34	A	10 15	E	4 07	TAU	19
277	4	Fr.	5 44	C	5 21	B	11 37	26	2¼	2½	8 09	A	11 A.M. 18	E	4 31	TAU	20
278	5	Sa.	5 45	C	5 19	B	11 34	27	3	3¼	8 54	A	12 P.M. 18	E	4 54	TAU	21
279	6	**F**	5 47	C	5 18	B	11 31	27	4	4	9 47	A	1 13	E	5 17	GEM	22
280	7	M.	5 48	C	5 16	B	11 28	27	4¾	5	10 48	B	2 02	E	5 40	GEM	23
281	8	Tu.	5 49	C	5 14	B	11 25	27	5¾	6	11 P.M. 57	B	2 43	E	6 02	CAN	24
282	9	W.	5 50	D	5 13	B	11 23	28	6¾	7	— —	–	3 17	E	6 25	CAN	25
283	10	Th.	5 51	D	5 11	B	11 20	28	7½	8	1 A.M. 10	C	3 47	E	6 48	LEO	26
284	11	Fr.	5 52	D	5 09	B	11 17	28	8½	8¾	2 26	C	4 13	D	7 11	LEO	27
285	12	Sa.	5 53	D	5 08	B	11 15	29	9¼	9¾	3 42	D	4 37	D	7 33	LEO	28
286	13	**F**	5 54	D	5 06	B	11 12	29	10	10½	5 00	D	5 01	C	7 56	VIR	0
287	14	M.	5 56	D	5 04	B	11 08	29	10¾	11¼	6 20	E	5 28	B	8 18	VIR	1
288	15	Tu.	5 57	D	5 03	B	11 06	29	11½	—	7 41	E	5 57	B	8 40	VIR	2
289	16	W.	5 58	D	5 01	B	11 03	29	12¼	12½	9 04	E	6 33	A	9 02	LIB	3
290	17	Th.	5 59	D	5 00	B	11 01	30	1	1¼	10 25	E	7 17	A	9 24	SCO	4
291	18	Fr.	6 00	D	4 58	B	10 58	30	1¾	2¼	11 A.M. 38	E	8 12	A	9 46	OPH	5
292	19	Sa.	6 01	D	4 56	B	10 55	30	2¾	3	12 P.M. 41	E	9 15	A	10 07	SAG	6
293	20	**F**	6 03	D	4 55	B	10 52	30	3¾	4¼	1 31	E	10 25	A	10 29	SAG	7
294	21	M.	6 04	D	4 53	B	10 49	30	5	5¼	2 10	E	11 P.M. 35	B	10 50	CAP	8
295	22	Tu.	6 05	D	4 52	B	10 47	31	6	6¼	2 41	E	— —	–	11 11	CAP	9
296	23	W.	6 06	D	4 50	B	10 44	31	7¼	7½	3 06	D	12 A.M. 44	B	11 32	AQU	10
297	24	Th.	6 07	D	4 49	B	10 42	31	8	8½	3 27	D	1 50	C	11 53	AQU	11
298	25	Fr.	6 09	D	4 48	B	10 39	31	9	9¼	3 46	D	2 54	C	12 14	AQU	12
299	26	Sa.	6 10	D	4 46	B	10 36	31	9½	10	4 05	C	3 57	D	12 35	PSC	13
300	27	**F**	6 11	D	4 45	B	10 34	31	10¼	10½	4 24	B	4 58	D	12 55	PSC	14
301	28	M.	6 12	D	4 43	B	10 31	31	10¾	11¼	4 44	B	6 00	E	13 16	PSC	15
302	29	Tu.	6 14	D	4 42	B	10 28	31	11½	11¾	5 08	B	7 03	E	13 35	ARI	16
303	30	W.	6 15	D	4 41	B	10 26	31	—	12	5 35	A	8 06	E	13 55	ARI	17
304	31	Th.	6 16	D	4 39	B	10 23	31	12½	12½	6 P.M. 09	A	9 A.M. 09	E	14s.14	TAU	18

O wild West Wind, thou breath of Autumn's being,
Thou from whose unseen presence the leaves dead
Are driven like ghosts from an enchanter fleeing,
Yellow, and black, and pale, and hectic red . . .
— *Percy Bysshe Shelley*

Farmer's Calendar

Nature gives bounty and variety, but it seldom gives consistency. Rather, what we can see of nature is full of caprice, trickery, and contradiction — to all of which we respond at least as gratefully as we do to order. No rules without exceptions, no patterns without contraries. No seasons without irregularities.

Consider the witch hazel, a common small and skinny tree of the hardwood forest. The witch hazel is blooming right now. Nearly half the year after other plants have bloomed, after the leaves of all other trees have fallen — after the witch hazel's own leaves have fallen, in fact — the spidery golden flowers appear like weak candles in the bare, gray woods.

The witch hazel, then, is stubbornly against nature, and to pagans and other fanciful people that has made it a thing passing strange, a piece of magic. Everybody knows that with this plant's cut branches you can dowse for water. In fact, though, if you can find water with witch hazel, you can do so with any kind of stick, switch, or rod; it's not the stick that finds water, it's you. Nevertheless, witch hazel is the traditional diviner's rod, and that, with the name of the tree itself, attests to its association with whatever is inexplicable, mysterious, dangerous. Witch Hazel. The old names for plants and animals are always important, for they were given by people to whom, say, a tree's blooming in the late fall was full of meaning. Whoever called this tree *witch* and believed that it was uniquely able to dowse for something like a mind or soul, and did so, I think, chiefly on the basis of finding each year the witch hazel blooming in the autumn woods long after all other vegetation had become still.

D.M.	D.W.	Dates, Feasts, Fasts, Aspects, Tide Heights	Weather ↓
1	Tu.	☾at ♋ • Roger Maris hit his 61st home run, 1961 • Tides {9.5 {9.7 •	*Jack*
2	W.	☾ at apo. • *A man is known by the silence he keeps.* • Tides {9.2 {9.6 •	*Frost*
3	Th.	♃ stat. • "The Captain Kangaroo" show debuted on CBS, 1955 • {8.9 {9.4 •	*is*
4	Fr.	**St. Francis of Assisi** • ♂♀☉ • Tides {8.5 {9.1 •	*a*
5	Sa.	*Mind unemployed is mind unenjoyed.* • Robert Goddard born, 1882 •	*tricky*
6	F	**19th S. af. P. • St. Faith** • ☾ runs high • {7.8 {8.7	
7	M.	Georgia Tech defeated Cumberland College in football, 222 to 0, 1916 •	*fellow;*
8	Tu.	Mrs. O'Leary's cow kicked over a lantern, Chicago, 1871 • Tides {7.7 {8.8 •	*watch*
9	W.	**St. Denys** • Leif Ericson Day • Tides {8.0 {9.2 •	*him*
10	Th.	*Porgy and Bess* opened in New York City, 1935 • Helen Hayes born, 1900 •	*turn*
11	Fr.	♂☾☾ • Eleanor Roosevelt born, 1884 • Tides {9.3 {10.2 •	*your*
12	Sa.	♂♀☾ • *Many a man's tongue has broken his nose.* • {10.1 {10.6 •	*garden*
13	F	**20th S. af. P.** • ☾ on Eq. • New ● •	*yellow.*
14	M.	**Columbus Day** • ☾ at peri. • Lillian Gish born, 1896 •	*Roll*
15	Tu.	☾at ♋ • ♂♀☾ • 113 mph wind in New York City, 1954 •	*up*
16	W.	♂♄☾ • Eugene O'Neill born, 1888 • Tides {10.9 {11.9 •	*your*
17	Th.	**St. Ethelred** • ♂♄☾ • Tides {10.6 {11.7 •	*sleeves,*
18	Fr.	**St. Luke** • ♂♆☾ • *Nothing dries sooner than a tear.* •	*rake*
19	Sa.	☾ runs low • Mary Walsh and Charles Cotton married in a balloon over Cincinnati, 1874 •	*some*
20	F	**21st S. af. P.** • Tides {9.0 {10.1 •	*leaves.*
21	M.	♂♃☾ • *A little neglect may breed great mischief.* • Tides {8.6 {9.6 •	*So*
22	Tu.	Sam Houston sworn in as President of Texas, 1836 • Tides {8.5 {9.3 •	*cold*
23	W.	Edson Arantes do Nascimento ("Pele") born, 1940 • Bryn Mawr College opened, 1885 •	*in*
24	Th.	Anna Edson Taylor went over Niagara Falls in a barrel, 1901 • Tides {8.9 {9.3 •	*the*
25	Fr.	**St. Crispin** • Mainland China admitted to U.N., 1971 • {9.2 {9.3 •	*river,*
26	Sa.	☾ on Eq. • First mules arrived in the United States, 1785 • Tides {9.5 {9.3 •	*the*
27	F	**22nd S. af. P.** • ♂♄☉ • Tides {9.7 {9.3 •	*fish*
28	M.	**Sts. Simon and Jude** • Full Hunter's ○ • Eclipse ○ •	
29	Tu.	☾ at apo. • −33°F. in Soda Butte, Wyoming, 1917 • Tides {9.8 {9.0 •	*start*
30	W.	*Self respect is the gate of Heaven.* • Charles Atlas born, 1894 • Tides {— {9.8 •	*to*
31	Th.	**All Hallow's Eve** • Harry Houdini died, 1926 •	*shiver!*

1985 NOVEMBER, THE ELEVENTH MONTH

On the 12th a total solar eclipse occurs in parts of the South Pacific, but most of us will experience only very high tides on this date, due to the near coincidence of the new moon and the year's closest approach of the moon to the earth. Before dawn on the 17th perhaps 10 Leonid meteors an hour can be seen coming from the south. On the 9th Halley's Comet passes upward through the plane of the earth's orbit but is still farther out than Mars until the 29th. Around the 16th the comet can be spotted in binoculars as a hazy patch of light, with maybe a short dim tail, as it passes just south of the beautiful Pleiades star cluster. The mighty comet has its first close approach to the earth on November 28th (still about 58 million miles away) but will be much closer and stirred to brightness and great tail length next March and April.

ASTRONOMICAL CALCULATIONS

☾	Last Quarter	5th day	15th hour	8th min.
●	New Moon	12th day	9th hour	21st min.
☽	First Quarter	19th day	4th hour	4th min.
○	Full Moon	27th day	7th hour	43rd min.

FOR POINTS OUTSIDE BOSTON SEE KEY LETTER CORRECTIONS—PAGES 86-90

Day of Year	Day of Month	Day of Week	☉ Rises h. m.	Key	☉ Sets h. m.	Key	Length of Days h. m.	Sun Fast m.	Full Sea Boston A.M.	Full Sea Boston P.M.	☽ Rises h.m.	Key	☽ Sets h.m.	Key	Declination of sun ° ′	☽ Place	☽ Age
305	1	Fr.	6 17	D	4 38	B	10 21	31	1¼	1¼	6 P.M. 49	A	10 A.M. 10	E	14S.34	TAU	19
306	2	Sa.	6 19	D	4 37	B	10 18	31	1¾	2	7 39	A	11 07	E	14 53	GEM	20
307	3	**F**	6 20	D	4 35	B	10 15	31	2½	2¾	8 36	A	11 A.M. 58	E	15 11	GEM	21
308	4	M.	6 21	D	4 34	B	10 13	31	3½	3½	9 42	B	12 P.M. 40	E	15 30	GEM	22
309	5	Tu.	6 22	D	4 33	B	10 11	31	4¼	4½	10 P.M. 51	B	1 17	E	15 48	CAN	23
310	6	W.	6 24	D	4 32	B	10 08	31	5¼	5½	— —	–	1 47	E	16 06	LEO	24
311	7	Th.	6 25	D	4 31	B	10 06	31	6	6½	12 A.M. 03	C	2 13	D	16 24	LEO	25
312	8	Fr.	6 26	D	4 30	B	10 04	31	7	7½	1 16	C	2 37	D	16 41	LEO	26
313	9	Sa.	6 27	D	4 28	B	10 01	31	8	8¼	2 31	D	3 00	C	16 59	VIR	27
314	10	**F**	6 29	D	4 27	A	9 58	31	8¾	9¼	3 48	D	3 24	C	17 16	VIR	28
315	11	M.	6 30	D	4 26	A	9 56	31	9½	10	5 08	E	3 52	B	17 32	VIR	29
316	12	Tu.	6 31	D	4 25	A	9 54	31	10½	11	6 31	E	4 25	B	17 48	LIB	0
317	13	W.	6 32	D	4 24	A	9 52	31	11¼	11¾	7 55	E	5 06	A	18 04	SCO	1
318	14	Th.	6 34	D	4 23	A	9 49	31	—	12	9 16	E	5 57	A	18 20	OPH	2
319	15	Fr.	6 35	D	4 23	A	9 48	30	12¾	1	10 27	E	6 59	A	18 35	SAG	3
320	16	Sa.	6 36	D	4 22	A	9 46	30	1½	1¾	11 A.M. 24	E	8 09	A	18 50	SAG	4
321	17	**F**	6 37	D	4 21	A	9 44	30	2½	2¾	12 P.M. 09	E	9 21	B	19 05	CAP	5
322	18	M.	6 38	E	4 20	A	9 42	30	3½	3¾	12 43	E	10 33	B	19 19	CAP	6
323	19	Tu.	6 40	E	4 19	A	9 39	30	4½	4¾	1 11	D	11 P.M. 42	C	19 33	AQU	7
324	20	W.	6 41	E	4 19	A	9 38	29	5½	6	1 33	D	— —	–	19 47	AQU	8
325	21	Th.	6 42	E	4 18	A	9 36	29	6½	7	1 53	D	12 A.M. 47	C	20 00	AQU	9
326	22	Fr.	6 43	E	4 17	A	9 34	29	7½	7¾	2 12	C	1 49	D	20 13	PSC	10
327	23	Sa.	6 45	E	4 17	A	9 32	29	8¼	8¾	2 30	C	2 51	D	20 26	PSC	11
328	24	**F**	6 46	E	4 16	A	9 30	28	9	9½	2 50	B	3 52	E	20 38	PSC	12
329	25	M.	6 47	E	4 15	A	9 28	28	9¾	10	3 12	B	4 55	E	20 49	ARI	13
330	26	Tu.	6 48	E	4 15	A	9 27	28	10¼	10¾	3 38	A	5 58	E	21 01	ARI	14
331	27	W.	6 49	E	4 14	A	9 25	27	11	11½	4 09	A	7 01	E	21 12	TAU	15
332	28	Th.	6 50	E	4 14	A	9 24	27	11½	—	4 48	A	8 04	E	21 22	TAU	16
333	29	Fr.	6 51	E	4 14	A	9 23	27	12	12¼	5 35	A	9 02	E	21 33	TAU	17
334	30	Sa.	6 52	E	4 13	A	9 21	26	12¾	12¾	6 P.M. 31	A	9 A.M. 55	E	21S.43	GEM	18

Dun shades quiver down the lone long fallow,
And the scared night shudders at the brown owl's cry;
The bleak reeds rattle as the winds whirl by,
And frayed leaves flutter through the clumped shrubs callow.
—Edwin Arlington Robinson

Farmer's Calendar

The geese passing overhead in a great arrow in the sky are first heard and often never seen at all, especially now. Each spring you're expecting them, but in autumn their voices are a surprise. For a moment it's not certain where that noise is coming from; sounds in the sky seem to come from everywhere. And then, geese overhead don't sound like themselves. Half a mile up in the sky they are talking or shouting, but their clamor comes down to us faintly, obscurely. They may sound like a creaking gate, a football game, a distant radio, barking dogs, a brook, a marching band. When you realize it's geese making that far racket, you look up and try to spot them, and you find them in their pointed files flung out against the sky beating south as straight as a line. When you first see them, they seem to go so slowly, but then they are out of sight, and in a minute more they are out of hearing.

The first flight of geese I remember taking special notice of was headed right down the line of Second Avenue in New York one fine, bright fall day 20 years ago. In New York you can't hear geese honking the way you can in the country because the city itself makes too much noise. Nevertheless, there they were, silent but eloquent, for there is something about the sight of geese flying north or south that plays tricks with what we know of time, as though a mirage has descended to beguile history. Geese were flying over Manhattan when that extraordinary island was a rocky woodland bright with squirrels and little birds; and for some reason when flying geese are in your thoughts that doesn't seem so long ago. What is it about the seasonal flights of geese that for a moment makes our world seem more temporary than it is?

D.M.	D.W.	Dates, Feasts, Fasts, Aspects, Tide Heights	Weather ↓
1	Fr.	**All Saints** • Barbed wire invented, 1873 • Tides {8.6 {9.5	*A ray*
2	Sa.	**All Souls** • Daniel Boone born, 1734 • Tides {8.4 {9.3	*of*
3	F	**23rd S. af. P.** • ☾ runs high • ♂♀ Spica • {8.1 {9.1	*sun,*
4	M.	Will Rogers Day • *An ounce of judgement is worth a pound of wit.*	
5	Tu.	Tatum O'Neal born, 1963 • Susan B. Anthony arrested for attempting to vote, 1875	*then*
6	W.	**St. Leonard** • Roses bloom in New Zealand • Tides {8.1 {9.0	*snow*
7	Th.	Narrows Bridge collapsed, Tacoma, Wash., 1940 • Tides {8.5 {9.2	*gun.*
8	Fr.	☿ Gr. Elong. E. (23°) • ♂♀ Antares • Tides {9.1 {9.5	*Gray*
9	Sa.	☾ on Eq. • ♂☾♀ • Great Lakes storm killed 200 people, 1913	*skies,*
10	F	**24th S. af. P.** • Kentucky outlawed dueling, 1801 • {10.6 {10.3	*and*
11	M.	**St. Martin** • **Veteran's Day** • ☾ at ♋ • ♂♀☾	
12	Tu.	Total Eclipse ☉ • New ● • ☾ at peri. • Tides {11.8 {10.6	*the*
13	W.	♂♀☾ • Year's highest A.M. tide: 12.0' • Paul Simon born, 1942	*first*
14	Th.	♂☾☾ • Claude Monet born, 1840 • Year's highest P.M. tide: 12.0'	*flake*
15	Fr.	☾ runs low • ♂♀☿ • Tides {10.2 {11.7	*flies.*
16	Sa.	Sadie Hawkins Day • -53°F. in Lincoln, Montana, 1959 • {9.8 {11.1	*Now*
17	F	**25th S. af. P.** • ♂♃☾ • {9.3 {10.5	*come*
18	M.	☿ stat. • Lincoln Deachey performed the first airplane loop-the-loop, 1913	*runny*
19	Tu.	*Neither abstinence nor excess ever renders man happy.* • Tides {8.7 {9.4	*noses*
20	W.	Pony Express stopped, 1861 • Dick Smothers born, 1939 • Tides {8.6 {9.0	*and*
21	Th.	*On this day so the winter.* • MGM Grand Hotel fire, Las Vegas, Nev., 1980	*freezy*
22	Fr.	**St. Cecilia** • ☾ on Eq. • ♂♄☉ • {8.9 {8.7	*toeses.*
23	Sa.	**St. Clement** • First jukebox installed, San Francisco, Calif., 1889	*Pull*
24	F	**26th S. af. P.** • Tides {9.4 {8.6	*on a*
25	M.	☾ at ☊ • ☾ at apo. • Joe DiMaggio born, 1914	*cardigan,*
26	Tu.	*Beauty is in the eye of the beholder.* • Tides {9.7 {8.6	*winter's*
27	W.	Full Beaver ○ • Pope Urban II preached the First Crusade, 1095	*going*
28	Th.	**Thanksgiving Day** • ☿ in inf. ♂ • {9.7	*to*
29	Fr.	Kilauea Volcano erupted in Hawaii, 1975 • Tides {8.5 {9.7	*start*
30	Sa.	**St. Andrew** • ☾ runs high • Youth Day in Upper Volta	*again!*

It matters not how long we live, but how. — Philip J. Bailey

1985	DECEMBER, THE TWELFTH MONTH

Before morning twilight on the 8th the southeastern United States can watch the crescent moon pass in front of Mars while the rest of the country gets to see a near miss. (This is the only occultation of the year.) All the other planets are near the sun this month. The winter solstice occurs at 5:08 P.M. EST on the 21st. On the nights of December 13-14 and 14-15, Geminid meteors will pour from high in the sky from late evening until morning twilight in numbers as great as 50 or 60 an hour. Early in the month country observers should see Halley's Comet with the naked eye for the first time in three-quarters of a century. On the 30th, in the west at nightfall, the comet is near the star Gamma in Aries, crossing the earth's orbit two days later.

ASTRONOMICAL CALCULATIONS

☾	Last Quarter	5th day	4th hour	2nd min.
●	New Moon	11th day	19th hour	55th min.
☽	First Quarter	18th day	20th hour	59th min.
○	Full Moon	27th day	2nd hour	31st min.

FOR POINTS OUTSIDE BOSTON SEE KEY LETTER CORRECTIONS—PAGES 86-90

Day of Year	Day of Month	Day of Week	☉ Rises h. m.	Key	☉ Sets h. m.	Key	Length of Days h. m.	Sun Fast m.	Full Sea Boston A.M.	Full Sea Boston P.M.	☽ Rises h.m.	Key	☽ Sets h.m.	Key	Declination of sun ° '	☽ Place	☽ Age
335	1	**F**	6 54	E	4 13	A	9 19	26	1½	1½	7 P.M. 33	B	10 A.M. 40	E	21s.52	GEM	19
336	2	M.	6 55	E	4 13	A	9 18	26	2¼	2¼	8 40	B	11 17	E	22 01	CAN	20
337	3	Tu.	6 56	E	4 12	A	9 16	25	3	3	9 49	B	11 A.M. 49	E	22 09	CAN	21
338	4	W.	6 57	E	4 12	A	9 15	25	3¾	4	11 P.M. 00	C	12 P.M. 15	D	22 17	LEO	22
339	5	Th.	6 58	E	4 12	A	9 14	24	4¾	5	— —	–	12 39	D	22 25	LEO	23
340	6	Fr.	6 59	E	4 12	A	9 13	24	5½	6	12 A.M. 11	D	1 02	D	22 32	VIR	24
341	7	Sa.	7 00	E	4 12	A	9 12	24	6½	7	1 24	D	1 24	C	22 39	VIR	25
342	8	**F**	7 01	E	4 12	A	9 11	23	7½	7¾	2 40	E	1 49	B	22 45	VIR	26
343	9	M.	7 01	E	4 12	A	9 11	23	8¼	8¾	3 59	E	2 18	B	22 51	VIR	27
344	10	Tu.	7 02	E	4 12	A	9 10	22	9¼	9¾	5 22	E	2 54	B	22 57	LIB	28
345	11	W.	7 03	E	4 12	A	9 09	22	10	10¾	6 44	E	3 40	A	23 02	SCO	0
346	12	Th.	7 04	E	4 12	A	9 08	21	11	11½	8 02	E	4 37	A	23 06	OPH	1
347	13	Fr.	7 05	E	4 12	A	9 07	21	11¾	—	9 08	E	5 45	A	23 10	SAG	2
348	14	Sa.	7 06	E	4 12	A	9 06	20	12½	12¾	10 00	E	6 59	B	23 14	SAG	3
349	15	**F**	7 06	E	4 12	A	9 06	20	1¼	1½	10 40	E	8 14	B	23 17	CAP	4
350	16	M.	7 07	E	4 13	A	9 06	19	2¼	2½	11 11	E	9 26	B	23 20	CAP	5
351	17	Tu.	7 08	E	4 13	A	9 05	19	3¼	3¼	11 36	D	10 35	C	23 22	AQU	6
352	18	W.	7 08	E	4 13	A	9 05	18	4	4¼	11 A.M. 58	D	11 P.M. 39	C	23 24	AQU	7
353	19	Th.	7 09	E	4 14	A	9 05	18	5	5¼	12 P.M. 17	C	— —	–	23 25	PSC	8
354	20	Fr.	7 09	E	4 14	A	9 05	17	6	6¼	12 36	C	12 A.M. 42	D	23 26	PSC	9
355	21	Sa.	7 10	E	4 15	A	9 05	17	6¾	7¼	12 55	B	1 44	D	23 26	PSC	10
356	22	**F**	7 10	E	4 15	A	9 05	16	7½	8	1 16	B	2 45	E	23 26	ARI	11
357	23	M.	7 11	E	4 16	A	9 05	16	8¼	9	1 41	A	3 48	E	23 26	ARI	12
358	24	Tu.	7 11	E	4 16	A	9 05	15	9	9¾	2 10	A	4 51	E	23 24	TAU	13
359	25	W.	7 12	E	4 17	A	9 05	15	9¾	10¼	2 46	A	5 55	E	23 23	TAU	14
360	26	Th.	7 12	E	4 18	A	9 06	14	10½	11	3 31	A	6 55	E	23 21	TAU	15
361	27	Fr.	7 12	E	4 18	A	9 06	14	11¼	11¾	4 24	A	7 50	E	23 18	GEM	16
362	28	Sa.	7 13	E	4 19	A	9 06	13	11¾	—	5 26	A	8 38	E	23 15	GEM	17
363	29	**F**	7 13	E	4 20	A	9 07	13	12¼	12½	6 32	B	9 19	E	23 12	CAN	18
364	30	M.	7 13	E	4 20	A	9 07	12	1	1¼	7 41	B	9 51	E	23 08	CAN	19
365	31	Tu.	7 13	E	4 21	A	9 08	12	1¾	2	8 P.M. 52	C	10 A.M. 19	E	23s.04	LEO	20

DECEMBER hath 31 days. 1985

Ring out the old, ring in the new,
Ring happy bells, across the snow:
The year is going, let him go;
Ring out the false, ring in the true.
—Alfred Tennyson

D.M.	D.W.	Dates, Feasts, Fasts, Aspects, Tide Heights	Weather ↓
1	F	**Advent** • Woody Allen born, 1935 • Tides {8.3 / 9.5} •	*Science*
2	M.	☌ ♅ Spica • First Model A Fords sold, with $385 price tag, 1927 •	*says*
3	Tu.	☌☿♀ • *Nothing is a man's truly but what he comes by duly.* • Tides {8.2 / 9.2} •	*the*
4	W.	Grapes ripe in Bolivia • 70°F. in Boston, Mass., 1982 • {8.3 / 9.1} •	*climate's*
5	Th.	☌♀♄ • Daniel C. Stillson patented the pipe wrench, 1876 •	*warming,*
6	Fr.	**St. Nicholas** • ☾ on Eq. • Tides {9.0 / 9.1} •	*but*
7	Sa.	Last manned flight to the moon (Apollo XVII) launched, 1972 • {9.6 / 9.3} •	*every*
8	F	**2nd S. Advent** • **Chanukah** • ☿ stat.	
9	M.	☾ at ☋ • *Deliberate slowly, execute promptly.* •	*wintertime*
10	Tu.	☌♅☉ • ☌☿☾ • ☌♄☾ • ☾ at peri. • {11.3 / 9.9} •	*it's*
11	W.	New ● • Max Born born, 1882 • Tides {11.7 / 10.0} •	*storming!*
12	Th.	29°F. in northern Florida, 1952 • George F. Grant patented the golf tee, 1899 •	*Polar*
13	Fr.	**St. Lucy** • ☾ runs low • Tides {11.8 / —} •	*cold*
14	Sa.	Halcyon Days begin • Roald Amundsen reached the South Pole, 1911 •	*paves*
15	F	**3rd S. Advent** • ☌♃☾ • Tides {9.6 / 11.0} •	*the*
16	M.	☌☿♃ • Boston Tea Party, 1773 • Noel Coward born, 1899 •	*way*
17	Tu.	☿ Gr. Elong. W. (21°) • *A threadbare coat is armor proof against highwaymen.* •	*for*
18	W.	Ember Day • Giant panda, Su-Lin, arrived in U.S., 1936 • Tides {8.8 / 9.1} •	*Santa's*
19	Th.	Al Kaline born, 1934 • ☾ on Eq. • Tides {8.7 / 8.6} •	*sleigh.*
20	Fr.	Ember Day • Pneumatic automobile tire patented, 1892 • Tides {8.7 / 8.3} •	*Cold*
21	Sa.	**St. Thomas** • Winter solstice 5:08 P.M. EST • Ember Day •	*and*
22	F	**4th S. Advent** • ☾ at ☊ • Tides {8.9 / 8.0} •	*clear,*
23	M.	☾ at apo. • -46°F. in Williston, N.D., 1983 • Tides {9.1 / 8.0} •	*holiday*
24	Tu.	*A good conscience is a continual Christmas.* • Tides {9.2 / 8.1} •	*cheer.*
25	W.	**Christmas** • ☌♆☉ • Tides {9.4 / 8.2} •	*With*
26	Th.	**St. Stephen** • James H. Nason patented the coffee percolator, 1865 •	*mittens*
27	Fr.	**St. John** • Full Cold ○ • ☾ runs high • Tides {9.7 / 8.4} •	*on,*
28	Sa.	**Holy Innocents** • Woodrow Wilson born, 1856 •	*we'll*
29	F	**1st S. af. Christmas** • ☌☿♅ •	*wave —*
30	M.	-50°F. in Bloomfield, Vermont, 1933 • Bert Parks born, 1914 • Tides {8.5 / 9.9} •	*so*
31	Tu.	**St. Sylvester** • New Year's Eve • Tides {8.7 / 9.8} •	*long!*

Farmer's Calendar

Some time before Christmas I lose my race against the snow. It started in September; now it's over. It's a race that probably isn't as important as I make it. With very few exceptions, the things I say I must get done before the snow comes are not things that, neglected, would threaten our safety, or our health, or even our comfort. Nevertheless, as winter approaches I feel a need to provide against it, even in unimportant ways, to make things safe, even though they are safe enough. And so each year there is a long tale of closing, tightening, nailing down, cleaning, raking, picking up, covering, burning, battening. I set about these jobs calmly, so as to do each of them right, but as the autumn wears on, I'm hurrying to get done before the snow begins, for a good snow will make half my list of jobs impossible and the other half irrelevant.

Always when snow comes I get caught with a few things still to do. The storm windows get on all right, and the foundation gets banked, but there are usually uncaulked cracks, or there's a new lilac that ought to have its own little snow fence and doesn't get it. I now realize that the fall jobs that don't get done are as important as the ones that do. I set my life up each autumn so that there will be these unfinished works at the end; I never make a list of jobs that has a last job. I also notice that when the snow finally comes to catch me not quite ready, I am content. I'm glad the snow has come. Am I alone in this? I think not. The autumn race to finish an unfinishable list of jobs before the winter comes down is less necessity than symbol. That there must be work left undone at the end and that we welcome the snow when it comes are signs that we know we must learn again each winter to submit.

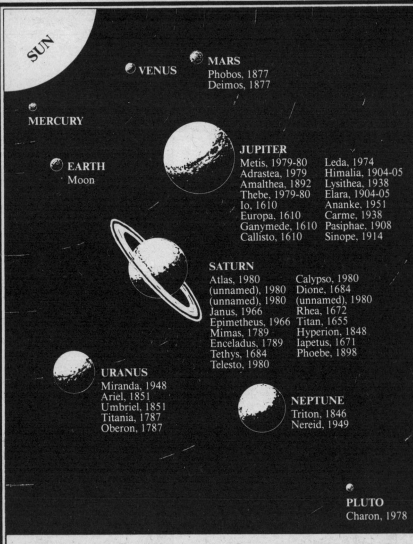

SUN

VENUS

MARS
Phobos, 1877
Deimos, 1877

MERCURY

EARTH
Moon

JUPITER

Metis, 1979-80	Leda, 1974
Adrastea, 1979	Himalia, 1904-05
Amalthea, 1892	Lysithea, 1938
Thebe, 1979-80	Elara, 1904-05
Io, 1610	Ananke, 1951
Europa, 1610	Carme, 1938
Ganymede, 1610	Pasiphae, 1908
Callisto, 1610	Sinope, 1914

SATURN

Atlas, 1980	Calypso, 1980
(unnamed), 1980	Dione, 1684
(unnamed), 1980	(unnamed), 1980
Janus, 1966	Rhea, 1672
Epimetheus, 1966	Titan, 1655
Mimas, 1789	Hyperion, 1848
Enceladus, 1789	Iapetus, 1671
Tethys, 1684	Phoebe, 1898
Telesto, 1980	

URANUS
Miranda, 1948
Ariel, 1851
Umbriel, 1851
Titania, 1787
Oberon, 1787

NEPTUNE
Triton, 1846
Nereid, 1949

PLUTO
Charon, 1978

How Many Moons Can You Name?

Galileo was the first to discover that a planet other than our own had natural satellites like our moon. Using his crude telescope in 1610, he could see four satellites of Jupiter, largest planet in the solar system. More moons were discovered as the centuries passed, but the last five years, since spacecraft have flown past Jupiter and Saturn, have produced a bumper crop, some so new that they have no names yet. The most complete list to date, compiled by J. Kelly Beatty of *Sky & Telescope* Magazine, is reproduced here with permission. Satellites are shown with their planets and listed in the order of their distance from the planet, nearest first, with the dates of discovery.

TIDE CORRECTIONS

Many factors affect the time and height of the tides: the coastal configuration, the time of the moon's southing (crossing the meridian) at the place, and the phase of the moon. This table of tidal corrections is a sufficiently accurate guide to the times and heights of the high water at the places shown. (Low tides occur approximately 6 hours before and after high tides.) No figures are shown for most places on the Gulf of Mexico, since the method used in compiling this table does not apply there. For such places and elsewhere where precise accuracy is required, consult the Tide Tables published annually by the Distribution Div. C44, National Ocean Survey, Dept. of Commerce, Riverdale, MD 20840.

The figures for Full Sea on the left-hand Calendar pages 48-74 are the times of high tide at Commonwealth Pier in Boston harbor. The heights of these tides are given on the right-hand Calendar pages 49-75. The heights are reckoned from Mean Low Water, and each day listed has a set of figures — upper for the morning, lower for the evening. To obtain the time and height of high water at any of the following places, apply the time difference to the daily times of high water at Boston (pages 48-74), and the height difference to the heights at Boston (pages 49-75).

	Time Difference Hr. Min.	Height Difference Feet		Time Difference Hr. Min.	Height Difference Feet
MAINE			Onset	−2 16	−5.9
Bar Harbor	−0 34	+0.9	(R.R. Bridge)		
Belfast	−0 20	+0.4	Plymouth	+0 05	0.0
Boothbay Harbor	−0 18	−0.8	Provincetown	+0 14	−0.4
Chebeague Island	−0 16	−0.6	Revere Beach	−0 01	−0.3
Eastport	−0 28	+8.4	Rockport	−0 08	−1.0
Kennebunkport	+0 04	−1.0	Salem	0 00	−0.5
Machias	−0 28	+2.8	Scituate	−0 05	−0.7
Monhegan Island	−0 25	−0.8	Wareham	−3 09	−5.3
Old Orchard	0 00	−0.8	Wellfleet	+0 12	+0.5
Portland	−0 12	−0.6	West Falmouth	−3 10	−5.4
Rockland	−0 28	+0.1	Westport Harbor	−3 22	−6.4
Stonington	−0 30	+0.1	Woods Hole		
York	−0 09	−1.0	Little Harbor	−2 50	*0.2
			Oceanographic		
NEW HAMPSHIRE			Inst.	−3 07	*0.2
Hampton	+0 02	−1.3			
Portsmouth	+0 11	−1.5	**RHODE ISLAND**		
Rye Beach	−0 09	−0.9	Bristol	−3 24	−5.3
			Sakonnet	−3 44	−5.6
MASSACHUSETTS			Narragansett Pier	−3 42	−6.2
Annisquam	−0 02	−1.1	Newport	−3 34	−5.9
Beverly Farms	0 00	−0.5	Pt. Judith	−3 41	−6.3
Boston	0 00	0.0	Providence	−3 20	−4.8
Cape Cod Canal			Watch Hill	−2 50	−6.8
East Entrance	−0 01	−0.8			
West Entrance	−2 16	−5.9	**CONNECTICUT**		
Chatham			Bridgeport	+0 01	−2.6
Outer Coast	+0 30	−2.8	Madison	−0 22	−2.3
Inside	+1 54	*0.4	New Haven	−0 11	−3.2
Cohasset	+0 02	−0.07	New London	−1 54	−6.7
Cotuit Highlands	+1 15	*0.4	Norwalk	+0 01	−2.2
Dennisport	+1 01	*0.4	Old Lyme	−0 30	−6.2
Duxbury	+0 02	−0.3	(Highway Bridge)		
(Gurnet Pt.)			Stamford	+0 01	−2.2
Fall River	−3 03	−5.0	Stonington	−2 27	−6.6
Gloucester	−0 03	−0.8			
Hingham	+0 07	0.0	**NEW YORK**		
Hull	+0 03	−0.2	Coney Island	−3 33	−4.9
Hyannis Port	+1 01	*0.3	Fire Island Lt.	−2 43	*0.1
Magnolia	−0 02	−0.7	Long Beach	−3 11	−5.7
(Manchester)			Montauk Harbor	−2 19	−7.4
Marblehead	−0 02	−0.4	New York City	−2 43	−5.0
Marion	−3 22	−5.4	(Battery)		
Monument Beach	−3 08	−5.4	Oyster Bay	+0 04	−1.8
Nahant	−0 01	−0.5	Port Chester	−0 09	−2.2
Nantasket	+0 04	−0.1	Port Washington	−0 01	−2.1
Nantucket	−0 56	*0.3	Sag Harbor	−0 55	−6.8
Nauset Beach	+0 30	*0.6	Southampton	−4 20	*0.2
New Bedford	−3 24	−5.7	(Shinnecock Inlet)		
Newburyport	+0 19	−1.8	Willets Point	0 00	−2.3
Oak Bluffs	+0 30	*0.2			

	Time Difference Hr. Min.	Height Difference Feet		Time Difference Hr. Min.	Height Difference Feet
NEW JERSEY			Fort Pierce Inlet	−3 32	−6.9
Asbury Park	−4 04	−5.3	Jacksonville		
Atlantic City	−3 56	−5.5	Railroad Bridge ..	−6 55	*0.10
Bay Head (Sea Girt)	−4 04	−5.3	Key West	+11 24	−9.1
Beach Haven	−1 43	*0.24	Miami Harbor		
Cape May	−3 28	−5.3	Entrance	−3 18	−7.0
Ocean City	−3 06	−5.9	St. Augustine	−2 55	−4.9
Sandy Hook	−3 30	−5.0	St. Petersburg ...	−9 53	−7.6
Seaside Park	−4 03	−5.4	Sarasota	−11 31	*0.22
PENNSYLVANIA			Suwannee River		
Philadelphia	+2 40	−3.5	Entrance	−9 01	−6.4
DELAWARE			**CALIFORNIA**		
Cape Henlopen	−2 48	−5.3	Carmel	−0 22	*0.5
Rehoboth Beach ...	−3 37	−5.7	Catalina Island ...	−1 23	*0.5
Wilmington	+1 56	−3.8	Crescent City	−2 05	−4.1
MARYLAND			Eureka	+1 35	−3.4
Annapolis	+6 23	−8.5	Laguna Beach	−1 38	*0.5
Baltimore	+7 59	−8.3	Long Beach	−1 30	*0.5
Cambridge	+5 05	−7.8	Los Angeles	−1 33	−4.7
Havre de Grace ..	+11 21	−7.7	Mendocino	+0 03	−4.4
Point No Point ...	+2 28	−8.1	Monterey	−0 31	−4.9
Prince Frederick ...	+4 25	−8.5	San Diego	−1 41	−4.3
(Plum Point)			San Francisco ...	+0 45	−4.4
VIRGINIA			Santa Barbara	−1 10	*0.5
Cape Charles	−2 20	−7.0	Santa Cruz	−0 34	−4.9
Hampton Roads ...	−2 02	−6.9	Santa Rosa Is.	−0 03	−4.5
Norfolk	−2 06	−6.6	**OREGON**		
Virginia Beach	−4 00	−6.0	Astoria	+2 21	−1.5
Yorktown	−2 13	−7.0	Empire-North Bend	+1 48	−3.4
NORTH CAROLINA			Gold Beach	+1 45	−3.4
Cape Fear	−3 55	−5.0	(Rogue R. Entrance)		
Cape Lookout	−4 28	−5.7	Tillamook	+2 28	*0.6
Currituck	−4 10	−5.8	**WASHINGTON**		
Hatteras			Aberdeen	+2 09	−0.1
Ocean	−4 26	−6.0	Bellingham	−6 18	−1.4
Inlet	−4 03	−7.4	Cape Flaherty	+1 26	*0.8
Kitty Hawk	−4 14	−6.2	Columbia River		
SOUTH CAROLINA			Entrance (Ilwaco)	+1 35	−2.2
Charleston	−3 22	−4.3	Everett	−6 30	+1.1
Georgetown	−1 48	*0.36	Long Beach	+1 07	*0.8
Hilton Head	−3 22	−2.9	Pacific Beach	+1 10	*0.9
Myrtle Beach	−3 49	−4.4	Port Townsend ...	−7 04	−1.6
St. Helena			Seattle	−6 21	+1.3
Harbor Entrance .	−3 15	−3.4	South Bend	+2 08	−0.2
GEORGIA			Tacoma	−6 14	+1.8
Jekyll Island	−3 46	−2.9	**ALASKA**		
Saint Simon's Island	−2 50	−2.9	Anchorage	−4 58	+17.5
Savannah Beach			Juneau	+3 08	+6.1
River Entrance .	−3 14	−5.5	Kodiak	+1 53	−1.7
Tybee Light	−3 22	−2.7	**CANADA**		
FLORIDA			Alberton, P.E.I. ...	−5 45**	−7.5
Apalachicola	−7 53	*0.18	Charlottetown, P.E.I.	−0 45**	−3.5
Cape Kennedy	−3 59	−6.0	Halifax, N.S.	−3 23	−4.5
Clearwater	−9 01	−6.4	North Sydney, N.S. .	−3 15	−6.5
Daytona Beach ...	−3 28	−5.3	St. John, N.B.	+0 30	−8.0
Everglades City	+16 12	−7.3	St. John's, Nfld. ...	−4 00	−6.5
Fort Lauderdale ...	−2 50	−7.2	Vancouver, B.C.	−5 25	+4.2
Fort Myers	−7 45	*0.12	Yarmouth, N.S.	−0 40	+3.0

* Where the value in the "height difference" column is so marked, height at Boston should be multiplied by this ratio.

** Varies widely; accurate only within 1½ hours. Consult local tide tables for precise times and heights.

Example: The conversion of the times and heights of the tides at Boston to those of Bristol, Rhode Island, is given below:

Sample tide calculation	High tide Boston (p. 60)	7:30 A.M.	Tide height Boston (p. 61)	9.7 ft.
May 30th, 1985:	Correction for Bristol	−3:24 hrs.	Correction for Bristol	−5.3 ft.
	High tide Bristol	4:06 A.M.	Tide Height Bristol	4.4 ft.

99 STRANGE BUT TRUE TALES

Heady brew for late-night reading.

Mysterious New England

Vampires of Rhode Island . . . Block Island's Fiery Ghost . . . Ancient Rock Carvings . . . Ghost Treasure Shaft of Bristol Notch . . . here are 49 tales that defy explanation. From the darker side of man and nature come hair-raising accounts of apples that dripped blood; the horrible truth behind Edgar Allan Poe's story, "The Cask of Amontillado"; the strange obsession of Hiram Marble; and the house designed in madness. Hundreds of photos and illustrations. 320 pages, 6" x 9" paperback, spine-tingling entertainment for only **$11.95**

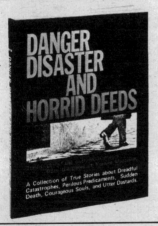

Danger, Disaster and Horrid Deeds

Death aboard the Herbert Fuller *. . . the killer ostrich . . . the rescue of Molly Finney . . . the great sea-water to gold swindle . . . 50 blood-chilling true stories bring to life scoundrels, strange accidents of fate, narrow escapes and brave rescues.* Relive the shocking events of historical New England from the tragic circus fire of 1944 to the Great Boston Fire of 1872, meet pirates like Black Sam Bellamy and the great swindler Rev. Prescott Jernegan. Perhaps you can solve the mysteries of the Phantom P-40, the *John Dwight* murders or the phantom ship *Mary Celeste.* Here are half a hundred ways to fill your nights with reading terror. 288 pages, 8½" x 11" paperback, hundreds of photos and illustrations, only **$10.95.**

Mystery Library Special: Buy both books for only $19.95 ($22.90 value)

Mail order to: **Yankee Books**
Dept. AL85
Depot Square
Peterborough, NH 03458

Amazing Animal Heroes

A collection of furred, feathered, and four-footed friends who have done some incredible things.

courtesy of Yolanda Jarvis

☐ HEROIC FEATS PERFORMED BY DOGS have become legendary, sometimes nearly mythic, in proportion. Two breeds, the St. Bernard and the New-foundland, seem to have evolved just for their ability to save lives on snowy mountains and in raging seas.

But there are other heroes in the animal kingdom. For example . . .

CATS

• In the winter of 1976 a voiceless, deaf, shorthaired cat named Baby saved the life of her master in Manitoba, Canada. Late one night Baby became aware that her master, Aurel Beriault, was in difficulty. Unable to meow, the little cat gamely jumped on the sleeping Mrs. Beriault's bed again and again until she awoke and discovered the problem. She rushed her husband to a hospital just in time to save him from what surely would have been a fatal heart attack.

• Sam, a six-month-old Manx cat, saved the lives of six people when his family's house caught fire in Orange, California, in 1973.

• Dumb-Dumb was a half-Siamese cat that attacked a burglar trying to break into her family's home in Wichita, Kansas, in 1978. The cat struck the would-be robber so suddenly and so fiercely that the intruder was actually felled, leading to his quick arrest.

• Mixy, a calico cat from Linden, New Jersey, meowed loud enough to awaken all the members of the Razwilavich family in time for them to escape from a devastating fire in their home in November of 1974.

• Rhubarb came into the life of Elsie Schneider in 1963 as a four-week-old Siamese female. Mrs. Schneider had lost her vision in 1954 but was still able to handle all her own household chores, so she decided to train Rhubarb to assist her. The remarkable cat quickly learned her mistress's needs and became, in effect, a seeing-eye cat for Mrs. Schneider for the next 17 years.

HORSES

• Indian Red, a Morgan/Quarter cross, was the first horse inducted into the Purina Animal Hall of Fame in October 1978. Helen Bumby had purchased the little gelding in 1974 because the horse had been neglected by his previous owner and was in very bad condition. Helen worked at a nearby horse farm in exchange for Indian Red's board and veterinary care and nursed the animal back to health. Almost as if to repay this kindness, Indian Red made a hero of his owner and himself on a bitterly cold, snowy day in December 1977. As Helen was riding Indian Red along a road near the barn where he was stabled, the horse suddenly began acting strangely. He stopped and refused to move. He kept whinnying and pawing the ground while he stared intently into the snow. Unable to see what was troubling the horse, Helen dismounted and looked more closely. To her amazement she found a helpless 77-year-old woman lying in a deep snowbank. Helen quickly summoned help and the woman was rushed to the hospital, where she made a complete recovery.

PIGEONS

• Cher Ami, like almost all pigeons whose acts of bravery have been recorded for posterity, was a military messenger pigeon. During his career Cher Ami delivered 12 messages from the Verdun front to his loft at Rampont during World War I. His last flight was by far his most amazing accomplishment. In October 1918 during a general advance of the 77th Division, a number of companies were cut off from support and surrounded by the Germans. The men were being attacked by heavy mortar and machine-gun fire when a French and American artillery barrage began to fall around them. So close was the shelling that the Americans were hit as heavily as the Germans. One after another, seven carrier pigeons were released with messages, but all of them were shot down by German marksmen. There was but one carrier left, Cher Ami. The message, "For God's sake, lift the fire," was placed in a capsule attached to his leg. Cher Ami took off and was almost immediately downed by a piece of shrapnel, but he managed to regain flight. His breast was pierced by a sharpshooter's bullet, but he flew on. A third shot tore off his right leg, leaving the

precious message capsule dangling by a tendon, and still the little creature flew on. Twenty-five minutes later the bird collapsed at his loft in Rampont. The message was relayed, the shelling stopped, and the so-called "Lost Battalion" was relieved. Cher Ami became a feathered celebrity, and even sported a wooden leg carved to replace the one lost in action.

• G.I. Joe saved a thousand British troops from a bombing in Italy during World War II. The troops had occupied a village suddenly evacuated by the Germans. G.I. Joe arrived at the airfield with a message from the British troops just as the bombing mission was to take off. He was decorated for this feat by the Lord Mayor of London.

• Black Halligan carried an urgent message from the 164th Infantry on Guadalcanal which revealed the position of 300 Japanese troops. He delivered the information despite the fact that he was wounded in the breast.

DOGS

• Chips, a tough German shepherd cross from Pleasantville, New York, is representative, albeit the most famous, of participants in the Dogs for Defense program during World War II. When he landed under fire in Sicily in July 1943, Chips was unusually disturbed. His handler, Private John P. Rowell, led Chips off to the flank so that the dog's barking and whining would not attract enemy fire on the company. As the man and dog advanced along the flank in the dawn light, what looked like a grass hut became barely visible ahead of them. It was a camouflaged pillbox. Private Rowell saw flames spurt from its wall as the hidden machine gun swept the beach. Suddenly Chips tore the leash from the handler's grip and streaked toward the pillbox. There was a brief turmoil of shrieks and low canine growls before an enemy machine gunner staggered out with Chips slashing at his throat. The other three members of the crew followed in surrender.

• In July 1961 Ramon C. Miller of Fresno, California, ran out of gas on a lonely road in the Mojave Desert south of Death Valley. With him was his Weimaraner Gretchen. Despite the fact that he had an artificial leg, Miller set off with Gretchen in search of assistance. After walking for nearly seven hours, Miller and his dog came to a sign that read simply "Springs." Following the path until noon of the following day, they reached a cave with a freshwater spring. Gretchen stayed at the cave with her crippled master for seven days without food, defending him from wild animals, until they were located by two rescuers.

• Eugene Harland of Almena, Wisconsin, took in a stray mixed-breed puppy in July 1979. Harland named him Batman and trained him to be a cow dog on his dairy farm. In the summer of 1982, Eugene and his wife went to round up a cow and her new calf in a wooded area on the farm. As Harland approached the cow, he told the dog to stay. Suddenly the cow charged the farmer, butted him to the ground, held him there with her head, and began flailing him with her hooves. When Batman heard Mrs. Harland scream, he broke command and rushed in, nipping at the enraged cow's legs until she retreated back to her calf. While Mrs. Harland helped her husband to safety, the dog stationed himself between the couple and the cow. Mr. Harland suffered cracked ribs, bruised lungs, and cuts requiring over a week in the hospital. Mrs. Harland reported that Batman refused to touch his food until the day her husband returned from the hospital.

FROGS

• In the late spring of 1972, a fire broke out in the science laboratory of a private grammar school in western New York (to remain nameless at the request of school officials). The students were quickly evacuated and grouped on the lawn when suddenly two sixth-grade boys broke from the crowd and dashed into the building by the rear door. Moments later both boys emerged, one of them clutching Horace, a large frog. As the two boys were being lectured for their recklessness by their biology teacher, Horace wriggled free and started hopping across the lawn, right into the path of a fireman who was rushing toward the side door of the building now spewing a cloud of thick black smoke. Horace, only recently having left the damp confines of his laboratory home, was wet, so when the poor fireman stepped on Horace he went flying. The fall stunned the man for a minute or two, during which time the roof of the laboratory collapsed in a flaming roar. Had the fireman made it into the side door, he surely would have perished in the holocaust. For saving the fireman's life, Horace was awarded a medal by the entire sixth-grade class, posthumously, of course.

Editor's note: Do you have a true story of a remarkable feat performed by an animal? Tell us about it and we will consider it for publication in *The Old Farmer's Almanac* for 1986. We will pay $50 for each true story we include in next year's issue. Send your stories to Animal Editor, *The Old Farmer's Almanac,* Dublin, NH 03444. □ □

Exciting Breakthrough For Suburban Gardeners!

At last!
Now there's a tiller/cultivator exclusively designed for small backyard gardens.

No longer do you have to choose between a yank-you-along *front-tine tiller* and a clumsy hard-to-guide expensive *rear-tine tiller.*

Now there's Mantis . . . the 20 pound wonder that makes every gardening job a breeze! Mantis starts with a flick of the wrist . . . turns on a dime . . . weeds an average garden in 20 minutes . . . and runs all day on a gallon of gas.

Mantis tills a full 8" deep, or delicately cultivates the surface for precision weeding.

The secret of Mantis' success is its exclusive "tine teeth" which spin at 240 revolutions per minute (*twice the speed* of most tillers). These *tine teeth* cut through soil, weeds and tough sod like a chain saw cuts through wood.

Women find the Mantis especially easy to maneuver.

Mantis is so easy to guide that you can cultivate right around plants, along crop rows and up tight to fences . . . without worrying about running into your growing flowers and vegetables.

And, with its easy-on/easy-off *precision attachments,* Mantis quickly becomes a *Planter/Furrower* . . . a *Border Edger* . . . a *Lawn De-thatcher* and *Aerator* . . . or a superb *Trimmer.*

MAIL ORDER BONUS

Get a FREE $41.00 Border/Edger! (If you hurry)

Cuts beautiful border edges along drives, walks, and gardens for professionally landscaped finish.

TIME CORRECTION TABLES

The times of sunrise, sunset, moonrise, moonset, and the rising and setting of the planets are given for Boston only on pages 48-74 and 36-37. Use the Key Letter shown there and this table to find the number of minutes that should be added to or subtracted from Boston time to give the correct time of your city. The answer will not be as precise as that for Boston, but will be within approximately 5 minutes. If your city is not listed, find the city closest to you in both latitude and longitude and use those figures. Canadian cities appear at the end of the list. For a more complete explanation see page 27.

Time Zone Code: −1 — Atlantic Std.; 0 — Eastern Std.; 1 — Central Std.; 2 — Mountain Std.; 3 — Pacific Std.; 4 — Yukon Std.; 5 — Alaska Hawaii Std.; 6 — Bering Std.

City	North Latitude ° '		West Longitude ° '		Time Zone Code	Key Letters A min.	B min.	C min.	D min.	E min.
Aberdeen, SD	45	28	98	29	1	+37	+43	+49	+55	+61
Akron, OH	41	5	81	31	0	+47	+44	+42	+39	+37
Albany, NY	42	39	73	45	0	+ 9	+10	+11	+11	+12
Albert Lea, MN	43	39	93	22	1	+24	+26	+29	+31	+34
Albuquerque, NM	35	5	106	39	2	+51	+37	+23	+10	− 4
Alexandria, LA	31	18	92	27	1	+68	+48	+27	+ 6	−14
Allentown-Bethlehem, PA	40	3	75	28	0	+26	+22	+18	+13	+ 9
Amarillo, TX	35	12	101	50	1	+91	+77	+64	+51	+37
Anchorage, AK	61	10	149	59	5	−58	−23	+13	+48	+83
Ardmore, OK	34	10	97	8	1	+76	+61	+45	+30	+15
Asheville, NC	35	36	82	33	0	+72	+59	+47	+34	+22
Atlanta, GA	33	45	84	24	0	+87	+71	+54	+38	+22
Atlantic City, NJ	39	22	74	26	0	+25	+19	+14	+ 8	+ 3
Augusta, GA	33	28	81	58	0	+78	+61	+45	+28	+11
Augusta, ME	44	19	69	46	0	−13	− 9	− 6	− 2	+ 2
Austin, TX	30	16	97	45	1	+94	+71	+48	+26	+ 3
Bakersfield, CA	35	23	119	1	3	+39	+26	+13	0	−13
Baltimore, MD	39	17	76	37	0	+34	+28	+23	+17	+11
Bangor, ME	44	48	68	46	0	−19	−14	−10	− 5	− 1
Barstow, CA	34	54	117	1	3	+33	+19	+ 5	− 9	−23
Baton Rouge, LA	30	27	91	11	1	+67	+44	+22	0	−23
Beaumont, TX	30	5	94	6	1	+80	+57	+34	+11	−12
Bellingham, WA	48	45	122	29	3	+ 1	+13	+25	+37	+49
Bemidji, MN	47	28	94	53	1	+15	+25	+34	+44	+54
Berlin, NH	44	28	71	11	0	− 8	− 4	0	+ 4	+ 8
Billings, MT	45	47	108	30	2	+16	+23	+29	+36	+42
Biloxi, MS	30	24	88	53	1	+58	+35	+13	− 9	−32
Binghamton, NY	42	6	75	55	0	+20	+20	+19	+19	+18
Birmingham, AL	33	31	86	49	1	+37	+21	+ 4	−12	−29
Bismarck, ND	46	48	100	47	1	+41	+50	+58	+66	+75
Boise, ID	43	37	116	12	2	+55	+58	+60	+63	+65
Brattleboro, VT	42	51	72	34	0	+ 4	+ 5	+ 6	+ 7	+ 8
Bridgeport, CT	41	11	73	11	0	+13	+11	+ 9	+ 6	+ 4
Brockton, MA	42	5	71	1	0	+ 1	0	0	− 1	− 1
Buffalo, NY	42	53	78	52	0	+29	+30	+31	+32	+33
Burlington, VT	44	29	73	13	0	+ 0	+ 4	+ 8	+12	+16
Butte, MT	46	1	112	32	2	+31	+38	+45	+52	+59
Cairo, IL	37	0	89	11	1	+33	+23	+13	+ 3	− 7
Camden, NJ	39	57	75	7	0	+25	+21	+16	+12	+ 7
Canton, OH	40	48	81	23	0	+47	+44	+41	+38	+36
Cape May, NJ	38	56	74	56	0	+29	+22	+16	+ 9	+ 3
Carson City-Reno, NV	39	10	119	46	3	+27	+21	+15	+ 9	+ 3
Casper, WY	42	51	106	19	2	+19	+20	+21	+22	+23
Chadron, NE	42	50	103	0	2	+ 6	+ 7	+ 8	+ 8	+ 9
Charleston, SC	32	47	79	56	0	+73	+55	+37	+19	+ 1
Charleston, WV	38	21	81	38	0	+58	+50	+43	+35	+28
Charlotte, NC	35	14	80	51	0	+67	+53	+40	+27	+13
Charlottesville, VA	38	2	78	30	0	+46	+38	+30	+22	+14
Chattanooga, TN	35	3	85	19	0	+85	+72	+58	+44	+31
Cheboygan, MI	45	39	84	29	0	+41	+47	+53	+59	+65
Cheyenne, WY	41	8	104	49	2	+20	+17	+15	+13	+10
Chicago-Oak Park, IL	41	52	87	38	1	+ 8	+ 7	+ 6	+ 5	+ 4

City	North Latitude ° ′	West Longitude ° ′	Time Zone Code	Key Letters A min.	B min.	C min.	D min.	E min.
Cincinnati-Hamilton, OH	39 6	84 31	0	+66	+60	+54	+48	+42
Cleveland-Lakewood, OH	41 30	81 42	0	+46	+44	+43	+41	+39
Columbia, SC	34 0	81 2	0	+72	+57	+41	+25	+10
Columbus, OH	39 57	83 1	0	+57	+53	+48	+44	+39
Cordova, AK	60 33	145 45	5	−72	−38	− 4	+30	+64
Corpus Christi, TX	27 48	97 24	1	+102	+75	+47	+20	− 7
Craig, CO	40 31	107 33	2	+33	+30	+26	+23	+19
Dallas-Fort Worth, TX	32 47	96 48	1	+80	+62	+44	+26	+ 8
Danville, IL	40 8	87 37	1	+15	+11	+ 6	+ 2	− 2
Danville, VA	36 36	79 23	0	+56	+45	+34	+23	+12
Davenport, IA	41 32	90 35	1	+21	+20	+18	+17	+15
Dayton, OH	39 45	84 10	0	+62	+58	+53	+48	+43
Decatur, AL	34 36	86 59	1	+34	+19	+ 5	−10	−24
Decatur, IL	39 51	88 57	1	+21	+16	+12	+ 7	+ 2
Denver-Boulder, CO	39 44	104 59	2	+26	+21	+16	+11	+ 6
Des Moines, IA	41 35	93 37	1	+33	+32	+30	+29	+27
Detroit-Dearborn, MI	42 20	83 3	0	+48	+48	+48	+48	+48
Dubuque, IA	42 30	90 41	1	+18	+18	+18	+19	+19
Duluth, MN	46 47	92 6	1	+ 7	+15	+23	+32	+40
Durham, NC	36 0	78 55	0	+56	+44	+32	+20	+ 8
Eastport, ME	44 54	67 0	0	−26	−22	−17	−12	− 7
Eau Claire, WI	44 49	91 30	1	+12	+17	+21	+26	+30
El Paso, TX	31 45	106 29	2	+63	+43	+23	+ 3	−17
Elko, NV	40 50	115 46	3	+ 5	+ 2	− 1	− 4	− 7
Ellsworth, ME	44 33	68 25	0	−19	−15	−11	− 7	− 3
Erie, PA	42 7	80 5	0	+37	+36	+36	+36	+35
Eugene, OR	44 3	123 6	3	+21	+25	+28	+31	+34
Fairbanks, AK	64 48	147 51	5	−81	−38	+ 4	+46	+88
Fall River-New Bedford, MA	41 42	71 9	0	+ 3	+ 2	0	− 1	− 2
Fargo, ND	46 53	96 47	1	+25	+34	+42	+51	+59
Flagstaff, AZ	35 12	111 39	2	+70	+57	+43	+30	+16
Flint, MI	43 1	83 41	0	+48	+49	+50	+51	+53
Fort Randall, AK	55 10	162 47	6	−43	−19	+ 5	+29	+53
Fort Scott, KS	37 50	94 42	1	+52	+44	+35	+27	+18
Fort Smith, AR	35 23	94 25	1	+60	+47	+34	+21	+ 8
Fort Wayne, IN	41 4	85 9	0	+61	+59	+56	+54	+52
Fort Yukon, AK	66 34	145 16	5	−98	−52	− 7	+38	+84
Fresno, CA	36 44	119 47	3	+37	+26	+16	+ 5	− 5
Gallup, NM	35 32	108 45	2	+57	+44	+32	+19	+ 6
Galveston, TX	29 18	94 48	1	+86	+61	+37	+12	−12
Gary, IN	41 36	87 20	1	+ 8	+ 6	+ 5	+ 4	+ 2
Glasgow, MT	48 12	106 38	2	− 1	+10	+21	+32	+43
Grand Forks, ND	47 55	97 3	1	+22	+33	+43	+53	+64
Grand Island, NE	40 55	98 21	1	+55	+52	+49	+47	+44
Grand Junction, CO	39 4	108 33	2	+43	+36	+30	+24	+18
Great Falls, MT	47 30	111 17	2	+21	+30	+40	+50	+59
Green Bay, WI	44 31	88 0	1	− 1	+ 3	+ 7	+11	+15
Greensboro, NC	36 4	79 47	0	+59	+47	+36	+24	+12
Hagerstown, MD	39 39	77 43	0	+37	+32	+27	+22	+17
Harrisburg, PA	40 16	76 53	0	+31	+27	+23	+20	+16
Hartford-New Britain, CT	41 46	72 41	0	+ 9	+ 8	+ 6	+ 5	+ 4
Helena, MT	46 36	112 2	2	+27	+35	+43	+51	+59
Hilo, HI	19 44	155 5	5	+124	+82	+39	− 3	−45
Honolulu, HI	21 18	157 52	5	+129	+90	+50	+11	−29
Houston, TX	29 45	95 22	1	+86	+63	+39	+15	− 8
Indianapolis, IN	39 46	86 10	0	+70	+65	+61	+56	+51
Ironwood, MI	46 27	90 9	1	0	+ 8	+16	+23	+31
Jackson, MI	42 15	84 24	0	+54	+53	+53	+53	+53
Jackson, MS	32 18	90 11	1	+56	+37	+18	− 1	−20
Jacksonville, FL	30 20	81 40	0	+89	+67	+44	+22	− 1
Jefferson City, MO	38 34	92 10	1	+39	+32	+25	+18	+11
Joplin, MO	37 6	94 30	1	+39	+29	+19	+ 9	− 1
Juneau, AK	58 18	134 25	3	+11	+41	+71	+101	+131
Kalamazoo, MI	42 17	85 35	0	+58	+58	+58	+58	+58
Kanab, UT	37 3	112 32	2	+66	+56	+47	+37	+27

City	North Latitude °	′	West Longitude °	′	Time Zone Code	A min.	B min.	C min.	D min.	E min.
Kansas City, MO	39	1	94	20	1	+46	+40	+34	+27	+21
Keene, NH	42	56	72	17	0	+ 2	+ 4	+ 5	+ 6	+ 7
Ketchikan, AK	55	21	131	39	3	+11	+36	+60	+85	+109
Knoxville, TN	35	58	83	55	0	+76	+64	+52	+40	+28
Kodiak, AK	57	47	152	24	5	−35	− 6	+23	+52	+81
LaCrosse, WI	43	48	91	15	1	+15	+18	+20	+23	+26
Lake Charles, LA	30	14	93	13	1	+76	+53	+30	+ 8	−15
Lanai City, HI	20	50	156	55	5	+127	+87	+46	+ 6	−34
Lancaster, PA	40	2	76	18	0	+30	+25	+21	+17	+12
Lansing, MI	42	44	84	33	0	+52	+53	+54	+54	+55
Las Cruces, NM	32	19	106	47	2	+62	+43	+24	+ 5	−13
Las Vegas, NV	36	10	115	9	3	+20	+ 9	− 3	−14	−26
Lawrence-Lowell, MA	42	42	71	10	0	− 1	0	0	+ 1	+ 2
Lewiston, ID	46	25	117	1	3	−12	− 5	+ 3	+11	+18
Lexington-Frankfort, KY	38	3	84	30	0	+70	+62	+54	+46	+38
Liberal, KS	37	3	100	55	1	+80	+70	+60	+50	+40
Lihue, HI	21	59	159	23	5	+133	+94	+56	+18	−20
Lincoln, NE	40	49	96	41	1	+48	+45	+43	+40	+37
Little Rock, AR	34	45	92	17	1	+54	+40	+26	+12	− 3
Los Angeles incl. Pasadena and Santa Monica, CA	34	3	118	14	3	+41	+25	+10	− 6	−21
Louisville, KY	38	15	85	46	0	+75	+67	+59	+52	+44
Macon, GA	32	50	83	38	0	+87	+69	+52	+34	+16
Madison, WI	43	4	89	23	1	+10	+12	+13	+14	+16
Manchester-Concord, NH	42	59	71	28	0	− 1	0	+ 1	+ 3	+ 4
McGrath, AK	62	58	155	36	5	−42	− 4	+35	+74	+112
Memphis, TN	35	9	90	3	1	+44	+30	+17	+ 3	−10
Meridian, MS	32	22	88	42	1	+49	+31	+12	− 7	−26
Miami, FL	25	47	80	12	0	+101	+70	+39	+ 8	−23
Miles City, MT	46	25	105	51	2	+ 3	+11	+18	+26	+34
Milwaukee, WI	43	2	87	54	1	+ 5	+ 6	+ 7	+ 8	+10
Minneapolis-St. Paul, MN	44	59	93	16	1	+18	+23	+28	+33	+38
Minot, ND	48	14	101	18	1	+38	+49	+60	+71	+82
Moab, UT	38	35	109	33	2	+48	+41	+34	+27	+20
Mobile, AL	30	42	88	3	1	+53	+31	+10	−12	−34
Monroe, LA	32	30	92	7	1	+62	+44	+26	+ 7	−11
Montgomery, AL	32	23	86	19	1	+40	+21	+ 2	−16	−35
Muncie, IN	40	12	85	23	0	+66	+61	+57	+53	+49
Murdo, SD	43	53	100	43	1	+52	+55	+58	+61	+64
Nashville, TN	36	10	86	47	1	+27	+15	+ 4	− 8	−20
New Haven, CT	41	18	72	56	0	+11	+ 9	+ 7	+ 6	+ 4
New London, CT	41	22	72	6	0	+ 8	+ 6	+ 4	+ 2	0
New Orleans, LA	29	57	90	4	1	+64	+41	+18	− 6	−29
New York, NY	40	45	74	0	0	+18	+15	+12	+ 9	+ 6
Newark-Irvington-East Orange, NJ	40	44	74	10	0	+19	+16	+13	+ 9	+ 6
Nome, AK	64	30	165	25	6	−69	−28	+14	+55	+97
Norfolk, VA	36	51	76	17	0	+42	+32	+22	+11	+ 1
North Platte, NE	41	8	100	46	1	+63	+61	+59	+57	+54
Norwalk-Stamford, CT	41	7	73	22	0	+14	+12	+ 9	+ 7	+ 5
Oakley, KS	39	8	100	51	1	+72	+66	+59	+53	+47
Ogden, UT	41	13	111	58	2	+48	+46	+44	+42	+39
Ogdensburg, NY	44	42	75	30	0	+ 8	+13	+17	+22	+26
Oklahoma City, OK	35	28	97	31	1	+73	+60	+47	+34	+21
Omaha, NE	41	16	95	56	1	+44	+42	+39	+37	+35
Ortonville, MN	45	19	96	27	1	+30	+35	+41	+47	+52
Oshkosh, WI	44	1	88	33	1	+ 3	+ 6	+10	+13	+16
Parkersburg, WV	39	16	81	34	0	+54	+48	+42	+37	+31
Paterson, NJ	40	55	74	10	0	+18	+15	+12	+10	+ 7
Pendleton, OR	45	40	118	47	3	− 2	+ 4	+10	+16	+23
Pensacola, FL	30	25	87	13	1	+51	+29	+ 6	−16	−38
Peoria, IL	40	42	89	36	1	+20	+17	+14	+11	+ 8
Philadelphia-Chester, PA	39	57	75	9	0	+26	+21	+17	+12	+ 8
Phoenix, AZ	33	27	112	4	2	+79	+62	+45	+29	+12
Pierre, SD	44	22	100	21	1	+49	+53	+57	+60	+64
Pittsburgh-McKeesport, PA	40	26	80	0	0	+43	+39	+36	+32	+29
Pittsfield, MA	42	27	73	15	0	+ 8	+ 8	+ 9	+ 9	+ 9

City	North Latitude ° '		West Longitude ° '		Time Zone Code	Key Letters				
						A min.	B min.	C min.	D min.	E min.
Pocatello, ID	42	52	112	27	2	+43	+44	+45	+46	+47
Poplar Bluff, MO	36	46	90	24	1	+39	+29	+18	+ 8	− 3
Portland, ME	43	40	70	15	0	− 9	− 6	− 4	− 1	+ 1
Portland, OR	45	31	122	41	3	+14	+20	+26	+32	+38
Portsmouth, NH	43	5	70	45	0	− 4	− 3	− 2	0	+ 1
Presque Isle, ME	46	41	68	1	0	−29	−21	−13	− 5	+ 3
Providence, RI	41	50	71	25	0	+ 3	+ 2	+ 1	0	− 1
Pueblo, CO	38	16	104	37	2	+30	+22	+15	+ 7	− 1
Raleigh, NC	35	47	78	38	0	+56	+43	+31	+19	+ 6
Rapid City, SD	44	5	103	14	2	+ 2	+ 5	+ 8	+12	+15
Reading, PA	40	20	75	56	0	+27	+23	+20	+16	+12
Redding, CA	40	35	122	24	3	+32	+29	+25	+22	+19
Richmond, VA	37	32	77	26	0	+44	+35	+26	+17	+ 8
Roanoke, VA	37	16	79	57	0	+55	+46	+36	+27	+17
Roswell, NM	33	24	104	32	2	+49	+32	+15	− 2	−18
Rutland, VT	43	37	72	58	0	+ 3	+ 5	+ 7	+10	+12
Sacramento, CA	38	35	121	30	3	+36	+29	+22	+15	+ 8
Salem, OR	44	57	123	1	3	+17	+22	+27	+32	+37
Salina, KS	38	50	97	37	1	+60	+53	+47	+40	+33
Salisbury, MD	38	22	75	36	0	+34	+26	+19	+11	+ 4
Salt Lake City, UT	40	45	111	53	2	+49	+46	+43	+40	+37
San Antonio, TX	29	25	98	30	1	+100	+76	+52	+27	+ 3
San Diego, CA	32	43	117	9	3	+42	+24	+ 6	−12	−30
San Francisco incl. Oakland and San Jose, CA	37	47	122	25	3	+43	+35	+26	+17	+ 9
Santa Fe, NM	35	41	105	56	2	+45	+33	+20	+ 8	− 5
Savannah, GA	32	5	81	6	0	+80	+61	+42	+22	+ 3
Scranton-Wilkes Barre, PA	41	25	75	40	0	+22	+20	+18	+17	+15
Seattle-Tacoma-Olympia, WA	47	37	122	20	3	+ 4	+14	+24	+34	+44
Sheridan, WY	44	48	106	58	2	+14	+19	+23	+28	+32
Shreveport, LA	32	31	93	45	1	+69	+51	+32	+14	− 5
Sioux Falls, SD	43	33	96	44	1	+38	+40	+42	+45	+47
South Bend, IN	41	41	86	15	0	+63	+62	+61	+59	+58
Spartanburg, SC	34	56	81	57	0	+72	+58	+45	+31	+17
Spokane, WA	47	40	117	24	3	−16	− 6	+ 4	+14	+24
Springfield, IL	39	48	89	39	1	+24	+19	+15	+10	+ 5
Springfield-Holyoke, MA	42	6	72	36	0	+ 7	+ 7	+ 6	+ 6	+ 5
Springfield, MO	37	13	93	18	1	+49	+39	+30	+20	+10
St. Johnsbury, VT	44	25	72	1	0	− 4	− 1	+ 3	+ 7	+11
St. Joseph, MO	39	46	94	50	1	+45	+40	+35	+30	+26
St. Louis, MO	38	37	90	12	1	+31	+24	+17	+10	+ 3
St. Petersburg, FL	27	46	82	39	0	+103	+76	+48	+21	− 6
Syracuse, NY	43	3	76	9	0	+17	+19	+20	+21	+23
Tallahassee, FL	30	27	84	17	0	+99	+77	+55	+32	+10
Tampa, FL	27	57	82	27	0	+102	+75	+48	+21	− 6
Terre Haute, IN	39	28	87	24	1	+16	+11	+ 6	0	− 5
Texarkana, AR	33	26	94	3	1	+67	+50	+33	+16	0
Toledo, OH	41	39	83	33	0	+53	+51	+50	+49	+47
Topeka, KS	39	3	95	40	1	+51	+45	+39	+33	+26
Traverse City, MI	44	46	85	38	0	+49	+53	+58	+62	+67
Trenton, NJ	40	13	74	46	0	+23	+19	+15	+11	+ 7
Trinidad, CO	37	10	104	31	2	+34	+24	+14	+ 5	− 5
Tucson, AZ	32	13	110	58	2	+79	+60	+41	+22	+ 3
Tulsa, OK	36	9	95	60	1	+64	+52	+41	+29	+17
Tupelo, MS	34	16	88	34	1	+41	+26	+11	− 4	−19
Vernal, UT	40	27	109	32	2	+41	+38	+34	+30	+27
Walla Walla, WA	46	4	118	20	3	− 6	+ 1	+ 8	+15	+22
Washington, DC	38	54	77	1	0	+37	+31	+24	+18	+11
Waterbury-Meriden, CT	41	33	73	3	0	+11	+ 9	+ 8	+ 6	+ 5
Waterloo, IA	42	30	92	20	1	+24	+25	+25	+25	+25
Wausau, WI	44	58	89	38	1	+ 4	+ 9	+14	+19	+24
West Palm Beach, FL	26	43	80	3	0	+97	+67	+38	+ 9	−20
Wichita, KS	37	42	97	20	1	+63	+54	+46	+37	+28
Williston, ND	48	9	103	37	1	+47	+58	+69	+80	+91
Wilmington, DE	39	45	75	33	0	+28	+23	+18	+13	+ 8
Wilmington, NC	34	14	77	55	0	+59	+44	+28	+13	− 2

City	North Latitude ° '	West Longitude ° '	Time Zone Code	Key Letters A min.	B min.	C min.	D min.	E min.
Winchester, VA	39 11	78 10	0	+41	+35	+29	+23	+17
Worcester, MA	42 16	71 48	0	+ 3	+ 3	+ 3	+ 3	+ 3
York, PA	39 58	76 43	0	+32	+27	+23	+18	+14
Youngstown, OH	41 6	80 39	0	+43	+41	+38	+36	+34
Yuma, AZ	32 43	114 37	2	+92	+74	+56	+37	+19
CANADA								
Calgary, ALTA	51 5	114 5	2	+18	+34	+51	+67	+83
Edmonton, ALTA	53 34	113 25	2	+ 6	+27	+48	+69	+90
Halifax, NS	44 38	63 35	−1	+21	+25	+30	+34	+38
Montreal, PQ	45 28	73 39	0	− 2	+ 4	+10	+16	+21
Ottawa, ONT	45 25	75 43	0	+ 7	+12	+18	+24	+30
St. John, NB	45 16	66 3	−1	+28	+34	+39	+45	+50
Saskatoon, SASK	52 10	106 40	2	−16	+ 2	+21	+39	+58
Sydney, NS	46 10	60 10	−1	+ 1	+ 9	+16	+23	+30
Thunder Bay, ONT	48 27	89 12	0	+49	+60	+71	+83	+94
Toronto, ONT.	43 39	79 23	0	+28	+31	+33	+35	+38
Vancouver, BC	49 13	123 6	3	+ 1	+14	+27	+40	+53
Winnipeg, MAN	49 53	97 10	1	+15	+29	+43	+57	+71

KILLING FROSTS AND GROWING SEASONS

Courtesy of National Climatic Center

City	Growing Season (Days)	Last Frost Spring	First Frost Fall	City	Growing Season (Days)	Last Frost Spring	First Frost Fall
Montgomery, AL	279	Feb. 27	Dec. 3	St. Louis, MO	220	Apr. 2	Nov. 8
Little Rock, AR	244	Mar. 16	Nov. 15	Helena, MT	134	May 12	Sept. 23
Phoenix, AZ	317	Jan. 27	Dec. 11	Omaha, NE	189	Apr. 14	Oct. 20
Tucson, AZ	261	Mar. 6	Nov. 23	Reno, NV	141	May 14	Oct. 2
Eureka, CA	335	Jan. 24	Dec. 25	Concord, NH	142	May 11	Sept. 30
Los Angeles, CA	*	*	*	Trenton, NJ	211	Apr. 8	Nov. 5
Sacramento, CA	321	Jan. 24	Dec. 11	Albuquerque, NM	196	Apr. 16	Oct. 29
San Diego, CA	*	*	*	Albany, NY	169	Apr. 27	Oct. 13
San Francisco, CA	*	*	*	Raleigh, NC	237	Mar. 24	Nov. 16
Denver CO	165	May 2	Oct. 14	Bismarck, ND	136	May 11	Sept. 24
Hartford, CT	180	Apr. 22	Oct. 19	Cincinnati, OH	192	Apr. 5	Oct. 25
Washington, DC	200	Apr. 10	Oct. 28	Toledo, OH	184	Apr. 24	Oct. 25
Miami, FL	*	*	*	Oklahoma City, OK	223	Mar. 28	Nov. 7
Macon, GA	252	Mar. 12	Nov. 19	Medford, OR	178	Apr. 25	Oct. 20
Pocatello, ID	145	May 8	Sept. 30	Portland, OR	279	Feb. 25	Dec. 1
Chicago, IL	192	Apr. 19	Oct. 28	Harrisburg, PA	201	Apr. 10	Oct. 28
Evansville, IN	216	Apr. 2	Nov. 4	Scranton, PA	174	Apr. 24	Oct. 14
Fort Wayne, IN	179	Apr. 24	Oct. 20	Columbia, SC	252	Mar. 14	Nov. 21
Des Moines, IA	183	Apr. 20	Oct. 19	Huron, SD	149	May 4	Sept. 30
Wichita, KS	210	Apr. 5	Nov. 1	Chattanooga, TN	229	Mar. 26	Nov. 10
Shreveport, LA	272	Mar. 1	Nov. 27	Del Rio, TX	300	Feb. 12	Dec. 9
New Orleans, LA	302	Feb. 13	Dec. 12	Midland, TX	218	Apr. 3	Nov. 6
Portland, ME	169	Apr. 29	Oct. 15	Salt Lake City, UT	202	Apr. 12	Nov. 1
Boston, MA	192	Apr. 16	Oct. 25	Burlington, VT	148	May 8	Oct. 3
Alpena, MI	156	May 6	Oct. 9	Richmond, VA	220	Apr. 2	Nov. 8
Detroit, MI	181	Apr. 25	Oct. 23	Spokane, WA	175	Apr. 20	Oct. 12
Marquette, MI	156	May 14	Oct. 17	Parkersburg, WV	189	Apr. 16	Oct. 21
Duluth, MN	125	May 22	Sept. 24	Green Bay, WI	161	May 6	Oct. 13
Minneapolis, MN	166	Apr. 30	Oct. 13	Madison, WI	177	Apr. 26	Oct. 19
Jackson, MS	248	Mar. 10	Nov. 13	Lander, WY	128	May 15	Sept. 20
Columbia, MO	198	Apr. 9	Oct. 24				

*Frosts do not occur every year.

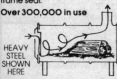
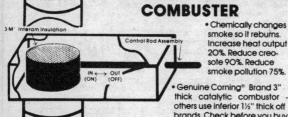

GREET

(BUT LITTLE KNOWN)

MOMENTS in Aviation History

by Don Bousquet

1902

Henry Masterson of Plattsburgh, New York, made the first heavier-than-air ascent using more than four thousand evening grosbeaks.

1914

Nunzio Lindbergh, half-brother of the transatlantic aviator, after his bid to become the first man to fly over the Pyrenees.

1930
Francis Perdue I
and his
thunderpullet;
an early attempt
at powering a
high-performance
aircraft on
chicken effluence.

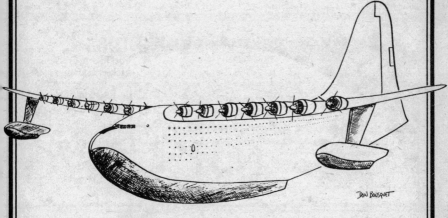

1948
Dwarfing the fabled Hughes "Spruce Goose," this
14-engine, all-wood leviathan (dubbed the
Mahogany Cacophony) was a top-secret postwar
project. Designed to send the entire population
of Trenton, New Jersey, back where it came
from, the flying boat sank while on sea
trials off Atlantic City.

1957
Rare view of the innovative Hudson
Hornet Custom Hollywood Airsedan.

1965
Voskhod II Cosmonaut
Aleksei Leonov poses
for a historic photo
during man's first
spacewalk.

1983
The free world is stunned by the launching of a Bulgarian space shuttle.

DON BOUSQUET

DON BOUSQUET

1984
Inflatable DC-10 developed by Goodyear for sale to Third World nations with limited hangar space.

AMAZING SUPER-GROWING SPECIES SOARS INTO A MAGNIFICENT TREE IN JUST ONE SINGLE YEAR!

Best of all, unlike most trees that demand constant care, constant pampering . . . about the only thing you do after you plant this super-growing wonder-hybrid is water it and enjoy it! That's why leading botanical gardens . . . landscape artists . . . garden editors . . . can't stop raving about its indescribable beauty . . . its trouble-free care . . . its surging, towering growth.

Small wonder that leading experts hail it in the most glowing terms . . . recommended it again and again for homeowners who want a stunning display of beauty . . . both a wind and privacy screen and deep, cool shade . . . and with practically no more work than a thorough watering each week!

VITAL STATISTICS FROM LEADING EXPERTS

MATURE GROWTH SIZE: as much as 40 to 65 feet
MATURE SPREAD: as much as 30 to 35 feet
ZONE OF HARDINESS: Hardy from the deepest South to as far North as Vermont, Minn., Quebec, British Columbia. Winter Hardy in areas where temp. drops as low as 30 degrees below zero.
LIGHT NEEDS: Grows beautifully in Sunny location.
DECORATIVE MERITS: Highly recommended by landscape architects as beautiful decorative specimens for homes, parks, highways, etc., where exceptional fast growth and beauty are required. Perfect for fast screening and privacy.
RAPID RATE OF GROWTH: Experts report growth rates on specimen trees that measure up to 8 FEET THE VERY FIRST YEAR ALONE. That's more than most shade trees grow in 3 . . . 4 . . . 5 . . . even 7 years. Yes, once established will grow ranch-house-roof high IN JUST ONE SINGLE YEAR, that's right—

The very next year after planting! Experts also report it soars an amazing 5 to 8 feet each year for YEARS thereafter. Naturally results are based on optimum growing conditions. Takes but 10 minutes to plant and normal care rewards you with a lifetime of beauty starting this very year.

CARE: Nothing special—just normal garden care. Water fully once weekly. Naturally resistant to most diseases, pests or insects.

JUST MINUTES TO PLANT— REWARDS YOU WITH A LIFETIME OF BEAUTY!

Here's a luxurious sight you don't have to wait half a lifetime growing—a matched pair of these towering show-pieces

Picture your patio bathed in the cool beauty of this show-stopping miracle tree from early spring to the first snows of winter.

Just a few minutes planting time—a few seasons' growing time, rewards you with twin towers of beauty.

© 1983, Spring River Nurseries, Inc., Spring River Road, Hartford, Michigan 49057

A *"rule of thumb,"* according to **Tom Parker,** *who has collected many hundreds from people in every state in the Union,* *"is a homemade recipe for making a guess . . . and falls somewhere between a mathematical formula and a shot in the dark."* *For instance . . .*

illustrated by **Bob Johnson**

EATING POTATOES

People will eat one and a half to two times the number of potatoes mashed that they would eat baked.

Ned Bounds, sawyer, Salmon, Idaho

AVOIDING A CRASH IN A CAR RACE

At high speed nothing stays in the same place for long. Aim your car at the spot where you see an accident start. Chances are the accident will have moved by the time you get there.

Joie Chitwood, former Indy driver and owner of the Joie Chitwood Thrill Show

LANDING A LEAR JET

A Lear jet 25G will float about 100 extra feet down the runway for each knot over its proper landing speed.

Richard Collins, pilot and writer

PLANNING A DINNER

Inviting more than 25 percent of the guests from the economics department for a university dinner party ruins the conversation.

Martha Farnsworth Richie, editor

CATCHING CRABS IN TEXAS

Crabbing season in Texas consists of all the months with the letter *r* in them. You can catch crabs during the other months, but they aren't good to eat.

David Hechler, writer, Rockport, Texas

SELLING THINGS BY MAIL

Most people selling things by mail need at least a 200 percent mark-up to make money. Don't pay more than $10 for something you sell for $30.

Jim Kobs, Kobs and Brady Advertising,
Chicago, Illinois

JUDGING THE AGE OF A CALF

A calf whose tail nearly reaches the ground is more than a year old.

Edward Dalrymple, dairy farmer

NURSING HOMES

Patients who are terminally ill are more likely to die after a holiday than before.

Jim Schlobohm, Oak Park, Illinois

STREAM FISHING FOR TROUT

Trout do most of their surface feeding in the upstream third of a pool.

Sheridan Anderson, author,
The Curtis Creek Manifesto

TREE ROOTS

The diameter of a tree trunk in inches is the radius of the root system in feet. *J. T. Schaefer, pilot*

WEANING A CALF

Wean a calf when it has gained 15 pounds over its birth weight. *Edward Dalrymple, dairy farmer*

CALLING IN SICK

In half of all cases, when an employee calls in sick, he's actually sick. *Walter Pitkin, literary agent*

ICE SKATING

You need to have three consecutive days of sub-20° weather before a pond will be safe for skating. *Holley Bailey, editor*

PREDICTING RAIN

The number of stars visible inside the ring around the moon is the number of days before rain. *Edward Saha, builder*

ESTIMATING THE SIZE OF YOUR FOOT

The distance from your elbow to your wrist equals the length of your foot. *Carla Corin, biologist, Eagles River, Alaska*

BUYING STOCK

Don't buy stock for a year after a presidential inauguration. For some reason, the market almost always goes down in that period. *The American Association of Individual Investors*

RAISING PIGS

When a sow conceives, make a notch just above the moon on your fingernail. When this mark grows off the end of the nail, the sow is about to give birth. *Doug Webb, Brooktondale, New York*

CHANGING YOUR SEX

A sex-change operation will age you five years. *A. A. Kennerly, New York City*

SELLING REAL ESTATE

Rental property should sell for about one hundred times its monthly rental income. *Tom Wolfe, writer*

THROWING AWAY CLOTHING

Wait one year before throwing out a piece of clothing. If you haven't worn it in a year, you will never miss it. *Betsy Wackernagel, Ithaca, New York*

PRUNING A TREE

After pruning a tree, paint all wounds that are larger than your thumbnail. *Betsy Wade, tree specialist*

CALLING FOR HELP

If you are assaulted, scream Fire! People are more likely to come to your aid than if you shout Help! *Boardroom Reports*

THE SURVIVAL RULE OF THREE

You can live three seconds without blood, three minutes without air, three days without water, and three weeks without food. *Sandy Figuers, geologist, El Paso, Texas*

RAISING MONEY
University fund raisers plan on getting one-third of their money from ten big contributors, one-third from one hundred medium contributors, and one-third from everyone else.

Anonymous university fund raiser

THE TRAVELING RULE OF TWO
When traveling, take twice the money and half the clothes you think you will need.

Betsy Wackernagel, Ithaca, New York

CASTRATING CALVES
Castrate a calf when his testicles are the size of a squirrel's head.

Veterinary pathologist,
Cornell University

USING A CHAIN SAW
Plan on spending half an hour on maintenance for each two hours of chain saw use.

Rob Weinberg, Tassajara Zen Mountain Center, Carmel Valley, California

GROWING CHRISTMAS TREES
You can plan on eventually harvesting four to five hundred Christmas trees for each one thousand seedlings you plant. *Jay Waring, tree grower and plant specialist*

FEEDING CATS
Feed your cat as much as it will eat in 30 minutes, two times a day.

Ronald Newberry, gardener

A MOUSE IN YOUR HOUSE
If you see one mouse in your house, you probably have a dozen.

C. H. Lacey, town historian,
Richford, New York

BETTING ON A HORSE
If you don't have much information before a race, bet on a horse that is swishing its tail straight up and down.

Donald Mycrantz, Tulsa, Oklahoma

POLITICAL CAMPAIGNS
Tall candidates with short names get elected twice as often as short candidates with long names.

Tom Wilbur, county commissioner,
East Lansing, Michigan

THE COLD RULE OF THREE
It takes three days to get a cold, three days to have a cold, and three days to get over a cold.

Veronica Cunningham, chemist,
Plattsburg, New York

BUYING A HOUSE
Don't pay more than twice your average annual income for a house.

Scott Parker, Beaumont, Texas

HITCHHIKING
When you're hitchhiking, look like who you want to pick you up.

Stewart Brand, publisher,
The CoEvolution Quarterly

HIRING BOYS
One boy's a boy; two boys — half a boy; three boys — no boy at all.

Margaret "Granny" Cochron,
102 years old

From *Rules of Thumb* by Tom Parker, published by Houghton Mifflin Company, Boston. Copyright 1983 by Tom Parker. Reprinted by permission of the publisher.

Anyone Can Make a Perfect Cup of Coffee

All it takes is perfect water at the perfect temperature, poured over the perfect beans freshly roasted and ground just to perfection.

by Leslie Land

illustrated by Margo Letourneau

☐ THE MELANCHOLY TRUTH IS THAT the two most commonly used American ways to make coffee make the worst coffee in existence. You'd think the main villain was instant coffee, for which 1,175,000 bags of green coffee (enough to make 4,272,727,200 cups) were imported last year. But the real offender is perked coffee, made in a percolator, glub-a-glub-a-glub, the inescapable sound of morning for several wholly misguided generations. Mostly it's awful because it is boiled, the one thing that coffee should never be. Boiling disperses the fragile, rich aromas that are so important to flavor, while it concentrates acids, extracts extra tannin, and intensifies bitterness.

For *absolutely* the best coffee you would have to start by roasting your own beans. Fragrance and flavor deteriorate quickly after green coffee is roasted, and from its ancient Middle Eastern beginnings to the turn of the present century, almost everyone everywhere who made coffee roasted the beans as needed. This is, however, a modest proposal, so we will simply insist that the coffee be as freshly roasted as possible, ground at the last minute.

Though the beans are obviously crucial, water is the main ingredient of coffee. If the water doesn't taste good, the coffee won't taste good. Avoid using very hard water or water that has been artificially softened, heavily chlorinated, or otherwise made to taste bad. In some places this means using bottled water.

Draw fresh cold water (hot might pick up impurities from the pipes) and put it on to boil. Use hot water to rinse the china, earthenware, stainless steel, glass, enamel, silver, or gold (but *not* tin or aluminum) coffeepot, so that it will be warmed up. Do the same with the cups. If you intend to use milk, put it in a double boiler to heat up gradually. Cream should be allowed to come to room temperature.

Decide which kind of coffee you want to make. Filtered coffee is light in body and aftertaste, but very clear, refreshing, and sediment-free. Steeped coffee is a heavier, richer product because none of the superfine flavoring compounds have been trapped and filtered out.

For filtered coffee: Put the pot where it will keep warm — in a larger pan of simmering water, on a heat-spreader, or at the side of the woodstove. When you hear the water about to boil, grind the coffee quite fine, not quite to powder. Put the filter-holder over the pot, line it with filter paper, and for each cup of coffee insert 1½ to 2 tablespoons of ground beans. Tamp down lightly, so the water will take more time to filter through. When the water boils, turn off the heat and let its temperature fall back a few degrees, then pour on only enough to dampen the coffee. Allow the grounds to swell for about two minutes, then add the rest of the water, in batches if necessary. Serve as soon as filtering is completed. (*Note:* Filter papers are pretty close to tasteless when they leave the factory, but will pick up strong odors — garlic, cheese, tobacco smoke — if stored near them.

For steeped coffee: Follow the instructions above, except:

(1) Be sure to use a wide-bottomed, high-spouted pot, so the grounds have plenty of chance to sink out of the liquid and stay sunk at pouring time.

(2) Grind the coffee (2 tablespoons per cup) only to the texture of rough cornmeal. Put it in the pot, pour on the not-quite-boiling water, and stir well.

(3) Let the coffee infuse for four minutes, stir again briefly, and let steep two to five minutes more, depending on how strong (and clear) you want the product to be. Dash in a few drops of cold water, which will sink through the hot coffee, carrying stray particles to the bottom of the pot. Serve at once, not letting the liquid sit around on the grounds for very long.

About that egg. Many recipes call for eggshell, egg white and shell, or an entire egg at the end of the process. The idea is to have the albumen in the egg bond with the floating coffee particles, carrying them out of the liquid. It isn't really necessary and it certainly isn't too tasty.

CHOOSING THE RIGHT BEANS

A well-stocked coffee store can be uncomfortably reminiscent of a well-stocked wine store, a place where it's easy to feel daunted by an exotic and unknown array. You can just taste until you figure out what you enjoy — unlike wine, almost all specialty coffee is pretty good, and even the most expensive is a bargain if you look at the cost per cup.

Although about a dozen species of coffee shrub *(coffea* genus) are cultivated, only two have major commercial importance. *Coffea robusta* is easier to grow than *Coffea arabica,* and more prolific, hence a great deal cheaper. Though rich in caffeine, it is bitter and poor-flavored. Robustas are mainly used as cheap fillers and for the manufacture of instant. Arabicas are labeled (and valued) according to place of origin. Generally speaking, the higher the elevation at which the coffee grew, the better the flavor will be.

The roast: Green coffee beans improve with age, but their flavor must be developed and made soluble by roasting. Heat breaks down fats and carbohydrates as it develops the coffeol, an oily, volatile, aromatic (and still somewhat poorly understood) substance that is the soul of the coffee. The longer the roasting, the darker the roast, which leads to a sort of false impression. Roasting reduces both acid and caffeine and brings coffee oils to the surface, so those sinister-looking shiny-black beans are actually much milder in effect than the ones that look like milk chocolate. The reputation of dark-roast coffee for bitter strength is more a function of the intense ways it is brewed than anything else.

And there you have it, all the ingredients for a flavorful, aromatic, bracing, soothing *perfect* cup of coffee.

You can savor the perfect cup of coffee by itself, or you might prefer what our grandmother always called "a little something sweet to go with." The coffee cakes following will fill the bill. □□

A Little Something Sweet to Go With

One or more of these recipes will surely strike your tastebuds as a wonderful complement to the perfect cup of coffee.

illustrated by Margo Letourneau

Pecan Sticky Buns

Sweet Dough:

> 2 packages active dry yeast
> ½ cup warm water (105° to 115°F.)
> 1¼ cups buttermilk
> 2 eggs
> 5½ cups all-purpose flour
> ½ cup butter or margarine, softened
> ½ cup sugar
> 2 teaspoons baking powder
> 2 teaspoons salt

Dissolve yeast in warm water in large mixer bowl. Add buttermilk, eggs, 2½ cups flour, the butter, sugar, baking powder, and salt. Blend 30 seconds with mixer on low speed, scraping sides and bottom of bowl. Beat 2 minutes on medium speed. Stir in 3 cups flour. (Dough should remain soft and slightly sticky.) Knead 5 minutes, or about 200 turns on a lightly floured board.

Filling:

> 2 tablespoons soft butter
> ½ cup sugar
> 2 teaspoons cinnamon
> ½ cup melted butter
> ½ cup firmly packed brown sugar
> 1 cup broken pecans

Divide dough in half, and roll into a 12×7-inch rectangle. Spread each half with 1 tablespoon soft butter, and sprinkle with ¼ cup sugar and 1 teaspoon cinnamon. Roll up halves, beginning at wide side. Seal well by pinching the seams. Cut each roll into 12 slices. Coat two 9-inch round cake pans with ¼ cup melted butter, ¼ cup brown sugar, and ½ cup broken pecans in each pan. Place 12 dough slices in each pan, leaving a small space between slices. Let rise until doubled. Bake in a preheated 375° oven for about 30 minutes. Invert pans onto serving plates. Makes 24 buns.

Cinnamon Swirls

> 2 packages dry yeast
> ¼ cup warm water
> 2 cups milk
> 4 tablespoons butter
> 2 eggs
> ½ cup sugar
> 7 to 8 cups flour
> 1 teaspoon salt
> 1 teaspoon cinnamon

Dissolve yeast in warm water and set aside. Scald milk and stir in butter until melted. When cooled beat in two eggs. Sift together the sugar, 6 cups of flour, salt, and cinnamon. Blend yeast and milk mixtures into the flour. Add more flour as needed to make a stiff dough. Turn out on floured board and knead until smooth. Place in greased bowl and turn to grease top. Let rise in warm place until doubled.

Filling:

    4 tablespoons softened butter
    ½ cup sugar
    1 tablespoon cinnamon

When dough has risen, turn out and punch down. Divide in half and roll each half about ½ inch thick. Spread each half with softened butter, and then the cinnamon and sugar that have been mixed together. Roll up as a jelly roll and slice into 1-inch pieces. Place in greased baking pan, just touching, cover, and let rise till doubled. Bake at 350° for 20 minutes. While still warm drizzle with Cinnamon Glaze. Makes 3 to 4 dozen.

Cinnamon Glaze:

    2 cups confectioner's sugar
    1 teaspoon cinnamon
    3 tablespoons milk
    dash of salt

Mix together until of spreading consistancy. Add more milk if it seems too stiff.

Sour Cream Cake

    1 cup butter
    2 cups sugar
    2 eggs
    1 cup sour cream
    1 teaspoon vanilla
    ½ teaspoon salt
    2 cups sifted flour
    1 teaspoon baking powder
    1 teaspoon baking soda

Streusel:

    ¼ cup brown sugar
    1 teaspoon cinnamon
    ½ cup pecans

Cream the butter, sugar, and eggs. In a separate bowl, mix the sour cream, vanilla, and salt. Sift together the flour, baking powder, and soda, and add half of it, then half of the sour cream mixture, to the butter mixture. Stir well and add remaining halves of sour cream and flour mixtures. Spoon half of batter into greased and floured tube pan. Mix streusel ingredients together until crumbly; sprinkle batter with half of the streusel. Spoon on remaining batter and sprinkle with remaining streusel. Bake at

350° for 45 minutes, or until cake tests done.

Note: This recipe may be halved and baked in an 8×8-inch cake pan.

Jewish Coffee Cake

Streusel:

    1 cup brown sugar
    2 tablespoons flour
    ¾ cup chopped nuts
    1 teaspoon cinnamon
    1 tablespoon melted butter

Mix all together until crumbly.

Cake:

    ½ cup butter
    1 cup sugar
    3 eggs
    2 cups flour
    1 teaspoon baking soda
    1 teaspoon baking powder
    ⅛ teaspoon salt
    1 cup sour cream (or ½ cup yogurt
        and ½ cup sour cream)
    1 teaspoon vanilla

Cream butter and sugar; add eggs and beat well. Sift dry ingredients together and add alternately with sour cream and vanilla to the butter mixture. Grease an angel food or bundt pan. Put half of streusel in pan, then half of batter, half of remaining streusel, rest of batter, and last streusel. Bake 55-60 minutes at 350°. Cool in pan for 10 minutes, then invert onto cooling rack.

Marzapyne

Dough:

    ½ pound cold butter
    2 cups flour
    1 tablespoon sugar
    1 teaspoon salt
    ½ cup water
    1 tablespoon white vinegar

Filling:

    2 medium eggs plus one yolk (save
        white)
    ½ cup sugar
    8 ounces almond paste
    ½ teaspoon lemon extract
    ½ teaspoon vanilla extract

To make dough, work like a pie dough, cutting cold butter into the flour. Add sugar, salt, and liquid ingredients gradually. Place in refrigerator. For filling, beat eggs and yolk. Beat in sugar. Beat in paste. Add lemon and vanilla extracts. Beat one minute. Place in refrigerator until firm.

Roll out dough into an 8×12-inch rectangle on a cookie sheet. Place filling in a tube shape down the long side, leaving space at either end to seal dough. Roll up, starting at the long side. Seal edges, brush outside with reserved lightly beaten egg white, and score every half inch with a sharp knife. Bake at 425° for 15 minutes, then at 350° for about 10 minutes or until browned and firm. Serves 10.

Cranberry Swirl Coffee Cake

½ cup softened butter (1 stick)
1 cup sugar
2 eggs
2 cups flour
1 teaspoon baking powder
1 teaspoon baking soda
½ teaspoon salt
1 cup yogurt
1 teaspoon vanilla
1 can (16 ounces) whole cranberry
　　sauce
½ cup chopped nuts

Preheat oven to 375°. Cream butter, then gradually add sugar and blend until fluffy. Add eggs, one at a time, beating after each addition. Sift together dry ingredients and add to batter alternately with yogurt. Add vanilla. Grease a tube pan and spread a thin layer of batter over the bottom. Stir the cranberry sauce so it is well mixed, then spread a thin layer of it over the batter. Add another layer of batter, a layer of cranberry sauce, a layer of batter and end with cranberry sauce. Sprinkle nuts over top, then bake for 55 minutes, or until toothpick inserted well into cake comes out clean. Cool in pan on rack for 5 minutes. Remove from pan and drizzle Almond or White Icing over the top. For a cherry-like flavor, substitute almond extract for the vanilla and top with Almond Icing. Makes 1 cake.

Almond Icing

1 cup powdered sugar
1 to 2 tablespoons water
1 teaspoon almond extract

Sift sugar, then add water gradually. Add almond extract, mixing until smooth. If icing is thick, add more water, a few drops at a time, until of thinner consistency.

White Icing

2 cups powdered sugar
2 tablespoons warm milk
1 to 2 teaspoon vanilla

Sift sugar, add milk and vanilla, and blend until smooth. For a thicker or thinner icing, adjust amount of milk used. For colored icing, add a drop or two of food coloring.

Polish Babka

½ cup soft butter
½ cup sugar
1 teaspoon salt
4 egg yolks
1 yeast cake or 1 package dry yeast
¼ cup lukewarm water
　　grated rind of one lemon
½ teaspoon cinnamon
5 cups flour
1 cup milk, scalded and cooled to
　　lukewarm
1 cup white raisins
1 egg yolk, beaten
2 tablespoons water
¼ cup chopped almonds

Cream butter and sugar in large mixing bowl. Add salt to egg yolks and beat until thick. Add to sugar and butter mixture. Add yeast softened in ¼ cup lukewarm water. Add lemon rind and cinnamon. Add flour alternately with milk and beat well to make a smooth batter. Add raisins and knead by hand until batter leaves the fingers. Let rise in warm place until double in bulk (about 1¼ hours). Punch down and let rise again until double in bulk.

Butter a fluted tube pan generously. Sprinkle with fine bread crumbs and fill with dough. Brush with mixture made by beating one egg yolk with two tablespoons water. Sprinkle with almonds and let rise again. Bake for 30 minutes in 350° oven.

Credit: Marzapyne is taken from *Best Recipes from New England Inns,* published by Yankee Books, Dublin, NH 03444 ($15.95); Cranberry Swirl Coffee Cake is taken from *Breads, Rolls, and Pastries* by the same publisher ($8.95). Both recipes are reprinted with permission. All other recipes are from *The Old Farmer's Almanac* files. □□

When Your Body Shivers at You

It means that your biological thermostat is trying to keep you from freezing to death — pay attention.

by Jay Butera
illustrated by Damian Henriques

☐ WHEN YOU STEP OUTSIDE ON A cold day, remember this: if your feet get cold, put your hat on. That might sound backwards, but there's a lot of logic behind this old saying. Your brain is the kingpin of your body's heating system. It stokes the biological furnace, sends fuel to the fires, and controls heat distribution within your body. So keep it warm! If your brain gets too cold, it can lose control of the energy system, and then death is not far behind.

Your body's thermostat is located in the front of the brain, just behind the bridge of your nose in an area called the hypothalamus. This mysterious piece of tissue is the most precise temperature regulator on earth. It's so sensitive that your body can usually maintain a temperature that varies no more than a couple of degrees from its optimal 98.6 degrees Fahrenheit. And it's a good thing. The human body can function properly only if it maintains internal temperatures within a very narrow range — 97 to 102 degrees on the average. If the body temperature drops below that range, the mechanisms of life slow down; and if the freeze continues, it can all grind to a halt.

The brain's first response to dropping temperatures is ruthless and self-

ish — it cuts off circulation of warmth-carrying blood in the hands and feet. This leaves those parts extremely vulnerable to frostbite, but it also conserves body heat for vital internal organs. This response is the body's attempt to "circle the wagons." Unfortunately, the hands and feet get left out in the cold; denied of their circulation, the temperature of these extremities can drop 30 or 40 degrees below normal while internal body temperatures warmed by the blood remain close to 98.6 degrees. If the temperature in the extremities dips below freezing, the tissues there may actually freeze, causing frostbite. But the brain must make a decision — cut off peripheral circulation and risk frostbite in the extremities, or risk a possibly fatal loss of body heat. Faced with this choice, the brain saves itself.

At the same time, the brain will try to ward off hypothermia (decreasing body temperature) by speeding up the body's metabolism, secreting hormones that make cell reactions quicken and make the body burn calories faster. Heat is the major by-product of cell reactions. Studies have shown that diets including adequate amounts of fats and carbohydrates (sugars) can help fuel this stepped-up metabolism and so warm the body. Badly chilled people may get a temporary boost by eating something sweet such as chocolates, but natural complex carbohydrates — such as those found in fruits, pasta, and whole-grain breads — will supply a more even source of energy.

If hoarding heat and fanning the metabolic fires can't keep the brain warm enough, and internal temperatures drop more than three or four degrees, the brain shifts the body into its next line of defense — shivering. Shivering, the involuntary contraction of muscles, is the body's emergency furnace. Tense muscles, chattering teeth, and shaking torsos are all reactions that generate heat within the body. In severe situations the net result of shivering can be five times as warming as normal metabolism alone. Similarly, voluntarily exercising your muscles can also create a tremendous amount of heat to warm your chilling bones.

If shivering muscles can't check a sliding body temperature, the situation can get extremely serious. Brain function grows ever slower with each dip in the mercury. When the internal reading reaches approximately 93 degrees, the impaired cerebral response becomes life-threatening. Slurred speech may be a sign that a hypothermia victim has reached this critical stage. Also, the person may be incapable of carrying out such simple, self-preserving tasks as zipping a jacket or striking a match. As the temperature drops even further, the victim's thinking becomes cloudy, and he may actually deny that he needs help and become angry with those who try to assist him.

As core temperatures reach 90 degrees and lower, the brain may become so chilled that it loses control of the heating mechanisms. Shivering ceases, and the brain seems to throw in the towel. Blood vessels in the extremities may begin to reopen, sending blood back into the hands and feet and giving the victim a temporary feeling of warmth. But these reactions only accelerate heat loss. As a final effort, the body may secrete thyroid hormone to try to spark more life into the metabolism, but this is often too late. Then the real enemies of the hypothermia victim arrive: apathy and drowsiness. As often happens, the victim may simply give in, lie down, drift off to sleep, and never wake again.

On the average, death occurs when the internal body temperature reaches 80.6 degrees — a fact determined in gruesome and inhumane experiments conducted by Nazi scientists during World War II. Eight prisoners in the Dachau concentration camp were immersed in water chilled to 39.2 degrees where they were observed until all eight died of hypothermia. The men survived this torture an average of just over one hour, and Nazi doctors gained

the dubious distinction of having clinically determined the average lethal low temperature for the human body.

On the other hand, doctors have been astonished by miraculous death-defying recoveries from accidental freezings. Modern physicians were baffled in 1981 when they witnessed the thawing and revival of Jean Hilliard, a 19-year-old woman who crashed her

car one night in Minnesota and tried to brave subzero temperatures by walking to find help. She collapsed just 15 feet from a friend's doorstep and wasn't found until the following morning after outside temperatures had dipped to 22 degrees below zero. Hilliard's stiff, frozen body was described as feeling like "a piece of meat out of a deep freeze." So hard was her tissue frozen that nurses could not puncture it with hypodermic needles or intravenous tubes, and no thermometer in the hospital had a scale low enough to record her temperature. Incredibly, after several hours wrapped in electric heating pads, Hilliard began to thaw and revive, and eventually she made a nearly complete recovery. "I can't explain why she's alive," her doctor said of her recovery. "It's a miracle."

So hard was her tissue frozen that nurses could not puncture it with hypodermic needles or intravenous tubes. . .

Those who survive such freezings may have entered an eerie state of suspended animation similar to that of some hibernating animals. During winter when food is scarce and the weather harsh, many animals go into hibernation, cooling their bodies to a point where metabolism enters slow motion, cutting requirements for food and energy and possibly putting growth and aging processes into a holding pattern. The Arctic ground squirrel, for example, has a normal body temperature nearly the same as a human's, but during hibernation the squirrel drops into a chilled state of 41 degrees. Its heart rate slows tremendously, and its blood becomes as thick as molasses.

Recently surgeons have attempted to simulate the suspended state of hibernation by putting a patient's body "on ice" during surgery. In 1982 doctors at Baltimore's Johns Hopkins Hospital pioneered a daring procedure in which they lowered a man's body temperature to 65 degrees and packed his head in ice in order to actually stop the man's heartbeat and breathing. This deathlike state enabled the patient's brain and other tissues to survive without oxygen and the nutrients normally supplied by the blood. Meanwhile,

doctors were able to remove a tumor close to the resting heart. Other operative procedures have taken human temperatures to below 40 degrees for short periods of time and successfully revived the patients.

Of course, most victims of accidental freezing aren't so lucky. Last year about 30,000 Americans died from exposure to the cold. Oddly, the majority of these deaths aren't caused by snow or arctic air — they happen indoors. "Most of these people are dying in their own homes," says W. Moulton Avery, director of the Center for Environmental Physiology in Washington, D.C. Each year thousands of people, particularly elderly people whose bodies may not respond vigorously to cold, slip slowly and quietly into hypothermia. An indoor temperature of 64 degrees is cold enough to slowly sap the life-sustaining heat from an inactive person. Often, for some reason, the elderly do not sense that they are cold. Their brains may fail to trigger the vital shivering response that is both the body's warning sign and its best defense against hypothermia. So they enter directly into the critical third stage of hypothermia, becoming disoriented, clumsy, and drowsy as their body temperatures tailspin in deceptive slow motion.

Many factors affect a person's ability to withstand cold and maintain body warmth. Females, for example, are somewhat better equipped to deal with cold than men of similar size because a woman's body generally contains more fat, which helps insulate them. Pound for pound, short people lose heat less rapidly than tall people because they have less surface area in contact with the environment. Scientists believe this explains why people native to arctic regions tend to be smaller than those indigenous to the tropics.

But besides such inborn adaptations, it appears that individuals can also adapt to a changing environment in relatively short order. Men stationed in the Arctic tend to gain extra pounds of insulating fat during the cold winter months just as the baleen whale takes on more than a ton of extra blubber in preparation for the freeze of winter. Many studies have shown that repeated exposure to cold can increase the body's ability to maintain warmth.

Brief exposures each day over the course of several weeks can "exercise" the heating system and actually improve your ability to tolerate frigid air. This may explain why Army scientists have observed much higher rates of cold-related injuries among soldiers from southern states who are assigned to cold areas without being given time to condition themselves to the environment. New England fishermen, on the other hand, may develop such high tolerance to the cold that their hands can function agilely at temperatures which would numb the fingers of most city dwellers.

But probably man's greatest method of adapting to life on a cold planet comes from his imagination. Man the dreamer and schemer has created hundreds of ways to warm himself, not from within but from without, by tapping sources of heat locked within the earth such as fire, oil, and atomic energy. But it's a warming thought to know that if all the outside sources grow cold, the body still has a few tricks of its own for keeping warm. □□

WIND/BAROMETER TABLE

Barometer (Reduced to Sea Level)	Wind Direction	Character of Weather Indicated
30.00 to 30.20, and steady	westerly	Fair, with slight changes in temperature, for one to two days.
30.00 to 30.20, and rising rapidly	westerly	Fair, followed within two days by warmer and rain.
30.00 to 30.20, and falling rapidly	south to east	Warmer, and rain within 24 hours.
30.20, or above, and falling rapidly	south to east	Warmer, and rain within 36 hours.
30.20, or above, and falling rapidly	west to north	Cold and clear, quickly followed by warmer and rain.
30.20, or above, and steady	variable	No early change.
30.00, or below, and falling slowly	south to east	Rain within 18 hours that will continue a day or two.
30.00, or below, and falling rapidly	southeast to northeast	Rain, with high wind, followed within two days by clearing, colder.
30.00, or below, and rising	south to west	Clearing and colder within 12 hours.
29.80, or below, and falling rapidly	southeast to northeast	Severe storm of wind and rain imminent. In winter, snow or cold wave within 24 hours.
29.80, or below, and falling rapidly	east to north	Severe northeast gales and heavy rain or snow, followed in winter by cold wave.
29.80, or below, and rising rapidly	going to west	Clearing and colder.

Note: A barometer should be adjusted to show equivalent sea level pressure for the altitude at which it is to be used. A change of 100 feet in elevation will cause a decrease of 1/10th inch in the reading.

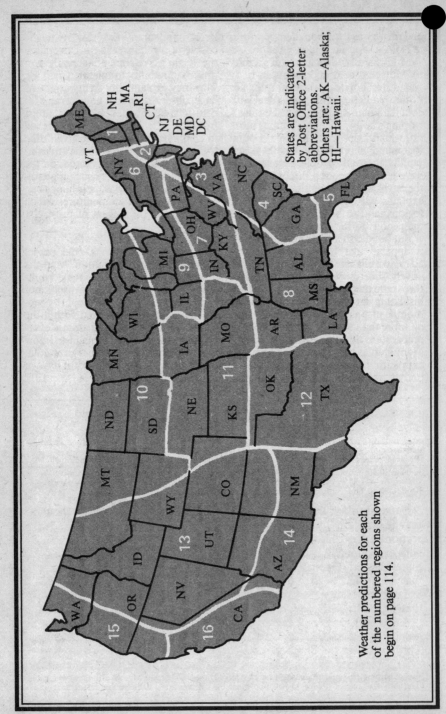

States are indicated by Post Office 2-letter abbreviations. Others are: AK — Alaska; HI — Hawaii.

Weather predictions for each of the numbered regions shown begin on page 114.

GENERAL WEATHER FORECAST
1984-1985

(For details see regional forecasts beginning on page 114.)

NOVEMBER THROUGH MARCH: Winter in most sections **east of the Rockies** is expected to be colder and drier than normal, with below-average total snowfall, despite relatively mild weather during much of November, December, and March and despite well-above-average snowfall in February and March. Above-normal precipitation is expected for Florida and from the central Great Plains to the eastern Ohio Valley, however, with above-average snowfall in the western Great Plains, northern New England, and the central Appalachians. Slightly milder than normal temperatures are anticipated in the northern Great Plains, the eastern Ohio Valley, and Florida. Watch for cold snaps extending well into the South during November and February and into Florida in January.

West of the Rockies, the mountain region may expect normal amounts of precipitation and generally below normal temperatures, while the Far West and Southwest will have milder than normal temperatures. Below-average precipitation is anticipated for the Northwest and slightly above for the Southwest. Central and northern California will be wetter than average, with heavy snow in the mountains.

APRIL THROUGH OCTOBER: Spring in the East will be warmer than normal but delayed by late-winter storms in early April. Warm and dry weather should then prevail through mid May, followed by heavy thunderstorms through June. The north-central part of the country should have a cool and wet spring, with the possibility of flooding at mid April and with heavy rains in May and June. Southern Gulf states and the southwestern Great Plains will be drier than normal. The **Northwest,** including the central and northern Rockies, will start out mild and dry through April and then turn cool and wet, while the reverse is anticipated for the **Southwest.**

Summer east of the Rockies is expected to be milder than normal except for the Southeast, which will be hotter than usual at midsummer. Most sections are expected to have above-normal rainfall in July and August, with exceptionally heavy thunderstorms in the central Atlantic and Gulf States, eastern Great Plains, and Great Lakes, where localized flooding may occur. The **western part of the country** will be warmer and drier than usual, except that central coastal sections will be cooler and more drizzly than normal, and the Southwest desert slightly cooler and drier than usual.

A cooler than normal **Fall** will prevail over most sections of the country despite a pleasant period of Indian summer-like weather at mid October. The Northwest and Southwest desert should be warmer than usual, however. September rainfall will be ample, but dry weather should prevail throughout the country during the month of October.

For regional boundaries, see map page 112

SUMMARY: *The winter is expected to be colder and drier than normal with below-average snowfall, but with large variations in temperature. After a brief cold snap at the beginning of November, generally mild weather, interspersed with cold waves, is anticipated for the balance of the year. Rainstorms should occur early in November, but precipitation is anticipated to be light thereafter until a storm in late December brings heavy rain to southern and heavy snow to northern sections. Cold spells are expected in mid-January and through February, with the north experiencing above-average snowfall during the latter month. March should be mild and very wet with considerable snowfall in the north.*

Alternating mild and cool spells are expected through the spring, with light precipitation, except for western sections that may have a wet May. Heavy thundershowers are anticipated for June that may result in local flooding and will bring well above average amounts of rainfall for the month.

From the latter part of June through August, temperatures are expected to be seasonably warm much of the time, with several cooler than normal periods interspersed with brief spells of hot weather. Thundershower activity should be sufficiently frequent as to bring close to normal amounts of rainfall to the region.

The fall is expected to be cooler than usual except for a period of Indian summer-like weather in mid-October. Showers in western and north-central sections in September should be quite heavy while the rest of the region is expected to be drier than normal; however, rain during early and late October will bring close to average amounts to most of the region.

Nov. 1984: Temp. 45° (0.5° above ave.); Precip. 3″ (1″ below ave.). 1-3 Cold snap, flurries north. 4-6 Heavy rain, seasonable. 7-10 Clear & mild. 11-15 Light rain, snow mountains. 16-18 Cold snap. 19-21 Mild, few showers. 22-24 Clear & warm. 25-27 Snow, cold. 28-30 Seasonable.

Dec. 1984: Temp. 34.5° (1° above ave.); Precip. 3.5″ (1″ below ave.). 1-5 Sunny, mild. 6-10 Warm, light rain. 11-13 Cold; snow north, showers south. 14-16 Severe cold. 17-19 Snowstorm north, rain south. 21-24 Flurries. 25-28 Cold, snow, then rain. 29-31 Mild, showers.

Jan. 1985: Temp. 26.5° (3° below ave.); Precip. 3.5″ (0.5″ below ave.). 1-2 Mild; rain & snow. 3-5 Cold, flurries. 6-9 Mild; rain south, snow mountains. 10-15 Severe cold, snow. 16-22

Clearing, then cold. 23-25 Rain, snow mountains. 26-29 Clearing. 30-31 Cold, snow south.

Feb. 1985: Temp. 26.5° (4° below ave.): Precip. 4″ (Ave.). 1-3 Cold, clearing. 4-6 Snowstorm north, rain & snow south. 7-9 Cold wave. 10-12 Snowstorm; sleet south. 13-19 Partly cloudy, cold. 20-23 Mild; rain, snow mountains. 24-28 Cold; flurries.

Mar. 1985: Temp. 41° (2.5° above ave.); Precip. 6″ (2″ above ave.). 1-4 Cold; snow north. 5-8 Milder; rain, snow mountains. 9-11 Some sun; rain south, snow north. 12-14 Mild; rain, snow mountains. 15-17 Sunny & mild, showers. 18-21 Rain south, snow north; cold. 22-24 Sunny, mild. 25-27 Rain, snow mountains; colder. 28-31 Clearing & milder.

Apr. 1985: Temp. 49.5° (1° above ave.); Precip. 2″ (1.5″ below ave.). 1-5 Sunny, cold; then rain, snow mountains. 6-11 Mild. 12-15 Cold snap, rain south, snow mountains. 16-21 Sunny & mild, few showers. 22-25 Cool, rain. 26-30 Clear & warm.

May 1985: Temp. 61° (2.5° above ave.); Precip. 2.5″ (1″ below ave.). 1-6 Sunny & warm, sprinkles. 7-9 Warm, rain. 10-12 Cool, rain. 13-15 Sunny, warm. 16-19 Partly sunny, mild. 20-25 Rain. 26-28 Warm, rain. 29-31 Cloudy, cooler.

June 1985: Temp. 69° (1° above ave.); Precip. 5″ (2″ above ave.). 1-3 Sunny & warm, showers. 4-9 Turning cool, rain. 10-12 Rain, warm. 13-17 Mostly sunny, hot. 18-22 Thundershowers, cool. 23-26 Warm, rain. 27-30 Seasonable.

July 1985: Temp. 71.5° (2° below ave.); Precip. 3″ (0.5″ above ave.). 1-5 Warm, few showers. 6-8 Rain, cooler. 9-12 Some sun, showers; warm. 13-15 Cloudy & cool, showers. 16-21 Sunny & hot; then cooler. 22-24 Rain, hot. 25-29 Sunny & warm. 30-31 Rain, cool.

Aug. 1985: Temp. 70.5° (1.5° below ave.); Precip. 3″ (0.5″ below ave.). 1-5 Rain, cool. 6-8 Sunny & warm; showers north. 9-12 Partly cloudy & pleasant. 13-16 Rain, cool, then warming. 17-22 Rain, warm. 23-26 Hot & humid. 27-29 Cool, showers. 30-31 Clear, warm.

Sept. 1985: Temp. 64.5° (0.5° below ave.); Precip. 2″ (1.5″ below ave.; 0.5″ above west & north). 1-2 Cool, showers. 3-6 Clear & hot. 7-11 Rain, then clearing; cool. 12-15 Rain, cool. 16-18 Clear & warm. 19-23 Rain, warm. 24-27 Sunny & cool, showers north. 28-30 Partly cloudy, showers.

Oct. 1985: Temp. 53.5° (1.5° below ave.); Precip. 3″ (0.5″ below ave.). 1-3 Rain, cold. 4-6 Partly cloudy, cool, few showers. 7-10 Clear & cold, frost inland; then showers. 11-15 Turning warm, clear & pleasant. 16-20 Partly cloudy, cool. 21-23 Rain. 24-27 Rain, warm. 28-31 Sunny, seasonable; then rain, cool.

For regional boundaries, see map page 112

SUMMARY: *The winter through November and December is expected to be milder than usual, then to turn progressively more severe through January and February before returning to milder weather in March. Snowfall should be lighter than normal, except average in January. A relatively dry November and January will alternate with a slightly wet December and February, then turn quite wet in March. Cold snaps should balance mild spells through November, but more extended mild periods are expected in December. Severe cold waves in mid-January and throughout February will more than balance brief mild spells. February, March, and up to mid-April should see stormy weather, with gale-force winds in March although mild temperatures will bring precipitation primarily as rain.*

Spring is expected to be warmer and drier than usual, particularly in central and southern sections, although cloudy, rainy, and cool periods are anticipated for mid-April, the second and fourth weeks of May, and early June. Thunderstorms during the latter two-thirds of June should make it a very wet month, particularly in the northwest. Except for a few brief warm periods in early May, no extensive hot spells are foreseen.

Thunderstorms are expected to be more numerous than usual through the summer, resulting in a wet, warm, and humid season. Several subnormal temperature periods may result in the monthly mean values being below normal. Sunny and warm periods are expected to alternate with rainy and cooler than normal ones through September and October before turning very cold at the end of the latter month.

Nov. 1984: Temp. 47° (Ave.); Precip. 3″ (1″ below ave.). 1-3 Cold snap. 4-6 Rain, mild. 7-9 Sunny & mild. 10-13 Rain, turning cold. 14-17 Cold snap, hard frost. 18-22 Sunny & mild, then cold. 23-25 Sunny, warm. 26-27 Rain, cold. 28-30 Partly cloudy, cold.

Dec. 1984: Temp 39° (3° above ave.); Precip. 4″ (0.5″ above ave.). 1-5 Sunny & mild. 6-9 Showers, mild. 10-12 Partly cloudy, colder. 13-15 Seasonable, then colder. 16-18 Rain, snow mountains, cold. 19-22 Clearing, milder. 23-26 Cold snap, flurries. 27-31 Rain, snow mountains; mild.

Jan. 1985: Temp. 30° (2° below ave.); Precip. 1.5″ (1.5″ below ave.). 1-4 Cold wave, flurries. 5-8 Rain & snow, mild. 9-13 Cold, cloudy. 14-16 Severe cold, snow. 17-19 Sunny, mild. 20-22 Cold, partly cloudy. 23-25 Rain & snow. 26-31 Sunny & mild.

Feb. 1985: Temp. 29° (4° below ave.); Precip. 4″ (1″ above ave.). 1-3 Snow, cold. 4-6 Rain, milder. 7-8 Clear, cold. 9-12 Rain & snow mixed, cold. 13-18 Partly cloudy, colder. 19-21 Moderate to heavy rain, mild. 22-25 Very cold, flurries. 26-28 Cold.

Mar. 1985: Temp. 42.5° (1.5° above ave.); Precip. 6″ (2″ above ave.). 1-2 Sunny, cold. 3-5 Sprinkles, flurries mountains. 6-9 Rain, then clearing. 10-13 Rain, gale winds; mild. 14-16 Partly cloudy. 17-21 Rain, cold. 22-24 Sunny, mild. 25-27 Rainstorm. 28-31 Cloudy & cold, then clearing & mild.

Apr. 1985: Temp. 52.5° (0.5° above ave.); Precip. 2.5″ (2″ below ave.). 1-4 Rain, snow north, unseasonably cold. 5-8 Sunny & mild, sprinkles. 9-11 Sunny, warm. 12-15 Moderate to heavy rain, snow north, cold. 16-20 Clearing, turning warm. 21-24 Cloudy, cooler, sprinkles. 25-30 Sunny & unseasonably warm.

May 1985: Temp. 64° (2° above ave.); Precip. 2″ (1.5″ below ave.). 1-2 Cloudy & cold. 3-5 Sunny, warm. 6-10 Cloudy, warm; light rain. 11-13 Rainstorm, cool. 14-17 Warming, partly cloudy, then rain. 18-21 Cloudy, then rain. 22-24 Mild, sprinkles. 25-27 Rain. 28-31 Partly sunny, mild.

June 1985: Temp. 71° (Ave.); Precip. 5.5″ (2.5″ above ave.). 1-3 Clear, hot. 4-8 Rain, cool. 9-10 Clearing, warm. 11-12 Thunderstorms. 13-15 Variable clouds, warm. 16-18 Rain. 19-20 Clear & pleasant. 21-27 Rain, warm. 28-30 Partly cloudy, mild; then showers.

July 1985: Temp. 74.5° (2° below ave.); Precip. 5.5″ (2″ above ave.). 1-4 Rain, then clearing. 5-7 Thunderstorms. 8-9 Sunny, warm. 10-13 Showers, cool. 14-16 Thundershowers, cooler. 17-20 Hot & humid. 21-22 Thunderstorms. 23-25 Clear, hot & humid. 26-30 Cloudier, milder. 31 Thunderstorms.

Aug. 1985: Temp. 73° (2.5° above ave.); Precip. 7.5″ (3″ above ave.). 1-3 Showers ending. 4-7 Rain, then warm. 8-11 Partly cloudy & mild. 12-14 Thundershowers, mild. 15-18 Clear & warm, then thunderstorms. 19-22 Thunderstorms. 23-26 Sunny, hot. 27-28 Showers, mild. 29-31 Sunny, cool.

Sept. 1985: Temp. 67° (1° below ave.); Precip. 3″ (0.5″ below ave.). 1-3 Showers, mild. 4-7 Clear, warm. 8-11 Partly cloudy, mild. 12-14 Rain, warm. 15-17 Showers. 18-21 Clear, warm. 22-24 Rain, cooler. 25-28 Partly cloudy, sprinkles. 29-30 Rain, cool.

Oct. 1985: Temp. 56° (1.5° below ave.); Precip. 2.5″ (0.5″ below ave.). 1-2 Heavy rain, cool. 3-7 Partly cloudy & cool. 8-10 Rain. 11-14 Clear & warm. 15-17 Cloudy, cool. 18-22 Showers. 23-24 Sunny & seasonable. 25-28 Rain, mild. 29-31 Rain, turning cold.

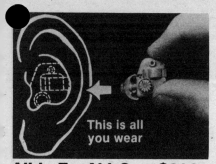

SUMMARY: *The winter as a whole is expected to be milder than normal (even though January and February may be considerably colder than usual) with below normal snowfall and precipitation despite some wet and snowy months. November should be sunnier and drier than usual, but with the temperature averaging about normal. December is expected to be quite mild and wet. A cold wave at mid-month should usher in the first major snowstorm of the season. In January a snowstorm in the second week may be followed by a protracted cold wave that will result in a colder than normal month. February's temperatures will be even lower, due to several brief cold spells; however, despite some moderate to heavy storms, only the mountain and northern sections are anticipated to get an average snowfall for the month. Following a stormy and cold first week, it is expected that March will be relatively mild.*

The spring may start out with a cold wave and snowstorm early in April and a storm at mid-month before a sunny and dry period sets in. After early May, temperatures should remain closer to normal. Heavy and frequent rains are expected from mid-May through June, although the Eastern shore may experience some drought.

Frequent and heavy thunderstorms through July and August should make for a cool and wet summer with flooding in northern sections after mid-July and more generally in mid-August.

September may be significantly drier than normal, but heavy rainstorms during October, interspersed with cold snaps, should make it a cool, wet month overall.

Nov. 1984: Temp. 48.5 (Ave.); Precip. 1″ (2″ below ave.). 1-3 Rain ending, cold. 4-6 Rain, mild. 7-9 Sunny & mild. 10-11 Rain, turning cold. 12-15 Cloudy, sprinkles, cold. 16-18 Clearing & warming; cold nights. 19-23 Sunny & warm. 24-27 Showers, turning colder. 28-30 Clearing, cold.

Dec.1984: Temp. 42° (3° above ave.); Precip. 4″ (1″ above ave.). 1-5 Clear, warm. 6-9 Rain, mild. 10-15 Partly cloudy, cold; sprinkles north. 16-18 Rain, snow north, cold. 19-22 Sunny, cold nights, mild days. 23-26 Cold, rain & snow. 27-28 Rain, mild. 29-31 Scattered showers, mild.

Jan. 1985: Temp. 33° (2° below ave.); Precip. 1.5″ (1″ below ave.). 1-4 Cloudy, cold; flurries north. 5-8 Rain changing to snow; colder. 9-11 Cloudy, very cold. 12-14 Severe cold; snow. 15-19 Clearing, mild. 20-22 Partly cloudy, season-able. 23-25 Rain & snow, cold. 26-29 Clear & mild. 30-31 Rain, snow mountains.

Feb. 1985: Temp. 34° (3.5° below ave.); Precip. 3″ (0.5″ above ave.). 1-3 Rain, snow mountains & north; cold. 4-8 Mild, rain; then clearing, cold. 9-11 Snowstorm north & mountains, rain east. 12-18 Cloudy & cold. 19-21 Rain, mild. 22-25 Rain & snow, turning cold. 26-28 Partly cloudy, cold.

Mar. 1985: Temp. 48° (2° above ave.); Precip. 4″ (0.5″ above ave.). 1-5 Cloudy & cold, few sprinkles. 6-8 Snowstorm. 9-11 Clearing & milder, showers. 12-14 Rain, mild. 15-17 Clear & warm, then cool. 18-21 Thunderstorms. 22-24 Sunny & warm. 25-27 Rain, colder. 28-31 Sunny, seasonable.

Apr. 1985: Temp. 57° (0.5° above ave.); Precip. 2.5″ (0.5″ below ave.). 1-4 Snowstorm, cold. 5-8 Partly cloudy, warming. 9-12 Clear, warm. 13-15 Snow, sleet & rain. 16-20 Clearing, very warm. 21-25 Rain, cold. 26-30 Clear & warm.

May 1985: Temp. 68.5° (2.5° above ave.); Precip. 4″ (0.5″ above ave.). 1-3 Mild, light rain. 4-6 Clear & hot. 7-9 Showers, warm. 10-12 Rain, warm. 13-15 Cloudy. 16-18 Warm, rain north. 19-23 Rain, then clearing. 24-26 Heavy rain, warm. 27-31 Cloudy, showers, then clearing.

June 1985: Temp. 75.5° (1° above ave.); Precip. 5.5″ (2″ above ave.). 1-4 Clear, hot. 5-9 Rain, milder. 10-11 Clear & hot. 12-17 Thundershowers; warm, then hot. 18-20 Sunny & milder. 21-24 Showers. 25-27 Rain, very warm. 28-30 Partly cloudy & cooler, then rain.

July 1985: Temp. 77.5° (1.5° below ave.); Precip. 5″ (1″ above ave.). 1-2 Rain, mild. 3-6 Sunny, warm; then rain. 7-8 Sunny & hot. 9-11 Thundershowers. 12-15 Partly sunny, milder, then showers. 16-20 Sunny, hot. 21-23 Heavy storm & flooding north, sunny & hot south. 24-26 Showers. 27-31 Showers, mild.

Aug. 1985: Temp. 76° (1.5° below ave.); Precip. 8″ (3.5″ above ave.). 1-4 Showers, hot. 5-7 Sunny & hot, few showers. 8-10 Rain south, milder. 11-15 Showers, then clearing. 16-18 Rain, some flooding east, warm. 19-22 Sunny, then thunderstorms, flooding. 23-26 Showers. 27-28 Rain, cool. 29-31 Clearing, mild.

Sept. 1985: Temp. 70.5° (0.5° below ave.); Precip. 1.5″ (1.5″ below ave.). 1-3 Showers, mild. 4-6 Sunny, showers south. 7-10 Rain northwest, warm then milder. 11-14 Rain, warm. 15-20 Clearing, hot; showers northwest. 21-23 Rain, warm. 24-29 Sunny & pleasant. 30 Rain.

Oct. 1985: Temp. 58° (1.5° below ave.); Precip. 7″ (4″ above ave.; ave. south). 1-2 Rain, cold. 3-5 Clear, cold snap. 6-10 Milder, then rain. 11-16 Clear and warm. 17-20 Torrential rains central & north, floods. 21-24 Clearing & warm. 25-28 Rain. 29-31 Rain, snow north; cold.

SUMMARY: *The winter is expected to be extremely variable, starting out warm and dry, becoming warm and wet in December, cold and dry in January, and then much colder and wetter through February and the first half of March, with above-average snowfall during this latter period. Temperatures should be well above normal through November and December except for cold spells at the middle of each month. Storms during December should come primarily as rain except for snow at mid-month. A severe cold snap in early January may result in a colder than usual month with below-normal amounts of precipitation. February is expected to be persistently colder than normal, with frequent and heavy storms, a pattern that may well continue through early March. Thereafter, it should be mild.*

Except for a storm at mid-month, April is expected to be quite dry and this condition may persist until mid-May. Heavy rains in late May and mid-June may bring well above normal rainfall, particularly to the north and west. Prolonged hot spells in early May and early June are expected in the north. Summer temperatures should be slightly above normal. Frequent thundershowers will bring above-average rainfall to Piedmont and the west although some eastern sections may be drier than usual.

Extended warm spells at mid-September and the latter part of October should be offset by cool periods, and precipitation is expected to be close to normal.

Nov. 1984: Temp. 51.5° (1° above ave.; 0.5° below south); Precip. 1″ (2″ below ave.; 1″ below south). 1-3 Clearing, cold. 4-7 Rain, warm, then clearing. 8-10 Showers, warm. 11-16 Frost. 17-24 Clear, warm. 25-28 Rain. 29-30 Cold, frost Piedmont.

Dec. 1984: Temp. 47° (4° above ave.; 2° above south); Precip. 5″ (1.5″ above ave.; 3″ above south). 1-6 Clear & warm. 7-9 Rain, warm. 10-14 Partly cloudy, cold. 15-17 Cold, rain, snow mountains. 18-20 Clearing, warming. 21-25 Clear & warm. 26-28 Rain. 29-31 Showers.

Jan. 1985: Temp. 39.5° (1° below ave.; 3° below south); Precip. 1.5″ (2.5″ below ave.; 1″ below south). 1-4 Cold, frost. 5-8 Rain; warm then colder. 9-11 Cloudy, cold. 12-14 Very cold; snow mountains. 15-17 Cold, then warming. 18-21 Sunny & warm. 22-24 Showers. 25-30 Clear, warm. 31 Showers.

Feb. 1985: Temp. 41° (2° below ave.; 4° below south); Precip. 5.5″ (1.5″ above ave.). 1-3 Rain, then clearing. 4-8 Rain; frost. 9-11 Rain, mild. 12-15 Sunny; rain central, cold. 16-18 Clear, cold. 19-21 Rain. 22-26 Clear, frost. 27-28 Rain, snow mountains.

Mar. 1985: Temp. 51.5° (1° above ave.; 2° below south); Precip. 6.5″ (1.5″ above ave.; 2.5″ above south). 1-2 Snow west, very cold. 3-5 Sunny, cold. 6-8 Snow, rain east. 9-14 Clearing, then rain, cool. 15-17 Sunny & warm. 18-21 Rain, warm. 22-24 Sunny. 25-27 Rain. 28-29 Clear & warm. 30-31 Rain.

Apr. 1985: Temp. 61.5° (1° above ave.; 2° below south); Precip. 1″ (2″ below ave.). 1-3 Rain & cool, then clear & warm. 4-6 Cloudy & cool. 7-12 Clear & warm, then cloudy. 13-15 Rain, cool. 16-19 Partly cloudy, cool; few showers. 20-23 Sunny & warm. 24-27 Sunny, cooler. 28-30 Clear, hot.

May 1985: Temp. 71° (2.5° above ave.; ave. south); Precip. 6.5″ (3″ above ave.; 0.5″ above south). 1-2 Rain, warm. 3-5 Cloudy & hot. 6-12 Showers, hot. 13-16 Cloudy, then clearing; cool. 17-20 Rain. 21-23 Sunny & warm. 24-27 Rain. 28-31 Cool, cloudy.

June 1985: Temp. 78.5° (3.5° above ave.; 0.5° above south); Precip. 6.5″ (3″ above ave.; 1″ below south). 1 Showers. 2-5 Sunny & hot. 6-12 Showers, hot. 13-18 Thundershowers, hot. 19-21 Rain, hot. 22-27 Sunny then showers. 28-30 Warm.

July 1985: Temp. 80.5° (2° above ave.; 0.5° above south); Precip. 6″ (2″ above ave.; 1.5″ below south). 1-4 Showers, cooler. 5-7 Rain. 8-10 Sunny & hot; showers south. 11-15 Showers, hot. 16-18 Clear, hot. 19-21 Showers. 22-25 Clear, hot. 26-31 Showers, cool.

Aug. 1985: Temp. 78.5° (0.5° above ave.; 0.5° below south); Precip. 3.5″ (0.5″ below ave.; 2″ above south). 1-4 Showers; hot north. 5-7 Clear & hot. 8-10 Thundershowers, milder. 11-15 Showers, mild. 16-18 Showers. 19-24 Sunny & hot, then showers. 25-28 Hot, showers. 29-31 Cloudy, cool.

Sept. 1985: Temp. 73° (1° above ave.; 1° below south); Precip. 4″ (0.5″ above ave.; ave. south). 1-2 Clear, warm. 3-6 Rain, cool. 7-8 Sunny. 9-12 Rain. 13-15 Hot, showers. 16-19 Clear, hot. 20-22 Hot, showers. 23-25 Showers, warm. 26-29 Clear. 30 Rain.

Oct. 1985: Temp. 61° (Ave.; 2° below south); Precip. 3″ (Ave.). 1-2 Rain, mild. 3-5 Clearing, cool. 6-8 Clear, warm. 9-11 Showers, mild. 12-15 Clear & warm. 16-18 Possible tropical storm offshore. 19-23 Sunny, warm. 24-26 Rain. 27-31 Rain, turning cold.

BEFORE

Mr. Sniffles sez....

....."NEW DOESN'T ALWAYS MEAN BETTER"

KONDON'S®
NASAL JELLY

HAS RELIEVED NASAL CONGESTION
SINCE 1889

GENTLE • QUICK • PLEASANT • SOOTHING

For over 90 years, **KONDON'S NASAL JELLY** has helped millions of sufferers from head colds, hay fever, sinus allergies. It relieves congestion, soothes membranes, promotes easy breathing.

AT YOUR PHARMACY — or send Check or Money Order — 1 Tube, **$2.25**; 6 Tubes **$10.50** — direct to:

KONDON MFG. CO.
P.O. Box EF-223
Croswell, Mich. 48422

AFTER

LYRIC CHOIR GOWNS

HELP YOU LOOK, FEEL AND
SOUND YOUR BEST.

Variety of styles, fabrics, colors • Quality crafts-manship • Thirty years experience • Satisfaction guaranteed Write today for free catalog and fabric samples.
Adult from $19.95
Youth from $16.95

LYRIC CHOIR
GOWN CO.

P.O. Box 16954 - S E
Jacksonville, FL 32216
(904) 725-7977

Great Hometown Cookery . . .

GREAT NEW ENGLAND RECIPES And The Cooks Who Made Them Famous. Features 37 favorite hometown cooks and their recipes. Over 275 recipes, 320 pages, 6"x9", hardcover. Only **$15.95** & **$1.50** postage & handling. Order from: YANKEE BOOKS, Dept. AL85, Depot Square, Peterborough, NH 03458.

Bag Balm

all-purpose
OINTMENT
helps *FAST*
Protection!

**LOADED
WITH
LANOLIN**

Money-Saving 10 oz. & Handy Purse-Size CANS

Try **BAG BALM Ointment** featured by A.P.; UPI; N.Y. Times; Wall Street Journal; Newsweek; Yankee; "On The Road" nationwide prime-time TV Show; others. ● Some people find **BAG BALM** helpful as a protective coating for Hands while Gardening, Fishing, other activities. 10 oz. **BAG BALM** $3 & 1 oz. Purse-Size $2.15 add 50¢ handlg. ea. Also try excellent, useful **TACKMASTER LEATHER Preservative-Conditioner-Cleaner.** PT. $3 add 50¢ hndlg. Dairy Association Co. 502 Lake St., Lyndonville, VT 05851.

For regional boundaries, see map page 112

SUMMARY: *The winter is expected to be wetter than usual and to have fluctuating temperatures, particularly in central and northern sections, that will average out to be cooler than normal. An extended cold wave at mid-November and a brief cold snap at the end of the month will be balanced by otherwise warmer than normal temperatures, while storms the first three weeks should bring well above-average rainfall. December will be warmer than usual; precipitation may be close to average except northern sections will have well above-normal amounts. Several frosts are expected in northern sections during January, while frequent rains are anticipated during the first half of the month. Several heavy storms during the latter part of February may make it a wetter than usual month, while cold snaps at the beginning and end could bring frost into southern sections. The cold is expected to last through the first week or more of March. Frequent and heavy rains will fall in central and northern sections in March.*

The early spring, through the first week of April, is expected to be cool and wet, but then through May most sections are anticipated to be dry. June may be quite wet, while temperatures remain fairly close to normal.

The summer is expected to be warmer and drier than normal with above-average daytime temperatures and fewer thundershowers than usual from mid-July to mid-August. Early and late periods of the summer, however, should see significant thunderstorm activity as well as milder temperatures.

The fall is expected to be drier than usual except for heavy showers in late September, with warmer than normal temperatures during the latter halves of September and October.

Nov. 1984: Temp. 65° (2° above ave.; 2° above north, 1° above south); Precip. 4″ (2″ above ave.). 1-5 Showers, warm. 6-10 Partly sunny then showers, warm. 11-15 Clearing, cold, frost north. 16-19 Showers, cool then warming. 20-24 Clear & warm. 25-28 Showers, warm. 29-30 Partly cloudy, cooler.

Dec. 1984: Temp. 62° (Ave.; 3° above north & south); Precip. 2″ (Ave.; 4″ above north). 1-2 Sunny, warm. 3-6 Cloudy, warm, showers. 7-9 Showers, warm. 10-14 Cloudy, cool; showers south. 15-17 Rain north. 18-21 Cool, frost north, rain south. 22-26 Clear, warm. 27-31 Rain, warm.

Jan. 1985: Temp. 56° (4° below ave.; 2° below north & south); Precip. 2″ (Ave.). 1-4 Showers, clearing & cooler. 5-9 Rain, warm. 10-14 Partly cloudy, cool, few showers. 15-17 Hard frost to south-central, clearing. 18-21 Sunny & warm.

22-24 Showers, very warm. 25-27 Cloudy, cool. 28-31 Clear, mild.

Feb. 1985: Temp. 57.5° (4° below ave.); Precip. 4″ (1″ above ave.). 1-4 Cold, then warmer, showers. 5-9 Frost to south. 10-12 Seasonable, showers. 13-15 Showers, warm. 16-18 Cloudy, cool. 19-21 Very warm, rain north. 22-24 Rain, cold. 25-26 Cold snap, frost. 27-28 Heavy rain.

Mar. 1985: Temp. 65° (2.5° below ave.; ave. north); Precip. 5″ (2″ above ave.; ave. south). 1-5 Variable cloudiness, showers, cold. 6-10 Rain, cold. 11-13 Clear & warm, then rain. 14-16 Sunny, very warm. 17-20 Warm, showers central & north. 21-26 Showers, warm. 27-31 Clear & warm.

Apr. 1985: Temp. 69.5° (2.5° below ave.; 0.5° below north); Precip. 3″ (1″ above ave.; 2″ below north). 1-2 Showers, cool. 3-5 Partly sunny & mild; rain south. 6-10 Clear & warm. 11-14 Clouds, warm, few showers. 15-18 Sunny & mild; cloudy & cool north. 19-21 Showers, cool. 22-25 Clearing, very warm. 26-28 Showers, mild. 29-30 Clear & hot.

May 1985: Temp. 77° (Ave.; 2° above north); Precip. 0.5″ (3.5″ below ave.). 1-4 Clear & hot. 5-10 Partly cloudy, warm; mild nights north. 11-13 Showers, mild. 14-16 Clear, seasonable. 17-19 Showers south. 20-23 Sunny, warm. 24-26 Showers north; seasonable. 27-31 Clear, hot; showers south.

June 1985: Temp. 80.5° (0.5° below ave.; 1° above north); Precip. 8″ (1″ above ave.; 2″ above north & south). 1-4 Showers, milder. 5-8 Showers. 9-11 Partly sunny, few showers. 12-15 Showers, hot. 16-18 Clear & hot. 19-22 Showers, hot. 23-28 Showers, milder. 29-30 Sunny.

July 1985: Temp. 84° (2° above ave.); Precip. 4.5″ (3″ below ave.; 4″ below south). 1-4 Showers, hot. 5-8 Rain. 9-15 Partly sunny, hot, few showers. 16-21 Showers, hot. 22-26 Clear, heat wave. 27-31 Showers, hot.

Aug. 1985: Temp. 83.5° (1″ above ave.); Precip. 5″ (1.5″ below ave.; 4″ below north & south). 1-4 Showers, hot. 5-7 Showers, partly sunny, hot. 8-10 Sunny & hot. 11-13 Rain north, showers south, seasonable. 14-17 Showers, seasonable. 18-23 Sunny, then showers. 24-29 Showers, sunny. 30-31 Rain, milder.

Sept. 1985: Temp. 80° (1° below ave.); Precip. 5″ (1″ below ave.; 1″ above north). 1-4 Showers, mild. 5-10 Showers, warm. 11-17 Partly sunny, few showers, hot. 18-24 Sunny, hot, few showers. 25-28 Showers south, sunny north, warm. 29-30 Rain.

Oct. 1985: Temp. 74° (1° below ave.; ave. north & south); Precip. 1″ (2″ below ave.). 1-3 Showers, cool. 4-6 Clearing north, rain south. 7-11 Clear, warm. 12-17 Partly sunny, few showers. 18-25 Clear & pleasant. 26-31 Showers.

6. UPSTATE N.Y. — TORONTO AND MONTREAL

For regional boundaries, see map page 112

SUMMARY: *The winter is expected to begin warmer and drier than normal, but then to change to progressively colder temperatures through February, with above-normal snowfall in February, March, and even April, despite below-average amounts of precipitation. Other than some cold periods in mid-November and mid-December, temperatures are anticipated to remain fairly mild in those months. Several storms of significance are expected in early November and shortly after mid-December. A brief cold snap after the first of the year and an extended cold wave the second week are expected to dominate temperatures in January. Frequent cold periods of progressively greater duration are anticipated through February; however, relatively mild nighttime temperatures are expected in March. Heavy snowstorms may arrive the second week of February and the first week of March.*

Spring is expected to be warmer and drier than normal, but with considerable variation in temperature. Frequent rains will bring the monthly totals close to average. There should be several cold spells in each month, with one in mid-April accompanying a snowstorm, but even greater periods of above-normal warmth are anticipated.

The summer is also expected to be drier than normal except that heavy thundershowers in central and eastern sections in July should make it a wet month there. Few extended periods of excessively high or low temperatures are anticipated.

An unseasonably warm period may occur after mid-September, but generally the fall is anticipated to be cooler than normal.

Nov. 1984: Temp. 40° (1° above ave.); Precip. 1.5″ (1.5″ below ave.; 0.5″ below west). 1-3 Cold snap, hard frost. 4-6 Rain, cold. 7-9 Clear, mild. 10-11 Rain, seasonable. 12-14 Cloudy, cold west. 15-17 Cold, light snow. 18-20 Mild, rain north. 21-23 Cloudy & cold, then warm. 24-27 Cold, rain & snow. 28-30 Cloudy.

Dec. 1984: Temp. 31.5° (3° above ave.; 5° above west); Precip. 2″ (1″ below ave.). 1-4 Rain north, clearing & mild. 5-7 Rain & snow, cold. 8-12 Clear, mild, then cold. 13-16 Snow, cold. 17-19 Snowstorm, cold. 20-23 Partly cloudy, milder. 24-26 Severe cold, light snow. 27-31 Mild, rain, snow mountains.

Jan. 1985: Temp. 20° (1° below ave., 2° below west); Precip. 1.5″ (1″ below ave.; ave. west). 1-4 Cold, snow. 5-8 Mild then cold, rain changing to snow. 9-15 Severe cold, flurries. 16-20 Milder, snow. 21-25 Cold then mild; sleet. 26-29 Partly sunny & mild. 30-31 Light snow.

Feb. 1985: Temp. 20° (3.5° below ave.); Precip. 1″ (1″ below ave.; 1.5″ above west). 1-3 Partly cloudy, cold east. 4-6 Mild, rain & snow. 7-8 Severe cold. 9-12 Heavy snowstorm. 13-17 Very cold, partly cloudy, snow west. 18-21 Milder, rain & snow. 22-28 Cold, flurries.

Mar. 1985: Temp. 37.5° (4° above ave.); Precip. 3.5″ (0.5″ above ave.). 1-4 Snow west, cloudy east; cold. 5-8 Warming, rain; snow mountains. 9-12 Light rain, warm. 13-16 Rain, snow mountains; mild. 17-21 Rain, floods; cold. 22-24 Milder. 25-27 Rain. 28-31 Sunny & mild.

Apr. 1985: Temp. 48° (1.5° above ave.; 0.5° below west); Precip. 2.5″ (0.5″ below ave.). 1-5 Rain; cold & snow west. 6-10 Showers, mild. 11-13 Turning cold, rain. 14-16 Snowstorm, cold. 17-21 Clearing & warming, rain north. 22-25 Cold, rain north. 26-30 Gradual warming, clearing.

May 1985: Temp. 61.5° (4° above ave.; 1° above west); Precip. 2.5″ (1″ below ave.). 1-4 Sunny, warm. 5-8 Rain, warm. 9-13 Turning cold, rain. 14-15 Sunny, warming. 16-19 Rain, warm. 20-22 Rain, cooler. 23-27 Rain, cool. 28-31 Sunny, warm east; cool, rain west.

June 1985: Temp. 67.5° (1° above ave.; ave. west); Precip. 2.5″ (0.5″ below ave.). 1-2 Clear & warm. 3-8 Showers, cool east. 9-12 Clear & warm, then rain. 13-15 Mostly clear, warm. 16-18 Showers, milder. 19-21 Cloudy, cool. 22-25 Showers, cool west. 26-29 Cloudy, cool west. 30 Showers north & west.

July 1985: Temp. 71.5° (Ave.; 2° below west); Precip. 5″ (2″ above ave.; 1″ below west). 1-3 Clear, hot. 4-6 Thundershowers; milder. 7-8 Clear east, cloudy west. 9-11 Showers, cool. 12-14 Cloudy, cool. 15-16 Thundershowers. 17-20 Sunny, mild. 21-24 Thundershowers. 25-30 Variable clouds, warm. 31 Showers.

Aug. 1985: Temp. 68° (1° below ave.); Precip. 2″ (1.5″ below ave.). 1-4 Thundershowers, milder. 5-7 Showers, cool. 8-12 Clearing, cool, then warm. 13-15 Thundershowers, mild. 16-18 Sunny, warm. 19-21 Thundershowers. 22-25 Sunny, warm east; cloudy, mild west. 26-28 Rain, cool. 29-31 Clear, seasonable.

Sept. 1985: Temp. 62° (1° above ave.); Precip. 2.5″ (0.5″ below ave.; ave. west). 1-2 Rain. 3-6 Clear, warm. 7-9 Rain, mild. 10-12 Clear, cool nights. 13-15 Rain, warm. 16-18 Clearing & warming. 19-22 Warm; showers. 23-24 Rain, cool. 25-30 Sunny & cool.

Oct. 1985: Temp. 48.5° (2° below ave.; 1° below west); Precip. 4.5″ (1.5″ above ave.; ave. west). 1-2 Heavy rain, cooler. 3-5 Cold snap, frost. 6-8 Sunny, mild. 9-11 Rain, cooler. 12-14 Clear & warm. 15-19 Partly sunny, cool. 20-24 Rain, then clearing & cold. 25-29 Rain, mild. 30-31 Snowstorm west.

7. GREATER OHIO VALLEY

For regional boundaries, see map page 112

SUMMARY: *The winter in the western section is expected to be colder and drier than normal, the eastern part to be wetter and milder than usual, with the whole region experiencing considerable variability within each month. November will be mild and wet except for a severe cold wave expected at mid-month. Unseasonably warm spells are anticipated for early and late December, with a possible snowstorm at mid-month and a heavy rainstorm to close out the year; January will be alternately cold and mild. Few severe storms are anticipated although eastern sections may have moderately heavy snows during the second week. February's temperatures should be below normal with several storms that may bring above-average precipitation. The eastern section may experience above-normal snowfall during a cold early March, but the balance of the month is anticipated to be mild.*

From late March through April, temperatures are expected to alternate from warm to unseasonably cold, but the balance of the spring should be very mild. A storm, with flooding, is anticipated at mid-April, while May and June should have average rainfall.

The summer should be cooler than usual in the west and warmer in the east, with thundershowers bringing above-normal precipitation, except possibly to some southwestern and eastern sections. Thundershowers in mid-July may cause some flooding.

After a very cool beginning the fall should be warmer than normal, with above-average rainfall in September. October may be quite dry in the western section, but wet in the east.

Nov. 1984: Temp. 40.5° (4° below ave.; 1° above east); Precip. 3″ (Ave.; 0.5″ above east). 1-3 Showers, then clearing. 4-6 Showers, mild. 7-9 Partly cloudy, cold. 10-14 Rain changing to snow, very cold. 15-17 Cloudy, very cold. 18-23 Warming. 24-27 Rain, cold. 28-30 Cloudy.

Dec. 1984: Temp. 40° (2° above ave.; 5° above east); Precip. 2.5″ (0.5″ below ave.). 1-5 Cloudy, cold west; sunny & mild east. 6-9 Showers, warm. 10-11 Cloudy, cold. 12-16 Snow, cold. 17-18 Snowstorm, cold. 19-21 Clearing, mild. 22-26 Sunny, turning warm. 27-31 Rain, mild.

Jan. 1985: Temp. 28° (2° below ave.; 1° above east); Precip. 1.5″ (1.5″ below ave.). 1-4 Cold snap; snow east. 5-8 Rain, mild; then snow, cold. 9-15 Severe cold, light snow. 16-20 Sunny, becoming mild. 21-24 Mild, rain. 25-27 Cloudy, cold. 28-31 Sunny, mild, then rain.

Feb. 1985: Temp. 30° (3.5° below ave.; 1° below east); Precip. 3″ (0.5″ above ave.; 2″ above east). 1-3 Rain, snow east, cold; then clear & mild. 4-7 Rain, changing to snow; cold. 8-11 Rain, snowstorm east; mild. 12-16 Very cold, light snow. 17-19 Clearing, turning mild. 20-23 Rain, then colder; snow. 24-28 Cold.

Mar. 1985: Temp. 45° (2° above ave.; 3° above east); Precip. 3″ (1″ below ave.; 1″ above east). 1-5 Cold, light snow. 6-8 Rain, snowstorm east; milder. 9-11 Clear, turning warm. 12-14 Rain, cold. 15-16 Clear & mild. 17-21 Rain, warm. 22-24 Cloudy & cold, then clear & mild. 25-27 Rain, cool. 28-31 Clear, warm, then rain.

Apr. 1985: Temp. 54° (0.5° below ave.; 2° above east); Precip. 3″ (0.5″ below ave.). 1-4 Rain, cold, snowstorm east. 5-8 Clear then showers; warm. 9-10 Clear, very warm. 11-15 Rain, snow & sleet east, turning cold. 16-19 Clearing, warming. 20-22 Very warm, showers. 23-25 Cloudy, cold. 26-30 Clear, very warm.

May 1985: Temp. 64° (Ave.; 3° above east); Precip. 4″ (Ave.). 1-5 Showers, then clear; very warm. 6-9 Rain, turning mild. 10-12 Rain, cool. 13-16 Showers, warming. 17-21 Rain, warm; then clearing & mild. 22-25 Rain, turning cool. 26-29 Cloudy, very cool. 30-31 Rain.

June 1985: Temp. 74.5° (1° above ave.; 5° above east); Precip. 5″ (1″ above ave.; ave. east). 1-5 Sunny & hot, rain east. 6-8 Showers, hot. 9-12 Sunny & hot, then rain. 13-15 Rain, seasonable. 16-18 Rain, turning cool. 19-22 Mild, few showers. 23-26 Rain, warm. 27-30 Cool, rain west, showers east.

July 1985: Temp. 76° (0.5°below ave.; 2° above east); Precip. 4″ (Ave.; 2″ below east). 1-3 Sunny & hot. 4-6 Partly cloudy, milder. 7-9 Seasonable; showers. 10-15 Warm, light rain. 16-20 Sunny, turning hot, few showers. 21-23 Sunny, hot; thunderstorms & floods east. 24-27 Showers, seasonably warm. 28-31 Sunny then rain.

Aug. 1985: Temp. 72° (3° below ave.; 1° above east); Precip. 4.5″ (1″ above ave.; ave. east). 1-4 Hot; rain central & east. 5-7 Showers, hot. 8-10 Showers west, warm. 11-14 Rain, cooler. 15-18 Sunny, warm; showers east. 19-21 Showers, warm. 22-25 Clear & warm. 26-28 Rain, cool. 29-31 Clearing, seasonable.

Sept. 1985: Temp 67.5° (1.5° below ave.; 3° above east); Precip. 4″ (1″ above ave.). 1-2 Light rain, warm. 3-5 Sunny, seasonable. 6-8 Showers, rain east. 9-11 Clear, warm. 12-14 Rain, warm. 15-17 Showers, seasonable. 18-20 Sunny, very warm. 21-24 Rain, turning cool. 25-27 Sunny, cool. 28-30 Showers, cold.

Oct. 1985: Temp 53.5° (3° below ave.; 1° above east); Precip. 1″ (1.5″ below ave.; 1″ above east). 1-2 Rain, showers west; cold snap. 3-7 Clear & warm. 8-10 Rain, warm. 11-14 Clear, warm. 15-17 Cloudy, seasonable. 18-21 Rain, east. 22-24 Clear & warm. 25-27 Rain, cool. 28-31 Sunny then rain; snow northeast; cold.

8. DEEP SOUTH

For regional boundaries, see map page 112

SUMMARY: *The winter is expected to be colder and drier than normal, but considerably snowier than usual in northern sections after the first of the year and with large variations in temperature from November through mid-March. Cold waves, with frost extending to central sections, are anticipated in the second and last weeks of November; December, by contrast, should be relatively mild. Storms through these two months will bring average rainfall to southern sections, but be less intense in the north. A severe cold wave is expected for mid-January, with a freeze extending to southern sections and accompanied by frequent light snows. The second half should be sunny and mild, after which frequent cold snaps through February and the first week of March are expected, together with some snowstorms in the north.*

Spring should be warmer than usual in southern sections and slightly cooler in the north. Temperatures are expected to be variable through April and May with a prolonged warm period occurring in early June. A dry spell may be in the offing for southern sections from late March through to mid-May, while more intense storms should bring close to normal rainfall to the north.

The summer is expected to be close to normal in the south and cooler than normal in the north, with a few brief periods of hot weather in July and early August. Heavy thundershower activity in the south during July and over the region in August will bring above-average rainfall then, but otherwise drier than normal conditions should exist.

Following heavy showers late September in the south, little rain is expected in the fall until the last few days of October. Temperatures may be well below normal in spite of an extended period of warm weather expected during mid-October.

Nov. 1984: Temp. 51.5° (3.5° below ave.); Precip. 4″ (Ave.; 1″ below north). 1-2 Cloudy, cold; rain northeast. 3-5 Rain, cool. 6-7 Sunny, mild. 8-10 Rain, turning cold. 11-15 Cold, frost; showers. 16-18 Clearing, warm days, cold nights. 19-23 Clear & warm. 24-27 Rain, cool. 28-30 Very cold.

Dec. 1984: Temp. 50.5° (2° above ave.); Precip. 5″ (Ave.; 2″ below north). 1-5 Clear, warm days, cold nights. 6-8 Rain, mild. 9-14 Sunny, cool. 15-17 Rain, snow north; cold. 18-20 Clearing, turning cold. 21-25 Sunny, warm. 26-28 Rain, cooler. 29-31 Rain.

Jan. 1985: Temp. 40.5° (5° below ave.); Precip. 2″ (3″ below ave.; 0.5″ above north). 1-3 Cold, cloudy. 4-6 Rain, mild. 7-14 Cold wave, inter-mittent snow. 15-21 Clear & mild. 22-24 Rain, cold. 25-29 Sunny, warm. 30-31 Rain, warm.

Feb. 1985: Temp. 45° (4° below ave.); Precip. 3.5″ (1″ below ave.; 1″ above north). 1-4 Rain, mild. 5-7 Cold snap, frost. 8-10 Cloudy & mild; intermittent rain. 11-13 Cloudy, cold. 14-15 Cold, rain. 16-18 Clear, mild. 19-21 Rain, cold; snow north. 22-26 Clearing, cold. 27-28 Cold rain; snow northeast.

Mar. 1985: Temp. 54° (2.5° below ave.); Precip. 5″ (1″ below ave.; ave. north). 1-4 Cold, light snow. 5-7 Rain, snow, heavy northeast. 8-13 Rain, cold. 14-16 Sunny & warm. 17-21 Warm, showers. 22-25 Sunny, then showers. 26-28 Sunny, warm. 29-31 Rain.

Apr. 1985: Temp. 65° (Ave.; 1° below north); Precip. 1″ (5″ below ave.; 1″ below north). 1-3 Sunny south, showers north. 4-6 Cold, cloudy, then clearing. 7-11 Cloudy & warm. 12-14 Rain, flooding. 15-19 Cloudy, rain; then clearing & warm. 20-22 Showers, warm. 23-28 Cloudy, then clear, warm. 29-30 Rain, mild.

May 1985: Temp. 72° (0.5° below ave.; 1.5° below north); Precip. 2.5″ (2.5″ below ave.). 1-3 Sunny south, rain north. 4-7 Cloudy & warm. 8-10 Showers. 11-15 Clear, warmer. 16-19 Showers. 20-21 Clear, warm. 22-24 Showers, mild. 25-27 Showers. 28-31 Clear, mild.

June 1985: Temp. 80.5° (1.5° above ave.; 0.5° above north); Precip. 1.5″ (1.5″ below ave.). 1-7 Clear & hot; showers northeast. 8-10 Showers, warm. 11-15 Showers, seasonable. 16-19 Cloudy, rain, cool. 20-24 Showers, then clearing. 25-27 Showers. 28-30 Clear & warm.

July 1985: Temp. 82° (Ave.); Precip. 5″ (0.5″ above ave.; 2″ below north). 1-3 Clear & hot; showers northeast. 4-6 Seasonable; showers. 7-10 Cloudy, showers south. 11-15 Thundershowers north, hot. 16-21 Showers, hot. 22-24 Clear & hot. 25-28 Thunderstorms, hot. 29-31 Showers, heavy south & east.

Aug. 1985: Temp. 81° (Ave.; 1.5° below north); Precip. 9″ (5″ above ave.; 1″ above north). 1-5 Showers, hot. 6-9 Showers, seasonable. 10-15 Thundershowers, mild. 16-18 Clear & warm. 19-27 Showers, mild. 28-31 Showers.

Sept. 1985: Temp. 75° (1.5° below ave.); Precip. 3.5″ (Ave.; 3″ below north). 1-4 Sunny & hot; showers south. 5-9 Sunny, hot; showers north. 10-13 Showers. 14-18 Clear, hot. 19-22 Showers; mild then warm. 23-26 Clearing, cool. 27-30 Clear, warm; then showers.

Oct. 1985: Temp. 63° (2° below ave.; 3° below north); Precip. 2″ (0.5″ below ave.; 2″ below north). 1-4 Showers, then clear & cold. 5-7 Cloudy, warmer. 8-10 Showers, mild. 11-15 Clear, warm days, cold nights. 16-22 Clear, warm, rain northeast. 23-26 Partly cloudy, mild. 27-31 Showers, cold snap.

SUMMARY: *The winter is expected to be extremely variable with temperatures averaging above normal through December, below normal through January and February, then warming up again in March. Precipitation is anticipated to be above average in the west and below in the east while the snowfall should be above average. Extended cold waves are expected in mid- and late November, mid-December, mid-January, early February, and another prolonged one from late February into early March. Following a moderately wet November the precipitation will be light through January despite possible snowstorms at the close of the year. February, however, should be quite wet and snowy while March is anticipated to have slightly below-normal precipitation but above-average snowfall in the north.*

Several cool, wet and even snowy periods, interspersed with sunny and warm spells, are expected through April while the early part of May should be warm before frequent rains and cooler temperatures prevail for the balance of the month. June will start out sunny and pleasant and end with cooler than normal temperatures; precipitation will be slightly above average for the month.

The summer should be relatively mild with only a few brief hot spells. July may have less rain than usual, but August and September should be wet.

The beginning of fall may see a severe cold wave and frost, after which mild conditions should prevail until another very cold snap arrives at the end of October. Following fairly heavy storms through mid-September, more moderate rains are expected throughout October, with the possibility of an early snowstorm in northern sections.

Nov. 1984: Temp. 40° (1° below ave.; ave. east); Precip. 3.5″ (1.5″ above ave.; 0.5″ below east). 1-2 Cold snap, frost. 3-5 Rain, slightly mild. 6-8 Sunny, mild. 9-13 Rain, changing to snow; cold. 14-16 Cloudy, cold. 17-19 Clearing, turning mild. 20-22 Sunny, mild. 23-25 Rain, very mild. 26-30 Cold, snowstorm, then clearing.

Dec. 1984: Temp. 34° (5° above ave.); Precip. 1″ (1.5″ below ave.). 1-3 Clear, mild. 4-6 Rain, mild. 7-10 Showers, mild. 11-13 Light snow, cold. 14-17 Cold, snow. 18-20 Cloudy, cold. 21-25 Sunny. 26-28 Rain, mild. 29-31 Cold, snow.

Jan. 1985: Temp. 22.5° (Ave.); Precip. 0.5″ (1.5″ below ave.; 1″ below east). 1-3 Cloudy, colder, snow. 4-6 Snowstorm, slightly mild. 7-12 Cold wave, then clearing. 13-16 Snow, cold. 17-20 Sunny & mild. 21-23 Rain, milder. 24-28 Clearing, warm. 29-31 Rain, snow north; mild.

Feb. 1985: Temp. 26° (1° below ave.; 4° below east); Precip. 4″ (2.5″ above ave.; 1″ above east). 1-2 Cloudy, cold; snow north. 3-5 Rain & snow, mild. 6-7 Clear & cold. 8-11 Snow, heavy west; cold. 12-15 Cold, snow. 16-18 Partial clearing, flurries, milder. 19-22 Snowstorm, turning cold. 23-26 Severe cold. 27-28 Snow, cold.

Mar. 1985: Temp. 39° (2° above ave.); Precip. 2.5″ (0.5″ below ave.). 1-5 Cloudy, cold, snow. 6-8 Milder, sleet, snow east. 9-11 Sunny & mild. 12-14 Rain, snow north; mild then colder. 15-19 Cold, showers, then rain. 20-22 Rain, snow north. 23-26 Sunny, mild; then rain, cool. 27-31 Sunny, then rain; mild.

Apr. 1985: Temp. 50° (0.5° above ave.; 2° above east); Precip. 2″ (2″ below ave.). 1-4 Cold, snowstorm. 5-8 Sunny, warm; showers. 9-11 Warm, rain, snow north. 12-15 Rain, warm. 16-19 Clearing, warm. 20-22 Rain, cool. 23-26 Sunny, warming. 27-30 Clear, warm, then rain.

May 1985: Temp. 60° (0.5° below ave.; 2° above east); Precip. 2.5″ (0.5″ below ave.; ave. east). 1-4 Sunny & warm, showers. 5-7 Rain, very warm. 8-11 Turning cool; rain. 12-14 Sunny, warm, showers north. 15-18 Rain, warm. 19-22 Rain. 23-25 Cool, showers. 26-29 Clearing & warming. 30-31 Rain.

June 1985: Temp. 68.5° (2° below ave.; 1.5° above east); Precip. 3.5″ (0.5″ above ave.; 0.5″ above east). 1-3 Clear & hot. 4-7 Showers, warm. 8-12 Partly cloudy then rain; cool. 13-14 Clear, warm. 15-18 Rain, turning cool. 19-21 Cool, scattered showers. 22-25 Rain, warm. 26-28 Cloudy & cool. 29-30 Showers.

July 1985: Temp. 74° (1° below ave.; ave. east); Precip. 3″ (1″ below ave.). 1-3 Sunny & hot; showers northwest. 4-6 Cloudy, mild; showers east. 7-10 Thundershowers. 11-14 Showers, mild. 15-19 Sunny & warm, rain south. 20-22 Clear, hot; showers north. 23-29 Rain then clearing; warm. 30-31 Rain, hot.

Aug. 1985: Temp. 70.5° (3° below east); Precip. 5″ (1.5″ above ave.). 1-6 Showers, warm. 7-9 Cloudy. 10-14 Thundershowers, cool. 15-17 Clear, warming. 18-20 Showers. 21-24 Sunny, warm. 25-27 Showers, turning cool. 28-31 Sunny, cool, then rain.

Sept. 1985: Temp. 65° (1° below ave.; 1° above east); Precip. 5″ (2″ above ave.; 1″ above east). 1-5 Showers then cloudy, warm. 6-8 Showers, cooler. 9-10 Sunny, warm. 11-13 Rain. 14-23 Showers, warm. 24-28 Turning cold, then rain. 29-30 Very cold, possible snowstorm west.

Oct. 1985: Temp. 50.5° (4° below ave.; 1.5° below east); Precip. 1.5″ (1″ below ave.; 1″ above east). 1-2 Rain east, possible snow west, very cold. 3-6 Clear, turning warm. 7-9 Rain, mild. 10-12 Sunny & warm. 13-17 Showers, cool. 18-20 Rain, cool. 21-24 Clear, very mild. 25-29 Rain, cold. 30-31 Very cold, snowstorm north.

"Because of My Feet I Just Couldn't Go On!"

"Thanks to Feathersprings®, I finally got a spring in my step again . . ."

"*Retiring as a golf professional was my own decision. Being forced to stop playing altogether was something my sore aching feet forced me to do. It got to the point where I would play a few holes and have to quit . . . because of my feet I just couldn't go on! I had tried everything and nothing seemed to work. Now, thanks to Feathersprings my feet are absolutely pain-free and I finally got a spring in my step again.*"
Jock Hutchison Jr., Retired Golf Professional
Northfield, Illinois

73% of all Americans over 18 have foot problems.
Anybody can develop foot problems . . . no matter what your age or walk of life. A young person with foot pain shouldn't be surprised, because there are over 300 types of perplexing problems your feet can develop.

Natural support breaks down and problems begin.
Each of your feet is made up of 26 bones, 56 ligaments and 38 muscles, joined in such a way to provide springy foundation for the whole body. Foot problems begin and multiply as soon as something happens to destroy nature's built-in support mechanism.

Feathersprings replace nature's support system.
It's true! Feathersprings, which are made in West Germany, actually restore the balanced, elastic support nature intended your feet to have. That's why Feathersprings have already brought instant, lasting relief to over 3,000,000 people of all ages, with all types of painful foot problems.

Feathersprings will relieve your foot pain.
We're so certain Feathersprings Flexible Foot Supports will relieve your pain that if they don't, we'll refund your money in full with no questions asked.

Don't needlessly suffer pain and discomfort for another day. Although most people think that foot pain is normal, the fact is that it's not. And you don't have to live with it. Write for our FREE Fact Report. There's absolutely no obligation and no salesperson will call. Just fill out and mail the coupon below.

What people say in unsolicited testimonials, about Feathersprings:

"*. . . I have thoroughly enjoyed the comfort Feathersprings have provided me. You would not believe the difference they have made my feet feel—before I had such pain when walking because I have severe callus' on both of my feet.*"
M.W.R./Richmond, VA

"*I want to thank you for refunding to me the full amount of what I ordered. I admire your company for this with no strings or red tape.*"
—G.K.M./Warwick, RI

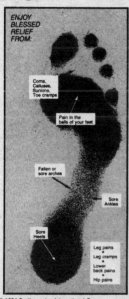

ENJOY BLESSED RELIEF FROM:

Corns, Calluses, Bunions, Toe cramps

Pain in the balls of your feet

Fallen or sore arches

Sore Ankles

Sore Heels

Leg pains • Leg cramps • Lower back pains • Hip pains

© 1984 Featherspring International Corp.
712 N. 34th Street
Seattle, Washington 98103

Since 1948

* Actual photo of a customer who sent us this letter.

SUMMARY: *The winter is expected to be extremely variable, but averaging out warmer than normal. Precipitation should be frequent but generally light despite above-average amounts of snowfall anticipated for late winter. Cold spells with snow are expected at the beginning and end of November, but December should be quite mild except for a cold period at mid-month. A snowstorm at the end of the year will usher in an intensely cold period that may last through the first half of January; however, the second half may be mild with little precipitation. Seasonal temperatures and frequent snowfall are anticipated through most of February, culminating in a severe cold snap that may extend into early March. The rest of March should be mild and quite wet in central and eastern sections, but drier than normal in the west.*

Following cold spells in the first and second weeks of April, sunny, mild, and dry weather is expected to prevail for the balance of the month, but thereafter frequent storms and subnormal temperatures should result in a cool and wet spring with the possibility of very heavy thundershowers in central sections at the end of May and in early June.

The summer is anticipated to be slightly milder than normal with frequent periods of subnormal temperatures and only a few brief hot spells, while frequent and occasionally severe thunderstorms in central and eastern sections should bring ample rainfall there and even some local flooding in early August. Far western sections, however, may expect less than normal amounts of rain.

Heavy rains are anticipated for September, culminating in a severe cold wave with snow and sleet at the end of the month. This will be followed by a warm and dry period through most of October before the arrival of another severe cold wave accompanying a snowstorm at the end of that month.

Nov. 1984: Temp. 33° (1° below ave.); Precip. 1″ (Ave.; 0.5″ below west). 1-2 Snow west, cold. 3-6 Clearing west, rain & snow east, cold. 7-9 Cold; sunny east, rain west. 10-14 Cold, snow. 15-20 Clearing, mild. 21-24 Rain changing to snow. 25-27 Snow west & north. 28-30 Sunny.

Dec. 1984: Temp. 25° (6° above ave.); Precip. 1″ (Ave.; 0.5″ below west). 1-6 Sunny, mild; showers east. 7-9 Rain, mild. 10-14 Sunny, cold, snow. 15-17 Snow, heavy central & east. 18-24 Sunny, mild, then cloudy. 25-28 Mild then cold; sleet. 29-31 Snow south, flurries north.

Jan. 1985: Temp. 14.5° (3° above ave.); Precip. 0.3″ (0.5″ below ave.). 1-6 Cold, flurries, then snowstorm. 7-12 Cold, flurries. 13-16 Mild

west, snow then mild east. 17-23 Sunny, mild; showers east. 24-28 Sunny, mild. 29-31 Mild west, colder east, snow north.

Feb. 1985: Temp. 19.5° (2° above ave.); Precip. 0.5″ (0.5″ below ave.). 1-4 Mild, flurries, snowstorm northeast. 5-10 Snow, then clearing. 11-15 Snow west & east; cold. 16-20 Flurries. 21-23 Severe cold, snow east. 24-28 Sunny east, then flurries; mild then snow west.

Mar. 1985: Temp. 33° (4° above ave.; 2° below west); Precip. 1.7″ (Ave.; 0.5″ above west). 1-3 Snow, cold. 4-9 Sunny, mild, then showers. 10-15 Cold, rain & snow. 16-22 Storm moving east, rain & snow. 23-28 Sleet, clearing & mild. 29-31 Rain, colder.

Apr. 1985: Temp. 50° (4° above ave.); Precip. 1.5″ (0.5″ below ave.; 1″ below west). 1-3 Snowstorm, cold. 4-8 Clearing, mild; showers west. 9-11 Rain, snowstorm north; cold. 12-15 Sunny, then showers. 16-19 Sunny, warm. 20-24 Cooler, rain. 25-27 Sunny, warm. 28-30 Rain.

May 1985: Temp. 56.5° (2° below ave.; 5° below west); Precip. 6″ (3° above ave.). 1-7 Intermittent rain; mild then cold. 8-10 Rain, cold. 11-14 Sunny, mild. 15-18 Heavy rain, cool. 19-22 Showers, cool. 23-28 Scattered showers, warming. 29-31 Rain.

June 1985: Temp. 66.5° (1.5° below ave.; 3° below west); Precip. 4″ (Ave.; 2″ below west). 1-4 Rain, mild. 5-7 Sunny, rain west. 8-10 Rain, warm. 11-13 Cloudy, warm. 14-16 Rain, turning cool. 17-20 Showers, mild. 21-24 Intermittent rain. 25-30 Cool, showers.

July 1985: Temp. 70° (3° below ave.; 5° below west); Precip. 3.5″ (Ave.). 1-3 Thundershowers, mild. 4-6 Cloudy, mild. 7-11 Intermittent showers. 12-14 Thundershowers, warm. 15-19 Sunny, warm then mild. 20-23 Thundershowers; mild west. 24-27 Sunny; showers west. 28-31 Showers.

Aug. 1985: Temp. 68.5° (2° below ave.); Precip. 3.5″ (Ave.; 1.5″ below west). 1-5 Thundershowers, heavy central & east; flooding. 6-8 Sunny, warm. 9-12 Showers. 13-16 Sunny, mild; showers west. 17-19 Rain. 20-24 Clear, turning hot. 25-27 Rain east, cloudy & cool. 28-31 Sunny then rain.

Sept. 1985: Temp. 58.5° (2° below ave.; 4° below west); Precip. 7″ (4.5″ above ave.; 3″ above west). 1-3 Cloudy, rain, warm. 4-6 Rain. 7-10 Sunny, warm. 11-16 Intermittent rain, hot. 17-22 Rain, turning cool. 23-25 Sunny, warming. 26-30 Severe cold, rain turning to snow.

Oct. 1985: Temp. 49° (0.5° below ave.; 1° above west); Precip. 1″ (1″ below ave.). 1-2 Frost, rain east. 3-6 Sunny, warm. 7-9 Rain, cool. 10-15 Sunny, warm. 16-20 Sunny, showers west & east. 21-24 Clear, warm. 25-27 Cold, frost, light snow. 28-31 Severe cold, snowstorm.

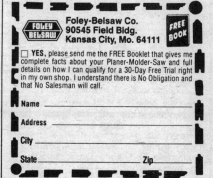

SUMMARY: *The winter is expected to be wetter and colder than usual while the total snowfall should be above average in the west, but normal in the rest of the region. November is anticipated to be cold and wet with a mild, dry period after midmonth. December, however, should have extended periods of mild weather, broken only by brief cold snaps at midmonth and the close of the year; the latter will usher in the first major snowstorm of the season, crossing the central and northern sections. A blizzard may be in the offing early in January, bringing a severe cold wave that may last until midmonth; this will be followed by an extended mild spell. February should be cold and wet with snow in central and northern sections. After a cold beginning, March will be relatively mild, with above-normal snowfall in the western and northern sections.*

The spring is expected to start out warmer and drier than normal, but then turn cool and wet. Frequent and often heavy rains in May and June will bring above-average rainfall to most of the region along with some flooding, but southwestern sections may be drier than usual.

After some cool periods in late June, temperatures should be close to the norm throughout the summer. Following heavy rains at the end of June, precipitation will be variable with heavy thundershowers in the north in mid-July, in the southwest in early August, and the southeast in late August.

Most of September may be quite warm but a severe cold wave, with snow and sleet in the north, may be in the offing for the last week and extending into early October. Thereafter, warm weather is anticipated until the arrival of another cold wave at the end of October. Heavy rains are anticipated in the west during September and October, but most of the region will be quite dry during the latter month.

Nov. 1984: Temp. 37.5° (1° below ave.; 3° below west); Precip. 3″ (1.5″ above ave.; 0.5″ above west). 1-5 Cold, rain; snow north. 6-7 Clear, cold. 8-11 Rain, cold. 12-15 Freeze; snow west. 16-21 Clear, warm. 22-24 Rain, cold. 25-27 Cold, rain & snow. 28-30 Clear, mild.

Dec. 1984: Temp. 32.5° (7° above ave.); Precip. 2.5″ (1.5″ above ave.; ave. west; 1″ below east). 1-3 Sunny, mild. 4-9 Cloudy, showers, cold. 10-13 Sunny, cold. 14-17 Cold, snow. 18-21 Clearing & warming. 22-25 Clear, mild. 26-27 Rain, turning cold. 28-31 Snow; rain southeast.

Jan. 1985: Temp. 18° (0.5° below ave.; 2° below south); Precip. 2″ (1″ above ave.; 0.5″ below

west, 1″ below central). 1-2 Cloudy, cold. 3-5 Snowstorm, blizzard. 6-10 Severe cold, snow. 11-13 Snow, heavy southeast, cold. 14-20 Cloudy, mild. 21-23 Rain, mild. 24-29 Sunny, warm. 30-31 Rain, warm.

Feb. 1985: Temp. 24.5° (Ave.; 2° below northwest); Precip. 1.5″ (0.5″ above ave.; 1″ above south, 2″ above east). 1-4 Cloudy, cold, snow; rain southeast. 5-7 Warming. 8-10 Mild, rain. 11-14 Cold, snow; rain southeast. 15-17 Sunny. 18-20 Snow, rain southeast. 21-25 Cold, snow, then clear. 26-28 Snow central & north.

Mar. 1985: Temp. 38° (3° above ave.; 1° below west); Precip. 2″ (Ave.; 1″ below south & east). 1-3 Cold, light snow. 4-6 Milder, snow; rain southeast. 7-10 Sunny, mild. 11-13 Rain, cool. 14-16 Sunny, mild. 17-21 Rain, sleet north; cold. 22-25 Rain. 26-28 Clear, warm. 29-31 Rain, snow north.

Apr. 1985: Temp. 52.5° (2° above ave.); Precip. 1″ (2.5″ below ave.; 0.5″ below east). 1-3 Cold; snow north, rain south. 4-9 Clear, warm. 10-13 Rain, cold. 14-17 Clearing, warm; showers. 18-19 Clear, warm. 20-23 Scattered showers, cooler. 24-27 Clear, warm. 28-30 Rain, mild.

May 1985: Temp. 60° (2° below ave.; ave. southeast); Precip. 6″ (2″ above ave.; ave. west; 1″ below east). 1-3 Warm, scattered showers. 4-10 Rain, cool. 11-13 Clear, warm. 14-16 Rain. 17-19 Rain, cool. 20-26 Intermittent rain, cool. 27-31 Clearing, warming, then rain.

June 1985: Temp. 72.5° (1° above ave.; 1° below south); Precip. 6″ (2″ above ave.; ave. northeast). 1-3 Sunny, hot. 4-6 Rain, mild. 7-10 Sunny, then rain; hot. 11-17 Rain, cool. 18-25 Cloudy, rain. 26-28 Mild. 29-30 Rain.

July 1985: Temp. 74.5° (2° below ave.; ave. east); Precip. 6″ (3″ above ave.; 1″ below east). 1-3 Cloudy, warm; rain north. 4-6 Clearing, showers west. 7-11 Sunny, hot; showers northeast. 12-25 Intermittent showers, hot. 26-28 Sunny, mild. 29-31 Showers.

Aug. 1985: Temp. 72.5° (1.5° below ave.); Precip. 2″ (1.5″ below ave.; 1.5″ above south). 1-4 Showers, hot. 5-7 Showers north; cloudy, milder. 8-12 Thundershowers, cooler. 13-16 Sunny, showers south. 17-19 Thundershowers. 20-25 Sunny, hot. 26-31 Showers, cool.

Sept. 1985: Temp. 65° (1° below ave.; 3° below south & east); Precip. 3″ (Ave.; 2″ above west, 2″ below southeast). 1-6 Showers; hot north & east. 7-13 Mild, showers. 14-16 Sunny, hot. 17-20 Rain, warm. 21-23 Rain. 24-28 Sunny, cool; showers. 29-30 Cold, rain; snow north.

Oct. 1985: Temp. 53° (1° below ave.); Precip. 1.5″ (1″ below ave.; 2″ below east, 1″ above southwest). 1-2 Clearing, cold, freeze. 3-6 Clear, warm. 7-9 Rain, mild. 10-16 Clear. 17-21 Sunny, rain west. 22-25 Scattered showers. 26-31 Cold, rain; snow north.

For regional boundaries, see map page 112

SUMMARY: *The winter is expected to be colder and drier than normal overall, but with large variations in temperature. November will be cold and wet with relief provided by a warm and dry third week. December will be mild early and late in the month, but cold and wet at midmonth. Thereafter, until early March, considerably less than normal precipitation is expected, except for heavy rains near the Gulf in early January. An extended cold wave, with frost extending to some sections of the Gulf, is expected the first half of January. The balance of the season should see mild periods during the first half of February and the middle of March more than offset by cold spells. Northern sections will receive above-average snowfall in February and March.*

Spring is expected to be cool and wet, with frequent rains from the second week of April to the second week of May causing some major flooding. Cool periods will more than compensate for brief warm spells.

In the summer milder than normal periods are anticipated in early July, late August, and early September. With the exception of central sections, the region will experience heavy and occasionally torrential rains during July and early August. Western and central sections should receive ample rainfall at the end of August and the first week of September.

A mild spell in late September extending into early October, and a cold wave at the end of October, should result in a cool fall. Rain will be above normal in central and northwestern sections, while the rest of the region will be comparatively dry.

Nov. 1984: Temp. 52° (3.5° below ave.; ave. west); Precip. 2" (0.5" below ave.; 2.5" above Gulf & east). 1-4 Cloudy & cold, then rain, heavy east. 5-7 Clear, mild. 8-11 Showers, cold. 12-16 Frost north, partly cloudy. 17-19 Clearing & warming. 20-23 Clear, unseasonably warm. 24-27 Rain, cold. 28-30 Frost central & north then warming.

Dec. 1984: Temp. 50.5° (2° above ave.; 4° above north); Precip. 2" (Ave.; 2" below southeast). 1-5 Sunny & mild, showers north. 6-12 Partly cloudy, few showers, cold. 13-17 Cold, rain, snow north. 18-20 Cloudy, cold. 21-24 Sunny & mild. 25-27 Rain, mild. 28-31 Partly cloudy, cold; showers east.

Jan. 1985: Temp. 42° (3° below ave.; 1° below north); Precip. 0.5" (1.5" below ave.; 0.5" below Gulf & west). 1-2 Cold snap. 3-5 Light rain, snow north. 6-13 Severe cold, freeze to Gulf. 14-17 Sunny, mild. 18-23 Partly cloudy, mild. 24-31 Clear & warm; then showers.

Feb. 1985: Temp. 49.5° (Ave.); Precip. 1" (1" below ave.). 1-4 Mild, then rain, colder. 5-11 Sunny, mild. 12-15 Showers, turning cold. 16-20 Sunny & seasonable, then rain. 21-23 Severe cold, frost central & north. 24-28 Mild, then rain, cold.

Mar. 1985: Temp. 55° (2° below ave.; 1° below north); Precip. 2" (1" below ave.; 3" below southwest). 1-3 Cold, snow north. 4-6 Rain, snow north. 7-9 Partly sunny, cold; rain east. 10-12 Showers, seasonable. 13-17 Sunny, warm; then rain northeast. 18-20 Few showers, warm. 21-28 Sunny, mild. 29-31 Rain, cold.

Apr. 1985: Temp. 63.5° (3° below ave.; 1° below north); Precip. 8.5" (4" above ave.; 1" above southeast). 1-4 Sunny, frost north. 5-9 Clear & warm, then cloudy. 10-12 Torrential rains, cold. 13-15 Clearing & warming. 16-18 Showers, warm. 19-22 Sunny & pleasant. 23-26 Rain, heavy north, then clearing; cool. 27-30 Heavy rain.

May 1985: Temp. 72° (2° below ave.; ave. west & Gulf); Precip. 5.5" (1" above ave.; 2" below Gulf & north). 1-4 Showers, warm. 5-9 Sunny, warm; showers northeast. 10-12 Showers, cool. 13-15 Sunny & warm. 16-19 Rain east, cool. 20-23 Clear & warm, then rain central and east. 24-28 Mild, showers. 29-31 Clear, hot west.

June 1985: Temp. 81° (1° below ave.; 1° above Gulf & west); Precip. 4" (1" above ave.; 3" above northeast). 1-8 Sunny & hot. 9-11 Rain, mild. 12-15 Rain east. 16-19 Sunny & hot; then showers, cool. 20-24 Partly cloudy,hot. 25-27 Showers, mild. 28-30 Hot.

July 1985: Temp. 84° (2° below ave.); Precip. 0" (2" below ave.; 3" above east, ave. west). 1-4 Hot; showers northwest. 5-7 Showers, milder. 8-11 Sunny north, thundershowers central & south. 12-15 Clear & hot; showers north. 16-20 Clear, hot. 21-25 Seasonable, few showers. 26-31 Sunny, milder.

Aug. 1985: Temp. 84° (1.5° below ave.; ave. Gulf); Precip. 3" (1" above ave.; 3" above east). 1-4 Showers, hot. 5-7 Seasonable, showers Gulf. 8-10 Showers, hot. 11-16 Few showers. 17-22 Sunny, then thundershowers. 23-25 Clear & hot. 26-31 Showers, mild.

Sept. 1985: Temp. 75.5° (3° below ave.; ave. Gulf); Precip. 4.5" (1" above ave.; 4" above northwest, 2" below Gulf). 1-2 Sunny & mild. 3-6 Showers, then clear. 7-13 Showers, warm. 14-18 Clear & hot, rain southwest. 19-21 Sunny, hot. 22-24 Showers, mild. 25-30 Clear, warm; rain north.

Oct. 1985: Temp. 64° (4° below ave.; ave. Gulf); Precip. 5" (2" above ave.; 2" below Gulf & northeast). 1-4 Clear, mild. 5-9 Showers, warm. 10-18 Clear & warm. 19-23 Rain, cool. 24-26 Sunny, mild. 27-29 Warm central & south, cool, showers north. 30-31 Showers, cool.

IS TAKING YOUR TEMPERATURE A HASSLE?

Can't See The Numbers? Can't Shake The Mercury All The Way Down? Has a Thermometer Ever Slipped Out Of Your Hand And Smashed On The Floor?

These annoyances are now a thing of the past. Finally a leading N.Y. physician has developed a thermometer that is safe and accurate for infants and children and is the perfect adult thermometer as well. Its numerals are large and easy to see, and the scales are color-zoned making them virtually mistake proof. Because of its practical size, it won't slip out of your hand and one or two snaps brings the mercury all the way down in a jiffy. It's designed with a natural stop point at the "Safety Shoulders" so over-insertion in the rectum of infants is prevented.

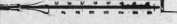

SAFTYTHERM® THERMOMETER

Act today, money back guarantee; Mail $3.95 plus $1.00 handling to SMB Celsius Co. Inc., P.O. Box 204, 25 Central Park Rd., Plainview, N.Y. 11803

For regional boundaries, see map page 112

SUMMARY: The winter is expected to be considerably colder than usual in the central and northern parts of the region and slightly colder in southern sections. The seasonal precipitation is anticipated to be close to normal, but with below-average snowfall. Following a cold beginning, November should be quite mild until the final week when a moderately severe cold period is expected. December should be warm despite a cold snap towards the end. Frequent snowstorms in the mountains during December will bring above-average amounts of snow to central and southern sections. A snowstorm and severe cold wave early in January are anticipated for central and northern sections, while mild weather should prevail in the south. The first half of February may be seasonable to mild before an extended cold period sets in that may persist into early March. Both February and March are expected to be colder and snowier than usual.

Following a cold beginning, the spring is expected to be fairly mild through most of April, with below-average precipitation, except in northern sections. Cool, wet periods will be frequent through May and June in the central and northern parts, while the south may have temperatures fairly close to normal with below-average precipitation.

The summer will be cool during the latter part of June, with brief hot spells occurring during July and August, and cool spells during early September. Precipitation will be light except in the south.

The fall should be sunny and warm except for a possible cold snap in early October. Temperatures will be seasonable for the remainder of the month with a continuation of subnormal precipitation.

Nov. 1984: Temp. 39° (1° below ave.; 1° above north); Precip. 2″ (0.5″ above ave.; 0.5″ below north). 1-4 Cold, rain, snow north; then clearing. 5-8 Rain, mild central & north; sunny south. 9-15 Sunny. 16-20 Rain, then clearing. 21-23 Rain & snow, cold. 24-27 Cold, sunny; snow north & east. 28-30 Sunny, cold.

Dec. 1984: Temp. 33° (3° above ave.); Precip. 1.5″ (0.5″ below ave.; ave. north). 1-5 Cold, then mild; showers. 6-9 Rain, snow mountains, cold. 10-13 Clear. 14-17 Cold, rain & snow. 18-24 Mild, rain, snow mountains. 25-29 Cold, snow. 30-31 Cold, snow west & south.

Jan. 1985: Temp. 20.5° (8° below ave.; ave. south); Precip. 1.5″ (Ave.; 1″ below south). 1-4 Cold, snowstorm. 5-9 Cold, snow then clearing. 10-12 Snow central & north, turning cold. 13-18 Cloudy, cold. 19-21 Snow central &

north, cloudy south. 22-26 Sunny, cold. 27-31 Sleet, snow mountains.

Feb. 1985: Temp. 30° (4° below ave.; 1.5° below south); Precip. 1.5″ (0.5″ above ave.; 1″ below south). 1-2 Rain & snow. 3-6 Cloudy, then sunny, mild. 7-16 Sleet; snow mountains. 17-20 Snow; clearing north. 21-23 Cold, clear. 24-26 Snowstorm, cold. 27-28 Sunny, cold.

Mar. 1985: Temp. 35.5° (5° below ave.; 1° below south); Precip. 1.5″ (0.5″ below ave.). 1-4 Cold, intermittent snow. 5-9 Sunny, cold; rain north. 10-14 Snow, then sunny & mild. 15-18 Sleet, snow mountains. 19-23 Cold, rain, snow. 24-27 Clearing. 28-31 Sleet, then clearing.

Apr. 1985: Temp. 53° (2.5° above ave.; 4° above north); Precip. 1″ (1″ below ave.; ave. north). 1-7 Clear, mild, rain north. 8-10 Rain, cool. 11-13 Clear, mild. 14-16 Showers, mild. 17-20 Sunny & warm, rain north. 21-25 Showers, then clear. 26-30 Cold, showers; snow south.

May 1985: Temp. 54° (5° below ave.; 1° below south); Precip. 3″ (1.5″ above ave.; 0.5″ below south). 1-4 Rain, snow mountains; cool. 5-7 Light rain; clearing & warming south. 8-12 Clearing, warm. 13-17 Cloudy, intermittent rain. 18-21 Showers, cold; sunny south. 22-28 Clearing, warm. 29-31 Scattered showers.

June 1985: Temp. 65° (3.5° below ave.; ave. south); Precip. 1″ (Ave.; 1″ above north, 0.5″ below south). 1-4 Cold, showers. 5-10 Sunny, warm; showers north. 11-15 Showers, cooler. 16-18 Sunny, cool. 19-22 Sunny & warm; rain north. 23-28 Showers, warm. 29-30 Rain.

July 1985: Temp. 76.5° (1° below ave.; 1.5° above south); Precip. 0.5″ (0.5″ below ave.; 1.5″ below south). 1-2 Cool, rain central & north. 3-8 Sunny, warm north, showers south. 9-11 Showers, hot. 12-18 Sunny, hot, showers north. 19-22 Rain, cool. 23-26 Clear, hot. 27-29 Sunny, hot. 30-31 Showers, partly sunny.

Aug. 1985: Temp. 76° (1° above ave.; 2° above north); Precip. 0.4″ (0.5″ below ave.; ave. south). 1-4 Showers, hot. 5-8 Hot, showers east & south. 9-14 Clear, hot; showers. 15-17 Mild, showers. 18-20 Clear, hot. 21-24 Scattered showers, hot. 25-28 Sunny, hot; showers north. 29-31 Showers, warm; cold north.

Sept. 1985: Temp. 62.5° (2.5° below ave.; 0.5° above south); Precip. 0.1″ (0.8″ below ave.). 1-4 Cool, showers north; mild south. 5-12 Cloudy, showers. 13-16 Thundershowers, mild. 17-19 Warm; showers north. 20-22 Cold, frost central & north; cloudy south. 23-30 Clear, warm.

Oct. 1985: Temp. 55° (2° above ave.); Precip. 0.5″ (0.7″ below ave.). 1-4 Sunny, warm. 5-8 Cool, showers north; warm south. 9-13 Clear, warm. 14-19 Turning cold, intermittent rain. 20-25 Clearing, warm. 26-31 Sunny central & south, rain & snow north.

14. SOUTHWEST DESERT

For regional boundaries, see map page 112

SUMMARY: *The winter will be warmer than usual until mid-February, and then have largely subnormal temperatures. Precipitation should be above average through early January before becoming considerably below normal for the balance of the season. November is expected to be warmer than normal into the final week, but then a cold wave and possible frost may occur. December should be milder than average up until Christmas, except for a wet and cool spell at midmonth. Cool waves and moderate rain at the end of December will extend into the second week of January. Frost may occur with these cold snaps. Mild and dry weather is then expected to persist until mid-February, when an extended cold spell is anticipated on into early March. Warm and dry periods should then alternate with cool and wet spells for the remainder of the month.*

Spring is expected to see fairly large variations in temperature through April and May, with the cooler spells outweighing the warmer in western sections and vice-versa in the east. April rains are anticipated to be above average, but May and June should be quite dry except for some rains in the east.

Milder than normal spells are expected in early and mid-July and the second week of August, but otherwise near normal hot weather is anticipated for the summer in the north, and generally hotter than average weather in the south. Fewer thundershowers than usual should occur in western sections, but more than normal in the east.

Slightly warmer than average values should prevail until mid-October in the west. In the east, a cold snap is expected at the end of September.

Nov. 1984: Temp. 61° (0.5° above ave.; 1° below south); Precip. 1.5″ (1″ above ave.). 1-4 Cool, showers west, then rain east. 5-15 Sunny, warmer. 16-18 Rain west; showers east, cool. 19-21 Clear, warm. 22-23 Rain, cold snap. 24-27 Frost west, sunny. 28-30 Clear & warm.

Dec. 1984: Temp. 55.5° (2.5° above ave.); Precip. 1.5″ (0.5″ above ave.; Ave. east). 1-6 Clear, warmer. 7-9 Partly cloudy, cool. 10-13 Clear & warm, cool east. 14-16 Rain, cool. 17-22 Partly cloudy, cool. 23-25 Clear & warm. 26-31 Cold, rain; then frost.

Jan. 1985: Temp. 54.5° (2° above ave.); Precip. 0.5″ (0.3″ below ave.). 1-3 Partly cloudy, cool. 4-6 Rain west; cold. 7-9 Frost, few showers east. 10-14 Sunny, cool. 15-18 Warm, few showers. 19-21 Seasonable west, cloudy & cold east. 22-26 Clear & warm, then cloudy & cool. 27-31 Sunny & warm.

Feb. 1985: Temp. 54° (2° below ave.); Precip. 0.1″ (0.5″ below ave.). 1-4 Partly cloudy, cool. 5-10 Clear & warmer. 11-13 Cloudy, cool. 14-17 Cloudy, frost; showers east. 18-20 Rain, cool. 21-25 Clearing, cool. 26-28 Few showers west, cloudy east; cool.

Mar. 1985: Temp. 57.5° (3° below ave.); Precip. 0.4″ (0.4″ below ave.; 1″ above south). 1-2 Partly cloudy, cold. 3-5 Rain, cold. 6-10 Clear & warm west, clearing east. 11-14 Cool, showers east, then sunny & warm. 15-18 Cloudy, cold. 19-21 Rain, warming. 22-27 Clear & warm. 28-31 Cloudy, mild, sprinkles.

Apr. 1985: Temp. 68° (Ave.); Precip. 0.8″ (0.5″ above ave.). 1-8 Clear & warm. 9-13 Cloudy, cooler, few showers. 14-16 Warm, then rain, cooler. 17-21 Partly cloudy, warm. 22-25 Clear & warm west, showers east. 26-30 Rain, cool, then clearing.

May 1985: Temp. 75° (2° below ave.; ave. east); Precip. 0″ (0.1″ below ave.). 1-2 Sunny & warm. 3-5 Mild, few showers. 6-8 Clearing, warmer. 9-13 Clear & warm; cloudy & cool east. 14-17 Cloudy, mild. 18-22 Partly cloudy, hot. 23-27 Clear, heat wave west; showers then rain east. 28-31 Sunny, hot.

June 1985: Temp. 85.5° (1° below ave.; 2° above east); Precip. 0″ (0.2″ below ave.; ave. east). 1-2 Partly cloudy, mild; hot east. 3-7 Sunny, hot. 8-12 Clear, hot west; few showers east. 13-16 Partly cloudy, cooler. 17-24 Sunny, hot. 25-28 Clear & very hot. 29-30 Cloudy, milder.

July 1985: Temp. 92° (Ave.; 2° above south); Precip. 1″ (0.4″ above ave.; 1.5″ below south & east). 1-3 Clear, hot. 4-7 Few showers, milder. 8-12 Sunny, hot. 13-15 Hot; rain east. 16-20 Sunny & hot, then thundershowers, milder. 21-23 Sunny, hot. 24-31 Sunny, continuing hot.

Aug. 1985: Temp. 89.5° (0.5° below ave.; 1° above south); Precip. 0.5″ (0.5″ below ave.; 2″ above east). 1-4 Partly cloudy, few showers, very hot. 5-13 Thundershowers, hot. 14-18 Sunny, hot. 19-22 Showers, heavy east. 23-25 Clear, hot. 26-29 Showers east, cooler. 30-31 Seasonably warm.

Sept. 1985: Temp. 85° (0.5° above ave.); Precip. 0.2″ (0.4″ below ave.; 0.5″ above south; ave. east). 1-3 Clear, hot. 4-6 Clear & hot west, rain east. 7-8 Cloudy, showers west. 9-11 Showers, hot. 12-17 Clear & hot, then showers west. 18-21 Clear & hot. 22-24 Showers east. 25-30 Clear; hot.

Oct. 1985: Temp. 74° (1° above ave.); Precip. 0″ (0.5″ below ave.; 0.5″ above east). 1-5 Clear, hot west, milder east. 6-8 Showers, warm. 9-14 Partly cloudy, seasonable, showers west. 15-19 Cloudy & mild, then rain east. 20-23 Rain, cool. 24-31 Mostly sunny & warm.

SUMMARY: *The winter is expected to be considerably milder than normal and to have slightly below-average rainfall and snowfall overall, but with great month-to-month variability. November should be mild through the third week before a cold wave and frost arrive while central and northern sections may get heavy rains and flooding late in the month. December should remain fairly mild with well above-average rainfall in lower elevations and above-average snowfall in the southern mountains. A severe cold wave is expected in early January that may persist through the third week in the southern part of the region. February is expected to be mild and wet with above-average precipitation in the south and above-average snowfall in the north. No large departures in temperature from the norm are anticipated for March while light precipitation should result in a fairly dry month.*

The spring is anticipated to start out comparatively warm and dry and become progressively cooler and wetter. Following a cold snap at the end of March, mild wet weather should prevail until another cool period arrives at the end of April. Several brief mild spells are anticipated during May, but more extended cool periods are expected in June with frequent rain during this period.

Several hot spells in both July and August should result in a warmer than normal summer with little precipitation.

The warm and dry weather is expected to continue on into the fall with hot, dry spells at the end of September and mid-October dominating the cool and slightly wet periods in between.

Nov. 1984: Temp. 48.5° (3° above ave.); Precip. 4″ (1″ below ave.; 2″ above north). 1-3 Rain, then clearing; cold. 4-9 Rain, mild. 10-13 Sunny, very mild. 14-16 Rain, cooler. 17-20 Heavy rain, floods in Willamette Basin. 21-23 Showers. 24-27 Clearing, cold, frost. 28-30 Sunny & mild, rain north.

Dec. 1984: Temp. 44.5° (3.5° above ave.); Precip. 10″ (3.5″ above ave.; 1″ above north). 1-5 Sunny & mild, then rain. 6-10 Rain, snow mountains. 11-16 Showers, snow higher elevations. 17-27 Rain, mild. 28-31 Rain, clearing north; cold.

Jan. 1985: Temp. 36° (3.5° below ave.; 1° above north); Precip. 3″ (3″ below ave.). 1-4 Showers, snow mountains; cold. 5-9 Severe cold wave. 10-13 Freezing rain, snow mountains. 14-16 Showers, cold north. 17-19 Sunny north, cold south. 20-22 Rain & sleet, cold south. 23-26 Clear & mild north, cloudy south. 27-31 Rain.

Feb. 1985: Temp. 44.5° (1.5° above ave.); Precip. 5″ (1″ above ave.; 0.5″ below north). 1-2 Clearing, mild. 3-9 Rain, snow mountains; mild. 10-15 Rain, cold. 16-19 Clear, cold. 20-23 Showers, cold. 24-28 Rain, snow mountains; cold wave, frost.

Mar. 1985: Temp. 46.5° (0.5° above ave.; 0.5° below north); Precip. 2″ (1.5″ below ave.; 0.5″ below south). 1-3 Rain, snow north, cold. 4-6 Sunny, then rain. 7-8 Clearing. 9-12 Rain, cold, then clearing. 13-17 Rain, snow mountains. 18-22 Rain, cold. 23-25 Clear, mild. 26-29 Rain, cold snap. 30-31 Clearing.

Apr. 1985: Temp. 55° (4.5° above ave.); Precip. 1″ (1.5″ below ave.). 1-5 Clear & warm, then rain. 6-8 Partly sunny, warm; rain south. 9-11 Cloudy, cool. 12-16 Sunny & warm, showers north. 17-21 Rain. 22-25 Clear, warm. 26-30 Rain, cool.

May 1985: Temp. 56.5° (Ave.); Precip. 3.5″ (1.5″ above ave.; 0.5″ above north). 1-4 Rain, cool. 5-8 Rain, continued cool. 9-12 Sunny, warm. 13-16 Rain, unseasonably cold. 17-20 Partial clearing, then rain, cool. 21-25 Mostly sunny, some rain, warming. 26-31 Rain, seasonable, then cool.

June 1985: Temp. 61° (1.5° below ave.); Precip. 2″ (0.5″ above ave.; 1.5″ above north). 1-4 Rain, cool. 5-9 Clearing, turning warm. 10-14 Rain, unseasonably cool. 15-18 Sunny, warm. 19-23 Rain, heavy north; very cool. 24-27 Clear, warm. 28-30 Rain, very cool.

July 1985: Temp. 71.5° (4° above ave.); Precip. 1″ (0.5″ above ave.; 0.5″ below north). 1-6 Heat wave, clear. 7-12 Partly cloudy, warm, sprinkles. 13-15 Rain, cooler. 16-17 Sunny & warm, showers north. 18-21 Rain, cool. 22-26 Clear, hot. 27-31 Sunny, warm.

Aug. 1985: Temp. 70° (2.5° above ave.); Precip. 0.5″ (0.7″ below ave.). 1-3 Few showers, cool. 4-6 Clearing, warm. 7-11 Showers, then sunny & warm. 12-14 Sprinkles, mild. 15-20 Sunny, turning hot. 21-24 Showers, warm. 25-28 Sunny, warm. 29-31 Rain, cool.

Sept. 1985: Temp. 65° (2.5° above ave.; 0.5° above north); Precip. 0.1″ (1.5″ below ave.). 1-2 Rain, warm. 3-6 Clear, warm. 7-11 Cloudy, cool, then turning sunny; rain north. 12-14 Intermittent rain. 15-18 Sunny, warm. 19-21 Cloudy, mild; showers north. 22-28 Clear, warm. 29-30 Cloudy, cool.

Oct. 1985: Temp. 57° (2.5° above ave.; 1.5° above north); Precip. 1.5″ (1.5″ below ave.; 2.5″ below south). 1-3 Cool, showers. 4-6 Showers, mild. 7-13 Alternately clear & warm, cloudy & seasonable. 14-19 Intermittent light to moderate rain, cool. 20-22 Clear & warm. 23-29 Partly cloudy, slightly mild. 30-31 Moderate to heavy rain, turning cold.

WE BUILD OUR STOVES WITHOUT COMPROMISE.

When considering a stove or fireplace insert, it's difficult to know what features are important. At Consolidated Dutchwest, our approach to your concerns is very straightforward. **We build in all the essential features right from the start.** We do not compromise on important features so that you won't have to either.

EVERY KEY FEATURE IS BUILT-IN

Our unique convection stoves and fireplace inserts have everything necessary for efficient, convenient, and safe burning of wood or coal. We start by using all cast-iron construction for maximum heat transfer and long life. Double wall construction creates circulating and radiant heat (blowers are available). Double-chambered baffles with an optional catalytic combustor provide exceptional efficiency. Consolidated Dutchwest convection stoves burn wood or coal (all parts necessary for each are standard), and come with an ashbin for easy cleaning, a shaker grate, dual air sources, front and side loading doors, glass windows, and a screen for open hearth burning.

Our designs not only stress performance, but safety and appearance as well. All models are airtight and fully tested to national and local standards. Each stove is carefully cast and assembled by hand. Federal-period styling, highlighted with solid brass trim, creates a classic sense of elegance and beauty.

FREE CATALYTIC COMBUSTOR

To introduce our new line of catalytic wood and coal stoves, and encourage the use of the latest developments in safe, clean woodburning, we will be giving away a free Corning Catalytic Combustor with every stove purchased this season. Contact us for more information.

For your FREE Color Catalogue, write or call (toll-free) today!

1-800-225-8277

(in Mass. call 617-747-1963)

16. CALIFORNIA

For regional boundaries, see map page 112

SUMMARY: *The winter is expected to be milder and wetter than normal in north-coastal sections while the interior and the south should be drier than usual. Snowfall should be above average in the central and northern Sierra Nevadas but below in the southern mountains. November will be warm until the last week when a cold wave may bring frost to northern interior sections. December should be mild, but colder than normal with above-average precipitation at the higher elevations. January will also be mild (despite an early cold wave that may bring frost to the Central Valley) with above-normal precipitation in the north; however, watch for a snowstorm in the southern mountains early in the month. Late January and early February may be stormy in the north with a possible freeze in interior sections toward the latter part of February. Temperatures will then be seasonable until the middle of March when heavy rains and snow are expected.*

Spring is anticipated to be near normal in the south, but colder and wetter than usual in the north with above-average snowfall in the Sierra Nevadas through May. After a sunny beginning, April should be cool with frequent showers. May through early June should see some cool, wet periods after which mild, dry weather is expected to prevail.

The summer should be sunnier than usual in the south, while the interior may experience brief heat waves at the beginning and end of July and in late August. Northern coastal sections are anticipated to be cloudy, cool, and wet.

After a cool beginning, the fall should be sunny and warm until mid-October. Thereafter, cloudy, wet periods will alternate with clear, hot spells to close out the month.

Nov. 1984: Temp. 58° (3.5° above ave.; 1° below interior); Precip. 1″ (1″ below ave.). 1-3 Sunny, mild. 4-8 Rain central & north, sunny south. 9-14 Sunny, warm. 15-17 Rain south, sunny north. 18-21 Rain north, showers south; mild. 22-26 Cool, frost central valley. 27-30 Clear; warm south, cold interior.

Dec. 1984: Temp. 54° (5° above ave.; 1.5° above south & interior); Precip. 6″ (2.5° above ave.; 1.5° above south & east). 1-2 Mild. 3-7 Rain, snow mountains. 8-12 Frost central valley. 13-16 Showers north, rain south. 17-20 Rain, snow mountains. 21-27 Rain north, sunny south. 28-31 Rain, snow mountains.

Jan. 1985: Temp. 53° (4° above ave.; 1.5° above south & interior); Precip. 6.5″ (1.5″ above ave.; 1″ below south). 1-5 Rain, snow mountains. 6-9 Cold; frost interior. 10-12 Showers north; sunny south. 13-18 Cold north, warm south. 19-21 Rain north, sunny south. 22-25 Clear. 26-31 Rain, snow mountains.

Feb. 1985: Temp. 54° (2.5° above ave.; 2° below interior & south); Precip. 4.5″ (1″ above ave.; 1″ below interior & south). 1-2 Clearing, cool. 3-11 Rain north, snow mountains, sunny south. 12-16 Sunny, cool interior. 17-21 Showers; frost central valley. 22-24 Showers north, sunny south. 25-28 Rain, snow mountains.

Mar. 1985: Temp. 53° (0.5° above ave.; 3° below interior); Precip. 2.5″ (Ave.; 0.5″ below south & interior). 1-4 Rain, clearing north. 5-13 Clear & warm. 14-19 Rain, cold; snow central Sierras. 20-25 Clearing & warming. 26-29 Cloudy, cold, showers. 30-31 Clear & warm.

Apr. 1985: Temp. 55.5° (0.5° above ave.); Precip. 3″ (1.5° above ave.; ave. interior). 1-3 Clear, warm. 4-6 Rain north, sunny south; warm. 7-10 Rain, showers desert; cool. 11-15 Cloudy, then rain. 16-21 Rain, cool. 22-26 Sunny, then cloudy; rain south. 27-30 Cloudy, warm.

May 1985: Temp. 56° (2° below ave.; ave. south); Precip. 1.5″ (1″ above ave.; ave. south & interior). 1-5 Rain, cold north. 6-12 Clearing. 13-16 Rain north, showers south. 17-20 Cool, rain north & interior. 21-25 Sunny, turning hot. 26-28 Cloudy, warm. 29-31 Rain, cool north.

June 1985: Temp. 57.5° (3.5° below ave.; ave. south, 1° below interior); Precip. 0″ (Ave.). 1-4 Cloudy north, sunny south. 5-9 Showers north. 10-16 Scattered showers, warm. 17-20 Cloudy & cool coast, sunny & warm inland. 21-27 Clearing. 28-30 Showers, cool north.

July 1985: Temp. 59.6° (2.5° below ave.; 2° above south & interior); Precip. 0″ (Ave.). 1-6 Warm, hot inland. 7-12 Clear & hot, cool coast. 13-16 Sunny, warm. 17-19 Showers, milder. 20-24 Mild south & inland, cool north & coast. 25-31 Hot south & inland, cool north & coast.

Aug. 1985: Temp. 59° (4° below ave.; 1° above south & interior); Precip. 0″ (0.1″ below ave.). 1-6 Sunny, warm south & inland; cloudy, cool north & coast. 7-12 Hot south & inland. 13-16 Cloudy north & coast, showers south. 17-19 Cloudy, hot inland & south. 20-27 Clear, hot; cool north & coast. 28-31 Cloudy, mild.

Sept. 1985: Temp. 60° (4° below ave.; 2° below south & interior); Precip. 0.2″ (Ave.; 0.2″ below south & interior). 1-5 Cloudy, mild. 6-11 Clearing, hot south. 12-14 Rain north; warm south. 15-20 Clear, warm. 21-23 Cloudy, mild. 24-27 Hot south & inland. 28-30 Cloudy.

Oct. 1985: Temp. 60° (0.5° below ave.; 1° above south & inland); Precip. 0.5″ (0.5″ below ave.). 1-5 Cloudy, cool north, warm south. 6-12 Clear, warm, cool north. 13-16 Cloudy, rain. 17-19 Showers north, warm south. 20-26 Clear, warm. 27-31 Cloudy, cool; showers north.

Indian Summer: What, Why, and When

☐ AFTER LABOR DAY HAS PASSED, IT seems that almost any warm day in the northern part of the United States is referred to by most people as "Indian summer." And while their error is certainly not of the world-shaking variety, they *are*, for the most part, in error.

Besides specific dates, there are certain Indian summer criteria to be met. Indian summer is warm, of course. In addition, however, the atmosphere during Indian summer is hazy or smoky, there is no wind, the barometer is standing high, and the nights are clear and chilly. Meteorologists describe these fall conditions as caused by conversion of a moving, cool, shallow polar air mass into a deep, warm, and stagnant anticyclone (high pressure) system, which has the effect of concentrating natural dust and smoke in the air near the ground and causing a large swing in temperature between day and night.

The more controversial aspect of Indian summer is the *time* of its occurrence. Or whether or not there *is* a certain time. Most would agree that warm days in the fall do not of themselves constitute Indian summer unless they follow a spell of cold weather or a good hard frost.

Beyond that, many references to Indian summer in American literature indicate a time of "late fall" or "after late October." This is in contrast, therefore, with the time of Indian summer in old England, which can come in September, known then as St. Augustine's

summer; in October, St. Luke's summer; or in November, St. Martin's summer. Those particular saints' days occur August 28, October 18, and November 11, respectively.

For the past 193 years this publication (as well as many other 19th-century almanacs) has always adhered to the saying, "If All Saints brings out winter, St. Martin's brings out Indian summer." Accordingly, Indian summer can occur between St. Martin's Day, November 11, and November 20. If the conditions that constitute Indian summer, described above, do not occur within those dates, then there is *no* Indian summer that year.

If there is a period of warm fall weather at a time other than between St. Martin's Day and November 20, then such a time could be correctly described as being *like* Indian summer.

Finally, why is Indian summer called Indian summer? Some say it comes to us from early Indians who believed the condition was caused by a certain wind emanating from the court of their God Cautantowwit or the Southwestern God. Others feel the term evolved from the fact that around the time of Indian summer, or shortly before it, the deciduous trees are "dressed" as colorfully as Indians.

The most probable origin of the term, in our view, goes back to the very early settlers in New England. Each year they would welcome the arrival of cold wintry weather in late October when they could leave their stockades without worrying about Indian attacks and commence preparing their fields for the following spring plantings. The Indians didn't like attacking in cold weather. But then came a time, almost every year around St. Martin's Day, when it would suddenly turn warm again, and the Indians would decide to have one more go at the settlers even though it was no longer their normal raiding season. "Indian summer," the settlers called it. ☐☐

The Night the Florida Keys Almost Washed Away

In 1935 a killer hurricane struck this chain of islands with such ferocity that it left little but death and destruction in its wake.

by Raymond Schuessler
illustrated by Austin Stevens

☐ FIFTY YEARS AGO, ON THE DAY before Labor Day in 1935, storm warnings were posted for south Florida when a low-pressure center was reported northeast of Turks Island in the Bahamas. On the Florida Keys the natives, wary of the power of tropical storms, began their usual rituals of battening down — stocking up on fresh water, tying down boats or sinking them with their engines removed, buying supplies of candles, kerosene, and canned food.

Soon the wind picked up and the palm trees groaned and genuflected. The day had turned gray and ominous, and the ground began to tremble from the pounding of angry waves. The barometer began to plummet to 29, then 28, then an awesome 27.15. The faces of people who were still outside began to bleed from the sharp, blowing sand. A flimsy automobile was lifted and thrown against a billboard as the winds began to roar like a runaway train.

This was a killer hurricane of immense power.

Through shuttered windows, people who were close enough eyed their railroad, a marvel of engineering that had been called the Eighth Wonder of the World. Henry Flagler, a multimillionaire who had made his fortune with Rockefeller, had built the railroad in 1905, leapfrogging it over a necklace of 29 islands for 156 miles from Miami to Key West. It had taken seven years to complete and was the most expensive shortline in American history. Hundreds of lives had been lost in its construction. But would the carefully built trestles and bridges, which had survived for 23 years through every kind of storm, withstand the fury of this massive hurricane whose winds began to scream at 200 miles an hour, gusting to 250? It was almost as if the sea had resented the intrusion and was now sending a storm to wreak vengeance.

The railroad and residents weren't the only vulnerable objects in the path. In 1934 President Franklin Roosevelt had put 700 of the vast army of unemployed men, many of them veterans, to work building a highway to parallel the railroad. These men were bedded down in flimsy shacks at camps from Snake Creek to Lower Matecumbe. The Veterans Administration had set up a plan to evacuate the workers in case of hurricane. On Labor Day, with the storm's intensity building, a call went through to the East Coast Railroad to send down a train from Homestead, on the mainland, to evacuate the highway workers and residents. But no train was available, and by the time a train and crew were found in Miami, it was already late in the day. The train finally left Homestead a little after 5 P.M., backing up toward the Keys on the one-track railroad, stopping often to clear away fallen trees and pick up hysterical evacuees.

At Snake Creek, a loose cable hooked the engine cab. It took an hour to free it. In three and a half hours the train had covered only 45 miles. Meanwhile the highway workers with their bundles of belongings huddled by the tracks, waiting fearfully as the storm shrieked around them.

The winds increased as pressure fell: soon the barometer would plunge to an incredible 26.35, the lowest reading

ever recorded on land. The pressure was so intense that refrigerator doors popped open, glass jars exploded, windows burst, and small animals and fish died. Many small animals were sandblasted to death by the 250-mile-an-hour winds.

The lighthouse keeper at Alligator Reef, J. A. Duncan, saw a huge wave at least 20 feet high rolling toward the 90-foot lighthouse. Clutching a ladder, he saw the wave crack over him and shimmy up to the top of the lighthouse.

This wasn't just a 20-foot surfer's wave; it was the whole ocean moving in at a level 20 feet higher than normal. Many could have survived except for this giant wall of water that washed over the islands. And the tremendous undertow that accompanied it sucked everything with it — people, wreckage, even entire islands.

Some people lashed themselves to trees and hung on while the wind and water lashed them mercilessly. Children floated by in beds, screaming. On Windley Key, the Becom family saw their house swept away and fought through the storm to huddle in their car. Turning the headlights on, they saw debris piling up on the windward side to form a barrier. Five frantic survivors who saw the headlights crowded in with the seven Becoms.

At Tavernier, Judge "Doc" Lowe, justice of the peace, had built a special hurricane shelter. He had poured a solid concrete foundation with a concrete house over it anchored by two huge chains. When the hurricane hit, Doc led his family to the shelter. As they nestled in the fortlike cubicle, a sudden gust lifted the whole kaboodle, concrete, chain, and all, into the air and cracked it. The family found itself in the water. Doc had his daughter's baby buttoned into his coat. Swept against a small tree, he hung on while he strapped his belt around the tree. The rest of the family clung to each other around the tree, holding children's heads above water. The wind howled and bent the tree in every direction dur-

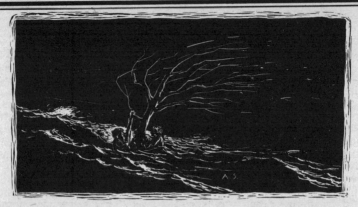

The rest of the family clung to each other around the tree, holding children's heads above the water . . .

ing the black night, but the tenacious family and the tiny tree rooted in coral rock held firm.

When the huge wall of water struck the rescue train at Islamorada late that evening, it uprooted the tracks and overturned 10 cars. Only the 106-ton locomotive *Schenectady* stood upright, its boilers flooded, sparing the lives of the engineer, fireman, and trainmaster. Thirteen people in the coaches survived by holding themselves and their children out of the water all night.

The hurricane's small calm center lasted at Lower Matecumbe Key for about 40 minutes and at the Long Key Fishing Camp for about 25 minutes, where the record-making barometric reading of 26.35 was registered.

By morning everything was gone — trees, buildings, bridges, railroads, docks, viaducts, and most of the highway workers and residents. Ten miles of Keys lay in utter destruction. Communities on the Keys — tight enclaves in which many people were often interrelated — were demolished. Many people simply vanished in the storm, never to be found. John Russell, postmaster at Islamorada, had 79 relatives on the Keys. After the storm, only he and 10 others were left.

Some bodies were found hanging in branches of uprooted trees. On one beach, Dr. G. C. Franklin of Coconut Grove found a hideous tableau of 39 men laid in a windrow just as the wind had mowed them down in death.

One man, still alive, leaned against a tree stump with a splintered 2 by 4 driven completely through him under the ribs. When doctors prepared to pull the wood out, the victim resisted. "When you pull it out, I'll die," he said. He asked for two bottles of beer. When he finished, he said, "Pull." The medics pulled, and the man died.

The full death toll was never known. There were 577 bodies found, but some say as many as 800 perished. Of these, 288 were the helpless highway workers. Luckily, 350 of the army veterans from the camps had gone to see a ball game in Miami and were spared. One of the first rescue workers to arrive on the Keys was novelist Ernest Hemingway, who wrote an article called "Who Murdered the Veterans?" The trouble with the railroad, many folks said, was that the high embankment for the tracks had blocked all channels between the Keys, giving the ocean no choice but to pound the land.

Key West had heard its last train whistle. The Overseas Railroad had died at sea, never to be rebuilt. But Henry Flagler had built well in spots. All the railroad's concrete viaducts of the 34 bridges stood. Today they support the Key West Highway.

For years after the storm, skeletons were found in hidden recesses. One rock pit yielded three autos with 1935 license plates and 10 skeletons. The skeletons still found occasionally in remote mangrove islands may have been victims of the 1935 storm, one of America's most violent natural disasters. □□

AMERICA'S MOST DESTRUCTIVE STORMS

The storms listed below are those on which there is fairly general agreement on their highly destructive stature. With a few exceptions, they are restricted to those occurring after 1890 because of population and valuation differences that make it impossible to assess earlier storms.

• *Most destructive tropical hurricane in loss of life:* the Galveston, Texas, hurricane of September 8, 1900, is estimated to have killed between 6,000 and 7,200 people, mainly by a tidal surge 20 feet high sweeping over the unprepared city. The highest exact-count hurricane death toll in the U.S. is 1,836 from the "San Felipe" hurricane of September 17, 1928, which literally blew Lake Okeechobee, Florida, out of its bed into the adjacent towns and farms.

• *Most destructive tropical hurricane in overall devastation:* the Great New England Hurricane of September 21, 1938, which devastated all or parts of six states with high winds, tidal surges, and river floods, killing an estimated 600. From a strictly meteorological standpoint, Hurricane Camille, which hit the Mississippi coast on August 17, 1969, is believed to be the most intense ever to hit the United States. Adequate warnings held the death toll to 144.

• *Most destructive hurricane-induced floods:* August 18-19, 1955, Pennsylvania to Massachusetts, by Hurricane Diane, with 172 dead and $700 million property loss; June 22, 1972, Pennsylvania and New York, by Hurricane Agnes, with 122 dead and $2.1 billion property loss.

• *Most destructive small-area flood:* Johnstown, Pennsylvania, flood of May 31, 1889. Cloudburst rains broke the dam on the Conemaugh River; city wiped out, 2,100 killed.

• *Most destructive wide-area flood:* March 25-26, 1913, on Wabash and other streams in Indiana and Ohio; Dayton, Ohio, totally under water; 467 dead, $147 million property loss.

• *Most destructive single-river flood:* Mississippi River in spring of 1927; 313 dead, $283 million property loss.

• *Most destructive thunderstorm-caused flood:* Rapid City, South Dakota (on Rapid Creek), June 9-10, 1972; 236 dead, $100 million property loss.

• *Most destructive single tornado:* March 18, 1925; track of 219 miles (longest on record) from Redford, Missouri, to Princeton, Indiana; 695 killed, 2,027 injured, $17 million property loss.

• *Most destructive tornado swarm:* April 3, 1974; 125 tornadoes in 11 midwestern and midsouthern states; 303 killed, 5,400 injured, property loss about $1 billion. The swarm of 60 or more tornadoes on February 19, 1884, in eight midsouthern and southeastern states is estimated to have killed 700 or 800 and caused enormous property loss.

• *Most destructive single-location tornado:* Natchez, Mississippi, May 7, 1840; most of city leveled, three steamboats sunk, 317 killed, property loss reported as at least $5 million in money of that period.

• *Most destructive snowstorm:* probably the Great East Coast blizzard of March 11-14, 1888. Snowstorms as a rule cause little direct destruction or loss of life, thus comparison is difficult. The 1888 blizzard, however, appears unrivaled for the magnitude of its disruption of commerce and transportation and for the estimated 100 or more persons who died of exposure in its drifts.

• *Most destructive Great Lakes storm:* the "Freshwater Fury" of November 9, 1913; eight large ore-carrying ships lost in Lake Huron; at least 200 drowned.

• *Most destructive ice storm:* January 28-February 1, 1951, in Tennessee and northern Mississippi, Alabama, and Georgia; estimated $100 million loss from downed trees, broken power lines, collapsed roofs; 25 dead, over 500 seriously injured.

Compiled by Andrew E. Rothovius

The Elephant We'll Never Forget

Sometime between 1796 and 1807 — records disagree — Hachaliah Bailey of Somers, New York, brought "Old Bet" to this country. She was quite a sensation, being the first "elyphunt" ever seen in America.

by Helen Reeder Cross

☐ HE LEFT NO LETTERS OR MEMOIRS that anyone can find. Only a few faded broadsides, moldy bills of sale, and a telling anecdote or two remain to give an inkling of his character. But from these it seems safe to assume that Hachaliah Bailey was a man with plenty of get-up-and-go, a virtue as much admired in the late 18th and early 19th centuries as now. It led him in later years to be dubbed "Father of the American Circus," even though Hach

Bailey never in his life saw a circus as we know it. To him "Educational Exhibit" would have been the proper title.

Besides enterprise, he also possessed imagination and daring. Imagine a backcountry man of the year 1796 risking $1,000 of his hard-earned cash to buy an elephant — a creature never before seen in America! Still, Hachaliah reasoned, who wouldn't be glad to pay a good round sum, say a quarter, for the educational privilege of being one of the first to see an "elyphunt"?

Hachaliah Bailey had been born in 1775, in the thriving village of Somers, which straddled the New York and Connecticut lines at the junction of two turnpikes. He apparently entered this world already blessed with a canny business sense. Before his twenty-fifth birthday he had acquired a wife named Mary. They lived in a fine brick home, and he had already begun to make a good living with shrewd land investments and cattle trading. He also owned a segment of the turnpike in front of his house. For its use he exacted tolls of all travelers.

Hach was certainly not a poor man when he began his elephant venture. Exactly how and when he got the notion to buy such a creature is uncertain. Later newspaper accounts and town records disagree. Some say it was as late as 1807. Others state that as early as 1796 Hachaliah bought the elephant from a man in Philadelphia named John Owen. There is a poster in the Elephant Museum in Somers giving that date for the showing of "a pachyderm" in that city.

John Owen is said to have been Hach Bailey's brother-in-law. For all one can be sure, Hachaliah may have bargained with Owen over a glass of ale in the Bull's Head Tavern, then had the elephant sent to him from Philadelphia.

The village of Somers rejects this story stoutly, defending its own long but only partly documented record as the original home of America's first elephant. They prefer the story that Hach's own brother, Theodorus Bailey, who was captain of the sailing ship *America,* transported an elephant already named "Old Bet" to New York at Hach's specific request. Theodorus had found the creature at an auction in London and bought it for the princely sum of $20!

A solid piece of evidence as to Bet's arrival in America is the mention in Greenleaf's *New Journal and Patriotic Register* of April 19, 1796. It states that, "The *America* has brought home an Elephant from Bengal in perfect health. It is the first ever seen in America, and is a very great curiosity."

Hach met the sailing vessel at the docks in New York and paid for the creature on the spot with cash from his pocket. Some say he walked Old Bet, tied to his wagon, the 50 or so miles to Somers (at night, so folks would not see his exotic purchase without paying for the privilege). Other accounts say he carried the pachyderm on a sloop that sailed her up the Hudson River to within a few miles of Somers.

Whichever story is true, one can imagine the scene at the wharf as Old Bet was unloaded after her long sea voyage from England. The first elephant in America! How the sight must have startled onlookers, few of whom had seen even a picture of such an animal. Why, she was a veritable behemoth, 15 feet 8 inches from trunk to tail, according to an early handbill. It was enough to send boys scrambling up lampposts, children into hiding behind their mothers' hoopskirts, and ladies into attacks of the vapors.

Once back in Somers, Hach kept his prize beast locked in his barn. From the first, no one had a glimpse of Old Bet without first crossing Hachaliah's palm with "One-eighth of a Dollar — Children Ninepence." Another broadside says it was "One Shilling." The wonder of viewing the mammoth creature spread like wildfire. Soon people were coming by wagon, horseback, and on foot to marvel at an animal from faraway India.

People soon lost all fear of her despite her great size. Hach was pleased. His "elyphunt" showed every sign of being a vein of pure gold. It was time to take Old Bet on the road.

So he did. He traveled always at night by lantern light. Old Bet followed at an elephant's normal pace of four miles an hour, tied by a rope to the back of Hach's wagon. She was like a faithful dog. When he reached a new town, Hach arranged to house and show the elephant in a farmer's barn.

All went well until the summer of 1816. Then in Waterboro, Maine, a man named Davis, who seems to have been something of a fanatic, actually did shoot Old Bet with a shotgun.

Later he devised a circular canvas enclosure that he carried rolled up in the wagon. Word of mouth brought people in droves to see her. "Elyphunt Day" was as exciting as Election Day.

Hachaliah soon began to develop the tricks and techniques of a natural showman. He had handbills printed. One described Bet as being "the greatest natural curiosity ever presented to the curious." He hired boys to hawk broadsides far and wide, paying them with a free look at the elephant.

Caring for the animal was no picnic. Like most elephants in captivity, Old Bet must have consumed at least 500 pounds of hay and 40 gallons of water daily, besides the vegetables and fruit for which elephants have a passion.

Providing all this was enough to wear out the strongest man. Many people paid their viewing fee with fodder, potatoes, corn, or oats, as well as produce fresh from the farm. One early source states that Bet's favorite treat was, of all things, gingerbread! Another tells of a farmer's bartering his whole family's admission to see the elephant with a two-gallon jug of home-distilled rum.

The work of managing all this soon led Hachaliah to hire a helper to drive a

supply wagon, which followed him and Bet on their nocturnal journeys. It was almost a little caravan. One summer Hach's helper was a teenager from Bethel, Connecticut, named Phineas.

Phineas also no doubt helped feed the beast and superintend her showers in nearby streams wherever they went. Then followed the dust bath that is particularly loved by Asiatic elephants. He may even have taught her a trick or two. One likes to think of Bet as gently picking up little girls with her trunk and setting them on her wide back for a ride. Did she also dance clumsily to a drumbeat? Did she learn to stand on her head? Did she flap her enormous ears when commanded?

We know that Asiatic elephants learn quickly and delight in their own cleverness. But though someone should have left a written description of Bet's possible accomplishments, no one did. As for her public, it seems to have been "educational" and entertaining enough for Old Bet's viewers simply to gaze, spellbound, at her strange shape and overwhelming size.

At some point over the years Hachaliah added a few monkeys and a bear to his little troupe. Proud of his Bet, he had trappings of a harness and saddle cloth made for her of red velvet trimmed with gold braid. Country eyes must have popped at the sight of the great creature decked out in such finery. Here was the germ of a circus, though Hachaliah could never have dreamed of the size and complexity into which traveling shows would grow after his time.

Each summer the little caravan went farther and farther afield. Records say they traveled north to Maine, south to the Carolinas. Quite naturally, Hach's neighbors back in Somers were envious of his success with Bet. The *Croton Falls News* of July 17, 1879, quotes an aged Benjamin Brown as having stated, "Why, in one season he [Hach] cleared $8,000 with that elephant!"

At one point Hachaliah must have decided to take a rest from his labors. There is a bill of sale in the Somers Museum which shows Benjamin Lent and Andrew Brown paying the sum of "$1,200 each for equal two-thirds use of Elephant for one year from the first day of the month, Bailey to furnish one-third of expenses from the first day of the month and the other men two-thirds. Dated August 13, 1808."

Also in the museum there is a small, crumbling book, undated and with no author named, which must have been inspired by this same transaction. Its steel engravings show the two men making such a quick fortune that Hachaliah tries to buy back his complete ownership rights before the year's end. They refuse. The story tells and pictures show Hach returning with a rifle which he holds to Old Bet's head. When asked what he intends to do, Hach announces blandly that he is about to shoot the critter.

"But you can't! She's ours as much as yours!" they reply in dismay.

"Oh, I don't mean to shoot the whole critter. Just my third," he calmly tells them. The little book ends happily with Hachaliah restored to full ownership of his pachyderm.

Apocryphal though the story probably is, it seems fitting for the character of Hach Bailey that emerges from the scanty old records. There is some validation for the anecdote in a separate 19th-century engraving that also shows Hachaliah threatening to shoot his third of the elephant.

All went well, apparently, until the summer of 1816. Then in Waterboro, Maine, a man named Davis, who seems to have been something of a fanatic, actually did shoot Old Bet with a shotgun. When questioned as to his reason, he complained that it was a sin for country people to waste so much money on the "foolishness" of seeing an elephant. As Bet expired, Hachaliah is quoted as saying, "There goes $30,000 of my money." This sounds a little callous, though the amount of his loss may well have been true.

From the profits of his more than 15-year association with the pachyderm, Hach built the Elephant Hotel as a kind of memorial to Bet. It still stands at the crossing of the two highroads in the center of the village of Somers. It is a handsome three-story brick structure of late colonial style with wide floorboards, high ceilings, paneled walls, and deep-set windows. Across its imposing front its startling name is emblazoned in large letters.

Atop a granite shaft in the middle of a grass plot in front of the building's entrance, Hach erected in the 1820s a small gilded statue of his elephant friend. Surely no traveler has ever passed the Elephant Hotel and the worn replica of Old Bet without asking for the story. Both are named in the National Register of Historic Places.

Hach died in 1845. His tombstone in the Somers cemetery is engraved with the legend: "Enterprise, Perseverance, and Integrity." To these qualities might have been added "Imagination and Daring." Old Bet has a separate memorial all her own. This one was erected in 1963 in Portland, Maine, the state of her demise, by the Sanford-Alfred Historical Society. It is a kind of civic expiation for the deplorable murder of the kindly beast.

But perhaps the greatest memorial to Hach and Old Bet was created in 1881. That was the year that the two biggest circuses in America joined forces to become "The Greatest Show on Earth." One of the co-founders was James Bailey, ward of a cousin of Hach Bailey. The other was the greatest showman of his age, Phineas Taylor Barnum, who had learned his art from a master. For he was the same Phineas who so many years before had driven the supply wagon for the first elephant in America. □ □

The Mighty (Tasty) Catfish

Herewith a confessed catfish eater offers his observations on this eminently catchable and cookable "poor man's trout."

by James Dodson

illustrations by Maryann Mattson

☐ I ONCE KNEW A PRESI-dential candidate who ran for the White House on the pledge to put fried catfish on every dinner plate in America. His name was Frank Stubbins. He was a small-time cattle farmer who lived in an eroding cinderblock house near the shores of Lake Seminole in the sun-baked sovereignty of West Florida. Frank, I must report, was not a very successful cattle farmer, but made up for his deficiency in that department by being a whale of a fisherman, specifically a terror to the catfish community in the finger coves close to his house. I don't know who was responsible for placing dreams of presidential grandeur in Frank's head, but it's easy enough to figure out why he chose to make catfish an important plank in his platform. Catfish, which are plentiful in southern lakes, were central to Frank's life. He caught and ate catfish almost every day of his life — catfish pancakes, catfish soup, catfish biscuits, catfish casserole. "I can make anything out of catfish," he once told me, showing me an aromatic catfish omelette he had just created.

Frank Stubbins, I suspect, could have gone on to become the Colonel Sanders of catfish, but he chose to run for president instead, an ambition that has brought low many great men. Of course, he never got out of the gate, presidentially speaking, even though he possessed many of the virtues one likes to see in a president. Part of the reason he never became president of the United States was because he placed catfish high on his political agenda. The sad truth is that while catfish is un-questionably the most democratic of panfish — anyone with a hook and a piece of string, a can of Vienna sausages, and ten minutes on his hands can catch one — there remains a substantial anticatfish bias in this country, the handiwork of snobby restaurateurs and the nation's powerful haute cuisine special interests.

Some brief historical perspective may be helpful. Before the South, a heaven-kissed region, briefly hauled itself to a certain measure of respectability under the klieg lights of native son Jimmy Carter's presidency, catfish, in the eyes of many connoisseurs, was largely regarded as a poor man's trout, the product of the region's many sluggish, muddy rivers and weedy lakes.

I have it on good authority that Jimmy Carter served catfish on fine china at the White House on several occasions, possibly one of his more notable achievements but also one that cost him dearly. My point is that having good intentions where catfish are concerned is simply not enough. As a national leader, a man in a position to deeply influence national thinking, Jimmy Carter may have made a noble if dooming gesture to expand the tastes of the Republic, but he clearly did not go far enough. Just look where it got him: today Jimmy Carter is back in Georgia making cane chairs in his basement. He and Frank Stubbins have political obscurity in common.

But I can't let this catfish die without a good kick.

Where I come from, more or less the same place Jimmy Carter comes from, a fried catfish supper that leaves your belly bulging and your arms lightly coated in lard grease is considered an expression of high social ascendancy, like a first communion or a birthday party where all the adults leave the room. This is because the South has long known what the rest of the country — indeed the world — has been slow to figure out by itself: that prepared almost any way, be it fried, skewered, bobbed, barbecued, filleted, fishcaked or even eaten raw, catfish is a marvelous delectation to the tongue — chewy, aromatic, light-meated, provoking an image in the mind of the eater of a more salutary period in the national experience when people sat on porch swings, spoke well of their elders, and let bygones be bygones.

But, gracious, don't take my word for it. Just attend a Baptist church lawn supper and revival preaching in Decatur, Alabama, sometime — a real hand-wringing time complete with lots of personal witnessing and cheerful blubbering in the name of the Lord and all things proper, after which everyone

---

I have it on good authority that Jimmy Carter served catfish on fine china at the White House on several occasions . . .

---

who is going to heaven, old sinner and new pilgrim alike, sits down to a delicious catfish fry, a real sugar-tea and Dixie-plate affair. Or, if you choose, drop in on a political supper at the National Guard armory in Level Cross, North Carolina, where one night several early autumns ago I saw Richard Petty, the famous race driver, not only declare his candidacy for county commissioner before a sweaty throng of hungry mothers and fathers and half-naked children, but also, in the space of about 13 minutes, wristwatch time, polish off a pile of fried catfish that would have fed a small pit crew.

Not long ago I had dinner with friends at a fancy seafood restaurant in Boston. Very ritzy place. The kind where waiters introduce themselves by Christian name and maintain an air of superior but glamorous boredom. When it came time to order, our waiter, who claimed his name was Victor, asked me what I wanted. I scanned the menu, which was written not only in longhand but also in a foreign language. "I'll have fried catfish," I said. "And don't skimp on the hushpuppies and coleslaw on the side."

There was an embarrassed silence at the table.

"I'm afraid," Victor said, sounding remarkably like Bette Davis, "you will have to go someplace else for *that*."

"I thought this was a fish restaurant," I said, not willing to let the issue escape unnoted. "You've got more fish on this menu than commodities on the New York Stock Exchange."

"This is a *seafood* restaurant," he said, "not a fish restaurant."

"Catfish live in the ocean," I said with dignity. "I happen to know this from personal experience."

"Lots of things live in the ocean," he said, "but we don't serve them here, either."

Well, you know what happened. I ordered a cheeseburger with raw onions. As I view the exchange now, I realize it was simply another moment in the difficult life of a catfish lover. Had I gathered my wits quicker, I might have had Victor sit down, take a load off for a few minutes, during which I would have brought him to an enlightenment not known in his circles since Paul struck out on the road to Tarsus.

Did Victor know, for instance, that a chap named Catfish Hunter, the former pitching ace of the Oakland A's, once won a Cy Young award against a field of nine other 20-game winners? Was he aware that, remarkably, in certain loci of the Mekong River of Laos and Thailand, the adult male catfish averages eight feet in length and weighs about 360 pounds, or roughly the size of a freshman defensive noseguard at the University of Alabama? Further, that 19th-century European records — Russian archival records, to be precise — show that catfish of an earlier time, *Anarhichas lupus* or wolffish, sometimes known as *Lupus marinus* and *Primelodus catus,* grew to the astounding size of 15 feet and 720 pounds without the benefit of steroids? Did it intrigue him that the scaleless catfish — long dismissed as a scavenger and a boob-fish among its peers, was classically extolled by no less an authority than the Roman poet Catullus for its natural scrappiness, its admirable courage and stubbornness — especially the sleeker and more streamlined channel cat? On that score, did he know that certain advanced tribal peoples of Africa ascribed important surefire fertility and spiritual properties to properly wielded bunches of dried catfish whiskers? And while we're on the subject of mothers and what they really want for you, Vic, did you know catfish, as a staple in the modern diet, has lower cholesterol content than most other fish, that catfish is an excellent source of protein, potassium, and thiamine, yet has a low sodium content — that, to phrase it another way, in a confused age beset by mung-bean parlors and salad-bar lines, the modest catfish is as nearly perfect a foodstuff as Our Creator made! And, finally, to clear up any lingering geographical myopia, did you know that catfish *is not* a fish exclusive to the Southern states but is, in fact, found in abundant supply in such alien places as Maine, New Jersey, Minnesota, Wyoming, and even Bakersfield, California?

Certain advanced tribal peoples of Africa ascribed important surefire fertility and spiritual properties to properly wielded bunches of dried catfish whiskers.

It pains me to admit I didn't have this conversation with Vic. Instead, I ate my cheeseburger in wounded silence and let the issue slide.

On one level I am ready to admit the rest of the world probably has a way to go to discover the culinary beguilements of catfish. But imagine my delight when not long ago a certain cookbook fell onto my desk. It's called *The Catfish Cookbook* (East Woods Press, 429 East Boulevard, Charlotte, NC 28203). It was as if God had dropped this book on my desk instead of the desk of a colleague who had never tasted catfish. Published by a firm in North Carolina, a catfish capital among the lower 48, the book offers 100 or more catfish recipes for the beginner and old hand alike, many of them prize-winning recipes from a contest sponsored by the Catfish Farmers of America, an organization that

has for years maintained a low political profile. Much of what's included isn't anything new to the devoted catfish lover, but the names conjure up magical interludes with fork and spoon. How could a responsible native son turn away from something called Catfish Andrew Jackson or Mississippi's Dixieland Catfish? There are also some regrettable concessions to the age we live in — dishes such as Hawaiian Catfish, Catfish Kiev, Catfish Pizza, Catfish Cantonese, Catfish Quiche, and something called Catfish Eldorado de Colorado, which sounds too much like something a Denver loan shark drives around in for me to enjoy. But overall it is a pleasing book to see, an indication that maybe times are changing.

Personally I subscribe to the Frank Stubbins formula for cooking catfish: all you need is a case of Dixie beer, a bowl of buttermilk, a large black skillet filled with enough bubbling lard to fill the wading pools of Hades, a bowl of dry self-rising cornmeal, and something protective to wear over your face so you don't burn your eyebrows off.

While you knock back the beer, you run the sliced catfish through the cornmeal in a manner that is not unlike the way a young girl goes through a shower after junior high school phys. ed. class. Then you hold the fillet approximately eight or nine inches over the grease, wait, and then drop it, leaping back quickly. The fish will cook in a matter of seconds and you'll need something reliable with which to fetch it out of the grease, like part of an old highway guard rail or an extra tire tool. But if you do it right, you'll soon be eating something truly wonderful, even if the state police do show up to inquire about what's really going on.

"Keep it simple" was Frank's motto where catfish and women were concerned, but also keep it interesting. For those of you who are less adventuresome, here is an unedited and relatively simple method for introducing yourself to catfish:

PLANTATION CATFISH

6 catfish
2 teaspoons salt
   Orange-Rice Stuffing
2 tablespoons melted fat or oil
2 tablespoons orange juice

Sprinkle fish inside and out with salt. Stuff fish. Close opening with small skewers or toothpicks. Place fish in a well-greased baking pan, 14″ x 11″ x 1″. Combine fat and orange juice. Brush fish with mixture. Bake in a moderate oven, 350°F. for 25 to 35 minutes or until fish flakes easily when tested with a fork. Baste occasionally with fat mixture. Remove skewers. Serves 6.

ORANGE-RICE STUFFING

1 cup chopped celery with leaves
¼ cup chopped onion
¼ cup melted fat or oil
¾ cup water
¼ cup orange juice
2 tablespoons lemon juice
1 tablespoon grated orange rind
¾ teaspoon salt
1 cup precooked rice
½ cup toasted, blanched, slivered almonds

Cook celery and onion in fat until tender. Add water, juices, orange rind, and salt; bring to a boil. Add rice and stir to moisten. Cover and remove from heat. Let stand 5 minutes. Add almonds and mix well. □□

The Ordeal of the First Car to Drive Across the Country

Traveling west to east, they encountered every imaginable hardship, including, in Wyoming, miles and miles of buffalo wallows . . .

by Lawrence Doorley

☐ IT ALL BEGAN AT THE UNIVERSITY Club in San Francisco in May of 1903, when Dr. Horatio Nelson Jackson of Burlington, Vermont, overheard a man at a nearby table ridiculing the newfangled horseless carriage. A passing fancy, the fellow sneered. In fact, he was willing to bet $50 that no automobile could be driven across the continent in less than 90 days. Dr. Jackson rose, stepped over to the man's table, extracted a $50 bill from his wallet, and announced he was covering the bet.

Wasting no time, Jackson, who was on his way back East after three years in the goldfields of Alaska, hastened to the livery stable where his Locomobile awaited him along with a young chauffeur-mechanic named Sewall Crocker. Jackson explained the bet and asked when they could leave. "Never make it," Crocker replied. The Locomobile was a steamer requiring lots of water and lots of attention. The only hope would be a gas-powered Winton. The very next morning they found a brand-new, two-cylinder, 20-horsepower, 1903 Winton touring car, just delivered from the Cleveland, Ohio, factory. At 1 P.M. on Saturday, May 23, Jackson tooted the bulb horn and the *Vermont,* as he had christened the car, pulled away from Market Street and headed for the Oakland ferry.

Every previous effort to cross the continent by car had foundered in the desert sands of Nevada. By taking a northern route through Oregon, Idaho, and Wyoming, Jackson felt they would have a better chance. But the dire warnings they had received about Oregon's roadless wastes proved all too accurate. The poor travelers wandered the desert like lost souls, bombarded with sand, tumbleweeds, and bitter alkali dust. They lost their cyclometers, which told them how many miles they had traveled, lost their cooking gear, had to pour their good water into the radiator and drink the foul alkali water themselves. With no such thing as a gas gauge, and the cyclometers gone, they ran out of gas. A coin was tossed; Crocker lost, and he set out afoot for Burns, 29 miles away. The next morning he reappeared with a secondhand bicycle, two gallons of gasoline, and three of benzine. Finally arriving in Burns, they filled up everything again and headed for Ontario, Idaho, 140 miles to the east.

Crossing the Snake River on a ferry and starting southeast along the tracks of the Union Pacific, Jackson and Crocker must have thought the worst was behind them. They were wrong. It began to rain, and the car slithered off the road into a mudhole. Using a block and tackle attached to a stake driven into the ground ahead of the car, Jackson and Crocker pulled the *Vermont* out of the mud. They did this nine times that day, reaching Caldwell, Idaho, at midnight after 16 hours on the road, having covered only 28 miles.

The next morning the town held a celebration for the distinguished visitors, complete with a dogfight between two bull terriers. The winner, a stoical-looking mutt named Bud, was offered to Jackson as a mascot. A place on the seat between the two men was made, a pair of goggles to protect his eyes from the dust was fashioned, and Bud became a part of the team.

Idaho continued to be troublesome. A deluge engulfed them on the way to Mountain Home, and they got caught in what had been a dry creek bed. This time the block and tackle failed to move them. The coin was tossed, and Crocker lost again. Six hours later he returned with a farmer and a four-horse team. Near Montpelier the ball bearings fell out of the front wheel. The coin was tossed, and Crocker headed for the nearest farm, perhaps by now muttering that it just might pay him to have a look at that coin. Several hours later, reliable old Crocker turned up with bearings he had salvaged from a junked mowing machine.

Wyoming proved no better than Idaho. The travelers encountered miles and miles of buffalo wallows which the rain turned into morasses. One of the deeper wallows gave them an idea. Unable to budge the car with the block and tackle by their own strength, Crocker suggested wrapping the cable around the rear axle and letting the car pull itself out. They used that method 16 times in one day.

Near Granger the road, such as it was, was completely washed out, and they turned north into a wasteland. For 36 hours they were without food and saw no other human beings. At last a lonely sheepherder directed them back to the Union Pacific tracks. The following day they crossed the Continental Divide and arrived in Rawlings on June 30.

By now excitement was mounting along the route, telegraphers having flashed news of the *Vermont*'s progress up and down the line. Schools were let out, work stopped, and whole families rushed for the nearest hamlet or cross-roads to see a real live automobile. From around the corner, or from far off on the western horizon, or down a dusty main street came the little Winton, piled high with equipment, tires tied on the front, more tires on the back, three dusty creatures on the seat, two of them waving — holy smoke! Was that a dog? With goggles on?

They were attracting attention back East now, and the newspapers in Omaha, Chicago, Cleveland, and New York began reporting each day's progress. In Cheyenne, on July 2, a long telegram from the Winton factory was waiting,

After covering 28 miles in 16 hours, they arrived in Caldwell, Idaho, where the town held a dogfight as part of the celebration staged for the travelers. The winner was "Bud," shown here, who traveled with them for the rest of the journey.

promising free parts from now on. Goodrich, in Akron, sent congratulations and offered free tires.

But there was disquieting news at Cheyenne. Two other cross-country attempts were underway from San Francisco, both by professional drivers. One team was driving a "curved dash" Oldsmobile, the other a specially built Packard with a new low gear designed for sand and mountain travel. Both teams were reported to be over the Sierras and far into Nevada.

That ominous information spurred Jackson and Crocker into greater efforts. Spurning hotel beds, they slept under the car. They reached true civilization, Omaha, in the dying twilight of a scorching Sunday, July 12, and by July 17 they were in Chicago. Crowds lined the roads across Indiana and into Ohio. At Elyria, a caravan of cars from the Winton factory met them and escorted them into Cleveland, where Bud was given a steak bone and Crocker and Jackson the keys to the city.

At 2:30 A.M. on July 23 they reached Rochester, New York, grabbed a few hours of sleep, headed down the Mohawk Valley, crossed the Hudson, turned south on the old Albany Post Road, and poured on the speed. The amazing little auto, seeming to sense it was in the homestretch, responded by hitting nearly 30 miles an hour with the wind behind it.

They sped through Rhinebeck, through Poughkeepsie — the street lights on to show them the way — crowds everywhere screaming encouragement, old Bud barking back at them. At Peekskill a delegation of Winton officials and Dr. Jackson's wife awaited them and joined in the last dash into the city. At 4:30 A.M., Sunday, July 26, 1903, they pulled up at the old Holland House at Fifth Avenue and 30th Street, the trip done in 63 days, only 45 of them actual traveling days. The Packard was in Nebraska; the Oldsmobile was out of touch somewhere in Wyoming.

The Winton people offered a $25,000 reward to anyone who could prove that Jackson and Crocker hadn't driven every inch of the way, except for the times they were pulled from mudholes by horses. No one ever claimed the reward. A meticulous investigation by the Smithsonian Institution convinced that eminent organization that the trip had been fairly made, and when Jackson offered the historic Winton to the Smithsonian in 1944 it was gratefully accepted. It's still there with much of its original equipment, billed as "The First Automobile to Cross the United States Under Its Own Power."

"They reached true civilization, Omaha, in the dying twilight of a scorching Sunday, July 12 . . . "

Jackson (left) and Crocker

Both Crocker and the Winton died young, but Jackson lived to be 82, serving with distinction in World War I, becoming one of the founders of the American Legion, publisher of a newspaper, owner of a radio station, and president of a bank. He also claimed another first when, two months after the grand cross-country drive was over, he became the first person to be arrested for exceeding the six-miles-an-hour speed limit in Burlington, Vermont. He cheerfully paid the five dollar fine. ☐ ☐

There Might Be Gold in Your Attic

As editor of Collectibles Illustrated, *the author is always being told, "You won't believe what I found!" Here are candidates for his personal list of all-time great collecting finds.*

by Charles J. Jordan

☐ EVERYBODY'S HEARD A STORY LIKE it: midwestern housewife, while rummaging through a box of "junk" in the attic of her recently departed grandmother's home, uncovers a cache of rare glass negatives dating back to the Civil War.

In some 15 years of writing stories for publications about collecting, I've met many people, collectors of everything from comic books to Ming Dynasty vases, who have heard of similar discoveries taking place in their own given fields. But I admit to experiencing only one major find of my own worthy of note in some two decades of active collecting: I once bought a beat-up book in Connecticut for a quarter, only to find it contained a handwritten note from circus showman P. T. Barnum to his grandson. I ultimately sold it through a New York autograph auction house for several hundred dollars. Consequently, most of the stories I tell involve other people and are sometimes two or three parties removed before they get to me.

A great many of the finds of the past decade or so have involved collectibles, stamps and photographs being the most celebrated of these. The greatest stamp story, hands down, involves a collector named William T. Robey, who made the purchase of a lifetime when he bought a sheet of new stamps at a Washington, D.C., post office back in 1918. The sheet contained 100 stamps of the United States 24-cent air-

mail issue, just printed. Robey immediately realized that the airplane pictured on all the stamps, a Jenny, was upside down. By the time postal authorities caught up with Robey, he wisely had decided not to part with his curiosities. A week later, he sold the sheet to a Philadelphia dealer for $15,000. Seven days later it changed hands again for $20,000. A few years ago a single "Inverted Jenny" sold for $135,000, making Robey's $24 purchase in 1918 worth $13.5 million by today's standards.

A considerable number of the most impressive photographic finds of the 20th century involve images of Abraham Lincoln. There are only 103 known photographs of Lincoln, and a good number of these have passed through the hands of Lincoln historian and collector Stefan Lorant, who has spent his lifetime tracking down photos of Honest Abe.

One of his greatest finds was based on the hunch he had that Francis Carpenter, an artist who had painted the huge canvas depicting the Emancipation Proclamation that now hangs in Congress, may have acquired photos of Lincoln on which to base his work. Lorant tracked down Carpenter's grandson, Emerson Carpenter Ives, who was in his mid-60s. Ives had inherited all of his grandfather's papers, which were stored in a large metal box. He spread the contents of the box out on the kitchen table — the artist's diaries, notebooks, letters, sketches — and a small cardboard box fell out. As Lorant remembers it, "My heart stood still." Inside the cardboard container was a glass negative, broken around the ends, but carrying the unmistakable image of the 16th President of the United States.

George Gilbert, a well-known expert in photographica, tells the story of two recent discoveries at West Coast and East Coast flea markets. "In 1972 at a San Francisco flea market, nine previously unknown daguerreotypes were found by two young men who paid $30 for the group," Gilbert explained.

"These were the only known images surviving from a series taken of Washington, D. C., by photographer John Plumbe, Jr." The photos captured the city of Washington at the very dawn of photography and included pictures of all the major office buildings and part of the Capitol, which was being built at the time. "To give you an idea of their value, just one photograph was sold to the Library of Congress for $12,000."

The East Coast find took place more recently. "Within the last three years," Gilbert recounted, "a young man from Connecticut, who happens to be a scout for collectors, uncovered 50 photographs of the Mexican War of 1848. These were found at a flea market near Poughkeepsie, New York. They were the first war pictures ever taken by an American photographer and were sold to a museum for over $100,000."

Tracing ownership of an item was the dilemma facing Timothy and Catherine Rude Sena of Worthington, Massachusetts, after they put down $1,400 for a single-action Colt revolver last summer. The gun, which surfaced at a flea market in Brimfield, Massachusetts, carried the engraved words: "Wyatt Earp — 1879." The engraving turned out to be the work of F. J. Durand, one of only two engravers who worked in the Dodge City, Kansas, area during 1879. A check of Colt's records showed that the gun was presented to Earp at a party of Republicans on September 5, 1879. The Senas have turned their find over to Regalia Incorporated of Los Angeles to be sold. The asking price is said to be $300,000, in case you're interested.

As often as not, memorabilia associated with figures who gained their notoriety on the other side of the law generate intense interest among collectors. The current world's record for a 20th-century autographed photo stands at $4,250 for a picture signed by Al Capone. At the John Dillinger Historical Museum in Nashville, Indiana, people flock to see Dillinger's "fake gun" that aided in his break from the

Lake County, Indiana, jail in 1934. The "gun," which Dillinger pulled on a guard at the prison, was actually carved from a wooden washboard and blackened with shoe polish. Newspaper accounts at the time said that Dillinger locked up the sheriff, eluded militiamen patrolling outside with submachine guns, and fled in the constable's own car. Three months later he was gunned down outside a Chicago theater by federal agents.

"They were the first war pictures ever taken by an American photographer and were sold to a museum for more than $100,000."

For 50 years the infamous weapon remained out of sight. Recently a private investigator who had worked for Dillinger's attorney died, his Iowa home was sold, and the couple who purchased it found the gun and documents supporting its authenticity in a specially fabricated furnace duct in the house. The item now joins others at the museum, including Dillinger's personal letters, photographs, and "lucky" rabbit's foot.

It's easy to understand the historical value of rare photographs of Abraham Lincoln, but souvenirs of our 20th-century popular culture are also attaining great value. The collecting world was rocked in 1982 when a prop from the motion picture *Citizen Kane* was sold by Sotheby's in New York City for $60,500. The prop was one of three "Rosebud" sleds made for the final scene of the classic film. (The actual one used in the motion picture was burned in the film's closing scene; the one sold by Sotheby's was a backup model.) The sled was discovered in 1977 by someone combing through a trash heap in a discarded prop vault at the old RKO studios in Hollywood.

And what about the famous Honus Wagner baseball card, which has been reported high and low in the press as being worth thousands of dollars? Wagner, who played for Pittsburgh, objected to his image appearing on cigarette tobacco cards and threatened to sue if they were not withdrawn immediately by the Sweet Caporal cigarette company. The company succeeded in pulling in most of the cards, but not all of them. Bill Mastro of Chicago, who has been collecting baseball cards since he was a kid, has owned three Wagner cards at various points in his collecting career. His first was purchased at a baseball card show and his third was won at an auction. It was his second Wagner card that Bill says brings back the best memories because its discovery came quite by chance and involved his grandmother.

"You know how grandmothers are," Mastro said. "They're always talking about their grandchildren. My grandmother likes to tell people about my baseball card collection. A friend of hers was cleaning out a priest's attic in New Jersey one day and found a cigar box of these old baseball cards from 1910. She called my grandmother to see if I wanted them. I did and paid her $500 for them. In the group was a Wagner card. At that time, 1974, the Wagner card was worth $1,000. By the time I sold it, it had appreciated several times in value. Today a good Wagner can bring $25,000 or more."

Is there gold in your attic? Bear in mind that each of these discoveries involved everyday people with a good knack for knowing a "hot" item when they saw one . . . and an incredible amount of luck. □□

JOIN
The Exciting New World Of
COLLECTIBLES

Whether you're a serious collector ... or simply someone who enjoys looking at the fascinating memorabilia of past decades, *Collectibles Illustrated* is as much fun to read as browsing through a really good flea market.

Beautiful full-color features highlight

from the popular to the most bizarre collections, as well as the collectors behind them.

Collecting tips, history, information on clubs, meets, shows and trends.

Collectibles Illustrated is for everyone — young and old!

Please enter my subscription for one year (6 bimonthly issues) of **COLLECTIBLES ILLUSTRATED** at only **$12.97.**

Name _____

Address _____

City _____ State _____ Zip _____

☐ Payment enclosed.   ☐ Please bill me.   Canadian and foreign subscriptions $15.97 (U.S. funds only).

COLLECTIBLES ILLUSTRATED, Depot Square, Peterborough, N.H. 03458   S5OFAIX

Replaceable You

Medical science can now replace an amazing number of body parts . . . at incredible prices.

by Ric Bucher

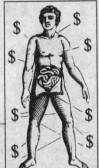

☐ MAN IS NOW A MARKETable quantity in the most literal sense. No longer can anyone rightly say, "You aren't worth a cent!" for even the most indigent being carries an inherent worth of over a million dollars.

You can attribute man's suddenly found astronomical value to advances in transplanting natural organs and implanting artificial ones. Last year in the United States, surgeons performed 103 heart transplants, 62 liver transplants, and 5,358 kidney grafts. Twenty-two heart and lung systems, the very core of man's internal organs, have been transplanted; 13 of these patients are still living.

Your marketability begins shortly after birth, and you have to sell neither soul nor limb. Umbilical cords, used to replace worn-out arteries in the body's extremities (synthetic arteries are used elsewhere), are purchased from nurses, who save them for a couple of dollars apiece. (Previously they were thrown in the trash.) Cutting your hair and clipping your nails are necessary chores of personal hygiene. Unbeknownst to most people, they are also a way to make a buck. It's a dying industry, but some wigmakers still purchase human hair. A half pound is needed to make a complete wig, and the maker generally pays $15 an ounce. Cosmetic companies purchasing fingernails are rarer yet, but those existing will pay $5 to $10 for nails over a half inch long. The only other marketable *and* dispensable part of the body is blood. In some places, mostly cities, donors are paid anywhere from $10 to $25 a visit.

Advances in other areas of medical science have increased the average man's means to money; the success with artificial insemination has brought a great demand for sperm donors. Once he has passed a battery of strict physical examinations, a donor is capable of earning $35 a visit.

Indispensable organs are not actually bought and sold, but each costs a specific amount to be replaced. The heart, the most romanced and revered organ in the human body, can be replaced by both artificial and genuine hearts; then again, there are people who displayed false hearts long before the first implant.

Human Spare Parts List*
Cornea: $2,500-$5,000
Bone Marrow: $60,000
Lung: $50,000-$150,000
Heart-Lung combo: $78,000-$92,000
Heart: $57,000-$110,000
Liver: $54,000-$238,000
Pancreas: $18,000-$50,000
Kidney: $25,000-$35,000

Artificial Parts
Ear: $8,000-$12,000
Lens Implant: $300
Wrist: $280-$295
Heart: $50,000-$80,000
Heart Valve: $2,000
Knee: $1,500-$2,000
Finger Joint: $99
Leg or Arm: $1,000-$3,000
Ankle: $700
Blood Vessel: $300
Toe Joint: $92-$99
Shoulder and Knee
  Ligament: $200-$500
Shoulder: $900
Elbow: $1,200
Hip: $1,000-$2,000

* All prices include parts and labor.

A Sharp Knife and Some Stout Thread

That was all the father-to-be had, or needed, to perform the first Caesarean delivery in America on a cold Virginia night in 1794.

by C. Brian Kelly

□ ONLY 25, MARRIED BARELY A YEAR, red-haired Pennsylvanian Jessee Bennett faced the most momentous decision of his young life, with two other lives — those of his wife and their unborn child — entirely dependent upon his skill and courage.

The scene was a log cabin in rural Edom, Virginia; the time was the wintry night of January 14, 1794, and the problem was obstructed delivery of Elizabeth Hog Bennett's baby. Hours after Elizabeth had gone into her difficult labor, it appeared that either mother or child must die.

Repeated attempts at a forceps delivery, Dr. Alexander Humphreys of nearby Staunton consulting, had failed. The next step normally would be craniotomy, forced removal of the infant from the birth passage by crushing its head and simply pulling it out, a fatal procedure.

The courageous mother, sure she would die, begged the two men to save her baby by any means possible. Jessee Bennett proposed a Caesarean delivery, which had never before been attempted in North America.

Oh, no, absolutely not, vowed the veteran practitioner Humphreys — he would have no truck with anything so risky. When Bennett became more insistent, Humphreys stomped out into the snowy night.

But Bennett, albeit somewhat untried, was himself a physician who had "read" his medicine in Philadelphia and completed his training at the University of Pennsylvania. Now, mind made up, he wasted no time. In minutes, Elizabeth was rendered unconscious by a large dose of laudanum; she was placed upon a makeshift table of two planks set across barrels. Two black servant women helped by holding her, and the patient's sister, Mrs. William Hawkins, also assisted.

"With one quick sweep of the knife," as one historian was to say, the gambling doctor made his incision. Seconds later he lifted forth the child — a girl. Then with the remark, "This shall be the last one," he quickly removed both of his wife's ovaries. By the flickering lamplight, he sewed up the wound with stout linen thread normally used in heavy clothing.

Amazingly, both mother and child lived to ripe old ages, as did Bennett himself, who later served as an army surgeon in the abortive "Whiskey Rebellion"; represented his subsequent home of Mason County, now West Virginia, in the Virginia General Assembly; and figured as a witness in the trial of Aaron Burr at Richmond.

Aside from saving his own wife and child, what Bennett had accomplished that January night was the first abdominal operation in America, the first Caesarean, and the first ovariectomy; but the nation's medical community would have no idea of his feat for another century or so. For many years the first Caesarean was credited to Dr. John Richmond of Newton, Ohio, for an abdominal delivery performed 33 years after Bennett's.

News of the real pioneer delivery was finally reported in 1891 by Dr. A. L. Knight, a family friend contributing to a history of the Great Kanawha Valley in West Virginia, an obscure citation to be "followed" by a report in the *West Virginia Medical Journal* nearly 40 years later (July 1929). Undoubtedly Bennett himself could have sped things up, but he is said to have once explained, "No doctor with any feelings of delicacy would report an operation he had done on his own wife." □□

Surefire Home Remedies for the Hiccups

A farmer in Iowa has tried them all — and he's been hiccuping for over 63 years.

by Tim Clark

illustrated by Bruce Hammond

☐ HICCUP, HICKE UP, HIKUP, HICKOP, hickhop, hecup, hiccop, hickup, hicket, hickok — it sounds like a bad attack of a condition that has plagued or amused (depending on your point of view) humanity since the dawn of time. In reality, it is a list of the different ways people have spelled the word in English, dating back as far as 1544, when the accepted medical practice was "to cast colde water in the face of him that hath the hicket."

The British, by the way, persist in spelling it "hiccough" (while still pronouncing it "hiccup"), which even their own Oxford English Dictionary suggests "ought to be abandoned as a mere error." Put that in your next cough of tea and drink it. But not too fast, for it might trigger an attack, along with eating too fast or too much, smoking, pregnancy, certain illnesses, exercising too strenuously, nervousness, laughing hard, or recent surgery.

Hiccups have nothing to do with coughing, nor are they, as some have supposed, unsuccessful efforts to inhale or to vomit. In fact, according to the world's leading authority on the biology of hiccups, the muscle spasm in the diaphragm that causes a sudden intake of air, ending with a "hic" as the glottis snaps shut, may be one of the most ancient behaviors in the animal kingdom, with links to breathing, digestion, and even reproduction.

Dr. Terence Anthoney, a specialist in animal behavior at Southern Illinois University, believes the hiccup originated millions of years ago as a gasp, a primitive form of breathing. Even now, he points out, some dying patients with respiratory problems begin to hiccup in the last moments of their lives, as if reverting to the most basic form of breathing. Eventually, more efficient forms of respiration were evolved, but when such improvements occur, Anthoney says, "Nature doesn't throw the old behavior away." It persists, held in reserve, perhaps adapting to some new function. In the case of hiccups, Anthoney believes that the new function was regurgitation of food in order to feed young, a behavior still found in many mammals. Along with the new behavior evolved the ability to close the glottis, to prevent food being sucked into the lungs, and thus was heard the primal "hic!"

Although human beings don't today regurgitate digested food for their young to eat (at least not in polite circles), Anthoney cautions against assuming that hiccups have no function. In years of study, he has found clues linking hiccups in infants to improved digestion, and his discovery that women, as a rule, have much more frequent bouts with hiccups than men has led him to investigate the possibility that hiccups may be connected with the human reproductive cycle. "The belief that hiccups have no purpose is a lot of hooey," says Anthoney. "It's just so common we don't look closely at it."

Although much of Anthoney's research has involved animals, one of his most fascinating cases was that of Charles Osborne of Anthon, Iowa, who started hiccuping one day in 1922 and hasn't stopped since. Osborne, a retired farmer and livestock trader, has been hiccuping anywhere from 10 to 40 times a minute for nearly 63 years — a total of somewhere around half a billion hiccups. Anthoney believes the cause of this phenomenon was a minor stroke Osborne suffered that day in 1922, while trying to lift a 350-pound hog, that destroyed a part of the brain that inhibits the hiccup response. Unlike many victims of prolonged hiccuping, who have lost great amounts of weight, or even died of exhaustion (Pope Pius XII suffered prolonged hiccuping before dying of a stroke in 1958), Osborne seems to have thrived. He is 90 years old, has fathered eight children, and since his first appearance on a radio program in 1936, has achieved a measure of worldwide celebrity. He is listed in the Guinness Book of World Records along with an unnamed young man admitted to an English hospital in 1769, whose hiccups could be heard at a distance of half a mile.

Prolonged hiccups can be stopped by surgery, but it can inhibit breathing, and so Charles Osborne prefers to live with his condition. He has, of course, tried thousands of folk remedies. One well-meaning friend fired both barrels of a shotgun behind him in an effort to startle the hiccups away, but nothing has worked.

Recent experiments with valproic acid have showed promise, but most people continue to rely on their own surefire home remedies. Most of them rely on forcing a deep breath, either by startling the victim or by increasing the

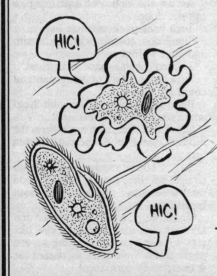

carbon dioxide content in the blood by breath-holding, hyperventilation, or breathing into a bag. Others appear to work by irritating nerve endings in the back of the throat when various substances are swallowed. Some depend on pure magic, such as the mystical numbers 3, 7, 9. And some have no rational explanation at all!

"The hickot is cured with sudden feare or strange newes" (1584).

"Sneezing doth cease the Hiccough" (Francis Bacon, 1626).

"You must in the very instant that the Hickup seizes the Party pull his Ring-Finger, and it will go off" (1727).

Cover your head with a pillow.

Spit on a rock, then turn it over.

Hold your breath and stick out your tongue.

Pant like a dog.

Bite your thumbs and blow hard against them for a minute.

Drink a glass of water with a pencil in your mouth.

Eat a spoonful of peanut butter.

Eat a spoonful of sugar.

Eat a spoonful of salt.

Eat a spoonful of vinegar.

Eat a spoonful of Worcestershire sauce.

Eat a spoonful of crushed ice.

Drink nine swallows of water from your grandfather's cup without taking a breath.

Drink water through a folded handkerchief.

Drink from the wrong side of the cup.

Drink water while holding your ears and nostrils closed.

Take a mouthful of water and swallow it in three gulps. Repeat three times while standing perfectly still and breathing through your nose.

Breathe into a paper bag.

Stand on your head for five minutes.

Stand on your head and drink a glass of water.

Lay over a chair on your stomach and drink a glass of water.

Put the head of a burnt match in your ear.

Place a matchstick on top of your head and count to nine.

In a baby, place two broom straws in the baby's hair.

Lay a broom on the floor, bristles to the right, and jump over it seven times.

Lay a broom on the floor and jump over it three times. Walk around it once, then leave it where it lies.

Hold your left elbow for seven minutes.

Hold a dime against the roof of your mouth for thirty minutes.

Wet a piece of red thread with your tongue, stick it to your forehead, and look at it.

Accuse the victim of something he has not done.

Turn your pockets inside out.

Stand nose-to-nose with the victim and stare at him.

Tighten a belt around your chest.

Stick your head under water and count to 25.

Place a wastebasket on your head and have somebody beat on it.

Say, "Nine sups from a cup cures the hiccups" three times without taking a breath.

Say, "Hiccups, hiccups, stand straight up; three sups in a cup are good for the hiccups" three times without breathing.

Stand in the middle of the road and say, "Hiccup, stickup, not for me, hiccup, stickup." (Ed. note: Keep an eye on the traffic while doing so, or the cure is likely to be permanent.) □□

OUTDOOR PLANTING TABLE, 1985

The best time to plant flowers and vegetables that bear crops above the ground is during the LIGHT of the moon; that is, between the day the moon is new to the day it is full. Flowering bulbs and vegetables that bear crops below ground should be planted during the DARK of the moon; that is, from the day after it is full to the day before it is new again. These moon days for 1985 are given in the "Moon Favorable" columns below. See pages 48-74 for the exact times and days of the new and full moons.

The three columns below give planting dates for the Weather Regions listed. (See Map p. 112.) Consult page 90 for dates of killing frosts and length of growing season. Weather regions 5 and the southern half of 16 are practically frost free.

Above Ground Crops Marked(*) E means Early L means Late	Weather Regions 1, 6, 9, 10, North 13		Weather Regions 2, 3, 7, 11, South 13, 15		Weather Regions 4, 8, 12, 14, 16	
	Planting Dates	Moon Favorable	Planting Dates	Moon Favorable	Planting Dates	Moon Favorable
*Barley	5/15-6/21	5/19-6/2, 6/18-21	3/15-4/7	3/21-4/5	2/15-3/7	2/19-3/6
*Beans (E)	5/7-6/21	5/19-6/2, 6/18-21	4/15-30	4/20-30	3/15-4/7	3/21-4/5
(L)	6/15-7/15	6/18-7/2	7/1-21	7/1-2, 17-21	8/7-31	8/16-30
Beets (E)	5/1-15	5/5-15	3/15-4/3	3/15-20	2/7-28	2/7-18
(L)	7/15-8/15	7/15-16, 8/1-15	8/15-31	8/15, 31	9/1-30	9/1-13, 29-30
*Broccoli (E)	5/15-31	5/19-31	3/7-31	3/21-31	2/15-3/15	2/19-3/6
(L)	6/15-7/7	6/18-7/2	8/1-20	8/16-20	9/7-30	9/14-28
*Brussels Spr.	5/15-31	5/19-31	3/7-4/15	3/21-4/5	2/11-3/20	2/19-3/6
*Cabbage Pl.	5/15-31	5/19-31	3/7-4/15	3/21-4/5	2/11-3/20	2/19-3/6
Carrots (E)	5/15-31	5/15-18	3/7-31	3/7-20	2/15-3/7	2/15-18, 3/7
(L)	6/15-7/21	6/15-17, 7/3-16	7/7-31	7/7-16	8/1-9/7	8/1-15, 8/31-9/7
*Cauliflower (E)	5/15-31	5/19-31	3/15-4/7	3/21-4/5	2/15-3/7	2/19-3/6
Pl. (L)	6/15-7/21	6/18-7/2, 7/17-21	7/1-8/7	7/1-2, 17-31	8/7-31	8/16-30
*Celery (E)	5/15-6/30	5/19-6/2, 6/18-30	3/7-31	3/21-31	2/15-28	2/19-28
(L)	7/15-8/15	7/17-31	8/15-9/7	8/16-30	9/15-30	9/15-28
*Corn, Sw. (E)	5/10-6/15	5/19-6/2	4/1-15	4/1-5	3/15-31	3/21-31
(L)	6/15-30	6/18-30	7/7-21	7/17-21	8/7-31	8/16-30
*Cucumber	5/7-6/20	5/19-6/2, 6/18-20	4/7-5/15	4/20-5/4	3/7-4/15	3/21-4/5
*Eggplant Pl.	6/1-30	6/1-2, 18-30	4/7-5/15	4/20-5/4	3/7-4/15	3/21-4/5
*Endive (E)	5/15-31	5/19-31	4/7-5/15	4/20-5/4	2/15-3/20	2/19-3/6
(L)	6/7-30	6/18-30	7/15-8/15	7/17-31	8/15-9/7	8/16-30
*Flowers	5/7-6/21	5/19-6/2, 6/18-21	4/15-30	4/20-30	3/15-4/7	3/21-4/5
*Kale (E)	5/15-31	5/19-31	3/7-4/7	3/21-4/5	2/11-3/20	2/19-3/6
(L)	7/1-8/7	7/1-2, 17-31	8/15-31	8/16-30	9/7-30	9/14-28
Leek Pl.	5/15-31	5/15-18	3/7-4/7	3/7-20, 4/6-7	2/15-4/15	2/15-18, 3/7-20, 4/6-15
*Lettuce	5/15-6/30	5/19-6/2, 6/18-30	3/1-31	3/1-6, 21-31	2/15-3/7	2/19-3/6
*Muskmelon	5/15-6/30	5/19-6/2, 6/18-30	4/15-5/7	4/20-5/4	3/15-4/7	3/21-4/5
Onion Pl.	5/15-6/7	5/15-18, 6/3-7	3/1-31	3/7-20	2/1-28	2/6-18
*Parsley	5/15-31	5/19-31	3/1-31	3/1-6, 21-31	2/20-3/15	2/20-3/6
Parsnips	4/1-30	4/6-19	3/7-31	3/7-20	1/15-2/4	1/15-19
*Peas (E)	4/15-5/7	4/20-5/4	3/7-31	3/21-31	1/15-2/7	1/20-2/5
(L)	7/15-31	7/17-31	8/7-31	8/16-30	9/15-30	9/15-28
*Pepper Pl.	5/15-6/30	5/19-6/2, 6/18-30	4/1-30	4/1-5, 20-30	3/1-20	3/1-6
Potato	5/1-31	5/5-18	4/1-30	4/6-19	2/10-28	2/10-18
*Pumpkin	5/15-31	5/19-31	4/23-5/15	4/23-5/4	3/7-20	—
Radish (E)	4/15-30	4/15-19	3/7-31	3/7-20	1/21-3/1	2/6-18
(L)	8/15-31	8/15, 31	9/7-30	9/7-13, 29-30	10/1-21	10/1-12
*Spinach (E)	5/15-31	5/19-31	3/15-4/20	3/21-4/5, 4/20	2/7-3/15	2/19-3/6
(L)	7/15-9/7	7/17-31, 8/16-30	8/1-9/15	8/16-30, 9/14-15	10/1-21	10/13-21
*Squash	5/15-6/15	5/19-6/2	4/15-30	4/20-30	3/15-4/15	3/21-4/5
*Swiss Chard	5/1-31	5/1-4, 19-31	3/15-4/15	3/21-4/5	2/7-3/15	2/19-3/6
*Tomato Pl.	5/15-31	5/19-31	4/7-30	4/20-30	3/7-20	—
Turnips (E)	4/7-30	4/17-19	3/15-31	3/15-20	1/20-2/15	2/6-15
(L)	7/1-8/15	7/3-16, 8/1-15	8/1-20	8/1-15	9/1-10/15	9/1-13, 9/29-10/12
*Wheat, Winter	8/11-9/15	8/16-30, 9/14-15	9/15-10/20	9/15-28, 10/13-20	10/15-12/7	10/15-28, 11/12-27
Spring	4/7-30	4/20-30	3/1-20	3/1-6	2/15-28	2/19-28

GARDENING BY THE MOON'S SIGN

The Outdoor Planting Table (opposite) shows how the phases of the moon can be used as a guide. Gardeners who use the moon's *astrological* sign (listed below) follow these rules: 1) When the moon is between New and First Quarter (see left-hand calendar pages 48-74 for moon phases), plant above-ground crops that produce seeds on the outside, and cucumbers, when the moon is in Taurus, Cancer, Virgo, Scorpio, Capricorn, or Pisces. 2) When the moon is between First Quarter and Full, plant above-ground crops bearing seeds inside the fruit when the moon is in Taurus, Cancer, Virgo, Scorpio, Capricorn, or Pisces. 3) When the moon is between Full and Last Quarter, plant below-ground crops when the moon is in Taurus, Cancer, Virgo, Scorpio, Capricorn, or Pisces. 4) When the moon is between Last Quarter and New, do not plant; use for destroying weeds, brush, pests, and for cultivating and plowing when the moon is in Aries, Gemini, Leo, Virgo, Libra, Sagittarius, or Aquarius.

Certain activities are best performed when the moon is in a certain sign: Prune to encourage growth when the moon is in Cancer or Scorpio. Prune to discourage growth when the moon is in Aries or Sagittarius. Set posts when the moon is in Aries, Gemini, Leo, Libra, Sagittarius, or Aquarius. Fill holes when the moon is in Taurus, Cancer, Virgo, Scorpio, Capricorn, or Pisces. Wean animals when the moon is in Sagittarius, Capricorn, Aquarius, or Pisces.

MOON'S PLACE IN THE ZODIAC

	Nov 84	Dec 84	Jan 85	Feb 85	Mar 85	Apr 85	May 85	June 85	July 85	Aug 85	Sept 85	Oct 85	Nov 85	Dec 85
1	AQU	PSC	ARI	GEM	GEM	LEO	VIR	SCO	SAG	AQU	PSC	ARI	GEM	CAN
2	AQU	PSC	TAU	GEM	CAN	LEO	LIB	SCO	CAP	AQU	ARI	TAU	GEM	CAN
3	PSC	ARI	TAU	CAN	CAN	VIR	LIB	SAG	CAP	PSC	ARI	TAU	CAN	LEO
4	PSC	ARI	GEM	CAN	LEO	VIR	SCO	SAG	AQU	PSC	TAU	GEM	CAN	LEO
5	ARI	TAU	GEM	LEO	LEO	LIB	SCO	CAP	AQU	ARI	TAU	GEM	LEO	VIR
6	ARI	TAU	CAN	LEO	VIR	LIB	SAG	CAP	AQU	ARI	TAU	GEM	LEO	VIR
7	ARI	TAU	CAN	VIR	VIR	SCO	SAG	AQU	PSC	ARI	GEM	CAN	LEO	LIB
8	TAU	GEM	CAN	VIR	LIB	SCO	CAP	AQU	PSC	TAU	GEM	CAN	VIR	LIB
9	TAU	GEM	LEO	LIB	LIB	SAG	CAP	PSC	ARI	TAU	CAN	LEO	VIR	SCO
10	GEM	CAN	LEO	LIB	SCO	SAG	CAP	PSC	ARI	GEM	CAN	LEO	LIB	SCO
11	GEM	CAN	VIR	SCO	SCO	CAP	AQU	PSC	ARI	GEM	CAN	VIR	LIB	SAG
12	GEM	LEO	VIR	SCO	SCO	CAP	AQU	ARI	TAU	GEM	LEO	VIR	SCO	SAG
13	CAN	LEO	LIB	SAG	SAG	AQU	PSC	ARI	TAU	CAN	LEO	LIB	SCO	CAP
14	CAN	VIR	LIB	SAG	SAG	AQU	PSC	TAU	GEM	CAN	VIR	LIB	SAG	CAP
15	LEO	VIR	SCO	SAG	CAP	AQU	ARI	TAU	GEM	LEO	VIR	SCO	SAG	AQU
16	LEO	VIR	SCO	CAP	CAP	PSC	ARI	TAU	GEM	LEO	LIB	SCO	CAP	AQU
17	VIR	LIB	SAG	CAP	AQU	PSC	ARI	GEM	CAN	VIR	LIB	SAG	CAP	PSC
18	VIR	LIB	SAG	AQU	AQU	ARI	TAU	GEM	CAN	VIR	SCO	SAG	AQU	PSC
19	LIB	SCO	CAP	AQU	PSC	ARI	TAU	CAN	LEO	LIB	SCO	CAP	AQU	PSC
20	LIB	SCO	CAP	PSC	PSC	ARI	TAU	CAN	LEO	LIB	SAG	CAP	PSC	ARI
21	SCO	SAG	CAP	PSC	PSC	TAU	GEM	CAN	VIR	LIB	SAG	CAP	PSC	ARI
22	SCO	SAG	AQU	PSC	ARI	TAU	GEM	LEO	VIR	SCO	CAP	AQU	PSC	TAU
23	SAG	CAP	AQU	ARI	ARI	GEM	CAN	LEO	LIB	SCO	CAP	AQU	ARI	TAU
24	SAG	CAP	PSC	ARI	TAU	GEM	CAN	VIR	LIB	SAG	AQU	PSC	ARI	TAU
25	SAG	AQU	PSC	TAU	TAU	GEM	LEO	VIR	SCO	SAG	AQU	PSC	TAU	GEM
26	CAP	AQU	ARI	TAU	TAU	CAN	LEO	LIB	SCO	CAP	AQU	ARI	TAU	GEM
27	CAP	AQU	ARI	TAU	GEM	CAN	LEO	LIB	SAG	CAP	PSC	ARI	TAU	CAN
28	AQU	PSC	ARI	GEM	GEM	LEO	VIR	SCO	SAG	AQU	PSC	ARI	GEM	CAN
29	AQU	PSC	TAU	—	CAN	LEO	VIR	SCO	SAG	AQU	ARI	TAU	GEM	CAN
30	PSC	ARI	TAU		CAN	VIR	LIB	SAG	CAP	PSC	ARI	TAU	CAN	LEO
31	—	ARI	GEM	—	CAN		LIB	—	CAP	PSC	—	GEM	—	LEO

The Natural Evolution of the Barn
Text and illustrations by Carl Kirkpatrick

☐ THE FARMER'S BARN HAD TO BE built wisely because invariably it housed his greatest assets, while making the most of available resources. Every new barn, therefore, was a "new and improved" version compared with past efforts, not only in construction materials and techniques, but also in orientation to the sun and prevailing winds as well as accessibility and general efficiency. The good builder employed knowledge gained from neighboring barns in his construction. The characteristic looks that we associate with barns are the result of this natural evolution.

Later farms came to specialize in certain crops, and barns became specialized as well (dairy, fruit, tobacco, poultry barns, etc.). Most of what we learned through this natural evolution is still widely employed in the barns of small farms today. As the cost of power rapidly increases, we will use still newer and more improved ideas in the continuing modification of the barn.

1 An early log barn with thatched roof. Mortaring the spaces between the lower logs kept cold winds out. Upper spaces were left open for circulation of air, which helped keep moisture under control. In early barns an open central hall provided a workspace to process grains, and a breeze for "winnowing." Storage was on either side.

2 A braced frame barn. Once sawn lumber was easily obtainable in the early colonies, most barns were of braced frame construction, which allowed larger and more adaptable structures. Air could circulate through the cracks between the boards. Large doors provided good light. Small barns could be attached horizontally with shed-roof additions on sides and back.

3 In the early 1700s farmers needed more room. Adding more stories in a new barn provided more space under the same roof area and on the same size foundation. Access to the barn was greatly improved if the barn could be situated on a hillside, allowing the farmer to drive in at several levels. Doors at opposite ends offered good cross-ventilation and allowed wagons to drive through. Rows of windows over the door became a popular method of letting in more light.

4 A Pennsylvania brick barn of the mid 19th century. Bricks were omitted in decorative patterns to let in air and light. Farmers adapted styles to whatever construction materials were most common in their area. Barns constructed of logs, stone, brick, or even cordwood were carried to a high degree of development. Also, the influence of various cultures and nationalities shows strongly from region to region. Many unusual examples survive.

5 The town dweller's barn became only large enough to accommodate the nonfarming homeowner's transportation animals, feed, equipment: the early garage. During the mid 1800s his barn was built to look like his house, being similarly sided in board-and-batten or clapboard and paint.

6 As more machines were invented to help the farmer increase his yield, the farmer's barn grew in size and efficiency, too. Simple devices such as trapdoors, hoists, ramps, chutes, and sliding doors were widely employed to move materials through the barn. The addition of a louvered cupola increased ventilation and added a dash of style.

7 **A round barn.** Fewer farmers had to provide for increasing numbers of nonfarming working people. In the mid 19th century experimental barns generated much interest among farmers in the efficient utilization of space and greatly influenced the layouts of later barns.

8 **A gambrel roof allowed more usable space** overhead than a gabled roof. With electricity providing light and ventilation, internal combustion engines replacing men and animals, and mass production techniques being employed wherever possible, many of the farmers' problems were overcome, and nature's direct influence in the design of barns was less crucial.   □□

Making the Most of Your Manure Pile

☐ LIKE WINE AND MEN, NO TWO MA-nures are made equal; like men, good and bad manure is determined by subtle and often intangible qualities; like wine, one's preference in manure is largely a matter of personal taste. The accompanying charts are intended as general guides for the backyard gardener. The best means of finding out what additives your garden needs is to have the soil, as well as the manure you intend to use, tested. This service will be provided free of charge by your local Extension Service if you simply send them samples.

Again as with wines, it is important how you store your manure. Manure is best kept in a pile, which makes it more likely to retain its nutrients and makes you less likely to accidentally step in it. The use of bedding (straw, sawdust, or mulch hay) will also help in preventing nutrients from evaporating or leaching into the ground. Bedding, as it decomposes over time, will also raise the or-ganic matter content of your manure; this is particularly beneficial with poultry and rabbit manure, which have a high nutrient content but are low in organic matter.

Most manures are best used in conjunction with a commercial fertilizer which will provide the nutrients your manure may be lacking. A "complete" fertilizer — one that contains a percentage of each of the three key nutrients nitrogen, phosphate, and potassium (potash) — is preferred. The results of the testing samples will tell you how much to add of each. Chemical fertilizers are generally less expensive than manure, but they will not provide the organic matter essential to maintaining rich soil.

Too much manure can be dangerous. A bushel of cow or horse manure is plenty for 50 square feet. Poultry, sheep, pig, or goat manure is potent enough to provide for 100 square feet per bushel.

TYPE OF MANURE	Water content	Primary nutrients (pounds per ton)		
		Nitrogen	Phosphate	Potash
Cow, horse	60-80%	12-14	5-9	9-12
Sheep, pig, goat	65-75%	10-21	7	13-19
Chicken:				
Wet, sticky and caked	75%	30	20	10
Moist, crumbly to sticky	50%	40	40	20
Crumbly	30%	60	55	30
Dry	15%	90	70	40
Ashed		none	135	100

TYPE OF GARDEN	Best Type of Manure	Best Time to Apply
Flower	cow, horse	early spring
Vegetable	chicken cow, horse	fall spring
Potato or root crop	cow, horse	fall
Acid-loving plants, (blueberries, azaleas, mountain laurel, rhododendrons)	cow, horse	early fall or not at all

GESTATION AND MATING TABLE

	Proper age for first mating	Period of fertility, in years	No. of females for one male	Period of gestation, in days	
				Range	Average
Ewe	90 lbs. or 1 yr.	6		142-154	147 151[8]
Ram	12-14 mos., well matured	7	50-75[2] 35-40[3]		
Mare	3 yrs.	10-12		310-370	336
Stallion	3 yrs.	12-15	40-45[4] Record 252[5]		
Cow	15-18 mos.[1]	10-14		279-290[6] 262-300[7]	283
Bull	1 yr., well matured	10-12	50[4] Thousands[5]		
Sow	5-6 mos. or 250 lbs.	6		110-120	115
Boar	250-300 lbs.	6	50[2] 35-40[3]		
Doe goat	10 mos. or 85-90 lbs.	6		145-155	150
Buck goat	Well matured	5	30		
Bitch	16-18 mos.	8		58-67	63
Dog	12-16 mos.	8			
She cat	12 mos.	6		60-68	63
Doe rabbit	6 mos.	5-6		30-32	31
Buck rabbit	6 mos.	5-6	30		

[1]Holstein & Beef: 750 lbs. Jersey: 500 lbs. [2]Handmated. [3]Pasture. [4]Natural. [5]Artificial. [6]Beef; 8-10 days shorter for Angus. [7]Dairy. [8]For fine wool breeds.

BIRD AND POULTRY INCUBATION PERIODS, IN DAYS

Chicken .. 21 Goose ...30-34 Guinea 26-28
Turkey .. 28 Swan ...... 42 Canary 14-15
Duck ... 26-32 Pheasant ..22-24 Parakeet 18-20

GESTATION PERIODS, WILD ANIMALS, IN DAYS

Black bear 210   Seal 330
Hippo 225-250   Squirrel, gray 44
Moose ... 240-250   Whale, sperm ... 480
Otter 270-300   Wolf 60-63
Reindeer ... 210-240

MAXIMUM LIFE SPANS OF ANIMALS IN CAPTIVITY, IN YEARS

Box Turtle   Elephant 84   Oyster
 (Eastern) .. 138   Giant Tortoise . 190   (Freshwater) 80
Bullfrog .... 16 Giraffe 28   Pig 10
Camel 25   Goat 17   Polar Bear .. 41
Cat (Domestic) . 23 Gorilla 33   Rabbit 13
Cheetah 16   Grizzly Bear ... 31   Rattlesnake .. 20
Chicken 14   Horse   Reindeer ... 15
Chimpanzee .. 37   (Domestic) .. 50   Sea Lion 28
Cow 20   Kangaroo...... 16   Sheep 20
Dog (Domestic) . 22 Lion 30   Tiger 25
Dolphin 30   Moose 20   Timber Wolf . 15
Eagle 55   Owl 68   Toad 36
                                              Zebra 25

REPRODUCTIVE CYCLE IN FARM ANIMALS

	Recurs if not bred	Estrual cycle incl. heat period (days)		In heat for		Usual time of ovulation
	Days	Ave.	Range	Ave.	Range	
Mare	21	21	10-37	5-6 days	2-11 days	24-48 hours before end of estrus
Sow	21	21	18-24	2-3 days	1-5 days	30-36 hours after start of estrus
Ewe	16½	16½	14-19	30 hours	24-32 hours	12-24 hours before end of estrus
Goat	21	21	18-24	2-3 days	1-4 days	Near end of estrus
Cow	21	21	18-24	18 hours	10-24 hours	10-12 hours after end of estrus
Bitch	pseudo-pregnancy	24		7 days	5-9 days	1-3 days after first acceptance
Cat	pseudo-pregnancy		15-21	3-4 days if mated	9-10 days in absence of male	24-56 hours after coitus

There's Nothing Like an Egg

Over easy, poached, or scrambled, this little calcified ellipsoid is surrounded by more myths and just plain old wives' tales than any other everyday food. Finally, a career poultry scientist sets the record straight.

by Bobby D. Barnett
illustrated by Anne Vadeboncoeur

☐ THE CHICKEN'S EGG IS THE SUBJECT of many myths and much mystery. A complex object in spite of its simple appearance, the egg contains all the chemical, biological, and nutritional material needed to make a microscopic speck on the surface of the yolk grow into a breathing, chirping chick that bursts through the shell to freedom.

Most eggs in today's marketplace are infertile and therefore incapable of producing chicks. Herein lie some of the mysteries of the egg. Both men and women have difficulty believing that millions of female chickens can grow to maturity, lay eggs for a year, and finally go to their reward in the soup kettle without seeing or missing a rooster. It may be presumptuous to say they don't miss males, but it is well established that hens lay as many eggs and are as healthy without male companionship. One frequently repeated myth is that the whitish, twisted material seen near the raw egg yolk is semen from the rooster. The myth persists despite the fact that most hens are virgins. This whitish material is actually thick albumen, which is part of a layer of dense egg white surrounding the entire yolk. Apparently its purpose is to help keep the yolk centered in the egg. This dense, cloudy albumen is especially prominent in fresh, high-quality eggs. When hens are mated, much of the semen stays in the lower part of the reproductive tract, but millions of sperm cells make their way up the tract. Only a few finally enter the yolk as it is engulfed by the extreme upper end of the oviduct. Only one spermatozoon actually unites with the yolk's genetic material to form that first cell of the new chick. Before the egg is laid, that cell

has divided several times, and the trained eye can distinguish fertile from infertile eggs by the appearance of the germinal disc. This is a spot on the yolk about the size of a match head, and the size is about the same whether the egg is fertile or infertile.

A modern myth concerning fertile eggs suggests that they are more nutritious or wholesome than infertile eggs. This is a part of the wisdom of the nutrition cult that holds that natural foods are more healthful than processed or less natural foods. (This ignores the fact that toadstools, pokeberries, and many other plant and animal products are toxic even though they are completely natural.) Perhaps a fertile egg is more natural than an infertile one, although infertile eggs occur among birds in the wild. Even so, it would be difficult, if not impossible, to demonstrate any nutritional difference between fresh fertile and infertile eggs. Of course, an *incubated* fertile egg changes rapidly, and the developing embryo converts egg material to muscle, bone, blood, and eventually all the tissues of a chick. At some point between the freshly laid fertile egg and the hatching chick, the contents of the egg would be nutritionally different from a fresh infertile egg. Some Asians consider incubated fertile eggs a delicacy. More than a delicacy, they consider them an aphrodisiac. They are probably as sexually stimulating as the ground rhinoceros horn preferred by some Africans for the same purpose.

The color of the chicken's egg shell is not well understood by consumers. In truth, the shell color is a genetic trait. This means that some breeds of chickens lay white-shelled eggs, some lay brown-shelled eggs, and some even lay bluish- or green-shelled eggs. A popular myth states that brown-shelled eggs have darker yolks than white-shelled eggs. The color of the yolk is determined by the feed. If the chicken eats grass, yellow corn, or other feedstuffs rich in yellow pigments, the yolk will be deep yellow in direct relation to the amount of yellow in the feed regardless of the breed of chicken or color of the shell. A modern myth states that the bluish-green egg of the South American Araucana chicken contains no cholesterol. If this were true there would cease to be Araucana chickens. Every living animal cell must contain cholesterol, and the germinal disk would never become a chick without cholesterol. By analysis, Araucana egg yolks are almost identical in their cholesterol content to eggs from the more popular breeds on a weight-for-weight basis.

While brown, white, and green eggs are essentially the same in nutritional value, there are definite preferences by individuals and by people in different regions of the country. New Englanders have almost convinced themselves that they make no distinction among colors of men, but they are unabashed bigots when it comes to their preference for eggs. They will accept any color as long as it is brown. Just why this is the case is a mystery. The fact that the American breeds were developed in New England and that all lay brown eggs is a clue. The popularity of these breeds in the Northeast, including the Rhode Island Red, New Hampshire, and Plymouth Rock, probably established the brown egg as the normal egg.

White-shelled eggs are preferred throughout most of the country, although pockets of brown-egg prejudice exist here and there. The Mediterranean breeds, of which the Single Comb White Leghorn is the most popular, lay white-shelled eggs. The smaller body size of the Leghorn re- duces feed consumption and makes this the most efficient producer.

Old wives' tales suggest that the shape of an egg indicates the sex of the chick that will hatch from it. Longer, more pointed eggs, according to this legend, will produce male chicks, while eggs that are more nearly round will produce female chicks. Unfortunately there is no truth to this myth. Commercial poultrymen would very much like to sex chicks before the eggs are incubated. Male chicks of the egg-laying types are normally killed at day-old, immediately after the sex is identified by examining the vent. This great loss could be eliminated if the fresh egg could be sexed. The "male" eggs could then be eaten. It is an interesting peculiarity of birds that the female determines the sex of the offspring as opposed to mammals in which the male determines the sex. That is, birds lay two kinds of eggs. About half are destined to be males and half females, yet scientists are unable to distinguish between the sexes before the eggs hatch.

Regardless of myths, mysteries, prejudice, or preference, the egg is a marvel of nutrition and economy. Whether white, brown, or even green, there is nothing like an egg. □ □

Three Ways to Hypnotize a Chicken

Oddly enough, high-strung birds are the easiest to put in a trance.

by Linda Riggins

☐ "I'VE BEEN HYPNOTIZING chickens since I was nine when the county 4-H agent in Milwaukee showed me how," says Dr. Doris White, a Bernardsville, New Jersey, chicken farmer who is also professor of elementary education at William Paterson College, *and* a chicken hypnotism instructor. "When he taught me, I thought everyone knew how to hypnotize chickens." She was wrong. She points out that "Some farmers are still surprised that a person can hypnotize chickens. But after they see me demonstrate how it's done, they go home and try it themselves."

Dr. White shows her audiences two methods of hypnotizing chickens. The Oscillating Finger Method is probably the easier of the two. Place the bird on its side with a wing under its body and hold it down gently. Make sure its head is flat on the table. To hypnotize the bird, use one finger of the free hand, moving the finger back and forth in front of the bird's beak from its tip (without touching it) to a point that is about four inches from the beak. Keep the finger in a line parallel to the beak.

The second technique is the Sternum Stroke Method. Gently put the bird onto its back. It may be necessary to use a book, purse, or other item to keep the bird from rolling onto its side. Hold the bird down. Lightly massage the bird's sternum, using the slightly spread thumb and index finger of one hand to do the stroking.

(*Editor's note:* A third technique, discovered buried in the files of *The Old Farmer's Almanac,* is the Chalk Line Method. Draw a straight chalk mark about a foot long. Hold the chicken with its beak on one end of the line, staring straight out at the chalk mark. In a few seconds, the chicken will be hypnotized.)

"A bird will stay hypnotized a couple of seconds, minutes, or hours," says White, although in her demonstrations they're "out" only for minutes. Regardless of the method used, a sudden movement or loud noise will bring the chicken out of the hypnotic trance.

White adds, "Pheasants go out faster than any other bird. Wild pheasants are very nervous and high-strung and usually very easy to hypnotize." In her demonstrations she is protective of pheasants because after they come out of hypnosis they are likely to hurt themselves unless they are carefully monitored.

Noting that domestic birds are more difficult to hypnotize than wild ones, she suggests that one reason may be that wild birds are using a survival skill when they submit to hypnosis.

White has reported the results of her experiments to several New Jersey science conferences and fairs. In one of her studies of 11 birds, the heart and respiration rates, when measured five minutes after hypnosis, were significantly lower than in the pre-hypnotic state. For example, in a Bantam White Cochin cock the heart rate before hypnosis was 457 beats per minute and the rate after hypnosis was 372. The rates for this bird's respiration were 22 and 20 breaths per minute respectively. The temperatures of nine of these birds went down or were unchanged in the post-hypnotic state. ☐☐

Unabridged List of All Our State Mottoes

R hode Island has the shortest; the most frequently mentioned words are "Liberty" and "Union"; and some, like New Mexico's, are a bit mystifying. But it's a safe bet that most Americans don't know their own state mottoes. This list should help . . .

Alabama
We dare defend our rights.

Alaska
North to the future.

Arizona
God enriches.

Arkansas
The people rule.

California
I have found it (Eureka).

Colorado
Nothing without Providence.

Connecticut
He who transplanted still sustains.

Delaware
Liberty and independence.

Florida
In God we trust.

Georgia
Wisdom, justice and moderation.

Hawaii
The life of the land is perpetuated in righteousness.

Idaho
It is perpetual.

Illinois
State sovereignty — national union.

Indiana
Crossroads of America.

Iowa
Our liberties we prize and our rights we will maintain.

Kansas
To the stars through difficulties.

Kentucky
United we stand, divided we fall.

Louisiana
Union, justice and confidence.

Maine
I direct (Dirigo).

Maryland
Manly deeds, womanly words.

Massachusetts
By the sword we seek peace, but peace only under liberty.

Michigan
If you seek a pleasant peninsula, look about you.

Minnesota
The star of the north.

Mississippi
By valor and arms.

Missouri
The welfare of the people shall be the supreme law.

Montana
Gold and silver.

Nebraska
Equality before the law.

Nevada
All for our country.

New Hampshire
Live free or die.

New Jersey
Liberty and prosperity.

New Mexico
It grows as it goes.

New York
Ever upward (Excelsior).

North Carolina
To be rather than to seem.

North Dakota
Liberty and union, now and forever, one and inseparable.

Ohio
With God, all things are possible.

Oklahoma
Labor conquers all things.

Oregon
The union.

Pennsylvania
Virtue, liberty and independence.

Rhode Island
Hope.

South Carolina
While I breathe, I hope.

South Dakota
Under God, the people rule.

Tennessee
Agriculture and commerce.

Texas
Friendship.

Utah
Industry.

Vermont
Freedom and unity.

Virginia
Thus always to tyrants.

Washington
By and by.

West Virginia
Mountaineers are always free.

Wisconsin
Forward.

Wyoming
Equal rights.

Betting Big on the Weather

The commodities market offers America's farmers, food processors, and speculators a legal forum for gambling on the growing season. In such a risky business the potential for either reward or disaster is great.

by Henry Dubroff
illustrated by Anne Fleming

☐ THE STRUGGLE BETWEEN THESE two superpowers has been going on for decades, and the well-being of every family in the free world depends on how skillfully each side plays its part. But the combatants in this all-important battle for survival are not the U.S. and the U.S.S.R.

This unarmed conflict is waged daily between "hedgers" — farmers and food-processing companies — and "speculators" — risk takers who are willing to bet millions on the value of a crop before the seeds are planted.

The conflict, a shoving match between traders clad in pastel-colored smocks, swirls into action each weekday at the major commodities futures markets in New York and Chicago.

If you doubt the importance of the futures market, consider this: Prices of basic commodities consumed by the entire world are set daily at the commodities exchanges. The exchanges are the free world's first line of defense against rapid food price swings that could cause mass starvation, bankrupt nations, and upend world economy.

For a pivotal conflict, the struggle between speculator and hedger has some very strange characteristics. For example:

• Face-to-face meetings between speculators and hedgers are extremely rare. Traders in the "pit" often work for both speculators and hedgers, so that when a futures contract is made or "struck," *it is impossible to tell one side from the other!*

• Futures contracts worth $1 trillion or more in soybeans, corn, orange juice, pork bellies, and other agricultural commodities are struck in the pits each year. However, 90 percent of all futures contracts are *canceled before delivery is taken on a single product!*

• The conflict between speculator and hedger has produced tactics that would confound General George Patton himself. But the single element that most often determines who wins and who loses is — *the weather!*

Commodities markets got their start as a way to break the iron grip that grain dealers held over the American farmer in the early 1800s. The grain companies knew that during four weeks every year — when the harvest came in — there would be a tremendous supply of grain brought to market, enough grain to cause prices to fall to a fraction of their pre-harvest price.

By the 1860s, the futures contract had evolved as the easiest way to solve the problem of the harvest-time price crash — and commodities exchanges were in business to stay. Futures contracts forced grain dealers to put a constant value on a crop from early winter to the end of the growing season, ending the annual price collapse.

"Simply put, a futures contract is an agreement to *make* or *take* delivery of a specific commodity of standardized quality or quantity, at a date in the future, made by open outcry in the trading pit," says the Chicago Board of Trade, the leading commodities exchange for the sale of wheat, corn, and soybean futures.

A simple trading pattern has emerged: If the market believes crops will be poor, futures prices generally will rise. But if the market believes in a bumper crop, futures prices usually will tumble (see box).

"The basic law of the commodities market is plain old supply and demand," said Christopher Stewart, who is a senior analyst at Merrill Lynch Commodities.

The battle to set prices in the pits is a constantly flowing struggle in which a contract held for just a few hours can bring tremendous rewards to a speculator. For speculators, *information* is the key to success.

It is Washington, D.C., in the spring of 1905. At 10:00 A.M. a man in panama hat and white suit strides briskly past the Agriculture Department offices, two hours before the release of the monthly cotton forecast. Glancing quickly at the building's facade, he hustles into a waiting carriage, heading for the nearest telegraph office. When the forecast is released, one New Orleans speculator has made a killing in the cotton futures market.

Each month the profits roll in like clockwork until a federal investigator notices a lowly Agriculture Department clerk suddenly lowering his win-

dow blind at 10:00 A.M. on an overcast morning shortly after the final cotton figures have been compiled. The Great Venetian Blind Scandal of 1905 cracks wide open.

Under questioning, the clerk confesses that he has turned his window into a giant bar graph, using the level of the venetian blind to signal the size of the crop forecast to a trading company scout passing by.

Today the USDA uses elaborate "lock-up" procedures, including the securing of all windows by locked blackout curtains, on the day the forecasts are compiled. So a dozen private forecasters talk to grain elevator opera-

The battle to set prices in the pits is a constantly flowing struggle in which a contract held for just a few hours can bring tremendous rewards . . .

tors, meteorologists, and secret sources, trying to outguess the USDA in pinpointing the size of the next year's harvest. Others use sophisticated computers to chart price patterns over decades — and even centuries.

Under the searing summer sun of 1983, townspeople throughout the Midwest took a look at withering crops and decided the USDA's August forecast of a 14 percent corn shortfall was too optimistic. They figured that the USDA's multi-billion-dollar program to pay farmers in surplus grain for acreage left fallow was going to have a big effect on supplies, too.

Barbers, coffee shop owners, even college professors became speculators, staking their financial future on "longs" — they bought futures contracts, figuring the price would go up. Some turned into big winners. Corn for December delivery jumped 48 percent to a near record $3.76 per bushel by summer's end, and year-end soybeans skyrocketed from $5.80 to nearly $10 per bushel. Belatedly, the USDA upped its estimated shortfall to 40 percent.

Analyst Stewart said the rapid swing in prices was a natural occurrence, one that vindicates the commodities market as a place of pure supply and demand economics. However, heads rolled at the USDA the next fall, and Congress launched an inquiry into the USDA's forecasting methods.

Conrad Leslie, an independent analyst in Chicago, said the commodities market "needs a new set of cloverleafs and road signs" as it ushers in the 21st century. Behind Leslie's concern is the fact that an entire new family of futures markets has grown up during the past decade. Trading in precious metals, U.S. Treasury bills, stock market indices, and other financial "commodities" now rivals the traditional agricultural futures market, making it tougher for the market to police itself.

Leslie is worried that two or three active speculators who buy and sell thousands of contracts each day could direct daily trading of a single commodity, tipping the scales too far in their favor. He wants consumers, farmers, and large brokerage houses to have greater representation on the exchanges' boards of directors to help police artificial price fluctuations.

One dramatic fluctuation occurred on the New York Mercantile Exchange in 1976, when a pair of potato processors allegedly tried to make a fortune speculating that prices would fall. When prices firmed, according to *The Wall Street Journal,* the pair failed to deliver on contracts worth nearly 50 million pounds of Maine potatoes, the largest default in commodities trading history. "The potato market never fully recovered," the *Journal* said. □ □

HOW THE MARKET REALLY WORKS

The battle between hedgers and speculators goes like this. Hedgers are either farmers or food processors. The farmer wants to cover his expenses in producing agricultural products. The food processor wants to cover his expenses in processing and delivering those products to the final consumers.

So the farmers "hedge" by selling contracts promising to deliver goods at a price that will cover their expenses if prices should fall. And food processors "hedge" by buying contracts to accept goods at prices they can afford, in case prices go shooting up. In both cases, the hedgers will lose money on the contracts if things don't go as they expected. But the protection against disaster is worth the loss in potential earnings. It's a sort of insurance policy.

So where do the speculators come in? They have no interest in selling corn or buying wheat. They are there to absorb the losses and reap the huge profits that the hedgers have insured themselves against.

Think of it as a game of "hot potato." Farmer Smith sells a contract to deliver 5,000 bushels of corn to Chicago at $3.55 per bushel, knowing that even under the worst conditions, it will cost him only $3.25 a bushel to produce the corn.

Who bought Farmer Smith's contract? Speculator Sharp, who is betting that the price of corn will go above $3.55. How high? He's guessing around $3.75, so he'll try to sell to some other speculator at that figure. The other speculator is guessing it will go even higher, and on it goes, the hot potato being tossed from speculator to speculator, until the music stops when the contract runs out on the date of delivery. By that time the food processor who actually wants the corn has usually stepped in and bought the contract.

The speculators buy or sell the contracts depending on whether they expect the price to rise or fall. Some will make money on the transactions, and some will get caught by changing conditions and lose. A few unlucky traders might end up holding the hot potato, an expired contract to accept delivery of 5,000 bushels of corn that nobody is willing to buy. Economists tell the story of a lonely figure knocking furiously at a neighbor's door on a cold evening in England in the 1930s. The desperate visitor couldn't unload his corn futures contract before the delivery date and wanted to use his neighbor's barn to store the corn before it was unloaded on his front lawn. The identity of the unhappy man? John Maynard Keynes, the father of modern economics, and an active commodities speculator.

Expert Advice On Catching, Keeping, Measuring, and Cooking Your Favorite Fish

A series of useful tips a pro has gleaned from a lifetime of angling.

by Bud Leavitt

"There's no place too far to go fishing," says Bud Leavitt, sportswriter, member of the Fishing Hall of Fame, and avid fresh- and saltwater fisherman. His fishing trips, from Honduras and Mexico across the United States and Canada and into Alaska, have been made in the company of such famous sportsmen as Ted Williams, Sam Snead, Prince Rainier, Curt Gowdy, and John Havlicek. Six days a week for 38 years, Bud Leavitt has written about his fishing exploits in a column for the *Bangor Daily News,* Bangor, Maine. His favorite fishing tips, drawn from a lifetime of angling, are listed here.

* * *

Fish tend not to bite during windy or stormy days, that is, when the barometer is falling. Use a good barometer and keep a salty eye on the water.

* * *

Spinning reels need only infrequent attention if used exclusively in fresh water. Reels that see saltwater service should be rinsed in fresh water and allowed to dry before storage. The easiest and surest method is to bring the entire outfit into the shower stall. A hot, soapy shower revives the fisherman after a hard day on the ocean and works wonders with a rod and reel.

* * *

Boston mackerel, strips of squid, and the white belly meat of summer flounder make excellent bait for game fish and food fish. Save good fishing time by preparing and freezing ready-to-use strip baits in advance. To prevent freezer burn, place baits in plastic margarine containers or fiber milk containers, label, and cover with water before freezing.

* * *

Nowadays many anglers release more fish than they keep, rightly figuring a fish is worth more alive in the water than dead in a pan. If you're without a scale and want to know the weight of a fish, measure its length and girth, then apply the measurements to this formula:

$$W = \frac{800}{L \times G^2}$$

Take the fish's length by measuring from the tip of the lower jaw to the bottom tip of the tail. Girth should be taken at the broadest part of the fish's body. In the above formula W is the fish's weight in pounds, L its length and G^2 is the girth squared.

* * *

Next time your children insist on chewing bubble gum when fishing, ask them to chew red gum. After the youngsters have chewed it a while, roll it into small chunks shaped like worms. Hook these in the middle to catch

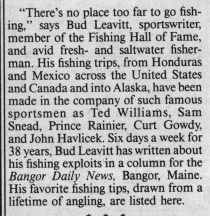

perch, bass, bluegills, crappies, and occasionally a wise old brook trout. You have to strike fast when you feel a nibble.

* * *

If you find yourself with a broken tip guide on your fishing rod and far away from the nearest tackle store, all is not lost. Find a safety pin, cut off the clasp end, and use the round loop of the pin for a guide. You can use monofilament to wind around the pin. If there is a woman in your party with some nail polish, use some to hold the windings.

* * *

Ever try to find a swivel in a tackle box with anywhere from one to 1,000 items in storage? Here's how you can do it in a hurry when a tackle change is necessary. String a dozen or so on a large safety pin and fasten the pin to the underside of your shirt pocket flap.

* * *

When cooking over an open fire, you can save yourself a lot of work scouring the outside of pots and pans if you first smear a thin coating of mud over them. Soot collects on the mud. After cooking tap the utensils and off comes the mud, soot and all.

* * *

The best dry fly fishing usually comes at day's last light, dusk, or when you can't see to change flies. A small pencil-size flashlight clipped to your fishing vest and aimed downward solves that problem nicely.

* * *

Empty cardboard milk cartons make excellent fire starters. For starting campfires, you can carry your supply easily by cutting off the ends of the cartons, slitting down one corner, and folding them flat. The paraffin-soaked cardboard will light when wet wood will sputter and refuse to burn.

* * *

You will always have a ruler with which to measure the length of your fish if you'll paint dots one inch apart on your fly or casting rod. Paint every fifth dot red. Paint as far as the biggest fish you would like to catch.

* * *

You must catch at least one trout or one perch to take advantage of one of these tips. The anal fin of a brook trout makes excellent bait. Cast the fin gently into riffles and pockets and retrieve it slowly. Belly strips of perch are good bait for bass, pickerel, musky, pike, and the occasional lake trout. Jerk the bait quickly on top of the water.

* * *

When fishing in a pond or lake, never pass up a half-sunken boat, or even a boat that is tied up offshore. Fish often lie in the shade of boats.

* * *

Fish belonging to the sunfish family — bass, bluegills, etc. — can be dressed by removing scales and skin with a pair of pliers. Start behind the head and keep pulling off skin.

* * *

A bicycle tire laid on the lawn can be a real help to improving your fishing technique. For either fly casting or bait casting, try landing your lure in the center of the tire. When you can put three out of four in the center, you are ready to talk to the trout — or salmon, bass, and such saltwater species as striped bass and weakfish.

* * *

When you don't have your watch, you may want to estimate how long it will be before dark. If the sun is shining, you can do this easily by facing the sun. Then stretch out your arms in front of you. Place one hand above the other with the little finger of one hand on the horizon. Then count the fingers — not thumbs — needed to blot out the sky between the horizon and the sun. Each finger represents 15 minutes of daylight.

* * *

For fish to be at its best on the table it must be properly frozen. One method is to put the fish in an empty milk carton, fill it with water, and then freeze. This way the meat is encased in ice, and the heavy material of the milk carton helps prevent freezer burn.

* * *

Use binoculars to check ponds for areas where there are moving fish, especially trout. The use of binoculars has accounted for more than a few outstanding catches. Rising trout show up on glass, and the smart fisherman knows what happens when fish are "working."

* * *

A smart Maine fisherman I know has a trick he uses to catch trout on Roach River, a Moosehead Lake tributary. He hangs his flashlight from a tree so it shines above — not on — the water of a likely pool. The light attracts insects, which in turn attract trout and landlocked salmon.

* * *

You can easily prevent hooks from becoming part of your thumb or from scattering all over your tackle box. Stop at the hardware store and pick up a small magnet. Put the magnet in the compartment where you store hooks. I know what I'm talking about. Nothing's funnier than a 245-pound outdoor writer walking into the local emergency center wearing a four-inch bass plug with one of the treble hooks in his fat thumb.

* * *

The really smart and sharp fishermen I know usually carry a tube of liquid cement in that already 101-pound pack that stores their fishing gear. The cement comes into play for plugging boat leaks, patching canoes and torn waders, tightening a loose rod ferrule, and even as a quick fire-starter. On a rainy day, there's nothing like it to start a warming fire or to boil up the tea pail.

* * *

Here's a salute to the man who invented Vaseline. A jar belongs in every outdoorsman's tackle box. It can be used as a lubricant, rust preventive, medication for insect bites, water repellent, and even as a floatant for fly lines and dry flies. A million-plus souls who fish and flounder around in fishing pools owe you one, Mr. Vaseline. □ □

BEST FISHING DAYS, 1985
(and other fishing lore from the files of *The Old Farmer's Almanac*)

Probably the best fishing time is when the ocean tides are restless before their turn and in the first hour of ebbing. All fish in all waters — salt or fresh — feed most heavily then.

Best temperatures for fish species vary widely, of course, and are chiefly important if you are going to have your own fish pond. Best temperatures for brook trout are 45° to 65° F. Brown trout and rainbows are more tolerant of higher temperatures. Smallmouth black bass do best in cool water. Horned pout take what they find.

Most of us go fishing when we can get off, not because it is the best time. But there are best times:

- One hour before and one hour after high tide, and one hour before and one hour after low tide. (The times of high tides are given on pages 48-74 and corrected for your locality on pages 78-79. Inland, the times for high tides would correspond with the times the moon is due south. Low tides are halfway between high tides.)
- "The morning rise" — after sunup for a spell — and "the evening rise" — just before sundown and the hour or so after. Still water or a ripple is better than a wind at both times.
- When there is a hatch of flies — caddis or mayflies, commonly. (The fisherman will have to match the hatching flies with *his* fly — or go fishless.)
- When the breeze is from a westerly quarter rather than north or east.
- When the barometer is steady or on the rise. (But, of course, even in a three-day driving northeaster the fish isn't going to just give up feeding. His hunger clock keeps right on working, and the smart fisherman will find something he wants.)
- When the moon is between new and full.

MOON BETWEEN
NEW & FULL

Jan. 1-6, 20-Feb. 5	July 17-31
Feb. 19-Mar. 6	Aug. 16-30
Mar. 21-Apr. 5	Sept. 14-28
Apr. 20-May 4	Oct. 13-28
May 19-June 2	Nov. 12-27
June 18-July 2	Dec. 11-27

"Magic" Indian Oil
CATCHES FISH LIKE CRAZY!

I made this remarkable discovery when my son went on his first fishing trip with me. We hired this old Indian guide in a small town in Wisconsin.

When our guide showed Mark how to bait his hook, I noticed that he rubbed something on the bait just before Mark put the line in the lake. Within minutes Mark had himself a beautiful bass. You can imagine how pleased I was and Mark, of course, wanted more.

So the whole thing was repeated—the guide put on the bait, rubbed it again, and up popped another beauty. Meanwhile, I sat there patiently waiting for my first fish.

This went on all morning. Mark caught 30 bass and I got eight.

When I pulled the boat in at noon and paid off our Indian guide, I noticed that a small, unusual seed had apparently fallen from the guide's pocket into the bottom of our boat.

"It works for me—wouldn't be without it."
D: Hulbutt, Duluth

The odor from the seed was quite strong and certainly different from anything I had ever smelled before. This was what he had rubbed on Mark's bait!

When we returned home the next day, I gave the seed to a chemist friend of mine. He analyzed it and duplicated it into a spray for me.

I could hardly wait for my next fishing trip. What I discovered on that trip was absolutely unbelievable. I have never before caught fish like that. Every time I baited my hook, I sprayed it and up popped another fish.

I tested some more. I put spray on one bait and nothing on another. The sprayed bait got the fish almost immediately. The unsprayed bait got some nibbles, but nothing more.

I gave some of my friends samples of the spray to try and the results were the same—they caught fish like never before.

I named my spray "CATCH FISH LIKE CRAZY" cause that's just what it does and it works with all kinds of fresh or salt water fish. It works equally well on artificial or live bait.

"I used your spray and caught all these fish"
J. Hannon, Chicago

Here's what fishermen say about my spray:

"What you say is true. I caught fish like crazy–it really works!"
K.S. Evansville, Ind.

"I read your ad and found it hard to believe–but sent for it anyhow cause I'm not very lucky–after one day, I'm a believer–I caught Snook and Sea Bass–it was easy!"
D.D. Naples, Fla.

"I always keep a can in my tackle box. It's fantastic!"
K.V. Highland Park, Ill.

OLD AND NEW MATHEMATICAL PUZZLES

Blanton C. Wiggin, Puzzle Editor

From many puzzles submitted by readers we have selected 15 classical, original, or timely puzzles for 1985. They are graded for difficulty, so that there should be something of interest for everyone. We hope you find them challenging. No calculus, computers, or tricks. We try to include specialized knowledge, if needed, in the puzzle statement.

We will award one prize of $50 for the best set of solutions to puzzles 12 through 15 received before February 1, 1985. The answers to these four are omitted here. These may sometimes require a chart or table of data from your local library.

We use a point system to judge the prize set. A basic, unadorned, correct answer is 20 points. For a thorough analysis, an elegant or novel answer, up to 5 points extra. Numerical errors lose only 2 or 3 points, if it is clear that the method is understood.

Explanations and Prize-Set Answers will be mailed after June 1 to anyone sending 50¢ and a self-addressed, stamped envelope to "Puzzle Answers," *The Old Farmer's Almanac,* Dublin, NH 03444.

We'll also pay $15 for any original puzzles we use in *The Old Farmer's Almanac* for 1986. Closing date for submissions is March 1, 1985. Entries become the property of Yankee Publishing Incorporated and cannot be acknowledged or returned. In addition to submitting a puzzle, please tell us the type of puzzle you like best, such as magic squares, geometry, time-rate-quantity, mazes, logic, number substitutions, etc.

From a group of good answers, we are happy to announce a first-time winner for 1984: Leon Kreidler, Sheboygan, Wis., with 88 points; followed by Walter Beveridge, Hartsdale, N.Y., 86; and past winner Newton Amos, St. Louis, Mo., 81. Other high scorers were Paul Nektaredes, Tarpon Springs, Fla., and Douglas J. Madea, Manheim, Pa.

Please submit your favorite puzzles and send your answers early for puzzles 12-15. Use a separate sheet for each puzzle or answer, and be sure each sheet has your name and address on it. Good luck!

Answers appear on page 200.

---

1. Russian Markets
Difficulty: 1

a. Carpenter Hammer charged Farmer Sickle a capitalistic 5 rubles to saw a board into 2 pieces. At that rate, what should he charge to make 4 pieces?

b. Sickle then challenged Hammer double or nothing to plow this pattern with one continuous line, never crossing itself. Did Sickle pay?

Matt McCullar
Fort Worth, Texas

2. Telling Time
Difficulty: 1

a. In England and some other countries 9-2-85 usually means February 9. In the U.S., most people think of September 2. During a year, how many dates can be confused?

b. During a single day, from one midnight to the next, how many times is the minute hand on a clock lined up with the hour hand?

Paul R. Erickson
Frankfort, Ill.

3. This and That
Difficulty: 2

This and That are whole numbers. This and That, plus ½ of This, and That again = 11. How much is This and how much is That?

Walter I. Christopher
Carmichaels, Pa.

4. Enlarged Pool
Difficulty: 2

Mr. Jones owns a square pool with a tree at each corner. He has decided to enlarge the pool, but being a lover of nature, he wants to save his trees. The pool must maintain its original shape, and no tree is to be moved or cut down.

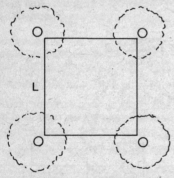

Suppose a side of the original pool is L. What is the maximum area of the enlarged pool?

Jose Diaz
Boston, Mass.

5. Short-Cut Math
Difficulty: 2

Quite obviously $\frac{26}{65} = \frac{2}{5}$ by canceling the sixes! What other fractions with denominators less than 100 reduce correctly by incorrect means?

Anita Burpee
Goffstown, N.H.

6. Double Vision
Difficulty: 3

a. If this three-dimensional object were constructed correctly, it would have four outside surfaces. However, someone goofed! How many outside surfaces does this "thing" have?

b. If the object were a true conventional picture frame instead, 1″ wide, what size picture, in whole inches on each side, would have an area equal to the face area of the frame?

M. A. Frost
Fort Worth, Texas

7. Peas, Beans & Barley
Difficulty: 3

a. Mark, Joe, and John, all farmers, went to the market one day to sell their produce. They offered the following bushels:

	peas	beans	barley
Mark	120	141	1050
Joe	115	149	1090
John	40	49	2200

If the peas sell for $5 a bushel and beans for $4, how much would the barley price have to be for John to receive more money for all his produce than Joe and Mark put together?

b. Feeling flush, John then bought some additional farm land for $10,000. Next day he felt differently and resold it for $10,200, but decided almost immediately that it was undervalued. He prevailed on his customer to sell back to him for $10,300 and sold it to someone else for $10,600 the third day.

How much did John gain or lose?

Eric Burgess
Greenwood, Tenn.

8. The One That Got Away
Difficulty: 3

We know that
— Fishermen tell tall tales.
— A flytier once said, "All flytiers are liars."
— No flytier is both honest and a liar.

Therefore, is the flytier a truth-teller feller or a tall-tale teller? Or are the facts contradictory?

V.V. Lloyd
Lynchburg, Va.

9. Espionage Express
Difficulty: 4

Four spies in trench coats sat in two facing bench seats as they rode the Orient Express. Two sat next to the window and two next to the aisle. The English spy sat on Mr. B's left. Mr. A wore a tan-colored coat. The spy in olive was on the German spy's right. Mr. C was the only cigar-smoker. Mr. D was across from the American spy. The Russian was in khaki and the English spy stared out the window on his left.

Who was the spy in the rust-colored coat?

Paula Reiter
Midwest City, Okla.

10. Deux and Zwei
Difficulty: 4

Can you substitute the same number for a letter each time the letter appears (or for a different digit in the last sum), for mathematically correct answers? Each problem is different, and there may be more than one answer to some. No left-hand zeros, please.

```
  T W O        E I N        V I N G T
× T W O        E I N          C I N Q
-------        E I N        + C I N Q
T H R E E     +E I N        ---------
               -----        T R E N T E
               V I E R
```

```
  I N S A N E      1 2 8 5 7
+ B R A I N      + 5 8 3 7 8
-----------      -----------
T E A S E R        7 1 2 3 5
```

Sidney Kravitz
Dover, N.J.

11. Endings
Difficulty: 4

a. What are the last three digits of 1985^{1985}?

b. What are the last three digits of 7^{9999}?

c. For what n is this true?
$$1324^n + 731^n = 1961^n?$$

Gary Gettel
Plano, Texas

12. Diagramless Cross-number
Difficulty: 5

Across or Down
— The year of this OFA.
— The sum of the six numbers in the puzzle is a perfect square.
— No number in this puzzle begins with zero, of course.
— Each of the ten digits is used only once in this puzzle.
— Only one of the six numbers is composite.
— Sorry you don't get a diagram or numbers, but if you make the first clue above go *across,* the solution is probably unique.

Bob Lodge
Seattle, Wash.

13. Look Alikes
Difficulty: 5

Here are 2 solid objects, a and b. The front, top, and side views of each are all the same.

A

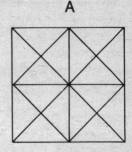

F, T & S

B

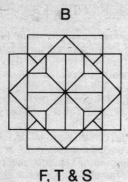

F, T & S

Can you draw a perspective or describe each? No wire, sheetmetal, or surface designs. Some solid lines may hide dashed lines as is customary in mechanical drawing, but there are no unshown purely dashed lines.

A.W. Mosenthal
Corinth, Vermont

14. Big Number
Difficulty: 5
What is special about:
8,589,869,056?

David Edgar
Hartford, Conn.

15. Curious Cubes
Difficulty: 5
a. How many unique ways can you arrange 5 equal cubes so that at least one face of each cube fully touches another cube? Partial, edge, and corner touching don't qualify. Simple rotations are not unique; mirror arrangements that cannot be rotated are.

b. If the cubes are dice, what is the maximum outside score that can be shown on an arrangement?

c. What is the maximum number of equal cubes whose faces can simultaneously touch the faces of a single cube of the same size? Partial touching OK; edges and corners not.

Fred Richardson
Lincoln, Mass.

THE 1984 SUPER PUZZLE ANSWER

Our 1984 Super Puzzle produced the most enthusiastic group of entrants we've seen in a long time. And smart! All entries had the correct answer: "R. B. Thomas," reference to our first editor and publisher, Robert Bailey Thomas, who started *The Old Farmer's Almanac* in 1792. There was a Puzzle Editor's typo (the basic hazard of puzzle editing and deadlines) in Clue S1, which should have referred to Mathematical Puzzle 6. We apologize. Fortunately, most people spotted it from the context and the logic of other clues. (Recognition of the error was a 1-point bonus.)

Highest scorers consistently worked backward and forward, tying together seemingly unrelated clues or trains of thought. As often happens, full background, reasoning, clarity, and citing of references separated the top answers from the others. The winner of the $500 prize was Robert M. Dierken of Kettering, Ohio, with an essentially perfect paper. Runners-up included David Lindsay, Silver Spring, Maryland; Marsha L. Farmer, Philadelphia, Pennsylvania; Randy Benjamin, Rockford, Illinois; R. N. Deardorff, Dayton, Ohio; Irma Simon, Vassalboro, Maine; and Michael Moore, Springfield, Illinois.

A full explanation is available for 50¢ and a self-addressed, stamped envelope. Send both to "Super Puzzle Answer," *The Old Farmer's Almanac,* Dublin, NH 03444.

WINNING RECIPES IN THE 1984 RECIPE CONTEST

In last year's Recipe Contest readers were asked to submit their favorite original stew recipes. The number and variety of responses were quite astounding and quickly made it clear that there is considerable flexibility in the definition of what constitutes a stew. There were meatless stews as well as stews featuring beef, chicken, sausage, squirrel, venison, kidney, and buffalo. A few cherished secret ingredients surfaced: tapioca for thickening, beer, angostura bitters, cracked bones, sliced lemon, green tomatoes, coffee, vodka, sweetbreads, and brains.

Techniques were as varied as the ingredients, but certain regional preferences were apparent. Readers from southern states advocated cooking stews in a large cast-iron pot, while pressure cookers and crock pots seemed to enjoy favor in the Northeast and the northern Midwest. Stew seems literally to reflect the idea that this nation is a melting pot, as the winners of the 1984 Recipe Contest show:

First Prize:
Tried and True Beef Stew

4 tablespoons flour
¼ teaspoon each: thyme, ground ginger, and summer savory
2-3 pounds beef chuck cut into 1½" cubes
2 tablespoons oil plus one tablespoon butter
1 large onion, thinly sliced
¾ cup dry red wine (optional)
4 cups beef stock (may be made with beef bouillon cubes)
2-3 whole bay leaves
salt and pepper
6 small carrots
6 pearl onions
4 medium potatoes peeled and quartered
½ package frozen green peas
3 tablespoons sour cream

Mix flour with thyme, ginger, and savory. Dredge meat with two tablespoons of this mixture and shake off excess. Heat shortening in heavy Dutch oven and brown meat thoroughly. Remove. Brown onion until quite dark and crisp, but do not allow to burn. Remove. Pour wine into drippings to deglaze pot; then add stock and bay leaves. Add salt and pepper to taste. Put meat and onions back into pot and simmer covered for 1½-2 hours or until tender. About 30 minutes before meat is done add carrots, onions, and potatoes. Add peas during last few moments of cooking. Thicken gravy with remaining two tablespoons of flour mixture and a little cold stock or water. Gradually whisk sour cream into thickened gravy being careful not to allow it to boil. Serves 6.   *Marion L. Brant*
Punta Gorda, Florida

Second Prize:
"In the Polish Fashion" Stew

½ pound thick-sliced bacon, cut into 1-inch lengths
1 pound pork stew meat, cut into 1-inch pieces
1 cup chopped onions
1½ cups coarsely chopped cabbage
1 cup coarsely shredded zucchini (do not peel)
1 can (4 ounces) mushroom stems and pieces
1 can (16 ounces) whole tomatoes
1 can (6 ounces) tomato paste
1 cup hot water
½ cup red wine vinegar
1 tablespoon granulated sugar
¼ teaspoon freshly ground black pepper
2 cups shredded and chopped sauerkraut
1 teaspoon black caraway seeds
½ pound thinly sliced smoked Polish sausage
½ cup pearl barley
2 tart apples, pared, cored, and chopped

Early on the day of serving, fry bacon in a Dutch oven until crisp; remove bacon and reserve. Add pork to bacon drippings and fry until pork is brown. Remove pork and reserve. Add onions, cabbage, and zucchini to remaining drippings and sauté until vegetables are a light brown. Stir in mushrooms with liquid, tomatoes with liquid, tomato paste, hot water, wine vinegar, sugar, pepper, sauerkraut, and reserved pork. Bring to a boil; reduce heat to maintain a simmer, cover, and continue simmering for 45 minutes, stirring occasionally. Add remaining ingredients and reserved bacon; bring to a boil; reduce heat to maintain a simmer, cover, and continue simmering 45 minutes. Shut off heat; let rest. Reheat before serving.

Note: This dish improves with reheating. I often make it one to two days before serving and store it covered in the refrigerator. Freezes well also. The flavor of the dish can be greatly enhanced by the addition of ½ cup vodka or Burgundy — I add this when I shut off the heat. I serve it with hot slices of dill cottage cheese bread and butter. This is my version of *Bigos,* the national dish of Poland. Serves 8-10. — *Jeanne Yunker*
Arlington Heights, Illinois

Third Prize:
Venison Stew

It's important to have the deer gutted and bled within the first half hour of killing. Then to age the meat, I hang the carcass for 48 hours before butchering, but no longer. (Some old-timers advocate hanging for at least *three* weeks. Urp!) Whatever method is used, the buttermilk marinade helps to draw out the "gamy" flavor without disguising the delicate, but different-from-beef flavor of the venison. Removing any body fat is important, too.

1½-2 pounds venison
1½-2 quarts buttermilk
¼ cup flour
5 strips bacon
2 quarts beer, any brand
3 medium potatoes
4 medium carrots
2 fat parsnips
2 large onions
3 celery stalks
1 can, or 1 pint frozen tomatoes
2 cloves garlic
any favorite available vegetable
water, as needed
5 juniper berries
7 coriander seeds
bay leaf
⅛ teaspoon ground cloves
1 teaspoon basil
1 teaspoon thyme
4 dried, pitted prunes

¼ pound mushrooms
teriyaki sauce, soy sauce, *or* salt, to taste
freshly ground black pepper

First, say thank-you to the deer-person. (If you don't like or don't need to eat venison, don't kill it, or it will never taste good no matter how you fix it.) Cut venison into bite-sized chunks. Remove any fat. Marinate in enough buttermilk to cover meat completely for 8 hours or overnight.

Pour off milk and give to livestock or dogs or compost. It won't be used in the actual cooking, but it is essential as a marinade. Lightly coat venison in flour. Fry bacon until crisp in a large, cast-iron Dutch oven or a 5- to 8-quart stew pot. Remove bacon and save. Brown venison *slowly* in bacon fat. Add one quart beer and simmer while chopping the following into stew-sized pieces: potatoes, carrots, parsnips, onions, and celery. Throw into stew pot and add one can tomatoes. Mince garlic and add with any other of your favorite vegetables, including chopped greens, but excepting winter squashes, which get mushy. When liquid has been reduced by half, add remaining quart of beer and enough water to make five quarts. Simmer 1½-2 hours. Season with a few juniper berries, crushed, and a few coriander seeds. Add a bay leaf, a "whisper" of cloves, the basil, thyme, and prunes, chopped. During the last half hour, add the mushrooms, either whole or quartered. Use a few shakes of teriyaki sauce, soy sauce, or salt to taste, but *not* all three.

Serve with crumbled bacon and freshly ground pepper.

Homemade sourdough bread or biscuits are great with this stew, or dumplings can be made during the last 15 minutes.

Note: Unless your kids have a really strange sense of humor, it's not good to tell them that they're eating "Bambi" or "Rudolph." However, if they're as weird as mine, you could add one maraschino cherry for the "nose" to the whole stew. The person who finds it gets to make a wish. (Maybe it's the isolation out here ... is nothing, not even Rudolph, sacred anymore?)
— *Marty Robinson*
Selma, Oregon

1985 Recipe Contest: Fresh Fruit Pie with Pastry

For 1985, prizes (first prize $50, second $25, third $15) will be awarded for the best original recipe for fresh fruit pie, including the appropriate pastry. All entries become the property of Yankee Publishing Incorporated, which reserves all rights to the material submitted. Winners will be announced in the 1986 edition of *The Old Farmer's Almanac.* Deadline is April 15, 1985. Address: Recipe Contest, *The Old Farmer's Almanac,* Dublin, NH 03444.

WINNING ESSAYS IN THE 1984 ESSAY CONTEST:

"The Tallest Tale I Ever Heard"

First Prize:

Zeke Thompson was a God-fearing man, but when it came to cursing, he was as intemperate as he was forcible. He had a talent for it. Zeke's oaths got to be infamous, so when folks got their danders up, they'd stop in and have him supply the high-quality abusive language they were after. One spring Zeke planted blueberry bushes in his meadow. A week later he went to check their progress and found that some beavers had built a dam that put a pond over the new planting. Well! He let out a whoop that turned three flocks of migrating birds back south again. The language wasn't blue; it was positively purple. The beavers came out, took the dam apart, and moved it two miles upstream. Zeke kept railing. The maple trees started pouring sap out into buckets, and when that didn't help, they pumped out preformed maple sugar candies in the shapes of heroes from Vermont history. The beavers took apart the second dam, and cut and stacked two cords of firewood.

It seemed like nothing would stop Zeke, but eventually he left off, though he claimed he still had plenty of new and interesting things to say. Even those bushes were mightily impressed. The next summer all Zeke had to do was hold a basket under a bush and sneer, and the blueberries would jump right in. — *Tom Hill*
Francestown, New Hampshire

Second Prize:

The tallest tale I ever heard is about a man who was fishing at a lake. His eye caught a gray squirrel in the trees near the shore. The tree limbs hung over the lake. In the lake was a stump with two nuts on it. The squirrel was desperately trying all his acrobatic gyrations in an effort to reach for the nuts. Just as he grabbed them, he lost his grip and fell into the water. Instantly the biggest fish the man had ever seen lunged up and swallowed the squirrel. The lake got calm again. Then the big fish jumped up out of the water and put the two nuts back on the stump.
Mrs. H.R. Bublitz
Waterford, New Jersey

Third Prize:

There once was a farmer who owned an old mule with a large open sore on his back. Unable to heal the sore, the farmer turned the mule out to pasture for his final days. Winters came and went with no sign of the old mule, so the farmer assumed he had died.

Then one fall day the farmer set out for the woods beyond the back pasture to hunt for squirrel. To his amazement, he saw something that looked like a tree moving. Upon closer inspection, he discovered the old mule walking along with a large oak and a smaller maple growing from his back. It seemed that an acorn and a maple seed had fallen into the sore on the mule's back, taken root, and grown. So being a resourceful man, the farmer cut down the oak tree and whittled a beautiful saddle from the stump. To this day the farmer can often be seen riding through his fields on the old mule. He left the maple tree standing, because he liked to ride in the shade.
Arthur E. Nolder, Jr.
Luthersburg, Pennsylvania

1985 ESSAY CONTEST

For 1985, prizes (first prize $50, second $25, third $15) will be awarded for the three best 200-word essays on this topic: "The Difference Between Men and Women." All entries become the property of Yankee Publishing Incorporated, which reserves all rights to the material submitted. Winners will be announced in the 1986 *The Old Farmer's Almanac.* Deadline: April 15, 1985. Address: Essay Contest, *The Old Farmer's Almanac*, Dublin, NH 03444.

RAINY DAY AMUSEMENTS

Answers appear on page 200.

What's in (the Middle of) a Name?
by George O. Pommier

Most of us are familiar with a few presidential middle names like Quincy, Fitzgerald, and Milhous, but there are lots of others. See how many of the middle names in the left-hand column you can correctly associate with the last names in the right-hand column.

1. Quincy	( )	(A)	Cleveland
2. Rudolph	( )	(B)	Roosevelt
3. Howard	( )	(C)	Adams
4. Birchard	( )	(D)	Hoover
5. David	( )	(E)	Ford
6. Gamaliel	( )	(F)	Garfield
7. Simpson	( )	(G)	Polk
8. Calvin	( )	(H)	Taft
9. Abram	( )	(I)	Arthur
10. Clark	( )	(J)	Jayes
11. Woodrow	( )	(K)	Krant
12. Grover	( )	(L)	Coolidge
13. Knox	( )	(M)	Eisenhower
14. Alan	( )	(N)	Harding
15. Delano	( )	(O)	Wilson

Old-Fashioned Girls
by Ida M. Pardue

If you grew up in the "good old days," you may remember all of these old-fashioned girls, most of whom have gone out of style. Try to match them with their true identities in the right-hand column.

1. Tin Lizzie	dance step
2. Black Maria	woman's loose, long gown
3. Susie Q	collar
4. Hello girl	free pass to a show
5. Patience	old Ford
6. Mary Jane	police van
7. Charlotte	baby garment
8. Annie Oakley	molded pudding
9. Mother Hubbard	telephone operator
10. Brown Bess	card game
11. Gertrude	old British firearm
12. Bertha	child's shoe

Rivers That Flow into Rivers
by Louis Hasley

Each of the 20 rivers listed below flows into one of the following: Arkansas, Colorado, Columbia, Hudson, Mississippi, Missouri, Ohio, Potomac, Rio Grande, Snake. Following each numbered river, write the name of the river into which it flows.

1. Arkansas _____
2. Canadian _____
3. Cimarron _____
4. Cumberland _____
5. Des Moines _____
6. Gila _____
7. Illinois _____
8. Missouri _____
9. Mohawk _____
10. Monongahela
11. Ohio _____
12. Pecos _____
13. Platte _____
14. Salmon _____
15. Shenandoah _____
16. Snake _____
17. Tennessee _____
18. Wabash _____
19. Wisconsin _____
20. Yellowstone _____

Figures Don't Lie!
by George O. Pommer

If you can fill in the proper numbers in each phrase below, they will add up to the total shown.

1. _____ if by sea	( )
2. _____ Keys to Baldpate	( )
3. Into the valley of death rode the _____	( )
4. Ali Baba and the _____ Thieves	( )
5. _____ Horsemen of the Apocalypse	( )
6. When you were sweet _____	(-)
7. _____ Downing Street	( )
8. _____ Leagues under the Sea	( )
9. _____ and One Nights	( )
10. _____ Nights in a Barroom	( )
11. Life Begins at _____	( )
12. The _____ Nights of Christmas	( )
13. House of _____ Gables	( )
14. Around the World in _____ Days	( )
15. The _____ Day War	( )
	21,834

Answers to
OLD AND NEW MATHEMATICAL PUZZLES
on pages 192-195

1. a. If stacked, R10; otherwise, R15.
   b. Sickle paid double:

2. a. 11 a month or 132.
   b. 23.

3. 6 & 1, or 2 & 4.

4. $2L^2$

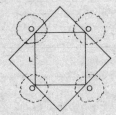

5. $\frac{19}{95}, \frac{16}{64}, \frac{49}{98}, \frac{46}{69} = \frac{64}{96}$ and others

6. a. 2.
   b. 3″ x 10″, or 4″ x 6″.

7. a. $32.317/bu
   b. $500 gain

8. Liar. If he were truthful, his statement would be incorrect. If a liar, the facts are possible.

9. The Englishman, Mr. D.

10.

138	821	94,851
× 138	821	6,483
19044	821	+ 6,483
	+ 821	107,817
	3284	

571072	74318
+ 49057	+13083
620129	87401

11. a. 625
    b. 143
    c. None. This is an example of Fermat's unproven Last Theorem. In this case, note the right-hand digits.

12-15. Prize set. See instructions, page 192.

Answers to
RAINY DAY AMUSEMENTS
on page 199

Middle Names:

1. C	6. N	11. O
2. E	7. K	12. A
3. H	8. L	13. G
4. J	9. F	14. I
5. M	10. D	15. B

Old Fashioned Girls:
1. Tin Lizzie/old Ford; 2. Black Maria/police van; 3. Susie Q/dance step; 4. Hello girl/telephone operator; 5. Patience/card game; 6. Mary Jane/child's shoe; 7. Charlotte/molded pudding; 8. Annie Oakley/free pass to a show; 9. Mother Hubbard/woman's loose, long gown; 10. Brown Bess/old British firearm; 11. Gertrude/baby garment; 12. Bertha/collar.

Rivers That Flow into Rivers:

Arkansas: 2, 3
Colorado: 6
Columbia: 16
Hudson: 9
Mississippi: 1, 5, 7, 8, 11, 19

Missouri: 13, 20
Ohio: 4, 10, 17, 18
Potomac: 15
Rio Grande: 12
Snake: 14

Figures Don't Lie:

1. 2	6. 16	11. 40
2. 7	7. 10	12. 12
3. 600	8. 20,000	13. 7
4. 40	9. 1,000	14. 80
5. 4	10. 10	15. 6

SECRETS OF THE ZODIAC

Famous Debowelled Man of the Signs

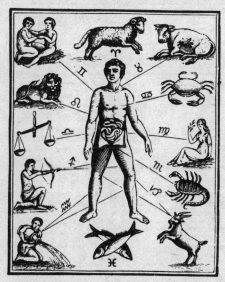

♈ Aries, head. ARI
  Mar. 21-Apr. 20

♉ Taurus, neck. TAU
  Apr. 21-May 20

♊ Gemini, arms. GEM
  May 21-June 20

♋ Cancer, breast. CAN
  June 21-July 22

♌ Leo, heart. LEO
  July 23-Aug. 22

♍ Virgo, belly. VIR
  Aug. 23-Sept. 22

♎ Libra, reins. LIB
  Sept. 23-Oct. 22

♏ Scorpio, secrets. SCO
  Oct. 23-Nov. 22

♐ Sagittarius, thighs. SAG
  Nov. 23-Dec. 21

♑ Capricorn, knees. CAP
  Dec. 22-Jan. 19

♒ Aquarius, legs. AQU
  Jan. 20-Feb. 19

♓ Pisces, feet. PSC
  Feb. 20-Mar. 20

Ancient astrologers associated each of the signs with a part of the body over which they felt the sign held some influence. The first sign of the zodiac — Aries — was attributed to the head, with the rest of the signs moving down the body, ending with Pisces at the feet.

When people ask you, "What's your sign?" they are usually referring to your *sun* sign — the section of the astrological zodiac the sun was in when you were born. The 12 sun signs are described on the following pages, with brief characterizations that are traditionally ascribed to each sign. When astrologers prepare a person's natal chart, however, they take into account the location within the astrological zodiac of the moon and all other eight planets at the exact time of birth in order to get a broad picture of the person's potential. For example, if you were born on October 15, 1950, at noon in Boston, Massachusetts, your sun sign (which indicates the deeper, more spiritual side of your personality) is Libra; your rising sign, or ascendant (generally descriptive of your outward nature and physical characteristics) is Capricorn; your moon sign (your instinctive or emotional side) is Sagittarius; Mercury (an indicator of mental activity) is in Libra; and so on.

Sun signs should not be confused with the *astronomical* position of the sun as listed on the left-hand calendar pages (48-74); because of precession and other factors, the astronomical and astronomical zodiacs do not agree. Many almanac readers have asked us which signs are best suited for various activities. Astrologers generally use moon signs for this information — see Gardening by the Moon's Sign, page 173. Below is a listing of other activities traditionally associated with sun signs and keyed to those signs on the following two pages.

A Cutting grass or brush, weeding.
B Cutting and setting posts or timbers.
C Cutting hay, pruning.
D Planting above-ground crops.
E Planting root crops, house painting.
F Harvesting crops or herbs.
G Breeding, setting hens, creating, baking.

H Weaning.
I Slaughtering.
J Operations, pulling teeth.
K Hairdos, sheep shearing, buying clothes.
L Business, gambling, taking risks.
M Fishing.
N Travel, marriage, romance.

ARIES

Symbol: ♈ Ruling planet: Mars. Element: Fire.
Dates: March 21-April 20.
Traits: Energetic, assertive, impulsive.
Compatible with Leo, Sagittarius, Gemini,
Aquarius.
Occupations: Exploration, the military,
entrepreneur, outdoor engineering, fireman.
Best for D, L, G, F, I

TAURUS

Symbol: ♉ Ruling planet: Venus. Element: Earth.
Dates: April 21-May 20.
Traits: Determined, persistent, loyal.
Compatible with Virgo, Capricorn, Cancer,
Pisces.
Occupations: Farming, the arts
(particularly music), work requiring
research, building, hand work.
Best for E, K, B, I, F, G

GEMINI

Symbol: ♊ Ruling planet: Mercury. Element: Air.
Dates: May 21-June 20.
Traits: Mentally active, talkative, versatile.
Compatible with Libra, Aquarius, Leo, Aries.
Occupations: Crafts, communications,
work dealing with intricate problems,
sales, small businesses.
Best for J, G, L, A, I, F

CANCER

Symbol: ♋ Ruling planet: Moon. Element: Water.
Dates: June 21-July 22.
Traits: Maternal, compassionate, thrifty.
Compatible with Scorpio, Pisces, Virgo, Taurus.
Occupations: Raising children, animals, or plants,
history, antiques, caring for elderly.
Best for D, M, K, G, I, A, C

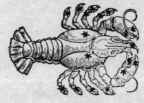

LEO

Symbol: ♌ Ruling planet: Sun. Element: Fire.
Dates: July 23-August 22.
Traits: Forceful, generous, creative,
well-organized.
Compatible with Sagittarius, Aries,
Libra, Gemini.
Occupations: Supervisor, actor, king,
activities requiring physical strength, bartender.
Best for K, B, A, F, N

VIRGO

Symbol: ♍ Ruling planet: Mercury. Element:
Earth.
Dates: August 23-September 22.
Traits: Analytical, discriminating, modest, neat.
Compatible with Capricorn, Taurus,
Scorpio, Cancer.
Occupations: Editor, medicine, chemistry,
research, accounting.
Best for J, K, L, A, I, F

LIBRA

Symbol: ♎ Ruling planet: Venus. Element: Air.
Dates: September 23-October 22.
Traits: Charming, diplomatic,
idealistic, indecisive.
Compatible with Aquarius, Gemini,
Sagittarius, Leo.
Occupations: Acting, the arts,
law and legal activities, politics.
Best for D, N, K, G, I

SCORPIO

Symbol: ♏ Ruling planet: Pluto. Element: Water.
Dates: October 23-November 22.
Traits: Passionate, intense, secretive, subtle.
Compatible with Pisces, Cancer,
Capricorn, Virgo.
Occupations: Teaching, work requiring
concentration, training animals,
psychiatry, surgery, detection.
Best for M, G, I, A

SAGITTARIUS

Symbol: ♐ Ruling planet: Jupiter. Element: Fire.
Dates: November 23-December 21.
Traits: Bountiful, frank, versatile, philosophical.
Compatible with Aries, Leo, Aquarius, Libra.
Occupations: Travel, politics, meteorology,
philosophy, religion.
Best for J, N, K, F, I, H

CAPRICORN

Symbol: ♑ Ruling planet: Saturn. Element: Earth.
Dates: December 22-January 19.
Traits: Ambitious, disciplined,
persevering, pessimistic.
Compatible with Taurus, Virgo, Pisces, Scorpio.
Occupations: Positions of trust, banking,
mountain climbing, coaching, engineering.
Best for J, G, I, H

AQUARIUS

Symbol: ♒ Ruling planet: Uranus. Element: Air.
Dates: January 20-February 19.
Traits: Humanitarian, independent,
inventive, aloof.
Compatible with Gemini, Libra, Aries,
Sagittarius.
Occupations: Teacher, social worker, astronomer,
astrologer, scientist, inventor.
Best for D, K, B, I, H, A

PISCES

Symbol: ♓ Ruling planet: Neptune.
Element: Water.
Dates: February 20-March 20.
Traits: Sympathetic, sensitive,
emotional, imaginative.
Compatible with Cancer, Scorpio,
Taurus, Capricorn.
Occupations: Medicine, teacher, fisherman,
dancing and the arts, clergy.
Best for D, M, B, G, I, H, C

CLASSIFIEDS

AGENTS WANTED

SELL CHRISTMAS and All Occasion Cards. Free literature upon request. Charm Cards, 2738 Broad, Dept. F, Austell, GA 30001.

SELL MANUFACTURER'S PERFUMES, popular fragrance. Write for details. Pavo Enterprises, Box 23057, San Jose, CA 95153.

EARN IMMEDIATE CASH selling Mason Shoes to neighbors, friends, relatives. No investment or experience needed. Call Toll Free 1-800-826-7030, Ext. 552, or write for a free selling kit. Mason Shoes, K-814, Chippewa Falls, WI 54774.

ASTROLOGY & OCCULT

LUCK CHANGING PROCESS Revealed. Fantastic Free Report. Acquire Instant Riches, Success, Love, Health, Power. MASSOC, Box 98-FA, Brooklyn, NY 11235.

WITCHCRAFT POWERS, Ancient secrets revealed by famous occult school. Box 1366, Nashua, NH 03061.

OCCULT CATALOG. Complete Spiritual and Occult needs. Large, informative. $1.00 handling. JOAN TERESA POWER PRODUCTS, P.O. Box 542-F, Safety Harbor, FL 33572.

GIFTED READER. Astrology: natal, horary, charts (date, time, place), $25. Tarot, $10. Other hermetic services. Yael Dragwyla, Box 1548, Goleta, CA 93116.

HOW TO CAST LOVE SPELLS — Bible Magic! Guaranteed. $6.00, Sandler, 19-F West Park, Merchantville, NJ 08109.

COMPLETE OCCULT DIGEST! 250 pages! Over 5000 Psychic, Magical, Spiritual Supplies. Books, Gifts, Jewelry, Charms, Talismans, Mystical Items. $2.00 (refundable). International, 8050-F Webb, North Hollywood, CA 91605.

MAGICK: Adepts/Students; Resource Contact Send $1.00: H..H..H..P.O. Box 86, Island Lake, IL 60642.

KNOW SECRETS of your stars. Madame Lee Fu's scientific ability to read stars has fascinated, amazed thousands. Let ASTROLOGY guide you to more success. If not afraid of truth, mail $4 for special reading. Give name, address, birthday, time if known. Madame Lee Fu, Box 107FO, Rheem, CA 94570.

FREE LUCKY AMULET with your lucky Numbers! Send birthdate, self-addressed stamped envelope. MYSTIC, Box 12279-R, Winston-Salem, NC 27107.

FREE CATALOG: Complete line herbs, lodestones, incense, perfumes, oils, sachets, baths, washes, occult sprays, crystal balls, etc. Asturo, Box 495, North Miami Beach, FL 33160.

NUMEROLOGY CHART — Your personal numbers interpreted. Shows your life cycles and trends. Yearly information from birth to age 79. Monthly information for current two-year period. $5.00. Send full birthname, birthdate. CYCLES, Dept. FA-N, 2251 Berkely Avenue, Schenectady, NY 12309.

YOU CAN CHANGE YOUR LUCK. You should have anything you want. Get Money, Power, Love, Justice. Send $1.00 for catalog of incense, oils, perfumes, witchcraft, Voo Doo spells and more. Since 1909. Ann Howard, Dept. FA-3, 200 West Sunrise Highway, Freeport, NY 11520.

BEE SUPPLIES

WE MANUFACTURE Cypress Bee Equipment and sell other Beekeeping supplies. Beginner book $2.75 — Free catalog. FORBES & JOHNSTON, Box 535, Homerville, GA 31634.

QUALITY EQUIPMENT BARGAIN prices. 10 sheets crimp 8½' foundation $5. Complete Hive $25. Complete Super $7.80. BRUSHY MOUNTAIN BEE FARM, Rt. 1, Box 135A, Moravian Falls, NC 28654. Send for free catalog.

BEER & WINEMAKING

MAKE BETTER BEER AND WINE and save. Free Catalog. Village Store, Box C51Y, Westport, MA 02790.

WINEMAKERS — BEERMAKERS — Free Illustrated Catalog — Fast Service — Large Selection: Kraus, Box 7850-YB, Independence, MO 64053.

BEER AND WINE Hobby. Complete home beer/wine-making supplies. Free catalog upon request. Beer and Wine Hobby, Box M, Melrose, MA 02176. (617) 665-8442.

BEERMAKERS! Our Free Catalog/Newsletter includes Kits, Kegs, Ingredients, Soft Drink Kits, and Information. William's Brewing, Box 461-FA, Oakland, CA 94604.

BOOKS

USED PAPERBACK BOOKS Several thousand novels, westerns, science fiction, comics etc. .25 each plus postage and handling. Books, Box 3770, Riverside, CA 92509.

PUBLISH YOUR BOOK! Join our successful authors. Publicity, advertising, beautiful books. All subjects invited. Send for fact-filled booklet and free manuscript report. Carlton Press, Dept OAV, 11 West 32 Street, New York 10001.

MONEY SAVING HOME REPAIR GUIDE, easy-to-follow instructions, plus photos and diagrams. This volume will teach anyone to fix cracked walls, repair carpets, patch concrete, restore a damaged roof. $4.95. L-Dee Sales, 904 Euclid, Dept. OFA5, Waycross, GA 31501.

SUPER MILAGE CARBURETOR how to build. Send for details. CDHE, P.O. Box 91174, Houston, TX 77291.

NEW BOOKS on Antiques and Collectibles. Write for list of over 1,100 books. The Collector's Book Shelf, Dept. F, Box 6, Westfield, NY 14787.

FREE BOOKLIST. Cooking, Health, Metaphysics, Pets, Sports, more. $2-5/bk. Marketplace, 341-D Rice Ranch Road, Orcutt, CA 93455.

GRACE LIVINGSTON HILL, other good clean reading. Send SASE. Callender House, 13742FF Callender, Southgate, MI 48195.

FREE Out-of-Print Rare Booksearch Service. Write: Yesterday's Gone, 2115 NE Division, Bend OR 97701.

GENEALOGIES. 2000 scarce old family histories. Catalog $2. Higginson Genealogical, 140 Derby Square, Salem MA 01970.

CUT YOUR MORTGAGE IN ½! Revealing report shows you how. $10, FFF, Box 4835, Framingham, MA 01701, or (617) 620-1027 24 hours!

FREE CASSETTE CATALOG. Best sellers professionally narrated, Unabridged. Buy/rent. Books In Motion, #1EY1, Veradale, WA 99037-0317.

WILDERNESS SURVIVAL! Homesteading, hunting, medical, gardening, selfdefense, crafts, military books. Free catalog. Aspen Cabin, Box 712, Prescott, AZ 86302.

BUSINESS OPPORTUNITIES

TAKE CATALOG ORDERS. We drop-ship 2500 best-selling specialty products. Lowest below wholesale prices. Immediate delivery. Spectacular home business opportunity. FREE BOOK. SMC, 9401 De Soto Ave., Dept. 358-46, Chatsworth, CA 91311.

EXTRA INCOME MAILING CIRCULARS! No Quotas/bosses. Set own hours! Division Headquarters, Box 464FA85, Woodstock, IL 60098.

MONEY PROBLEMS? Write Us. Immediate loans and outright grants to individuals refused elsewhere. 98% eligible. Associates, Box 98-FA, Brooklyn, NY 11235.

MINIATURE GOLF COURSES. Indoors. Outdoors. $4,950. Terms available. MINI-GOLF, 202 Bridge, Jessup, PA 18434 (717) 489-8623.

I'LL HELP YOU get started in mailorder, give you personal attention, evaluate your ideas. Serious beginners only. Jay Reiss Advertising, 2444 Wilshire #609-F, Santa Monica, CA 90403. (213)453-8859.

400,000 BARGAINS BELOW WHOLESALE. Liquidations . . . Closeouts . . . Job Lots . . . Single Samples. Free Details. Bargain Hunters Opportunities, Box 730-OFA, Holland, MI 49423.

MAILORDER OPPORTUNITY! Start profitable home business in America's fastest growing industry. Nationally known authority will teach you. No experience or product investment required. Information free. Mail Order Associates, Dept. 781, Montvale, NJ 07645.

BOOKS!! MONEY OPPORTUNITIES, Energy, Success, Sports, Pets, Religious, Others. Catalog — $1.00. New Idea Book Co., Box 3416-FA, Greensburg, PA 15601.

PIANO TUNING PAYS. Learn at home with correspondence course. Write: ASPT, 17050 Telfer Dr., Morgan Hill, CA 95037.

MAKE MONEY at home raising fishworms. Soilless, odorless method. Complete raising, marketing instrucitons. SHIELDS PUBLICATIONS, Box 669 E, Eagle River, WI 54521.

FREE LITERATURE. Raise Fishworms, Crickets. Redworms — 1000 — $8.95, 5000-$42.50. Book — How, Where to Sell with Order. Carter Farm-19, Plains, GA 31780.

$500.00 WEEKLY, ($1.00 — Pound Up!) Recycling "Junked" Tires at Home! (Rush Stamp). LaValleys-OFA, Fountain, FL 32438.

PROVEN STEP-BY-STEP SHORTCUTS to becoming rich with NO large investment. FREE DETAILS. Cardinal, Dept. OF1, Box 55, Palo Alto, CA 94302.

WE PAY CASH for articles clipped from discarded newspapers and magazines. Free list. Datag, Box 226, Matlacha, FL 33909.

5 EASY STEPS To Success!! Wealth, Success Secrets Revealed. Shows How To Start, Ways To Make Extra Money. Only $16.95. Satisfaction Guaranteed. Char-Mar, Inc., Box 1678-SA, Morristown, TN 37816-1678.

EARN MONEY selling rings, jewelry, buckles, watches-buy direct. 100% below retail. Catalog $1.00 (refundable). Anka-FA, 90 Greenwich Ave., Warwick, RI 02886.

BORROW $30,000 without interest! All eligible. Repay anytime. Free details! Infohouse-OFA, 808 Post, San Francisco, CA 94109.

AUSTRALIA WANTS YOU! Jobs! Big Pay! Transportation! Newest handbook — $2.00. AUSTRALIAN INTERNATIONAL, Box 191707-JM, Washington, DC 20036.

OVERSEAS EMPLOYMENT OPPORTUNITIES! All occupations! $20,000 — $65,000+. Free Report! EMPLOYMENT INTERNATIONAL, Box 19760-JM, Indianapolis, IN 46219.

CLIP NEWSPAPER ITEMS for $2.00 to $25.00 each. No investment. Send 50¢ for details. Cardinal Publishing, 2071-C54 Emerson, Jacksonville, FL 32207.

MAKE an extra $200 a month part time, one hour a week from your kitchen table. No experience, educational requirements. For details write: Andrew Lemon, 1801 E. Compton Blvd., Compton, CA 90221.

STAY HOME! Make Money Addressing Envelopes. Valuable Details 20¢. Lindco, 3636-FA Peterson, Chicago, IL 60659.

VINYL'S WHERE THE MONEY IS! Professionally repair, refinish, recolor furniture, luggage, car tops. Quick, easy. Two small $20 jobs a day earn you $1,000 a month. Homes, cars, offices, restaurants, unlimited customers. Start earning after a few days practice. Sensational details free. VIP, 2016 Montrose, Chicago 60618.

LYRICS, POEMS for musical setting and recording. $1,000.00 for best poem. Satisfaction guaranteed. Talent 17 (FA) Longwood Road, Quincy, MA 02169.

FREE RHYMING DICTIONARY. Songpoems! Songs! Needed. Songpoems must be submitted to receive rhyming dictionary. Immediate replies. Possible publishing contract. Betty's Music Makers, 6994 — 15th Avenue, North. Dept. WX, St. Petersburg, FL 33710.

PLAY GOSPEL SONGS by ear! Add chords. Piano, organ. 10 easy lessons $5.98. "Learn Gospel Music." Chording, runs, fills, basses. 20 lessons $6.98. Both $12. Davidsons, 6726FA Metcalf, Shawnee Mission, KS 66204.

OF INTEREST TO ALL

FREE. TRUTH about evil spirits. Golden Opportunity. Must reading. Ruth Fish, 948-K Maxwell, Nashville, TN 37206.

WORK CLOTHES — Save 80%. Shirts. Pants. Coveralls. Free folder, write: Galco, 4004 East 71st Street — Dept. OF-2, Cleveland, OH 44105.

LEARN FLOWER ARRANGING. Start business or hobby. Study at home. Free booklet. Lifetime Career School, Dept. B-116, 2251 Barry Ave., Los Angeles, CA 90064

FREE! World's Most Unusual Novelty Catalog. 1800 Jokes, Tricks, Science, Sports, Hobbies. Johnson-Smith, C-6029, Mt. Clemens, MI 48045.

FAMILY TREE RESEARCH! Have all released U.S. census records 1790-1910, for every county, every state, etc. Walter White, Room 16-A, 340 North Main St., Columbia City, IN 46725.

MAKE BIG PROFITS Buying, Selling at Flea Markets. Secrets Revealed. Only $2.95. Char-Mar, Inc., Box 1678-FA, Morristown, TN 37816-1678.

CHAMBERLAIN LOTION preferrd dry skin corrective for six decades. If you store can't supply, write Chamberlain, Box 3570, Des Moines, IA 50322.

FREE MONEY from Washington D.C. New Money Book Reveals Government Secrets. Guaranteed Results. Write GOVERNMENT CASH, 12610 Central, Suite 110G, Chino, CA 91710.

MAKE YOUR OWN will! Complete kit, how to book, $2.95. Katherine's Lt., Dept. H, 13269 Lamplite Lane, Lakeside, CA 92040.

NEED CREDIT? Get MasterCard, others without credit check. Guaranteed! Other credit secrets. Details. S.A.S.E. to: Inflation Reports, FA5, Box 60148, Los Angeles, CA 90060.

PHOTO ID. Sealed in plastic. Good in all states, provinces. Fast. GUARANTEED. Free birth certificate. Send $6.00 (2/$10.00), photo, name, address, height, weight, hair, eyes, birthdate. Cardinal Publishing, 2071-124 Emerson, Jacksonville, FL 32207.

INCREASE THE 17% above your IQ 110 by legalized genetic improvement. (Read) Revolution of the Saints by Walzer. B. Inquizative, Box 871, Topeka, Kansas.

MONEY PROBLEMS SOLVED FOREVER. Get Everything You Want. Secret Book — Guaranteed — No Work Involved. Write EASY MONEY, 12610 Central, Suite 110M, Chino, CA 91710.

TWELVE MONTH BIORHYTHM CHARTS — $4.00. Send birthdate and year. John Morgan, 1208 Harris, Bartlesville, OK 74006.

CAPTURE THE HIGHLIGHTS of your life! — the Sights/Sounds/Sentiments with My Lifetime Book. Finest life-story organizer available. Handsome loose-leaf album, hundreds of life-history sheets, photo-sheets, 6 cassette holders, $29.95. Money order, VISA, MC. Satisfaction guaranteed. Personal History Systems, Inc., P. O. Box 8000, Wheeling, WV 26003.

FREE RENT & Utility Bills. Live Anywhere You Want. Absolutely Guaranteed Results. FREE Information. NEVER PAY RENT AGAIN, 12610 Central, Suite 110R, Chino, CA 91710.

DRAFT HORSES, FARMING NOSTALGIA. $10.50/yr. The Evener Magazine, Dept. 80, 29th & College, Cedar Falls, IA 50613.

"BINGO MEANS MONEY!" New Booklet Reveals Jackpot Winning Secrets. $2.00 Guaranteed. Kennedy Press, 372-F4, Absecon, NJ 08201.

FREE FIREWOOD for your fireplace & No Cost Energy Savers. Complete Information. Guaranteed Results. Send $5, FIREWOOD, 12610 Central, Suite 110F, Chino, CA 91710.

PERSONALITY ANALYSIS REVEALS your potential for success. Improve: relationships, communication skills. Personal Development, #Y1, Veredale, WA 99037-0317.

GET CASH GRANTS — from Government. (Never repay.) Also, loans. All ages eligible. Information, $2 (refundable). Surplus Funds-OF-G, 1000 Connecticut Ave. NW, Washington, D.C. 20036.

COMPUTERIZED BIORHYTHM CHARTS. 5 Years. Send $5, Birthdate/Year. 12610 Central, Suite 110B, Chino, CA 91710.

COATS OF ARMS 500,000 names, 32 countries. FREE CATALOG. The Ship's Chandler, Dept. F, Wilmington, VT 05363.

OF INTEREST TO WOMEN

FREE QUILT PATTERNS in "Quilter's Newsletter Magazine," plus Catalog Illustrating Hundreds of Quilt Patterns, Quilting Stencils, Quilting Books, Supplies, Kits, Fabrics — $2.00. Leman Publications, Box 501-F16, Wheatridge, CO 80033.

WEAVERS-COMPLETE catalog. Samples, and low prices on warps, fillers, looms, parts, etc. Send 25¢. If you have loom, advise make, weaving width. OR. RUG COMPANY, Dept. 0418, Lima, OH 45802.

SILK! Save 50% on India fabrics. Swatch $1. Schoonover's 1938 Wildwoods, Glendale Hts. IL 60139.

EARN $400 A MONTH AT HOME in own business, spare time, doing only two $10.00 Invisible Reweaving/Reknitting jobs a day. Good money paid for making cuts, tears disappear from fabrics. Details mailed free. Fabricon, 2051 Montrose, Chicago 60618.

PERSONALS

SINGLE? WIDOWED? DIVORCED? Happy Matchmaker Club offers opportunity for sincere permanent relationship. Don't be lonely anymore! Free information. Box 312-F, Glen Oaks, NY 11004.

DON'T DIVORCE YOUR KIDS! Helpful handbook, "101 Ways to Be A Long-Distance Super-Dad" Highly recommended. $6.95 postpaid. Free details. Blossom Valley Press, Box 4044F, Mountain View, CA 94040

CASH LOANS! Borrow by mail, $500.00 to $25,000. Free details, application! LTD-FD, Box 937, Ft. Lauderdale, FL 33302

BORROW $25,000 "OVERNIGHT." Any purpose. Keep indefinitely! Free Report! SUCCESS RESEARCH, Box 19739-JM, Indianapolis, IN 46219.

TELL FORTUNES with ordinary playing cards. Gypsy Method. Lucky numbers. Details free: Cleveland, Dept. F, 505 No. Lakeshore, Chicago, IL 60611.

LEARN WITCHCRAFT for protection, success and serenity. Gavin & Yvonne Frost, world's foremost Witches, now accepting students. Box 1502-0, New Bern, NC 28560.

CHANGE LUCK with our powerful Good Luck products: Trimurti powders, oils; Psychic Bath Conditioner, Floor Wash, Lucky Amulets, Charms, Rituals; Lucky Numbers. Send $1.00 for details and three Lucky Secrets. Psychic Authority, Box 10460-A7, Jacksonville, FL 32247.

$LOANS! ON SIGNATURE to — $100,000! Any purpose. Write: ELITE, Box 206-FA, East Rockaway, NY 11518.

IS CURLY HAIR the wave of the future? Can kinks be worked out? Can there be a permanent solution? You hold the answer!

I AM EXPERIENCED in helping people with their problems through candles, herbs, baths and prayer. We work together-You Will Never Be Alone Again. Hundreds of people are happier and satisfied. Write to MARTHA, Dept. F, 200 West Sunrise Highway, Freeport, NY 11520.

PLANTS & SEEDS

CARNIVOROUS, woodland terrarium plants, supplies, book. Illustrated catalog free. PETER PAUL'S NURSERIES, Canandaigua, NY 14424.

WEED-FREE GARDENING Plus 87% Greater Yields!! No Tilling, Cultivating, Chemicals. Ideal for Herbs, Vegetables. Guaranteed! Free Proof. Lexigrow, Box 1491-FA, Indianapolis, IN 46206.

THREE RED INDIAN cling peach trees, $15.00; 25 Concord Grapevines, $20.00; postpaid. List free. Ponzer Nursery, Rolla, MO 65401.

FREE CATALOG: We're famous for Watermelon, Cantaloupe and other Superior Quality Seed: Bean, Corn, Okra, Tomato, etc. Free catalog on request. Willhite Seed Company, Box 23, Poolville, TX 76076.

NEW — OLD — RARE — TOMATO VARIETIES! Free Catalog. Jersey Devil Tomato Seeds $1.00. The Tomato Seed Company, P. O. Box 323 F, Metuchen, NJ 08840.

ORCHID CACTI, Christmas, Easter, Rattail Cacti, Hoyas. Color Catalog $1.00. California EPI Center, Dept. OF85, Box 1431, Vista, CA 92083.

MUSHROOM GROWING EQUIPMENT, supplies catalog $2. Gourmet Black Tree Mushroom farm $25. GPA, INC., Box 722, Bryn Mawr, PA 19010.

FREE CATALOG: Unusual seed varieties; plus wide selection of tomatoes. GROW: 3-foot long Carrots, chocolate-colored Sweet Peppers, Tomatoes green when ripe and more. GLECKLER'S SEEDMEN, Metamora, OH 43540.

POULTRY

SEND 50¢ FOR our catalog featuring over 35 Standard and Rare Exotic breeds. Ship parcel post. Guaranteed 100% live arrival. Allen Hatchery, Inc., Box 46-95, Windsor, MO 65360. Phone (816) 647-3101.

QUAIL AND EQUIPMENT catalog. Also info: "How to Produce and Sell Quail Year Around" Send 25¢ GQF Manufacturing, P. O. Box 1552-OF, Savannah, GA 31498.

FREE PICTURE CATALOG. Goslings, Ducklings, Turkeys, Chicks, Guineas, Gamebirds, Bantams, Swans. Equipment. Hoffman Hatchery, Gratz, PA 17030.

WORLD FAMOUS COLONIAL CHICKS. 300-egg Pedigree-Bred enriched. 17 leading breeds and crosses for eggs and meat. Also new "Mini" layers — eat less feed than Bantams, lay far more eggs. Over 80% large. Up to 100 or more heavy-breed chicks FREE. Get introductory offer. For FREE COLOR CATALOG write nearest address: COLONIAL POULTRY FARMS, INC. Dept. 771, Pleasant Hill, MO 64080; Effingham, IL 62401; or Fairbault, MN 55021.

ALL NEW FREE CATALOG. Featuring over 100 varieties with beautiful color breed pictures, history and descriptions. Everything from Giants to Bantams. Country's largest selection and most experienced shipper of baby chicks. 68 years supplying large, small, hobby flocks for eggs, meat, exhibition. Order as few as one of a kind. Free 4-H, FFA, surprise gift offers. Guaranteed safe shipment entire U.S. MURRAY McMURRAY HATCHERY, B100, Webster City, IA 50595.

HARDY GOSLINGS, UNUSUAL DUCKLINGS. Chicks. Illustrated catalog and book list $1.00, deductible. Pilgrim Goose Hatchery, OF-85, Williamsfield, OH 44093.

...TRY RAISING — an American tradition. ...by this business or hobby pastime by beginning your flock today!

BABY CHICKS — Over 40 varieties of rare and fancy breeds, old time favorites, Bantams, plus nation's best popular laying breeds. Chicks for every requirement, commercial, poultryman, small raiser, 4-H boy and girl and hobbyist. Poultry show winners coast-to-coast. Safe shipment all 50 states and possessions. Send 50¢ for Big colorful catalog. Marti Poultry Farm, Box 27-51, Windsor, MO 65360.

BABY DUCKS TURKEYS, Guineas, Pheasants, Chukar, Bantams, Ducklings, Goslings, Peafowl, Hatching Eggs, Packaged Bees, Queens, Hives, Supers, Garden Herbs, Mushrooms: Poultry, Grain, Food, Rabbit, Apiary, Pork, Insect, Garden Equipment. Send $1.00 for our 32 page supermarket catalogue "Farming USA." Insured shipments all 50 states and possessions. HOCKMANS, Box 7187-H5, San Diego, CA 92107.

FREE — Five Free Chicks with each order. Raise chickens (also Bantams and Ducks) for meat and eggs. We ship parcel post all 50 states. Send 50¢ for big picture catalog. Shows over 35 rare, exotic and standard breeds. 25 chicks low as $6.95; 50 for $8.95; 100 for $13.95. fob. Clinton Hatchery, Inc., Box 548-ГA, Clinton, MO 64735. Telephone 010-085-8500.

BANTAMS, RARE and Standard Breed Chicks. Incubators, Books, Medications, Poultry Equipment. Gamebird Hatching Eggs. Send 50¢ for new color catalog. Crow Poultry & Supply, Box 106-18, Windsor, MO 65360.

GOSLINGS, DUCKLINGS, turkeys, chicks, pheasants, bantams. Colorful catalog $1.00, deductible. Heart of Missouri Hatchery, Box 954FA, Columbia, MO 65205-0954

FREE 1985 COLOR CATALOG. Raise birds year round. Incubators, brooders, cages, feeders, fountains, how-to-books. Marsh Farms, Box 7, Garden Grove, CA 92642.

REAL ESTATE

NOTHING DOWN! 2-10 acre parcels of Ozarks forest. No down payment. Private financing. Shelton Realty, Box 1fa, Willow Springs, MO 65793 1-417-469-3177.

MISSOURI-OZARKS, properties of all sizes, types. Free information, contact Joe Baker, Century 21 Baker Realty, Box 266, Willow Springs, MO 65793.

FREE SEASONAL EDITION CATALOG! Over 5000 properties, 2000 pictures! Values in every type real estate, many owner financed! From 600 offices in 43 states. Get your FREE copy NOW! STROUT REALTY, P. O. Box 431, Dept. 5940, Clifton Park, NY 12605. Call toll free: 1-800-641-4266.

480,000,000 ACRES VALUABLE GOVERNMENT LAND. Now available low as $6.80 per acre. Campsites, farms, homesites. Fabulous business opportunities. Lastest report — $2. Satisfaction guaranteed. American Land Disposal, Box 913-OFA, Holland, MI 49423.

REAL ESTATE FOR SALE . . . 500 offices, 45 states! 30,000 listings on computer, 16,000 under $50,000, others with prices ranging up to several million dollars. Free printouts and regional catalogs . . . UNITED FARM AGENCY, INC., 175-YF North Street, Boston, MA 02113. Ph. Toll-Free: 1-800-821-2599.

GOVERNMENT LANDS . . . From $7.50/ACRE! Homesites, farming, vacationing, investment! "Land Buyer's Guide" PLUS nationwide listings — $2.00 (guaranteed). LANDS, Box 19107-JM, Washington, DC 20036.

TENNESSEE FARM, Mountain & Investment properties. Easy Financing. Free Brochures. Kay Realty, Rogersville, TN 37857. (615) 272-9321.

MAINE BUSINESS OPPORTUNITY LISTING MAGAZINE, containing over 100 offerings of all types of businesses. Send $2.00 for your copy today! MAINCO Realty, Inc., POB 266-46, 65 Oak Street, Boothbay Harbor, ME 04538. (207) 633-3483.

WEST VIRGINIA, farms, acreage, riverproperty . . . rural tracts, homes . . . Jones Realty, Rt. 86, Box 99FA, Jumping Branch, WV 25969. (304) 466-4246.

TENNESSE ACREAGE. Five Acres — $2,500. 21 Acres — $9,000. Terms. (615) 833-5280. Free Brochure, Charles Smith, Box 110152, Nashville, TN 37222.

RELIGION

FREE BIBLE COURSE. Diplomas upon completion. Zion Faith College, P. O. Box 804, Caldwell, ID 83606-0804.

SPIRITUAL, RELIGIOUS POEMS wanted for musical setting recording. $1,000.00 for best song. Chapel Recording (FA), Box 112, Wollaston, MA 02179 (Talent Co.)

WAS THERE REALLY A FLOOD? Is the story of Abraham fact of fiction? Could Moses have written the Genesis account nearly 4,000 years ago? Get free booklet "Archaeology Proves The Bible," Bible Answers, Dept. 12, Box 60, General Post Office, NY, NY 10116.

BECOME an ordained Minister. Free ministerial credentials, legalize your right to the title "Reverend." Write Church of Gospel Ministry, 486-OF Skyhill Court, Chula Vista, CA 92010.

STAMPS & COINS

10 ISRAEL STAMPS Free to approval applicants. W-B Stamp Co., FA, Wilkes-Barre, PA 18703.

WHEAT BACK PENNIES. 50 old pennies only $4.00. Chandler, Box 9019, Akron, OH 44305.

STAMPS: Old Attic Accumulation! Many 19th Century. U.S. or WORLDWIDE $6.95/oz., D'Angelo, 21213B Hawthorne. #5600-A, Torrance, CA 90509.

UNITED NATIONS 3 Complete Mint Sets only 25¢ with approvals. Cornetta, POB 1509US, Lake Placid, FL 33852.

WANTED

GINSENG, write for free price list. Snowiss Fur Company, East Third, Williamsport, Pa 17701.

INVENTIONS, IDEAS, new products wanted! Industry presentation/national exposition. 1-800-528-6050. Arizona, 1-800-352-0458. X831. IMI-FA, 701 Smithfield, Pittsburgh, PA 15222.

INVENTORS! If you have an invention for sale or license, write for free booklet explaining how we can help you. Kessler Sales Corp., C-4210, Fremont, OH 43420

TV GUIDES, 1948-84. Highest prices paid. TV Guide Specialists, Box 20-OFA, MaComb, IL 61455.

ANECDOTES AND PLEASANTRIES

A motley collection of amazing if sometimes useless facts, strange stories, and questionable advice kindly sent to us during 1984 by readers of this 193-year-old publication.

FINALLY, SOME STATISTICS THAT MAKE US LOOK GOOD!

Last year the Agriculture Department disputed the popular notion that Americans have the highest per capita "disposable income" in the world, but spend high percentages on food, soft drinks, alcoholic beverages, and tobacco compared with foreigners.

The Swiss, they reported, had a disposable income per head of $13,823; followed by the Danes, $11,666; the Swedes, $11,309; the West Germans, $10,837; and the Belgians, $10,202. Americans, who averaged $9,595, are barely ahead of the French, $9,509, and the Dutch, $9,507.

But Americans spent only 12.7 percent of their meager disposable income on food at home. The Canadians spent 14.5 percent; the Dutch, 15 percent; Australians, 17.1 percent; the British, 17.3 percent; the Poles, 28.3 percent; and the Soviets, 33.7 percent.

Americans spent 0.8 percent on soft drinks; the Thais led with 3.2 percent.

Americans were a sober 47th in alcoholic beverage spending, tied with Sudan. The Southern Irish and Poles led, each with 12.1 percent. Close behind were the Hungarians, 11.6 percent, and the Soviets, with 10 percent.

Americans tied with the Japanese for the 50th ranking in tobacco spending, of 1.3 percent. Citizens of Malta led with 5 percent.

So there.

THE WORST POSSIBLE OPENING SENTENCE FOR A NOVEL

From the annual "worst opening sentence" competition conducted by the English Department at San Jose State to which more than 4,000 entries were submitted from all over the country as well as from Thailand, Kenya, Papua New Guinea, and Saudi Arabia, here is the winner:

"The lovely woman-child Kaa was mercilessly chained to the cruel post of the warrior-chief Beast, with his barbarian tribe now stacking wood at her nubile feet, when the strong, clear voice of the poetic and heroic Handsomas roared, 'Flick your Bic, crisp that chick, and you'll feel my steel through your last meal.'"

For that, Steve Gorman of Pensacola, Florida, received an award of a word processor.

The runner-up was Joan C. Gilliam of Houston, Texas, who received a 30-volume set of the works of a minor Victorian novelist named Sir Edward Bulwer-Lytton. Her opening sentence:

"I had left the barbecue quite hurriedly with sketchy directions to the ladies' room 'out back,' and now faced a black cow wearing one red earring standing beneath an ill windmill, bladeless and bent from years of prevailing winds, as she watched me with

bovine detachment, my heels sunk arch-deep into the mire . . . I hate the country!"

Entries are judged on anticlimax, wordiness, misplaced modifiers, overblown triteness, and parody.

Information courtesy of The New York Times

EXACTLY HOW MUCH IS ONE CORD OF WOOD?

1. 12 dining room tables
2. 7½ million toothpicks
3. 1,200 editions of the *National Geographic*
4. 942 one-pound books
5. 4½ million commemorative postage stamps
6. 30 Boston rocking chairs

According to the Paper Industry Information Office

WHY GEORGE WASHINGTON'S GARDENER ALWAYS LOOKED FORWARD TO CHRISTMAS
(and why Easter was only half as pleasant)

The following is the exact wording of the contract drawn up between President George Washington and one Philip Bater, his gardener at Mt. Vernon. It's dated April 23, 1787.

Article of Agreement made this twelfth of April Anno Domini one thousand seven hundred and eighty-seven by and between Geo. Washington Esq.

of the Parish of Truro in the County of Fairfax, State of Virginia, on one part, and Philip Bater, Gardener, on the other. Witness, that the said Philip Bater, for and in consideration of the covenants herein, doth promise and agree to serve the sd. George Washington, for the term of one year, as a Gardener, and that he will during said time, conduct himself soberly, diligently, and honestly — that he will faithfully and industrially perform all and every part of his duty as Gardener to the best of his knowledge and abilities, and that he will not, at any time, suffer himself to be disguised with liquor, except on the times hereafter mentioned.

In consideration of these things being well and truly performed on the part of the sd. Philip Bater, the sd. Geo. Washington doth agree to allow him (the sd. Philip) the same kind and quantity of the provisions as he has heretofore had; and likewise, annually, a decent suit of clothing befitting a man in his station; to consist of a Coat, Vest, and breeches; a working Jacket and breeches, of homespun . . . besides: two white shirts; three check Ditto; two pair of yarn stockings; two pair of thread Ditto; two linnen pocket handkerchiefs; two pair of linnen overalls; as many pair of Shoes

as are actually necessary for him; 4 dollars at Christmas with which he may be drunk 4 days and 4 nights; 2 dollars at Easter to effect the same purpose; two

FIVE COMMON MISCONCEPTIONS ABOUT BIBLICAL EVENTS

WRONG	RIGHT
There were three Wise Men.	There is no reference in the New Testament to the exact number of Wise Men.
The forbidden fruit eaten by Adam and Eve was an apple.	The word "apple" does not appear in *Genesis*. The Bible only says the couple ate from the fruit of the Tree of Knowledge of Good and Evil.
Jonah was swallowed by a whale.	There is no reference to a whale. Jonah was swallowed by a "big fish."
Elijah went to heaven in a fiery chariot.	Elijah was separated from his companions by a fiery chariot but was taken to heaven in a "whirlwind."
King Solomon owned mines.	There is no biblical reference to King Solomon's mines.

Courtesy of John Hutchins

dollars also at Whitsuntide, to be drunk two days; a Dram in the morning and a drink of Grog at dinner or at noon.

For the true and faithful performance of all of these things the parties have hereunto set their hands this twenty-third of April Anno Domini 1787.

It was signed by both parties and two witnesses. *Courtesy of Elizabeth Powers*

WHEN IS EASTER? CAN IT COINCIDE WITH PASSOVER? (and stuff like that)

The rough "rule of thumb" for determining the date of Easter each year is as follows:

Easter is to be celebrated on the first Sunday after the day of the first full moon which falls on or after the day of the vernal (Spring) equinox.

Use this rough rule and you'll be correct about 83-84 years out of each century. You'll be wrong 16-17 times in a hundred years because both the full moon and vernal equinox are, in this rule, determined by calculations and assumptions of the early Christian church rather than by modern astronomy. Thus the ecclesiastical vernal equinox is *always* on March 21st, whereas the actual vernal equinox sometimes also falls on the 20th and sometimes on the 22nd. The old-time ecclesiastical moon tends to be as much as a day *after* the actual astronomical moon.

Thus the 16 percent to 17 percent margin of error. The lengthy calculations that ensure 100 percent accuracy would require too much space here, but you can trust that this annual publication will always contain the correct date. Guaranteed.

Some might be interested to know that Easter can and sometimes does coincide with Passover. Recently the two have coincided in 1954 (April 18) and 1981 (April 19). They will do so in 2123 (April 11) and 2143 (March 31). March 22nd is the earliest possible date for Easter. It has not fallen that early since March 22, 1818, and will not again until 2285.

The latest date is April 25, on which it fell last in 1943 and will next in 2038.

Information courtesy of Francis P. Larkin

A READER'S PLEA FOR IDENTITY

The following letter was sent to *The Old Farmer's Almanac* several months ago from a man in Sneeds Ferry, North Carolina. In all honesty, we're not sure how best to reply. Can anyone help? **Ed.**

Dear Editor of The Old Farmer's Almanac *(Dublin, NH 03444):*

Here's my situation and I hope you can straighten things out for me. My wife's grandfather was named Jerry Jarman. His best friend was Henry Heath. Tragically, both lost their wives in death and each was left with children to care for. Also, each had a daughter old enough to court. Well, Jerry Jarman courted and married Henry Heath's daughter, Lou, which made Henry Jerry's father-in-law and Jerry Henry's son-in-law.

To complicate matters, Henry Heath then courted and married Jerry Jarman's daughter, Eva. Now Jerry became Henry's father-in-law and Henry became Jerry's son-in-law. Of course, Henry was already Jerry's father-in-law and now he was his son-in-law. Same with Jerry, so in a manner of speaking one could say each became his own father-in-law and his own son-in-law.

In the same way, Jerry and Henry's new wives, Lou and Eva, became each other's own mother-in-law and daughter-in-law. Naturally enough, complications mushroomed when both couples were blessed with children, then more children, all of whom had such a confusion of double stepfathers and stepmothers, double nephews, and double grandfathers-in-law that in several generations no one knows who is who.

Well, 37 years ago I married one of the granddaughters. I do know my wife's maiden name was Sudie Marie

THE CANNON THAT FIRES CHICKENS AT AIRPLANES
(Included here specifically for chicken-trivia enthusiasts)

In order to help reduce accidents caused by jet airplanes hitting birds, a cannon has recently been developed at Langley Air Force Base in Langley, Virginia, which shoots whole four-pound (dead) chickens at airplanes. The chickens are aimed at engines, windshields, and landing gear to determine how much damage such collisions can cause; they are traveling about 700 miles an hour on impact.

Jarman, granddaughter of Jerry Jarman and daughter of Claude Jarman. But when you consider the Heaths, does it mean she's her own grandmother-in-law?

[signed]

Garland Wesley Brinson (I think)

HOW TO MAKE A CLOUD IN A BOTTLE

Place ¼ cup of water in a clean bottle that is fairly big in diameter and has a small mouth. Set the bottle on a table and shine a flashlight through it in such a way that the beam of light is at right angles to the viewer. Apply pressure to the bottle by blowing into it as if trying to blow up a balloon. Release the pressure and see what happens. A very few cloud droplets may be visible, reflecting from the beam of light. Now light a match and hold it near the opening of the bottle. Blow the match out. It is not necessary to get any of the visible smoke into the bottle. Repeat the process of pressurizing the air and releasing the pressure. With enough change in pressure, a white cloud should appear, filling the bottle with thousands of tiny cloud droplets, each reflecting the light. If pressure is again applied, the cloud will disappear; releasing the pressure will bring it back as before.

This experiment can be done in a few minutes and it never fails (well, hardly ever) to cause even the most nonscientific person to gasp at what a little dirt (the combustion particles from the match) will do.

Courtesy of Mark Urbaetis

WHEN YOUR NAUGHTY PET MAKES A WET BOO BOO ON THE CARPET

1. Blot the affected area with clean white cloths or paper towels until none of the urine shows on the absorbent material.
2. Next, use a spray or a sponge to lightly flush the area with tap water. Do not overwet the carpet.

3. Blot dry with the same type of absorbent material.
4. Next, mix a teaspoon of a dishwashing powder detergent with a cup of lukewarm water. Apply the solution into the carpet pile with your fingers.
5. Blot dry. Then flush as described in step 2. Blot until area is as dry as possible.
6. Dampen the area with a solution of equal parts of water and white vinegar and allow it to remain for a few minutes. Then absorb the solution until the carpet is as dry as possible.
7. Finally, place a one-inch layer of the same absorbent material on the treated area and weight it down with a heavy object. Leave it in place for eight hours.

Information courtesy of A.S. Garstein

FIFTY NIFTY ALL-PURPOSE RULES WHICH EVERY THINKING PERSON ALIVE AND WELL ON THIS PLANET QUITE POSSIBLY OUGHT TO BEAR IN MIND

(1) Dress warmly. (2) *Keep out of reach of children.* (3) Close cover before striking. (4) *Fasten your seat belt.* (5) Shake well before using. (6) *Do not remove tag under penalty of law.* (7) Check your expiration date. (8) *No salesman will call.* (9) Cross between yellow lines. (10) *If pain persists, see your doctor.* (11) Leave a message when you hear the beep. (12) *See back of package for representative sample.* (13) Squeeze left. (14) *Assemble in minutes with just a screwdriver.* (15) Proceed at your own risk. (16) *Last bus departs at 6:50 P.M.* (17) Employees must wash hands before leaving rest room. (18) *In emergency pull handle.* (19) Enclose self-addressed stamped envelope. (20) *Bridge freezes before road.* (21) Do not use pennies. (22) *Do not inhale.* (23) Sit up straight. (24) *Call your mother.* (25) Use waste receptacle provided. (26) *Watch your hat and coat.* (27) Tear along dotted line. (28) *Lift here.* (29) Do not talk to operator of this vehicle.

continued

Anecdotes and Pleasantries *continued*

(30) *The management reserves the right.* (31) The management cannot be held responsible. (32) *Void where prohibited.* (33) F.O.B. Buffalo. (34) *State residents include applicable tax.* (35) Dry clean only. (36) *Use no hooks.* (37) This man may be armed and dangerous. (38) *Satisfaction guaranteed or your money back.* (39) Try another se- lection. (40) *Escalators temporarily out of order.* (41) Do not feed the elephants. (42) *This offer cannot be repeated.* (43) In case of a knockdown, go to a neutral corner. (44) *Violators will be prosecuted.* (45) If no answer, keep trying. (46) *Substantial penalty for early withdrawal.* (47) All entrées include choice of potato or salad. (48) *Lifeboat drill is mandatory.* (49) Do not write in this space. (50) *Dress warmly.*

by Bill Conklin

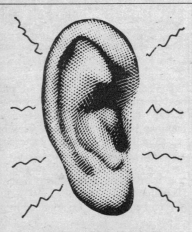

CURING AN EARACHE
Three Methods — à la 1889

• Take a small piece of cotton batting or cotton wool, make a depression in the center with the finger, and then fill it up with as much ground pepper as will rest on a five-cent piece; gather it into a ball and tie it up; dip the ball into sweet oil and insert it in the ear, covering the latter with cotton wool, and use a bandage or cap to retain it in its place. Almost instant relief will be experienced.

• Roast a piece of lean mutton, squeeze out the juice, and drop it into the ear as hot as can be borne.

• Roast an onion and put it into the ear as hot as can be borne.

From a copy of Burroughs' Encyclopedia, 1889. Reprinted by Miggs Burroughs and available through Brayden Books, 719 Post Road East, Westport, CT 06880.

WHO WERE MR. FAHRENHEIT AND MR. CELSIUS?

Gabriel Daniel Fahrenheit was born in Danzig, Poland, in 1686. His parents died when he was 15 years old, and his guardian sent him to Amsterdam, where he found work in the field of manufacturing scientific instruments. He traveled widely and in 1717, at age 31, set himself up as an independent craftsman. By 1724 his skills were so highly recognized that he was admitted to membership in the Royal Society despite his total lack of formal scientific schooling and training.

His field covered a wide variety of scientific research, but he became best known for his development, in the period 1708-1717, of the thermometer whose scale presently reflects the freezing and boiling points of water as 32 and 212 degrees respectively.

Fahrenheit died in 1736, at which time Anders Celsius, in Sweden, was experimenting with thermometers.

Anders Celsius, born in Uppsala, Sweden, in 1701, studied at the University of Uppsala where his father had been Professor of Astronomy, and in 1730 assumed that post himself.

continued

He devoted many years to observations of the aurora borealis and participated in a complex meridian measurement that confirmed one segment of Newton's theory regarding the state of the poles.

He wrote many papers but remains best remembered as the inventor of the Celsius thermometer, which is primarily the application of the metric system to its scale.

Originally he established the boiling point of water as zero degrees and the freezing point as 100. This was in 1742, two years before his death.

The presently used system, with the scale reversed, was introduced by the University in 1747, and became the standard in all countries using the metric system.

by Earl O. Nielsen

Author's Note: A simple (even simpler if you round out the numbers) method for converting Fahrenheit to Celsius: Fahrenheit times .555 minus 17.76 equals Celsius. Or $C = (F \times .555) - 17.76$.

THE GOLDEN RULES
(It's true in all faiths)

Brahmanism: This is the sum of duty: Do naught unto others which would cause you pain if done to you.
Mahabharata 5: 1517

Buddhism: Hurt not others in ways that you yourself would find hurtful.
Udana-Varga 5: 18

Confucianism: Surely it is the maxim of loving kindness: Do not unto others what you would not have them do unto you. *Analects 15: 23*

Taoism: Regard your neighbor's gain as your own gain and your neighbor's loss as your own loss.
T'ai Shang Kan Ying P'ien

Zoroastrianism: That nature alone is good which refrains from doing unto another whatsoever is not good for itself. *Dadistan-i-dinik 94: 5*

Judaism: What is hateful to you, do not to your fellowman. That is the entire Law; all the rest is commentary.
Talmud, Shabbat 31a

Christianity: All things whatsoever ye would that men should do to you, do ye even so to them; for this is the Law and the Prophets. *Matthew 7: 12*

Islam: No one of you is a believer until he desires for his brother that which he desires for himself. *Sunnah*

Courtesy of Elizabeth Pool

The Will in the Willow, the Flow in the Flower

Are the trees in your garden just standing there passively twiddling their twigs, or might there be something up their stems you never dreamed could really be?

Text and illustrations by
Guy Murchie

☐ DID YOU KNOW THAT A WILLOW actually has a will of its own, a will that tells it how to root and shoot? And have you heard that the petals of most flowers literally flow into their beautiful shapes like water gurgling down a brook, only much slower?

These are beautiful stories, but true, and they convey important messages to us out of the mystery of the world. First let's take a willow twig or, in fact, any small piece of a living willow tree. It may look innocent enough, but actually it has what amounts to a primitive mind. For it knows its top from its bottom by means of its genes and their built-in instructions on how to grow. Thus, if you cut the twig off in spring and plant it in moist soil, it will sprout both roots and shoots. Indeed it is more than an organism: it is organized. It feels a definite polarity so that, even if you forget which end of the piece of willow was nearer the roots of its mother tree, the piece itself cannot possibly forget. If the wrong end is planted in the ground, the twig will in effect turn itself around by sprouting roots at the upper end that will grow downward into the earth while shoots rise out of the soil from the bottom end to form a clump of willows, one of which a few decades later may become a beautiful big willow tree with no trace left of the misplaced twig.

But polarity does not mean that any particular cell in the planted piece of willow is predestined to sprout a root instead of a shoot or vice versa, for the cell's action depends on its position in *relation* to the rest of the piece. If your cut puts the cell at the root end of the piece, it will sprout a root. But if you cut it so the same cell comes at the shoot end, it will grow a shoot. No matter how small the grains you cut willow into, they keep their root-shoot polarity as surely as crumbs of magnetized iron keep their north-south polarity, and this will in willow asserts itself right down to hollow statolithic cells that

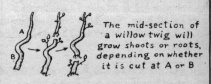

The mid-section of a willow twig will grow shoots or roots, depending on whether it is cut at A or B

contain dense, loose starch grains that keep rolling to the bottom of the cells in response to gravity, thus apprising the twig (which somehow "feels" them) which ways are up and down!

But there is something besides gravitational polarity that guides the growth of all trees and plants. And that is a group of hormones, the first and best known of which was proven to exist only as recently as 1928. It is called auxin. Shortly after its discovery a curi-

the flow in flowers

milk splash & polyp in sea

ink in water & small jellyfish

fusel oil in paraffin

medusoid jellyfish

DYNAMICS OF LIVING FORMS

ous intrarelation between different branches on the same tree began to attract the attention not only of botanists but even of a few philosophers. It had been noticed that cutting off the topmost or leading stem of a pine tree induces the lateral branches just below it to start bending upward in what seems to be an attempt to replace the lost leader. At least that is the ostensible purpose of the reaction if one can believe there is any purpose in nature.

The most remarkable part of the tree's response to the emergency, however, comes after the first scramble upward by competing lateral branches, when the tree somehow singles out one (rarely two) from among these rising candidates and elevates it in a few growing years to the vacant vertical throne. The problem of succession is thus usually settled without a serious battle as the chosen prince of branches swings to the central supreme position with a seeming crown of authority while the other limbs drop placidly back to their accustomed places as if they recognized their new sovereign.

How they recognize him is hard to say. It is known only that the cutting off of the top stem causes new wood of a different kind to appear at the base of the nearest lateral branches, but how one of these is selected for honor and the others are denied it remains a mystery. The only thing reasonably sure is that some sort of a cooperative decision gets to be agreed upon by the branches,

if not by the whole organism. One might consider it the result of a kind of secret conference within the cells of the tree, perhaps involving a process analogous to voting in which proximity and responsiveness are at a premium, and messages travel through the mysterious mediums of hormone chemistry.

In case you are wondering now what all this has to do with the flow in flowers, please note that flowing has a strong component of geometry, and that geometry is a common denominator not only in the polarity of twigs and the intrarelations of branches, but also in the unfolding of buds as they burst into flowers. A famous Scottish biophysicist named D'Arcy Thompson was studying the dynamics of raindrops, bubbles, and splashes at the end of the last century and, with the aid of high-speed photography, he noticed that when a round pebble falls into calm water, its downward pressure after impact pushes a "filmy cup of water" upward all around, which "tends to be fluted in alternate ridges and grooves, its edges ... scalloped into corresponding lobes and notches, and the projecting lobes ... into drops or beads ..." Although this creation lasts but a tiny fraction of a second, the photographs showed it to have a beautiful, symmetrical, flowerlike form put there by the same sort of dynamic forces that generally infuse the flow into flowers, only many millions of times faster. Of course it was a new concept in those

sand on steel
at 7800 cycles
per second

liquid tiles

CYMATICS

vibrating
soap bubble

a "fishbone" in glycerine

a chord from Bach's Toccata in D minor

days, but the recent proliferation of time-accelerated and time-decelerated movies has made it much clearer, demonstrating dramatically the extraordinary parallels between fluid turbulence and the relatively solid forms of life; between a lacteal crown of two dozen beadlike points tossed up in a splash of milk and certain polyps in the sea with two dozen vertical tentacles surmounting a similar cuplike body; between columns of ink sinking in water or fusel oil in kerosene and various medusae jellyfish; even between the furrowed torsos of protozoans, the fluting of instable sleeves of plasma in a jet engine, and the gadrooned blossoms of gentians and lilies.

Of course there is wave action in all these examples, action which in the plural, at a high enough pitch, would be considered as vibrations which, when artfully varied and harmonically blended, become music. On the other hand, in graphic screen form they may conjoin themselves into moiré art. Waves and the oscillations that generate them are among the most universal of phenomena and familiar today in tides, winds, weather, rivers, ocean currents, magnetic lines of force, earthquakes, sound, sunspots, radiation belts in space, meteor showers, galactic gyrations, mass migrations of fish, birds, insects, microbes, mammals, man, etc. But two centuries ago almost nothing was known about the dynamics of waves or what creates them, nor was it until just before the French Rev-

olution that an imaginative German scientist and musician named Ernst Chladni discovered that, if he covered a metal plate with sand and vibrated it with his violin bow, the sand would be rapidly shaken away from most of the plate, disposing itself as if by magic in a pattern of nodal axes along which the plate was almost motionless.

It was a kind of Pythagorean revelation from which gradually emerged the science of cymatics in which modern researchers use crystal oscillators to test a wide variety of materials, in effect sewing sand into lace and weaving honey into tapestries, the texture becoming finer as the pitch rises. They also induce cream or iron filings to dance, liquid to mold rows of quavering "roof tiles," glycerine to create a fishbone spine, a soap bubble to form a breathing hexagonal prism, and even a film of oil to ripple into subtle recordings of every kind of music from a ditty to a symphony. As such phenomena are found to exist not only on land and sea but in every snowflake, every dancing drop of rain, and every bolt of lightning in the sky, it is becoming increasingly easy to surmise that there is a fundamental law at work here ordering the textures, shapes, and indeed the very being of everything in the universe. □ □

If you want a copy of Guy Murchie's 700-page book *The Seven Mysteries of Life* (featured in *The Old Farmer's Almanac* in recent years), inscribed and postpaid, send $20 to Guy Murchie, Marlborough, NH 03455, or send $13 for the same book in paperback.

1 9 8 4

JANUARY
S	M	T	W	T	F	S
1	2	3	4	5	6	7
8	9	10	11	12	13	14
15	16	17	18	19	20	21
22	23	24	25	26	27	28
29	30	31	—	—	—	—

FEBRUARY
S	M	T	W	T	F	S
—	—	—	1	2	3	4
5	6	7	8	9	10	11
12	13	14	15	16	17	18
19	20	21	22	23	24	25
26	27	28	29	—	—	—

MARCH
S	M	T	W	T	F	S
—	—	—	—	1	2	3
4	5	6	7	8	9	10
11	12	13	14	15	16	17
18	19	20	21	22	23	24
25	26	27	28	29	30	31

APRIL
S	M	T	W	T	F	S
1	2	3	4	5	6	7
8	9	10	11	12	13	14
15	16	17	18	19	20	21
22	23	24	25	26	27	28
29	30	—	—	—	—	—

MAY
S	M	T	W	T	F	S
—	—	1	2	3	4	5
6	7	8	9	10	11	12
13	14	15	16	17	18	19
20	21	22	23	24	25	26
27	28	29	30	31	—	—

JUNE
S	M	T	W	T	F	S
—	—	—	—	—	1	2
3	4	5	6	7	8	9
10	11	12	13	14	15	16
17	18	19	20	21	22	23
24	25	26	27	28	29	30

JULY
S	M	T	W	T	F	S
1	2	3	4	5	6	7
8	9	10	11	12	13	14
15	16	17	18	19	20	21
22	23	24	25	26	27	28
29	30	31	—	—	—	—

AUGUST
S	M	T	W	T	F	S
—	—	—	1	2	3	4
5	6	7	8	9	10	11
12	13	14	15	16	17	18
19	20	21	22	23	24	25
26	27	28	29	30	31	—

SEPTEMBER
S	M	T	W	T	F	S
—	—	—	—	—	—	1
2	3	4	5	6	7	8
9	10	11	12	13	14	15
16	17	18	19	20	21	22
23	24	25	26	27	28	29
30	—	—	—	—	—	—

OCTOBER
S	M	T	W	T	F	S
—	1	2	3	4	5	6
7	8	9	10	11	12	13
14	15	16	17	18	19	20
21	22	23	24	25	26	27
28	29	30	31	—	—	—

NOVEMBER
S	M	T	W	T	F	S
—	—	—	—	1	2	3
4	5	6	7	8	9	10
11	12	13	14	15	16	17
18	19	20	21	22	23	24
25	26	27	28	29	30	—

DECEMBER
S	M	T	W	T	F	S
—	—	—	—	—	—	1
2	3	4	5	6	7	8
9	10	11	12	13	14	15
16	17	18	19	20	21	22
23	24	25	26	27	28	29
30	31	—	—	—	—	—

1 9 8 5

JANUARY
S	M	T	W	T	F	S
—	—	1	2	3	4	5
6	7	8	9	10	11	12
13	14	15	16	17	18	19
20	21	22	23	24	25	26
27	28	29	30	31	—	—

FEBRUARY
S	M	T	W	T	F	S
—	—	—	—	—	1	2
3	4	5	6	7	8	9
10	11	12	13	14	15	16
17	18	19	20	21	22	23
24	25	26	27	28	—	—

MARCH
S	M	T	W	T	F	S
—	—	—	—	—	1	2
3	4	5	6	7	8	9
10	11	12	13	14	15	16
17	18	19	20	21	22	23
24	25	26	27	28	29	30
31	—	—	—	—	—	—

APRIL
S	M	T	W	T	F	S
—	1	2	3	4	5	6
7	8	9	10	11	12	13
14	15	16	17	18	19	20
21	22	23	24	25	26	27
28	29	30	—	—	—	—

MAY
S	M	T	W	T	F	S
—	—	—	1	2	3	4
5	6	7	8	9	10	11
12	13	14	15	16	17	18
19	20	21	22	23	24	25
26	27	28	29	30	31	—

JUNE
S	M	T	W	T	F	S
—	—	—	—	—	—	1
2	3	4	5	6	7	8
9	10	11	12	13	14	15
16	17	18	19	20	21	22
23	24	25	26	27	28	29
30	—	—	—	—	—	—

JULY
S	M	T	W	T	F	S
—	1	2	3	4	5	6
7	8	9	10	11	12	13
14	15	16	17	18	19	20
21	22	23	24	25	26	27
28	29	30	31	—	—	—

AUGUST
S	M	T	W	T	F	S
—	—	—	—	1	2	3
4	5	6	7	8	9	10
11	12	13	14	15	16	17
18	19	20	21	22	23	24
25	26	27	28	29	30	31

SEPTEMBER
S	M	T	W	T	F	S
1	2	3	4	5	6	7
8	9	10	11	12	13	14
15	16	17	18	19	20	21
22	23	24	25	26	27	28
29	30	—	—	—	—	—

OCTOBER
S	M	T	W	T	F	S
—	—	1	2	3	4	5
6	7	8	9	10	11	12
13	14	15	16	17	18	19
20	21	22	23	24	25	26
27	28	29	30	31	—	—

NOVEMBER
S	M	T	W	T	F	S
—	—	—	—	—	1	2
3	4	5	6	7	8	9
10	11	12	13	14	15	16
17	18	19	20	21	22	23
24	25	26	27	28	29	30

DECEMBER
S	M	T	W	T	F	S
1	2	3	4	5	6	7
8	9	10	11	12	13	14
15	16	17	18	19	20	21
22	23	24	25	26	27	28
29	30	31	—	—	—	—

1 9 8 6

JANUARY
S	M	T	W	T	F	S
—	—	—	1	2	3	4
5	6	7	8	9	10	11
12	13	14	15	16	17	18
19	20	21	22	23	24	25
26	27	28	29	30	31	—

FEBRUARY
S	M	T	W	T	F	S
—	—	—	—	—	—	1
2	3	4	5	6	7	8
9	10	11	12	13	14	15
16	17	18	19	20	21	22
23	24	25	26	27	28	—

MARCH
S	M	T	W	T	F	S
—	—	—	—	—	—	1
2	3	4	5	6	7	8
9	10	11	12	13	14	15
16	17	18	19	20	21	22
23	24	25	26	27	28	29
30	31	—	—	—	—	—

APRIL
S	M	T	W	T	F	S
—	—	1	2	3	4	5
6	7	8	9	10	11	12
13	14	15	16	17	18	19
20	21	22	23	24	25	26
27	28	29	30	—	—	—

MAY
S	M	T	W	T	F	S
—	—	—	—	1	2	3
4	5	6	7	8	9	10
11	12	13	14	15	16	17
18	19	20	21	22	23	24
25	26	27	28	29	30	31

JUNE
S	M	T	W	T	F	S
1	2	3	4	5	6	7
8	9	10	11	12	13	14
15	16	17	18	19	20	21
22	23	24	25	26	27	28
29	30	—	—	—	—	—

JULY
S	M	T	W	T	F	S
—	—	1	2	3	4	5
6	7	8	9	10	11	12
13	14	15	16	17	18	19
20	21	22	23	24	25	26
27	28	29	30	31	—	—

AUGUST
S	M	T	W	T	F	S
—	—	—	—	—	1	2
3	4	5	6	7	8	9
10	11	12	13	14	15	16
17	18	19	20	21	22	23
24	25	26	27	28	29	30
31	—	—	—	—	—	—

SEPTEMBER
S	M	T	W	T	F	S
—	1	2	3	4	5	6
7	8	9	10	11	12	13
14	15	16	17	18	19	20
21	22	23	24	25	26	27
28	29	30	—	—	—	—

OCTOBER
S	M	T	W	T	F	S
—	—	—	1	2	3	4
5	6	7	8	9	10	11
12	13	14	15	16	17	18
19	20	21	22	23	24	25
26	27	28	29	30	31	—

NOVEMBER
S	M	T	W	T	F	S
—	—	—	—	—	—	1
2	3	4	5	6	7	8
9	10	11	12	13	14	15
16	17	18	19	20	21	22
23	24	25	26	27	28	29
30	—	—	—	—	—	—

DECEMBER
S	M	T	W	T	F	S
—	1	2	3	4	5	6
7	8	9	10	11	12	13
14	15	16	17	18	19	20
21	22	23	24	25	26	27
28	29	30	31	—	—	—

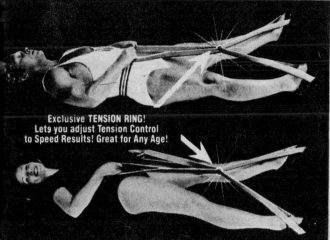

The Most Beautiful Songs of Faith Ever Recorded!

Gospel's Top 20

Featuring:

The Greatest Country Singers Of All Time!

In Over 500,000 Homes!

The Songs You Love

ROCK OF AGES
Johnny Cash

WHISPERING HOPE
Jim Reeves

PEACE IN THE VALLEY
Loretta Lynn

CHURCH IN THE WILDWOOD
The Statler Brothers

HOW GREAT THOU ART
Tammy Wynette

BEYOND THE SUNSET
Hank Williams

ON THE WINGS OF A DOVE
Billy Walker

AMAZING GRACE
Johnny Cash

ONE DAY AT A TIME
Marilyn Sellars

THE OLD RUGGED CROSS
David Houston

I SAW THE LIGHT
Roy Acuff

OLD TIME RELIGION
Charlie Rich

PRECIOUS MEMORIES
Kitty Wells

IN THE GARDEN
David Houston

THE BIBLE TELLS ME SO
Roy Rogers

IT IS NO SECRET WHAT GOD CAN DO
Tammy Wynette

IN THE SWEET BY AND BY
Johnny Cash

WILL THE CIRCLE BE UNBROKEN
The Carter Family

WHEN THE SAINTS GO MARCHING IN
Chuck Wagon Gang

WHEN THEY RING THOSE GOLDEN BELLS
Loretta Lynn

We proudly offer you one of the most inspiring and beautiful listening experiences of your life.

Here, in this beautiful treasury, are the most loved songs of faith and inspiration ever written . . . sung by the most loved country singers in history.

Yes, you get legendary stars like **LORETTA LYNN . . . JOHNNY CASH . . . JIM REEVES . . . THE STATLER BROTHERS . . . HANK WILLIAMS . . .** and all the others listed on the left. And every single song has been selected as the most beautiful recording ever made of that song! You'll thrill to richly beautiful recordings of **THE OLD RUGGED CROSS . . . AMAZING GRACE . . . ROCK OF AGES . . . CHURCH IN THE WILDWOOD . . .** and 16 MORE! You even get the original hit recording of the beloved favorite that gives you strength each day: **ONE DAY AT A TIME.**

Offer Will Not Be Repeated

No collection of music you've ever owned will give you so much continuous joy and inspiration as this one. After listening to it just once, if you don't agree, simply return it for full refund. It's not sold in any store. Be sure to mail the no risk coupon now.

MAIL TODAY · NOT IN STORES

THE BIGGEST ADVANTAGE OF A NEW POULAN CHAIN SAW MAY BE THE GUY WHO SELLS IT TO YOU.

AFTER ALL, HE SHOWED YOU THE BEST VALUE ON THE MARKET, DIDN'T HE?

When you buy a Poulan chain saw, you get a combination of quality and price that adds up to old-fashioned value. All the features and performance you want at a price you'll love. But you also get a Poulan dealer. A man who knows chain saws. Who can help you select the right one for the job.

Poulan

And who'll be ready to help if you have a problem. In fact, he knows so much about chain saws that, chances are, he can even tell you how to pronounce our name ('Pō-len). See a Poulan dealer today.

MADE IN U.S.A.

BEAIRD-POULAN/WEED EATER
5020 FLOURNOY-LUCAS ROAD
SHREVEPORT, LOUISIANA 71129

Poulan®
NO MATTER HOW YOU SAY IT,
THE NAME MEANS QUALITY.

SEE THE YELLOW PAGES UNDER "SAWS" FOR YOUR NEAREST DEALER

ISBN 0-89909-040-

0 140216

55